FAMILY FAVORITES
VARIETY PUZZLES 48

This collection of puzzles has been selected by the editors of Penny Press for the enjoyment of your entire family.

Penny Press is the leading publisher of puzzle books and magazines exclusively. Its publications are recognized for the excellence of their editorial quality and graphic presentation. A list of Penny Press publications appears on the following page.

PennyPress ®

PENNY PRESS PUZZLE PUBLICATIONS

✦ PUZZLE MAGAZINES ✦

All-Star Word Seeks
Approved Easy & Fun Variety Puzzles
Approved Variety Puzzles
Classic Variety Puzzles Plus
  Crosswords
Easy Crossword Express
Family Variety & Crosswords
Family Variety Puzzles & Games
Favorite Easy Crosswords
Favorite Fast & Easy Crosswords
Favorite Fill-In
Favorite Quick & Easy Crosswords
Garfield's Word Seeks
Good Time Crosswords
Good Time Easy Crosswords
Good Time Variety Puzzles
Master's Tournament Variety Puzzles
Master's Variety Puzzles

Merit Variety Puzzles & Games
Original Logic Problems
Original Logic Problems
  British Edition
Penny's Famous Fill-In Puzzles
Penny's Fill-In Puzzles
Penny's Finest Favorite Word Seeks
Penny's Finest Good Time Word Seeks
Penny's Finest Super Word Seeks
Spotlight Celebrity Word Seek
Spotlight Movie & TV Word Seek
Ultimate Favorite Variety Puzzles
Ultimate World's Finest Variety Puzzles
Variety Puzzles and Games
Variety Puzzles and Games Special
  Issue Plus
Word Seek Puzzles
Large-Print Word Seek Puzzles

✦ SPECIAL COLLECTIONS ✦

Selected Anagram
  Magic Square
Selected Brick by Brick
Selected Codewords
Selected Crostics
Selected
  Crypto-Families
Selected Cryptograms
Selected Diagramless
Selected Double
  Trouble

Selected Flower Power
Selected Frameworks
Selected Letterboxes
Selected Match-Up
Selected Missing List
  Word Seeks
Selected Missing
  Vowels
Selected Patchwords
Selected Places, Please
Selected Quotefalls

Selected Share-A-Letter
Selected Stretch Letters
Selected Syllacrostics
Selected The Shadow
Selected What's Left?
Selected
  Wizard Words
Selected Word Games
  Puzzles
Selected Zigzag

✦ PUZZLER'S GIANT BOOKS ✦

Crosswords   Sudoku   Word Games   Word Seeks

✦ ✦ ✦

Family Favorites Variety Puzzles, No. 48. Published four times a year by Penny Press, Inc., 6 Prowitt Street, Norwalk, CT 06855-1220. On the web at pennydellpuzzles.com. Copyright © 2011 by Penny Press, Inc. Penny Press is a trademark registered in the U.S. Patent Office. All rights reserved. No material from this publication may be reproduced or used without the written permission of the publisher.

Printed by Quad/Graphics, Taunton, MA U.S.A 12/12/11

AROUND THE BLOCK

Find your way from Start to Finish by passing through all the white squares one time only. You may move up, down, and across, but not diagonally.

Solution on page 267

START

FINISH

WHEELS

Answer the clues for the 6-letter words which go clockwise around the inner circles. Three letters of each are given. Then rearrange the three letters you added and place them in the adjoining spaces in the outer circle. The result will be a quotation which you can read by starting at the arrow and proceeding clockwise.

Solutions on page 267

A. CLUES

1. Deliver a sermon

2. Bear, as the cost

3. Steadfastly

4. Mysterious

5. Bestow

6. Seafarer

7. Obstruct

8. Transfer

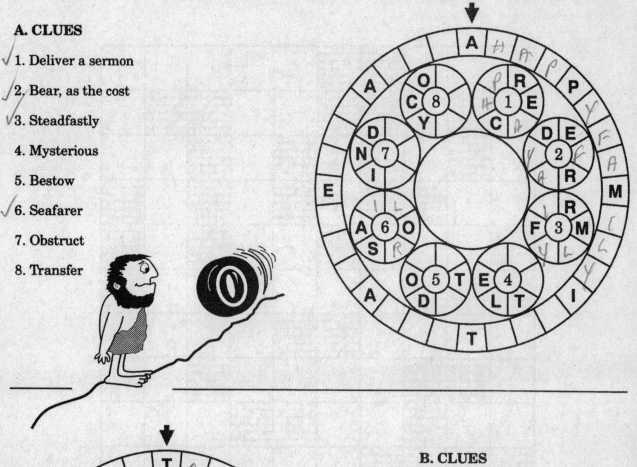

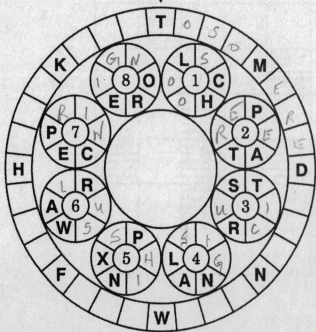

B. CLUES

1. Academy

2. Reiterate

3. Countrylike

4. Traffic device

5. Statue in Egypt

6. Massive sea animal

7. Noble title

8. Pay no attention to

6

BULL'S-EYE SPIRAL

This is a new target for those who can think in circles. The game works two ways, outward and inward. If you are outward bound, guess the word that fits clue 1-8 (the numbers correspond to the number of letters in the answer). Then go on to clue 9-14 and so on. If you're stuck with an outward-bound word, try the inward clues. Work both ways to hit the Bull's-Eye.   Solution on page 267

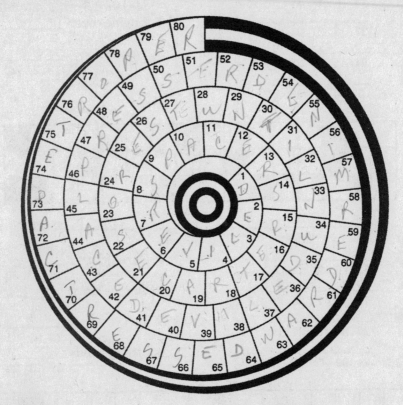

OUTWARD	INWARD
1-8. Distributes mail	80-73. Gave the news
9-14. Trendsetters	72-66. Leading lady
15-21. Go over again	65-60. Duke of Windsor
22-27. Most painful	59-54. Royal fur
28-32. Up to the time of	53-47. Chest of drawers
33-36. Unclothed	46-42. Location
37-40. Reside	41-35. Prepared stuffed eggs
41-45. Transfer pattern	34-30. Dark
46-52. Ironer	29-26. Eccentrics
53-57. Jeans material	25-21. Unevenly worn
58-63. Sketch anew	20-14. First Family before the Reagans
64-70. Sweet course	13-8. Summaries
71-75. Military student	7-1. Abused verbally
76-80. Lassoer	

7

QUOTAGRAMS

Fill in the answers to the clues below. Then transfer the letters to the correspondingly numbered squares in each diagram. Each completed diagram will contain a quotation.

Solutions on page 267

A.

1. College head — ___ ___ ___ ___
19 7 32 11

2. Jiffy — ___ ___ ___ ___ ___ ___
23 17 27 21 3 8

3. Faithful — ___ ___ ___ ___ ___
34 15 33 28 6

4. Not spicy — ___ ___ ___ ___ ___
5 30 22 36 14

5. Great pleasure — ___ ___ ___ ___ ___ ___ ___
1 26 29 10 37 25 18

6. Engine cover — ___ ___ ___ ___
9 4 2 31

7. Powerful — ___ ___ ___ ___ ___ ___
13 24 20 35 16 12

1	2		3	4	5	6	7		8	9	10	11	12	13	
14	15		16	17	18		19	20	21	22	23		24	25	26
27		28	29	30		31	32	33		34	35	36	37		

B.

1. Vista — ___ ___ ___ ___ ___
12 10 44 41 2

2. Pertinent — ___ ___ ___ ___ ___ ___ ___ ___
16 13 7 25 3 18 36 38

3. Influences — ___ ___ ___ ___ ___
27 20 6 22 14

4. Selection — ___ ___ ___ ___ ___ ___
34 39 42 32 28 8

5. Chronicles — ___ ___ ___ ___ ___ ___
15 43 30 40 19 1

6. Female fox — ___ ___ ___ ___ ___
31 35 9 17 33

7. Tart — ___ ___ ___ ___
23 29 11 5

8. Strong winds — ___ ___ ___ ___ ___
37 21 24 4 26

1	2	3	4	5	6	7		8	9	10	11	12	13	14		15
16	17		18	19	20	21	22	23		24	25	26	27		28	29
30	31	32	33	34	35	36	37		38	39	40	41		42	43	44

C.

1. Taught one-on-one — ___ ___ ___ ___ ___ ___ ___
43 25 9 15 38 45 5

2. Lamb — ___ ___ ___ ___ ___
49 44 13 35 3

3. Son — ___ ___ ___ ___
18 48 6 42

4. Evaluate — ___ ___ ___ ___ ___ ___ ___ ___
46 27 33 16 11 29 36 4

5. Welcome — ___ ___ ___ ___ ___
47 23 7 19 26

6. Jester — ___ ___ ___ ___ ___ ___ ___
24 22 14 40 21 41 8

7. Baptize — ___ ___ ___ ___ ___ ___ ___ ___
31 20 28 32 10 17 1 30

8. Take it easy — ___ ___ ___ ___ ___
12 39 34 37 2

1	2	3	4	5	6	7	8	9	10		11	12	13		14	15	16		17
18	19		20	21	22	23		24	25	26		27	28	29	30	31	32	33	34
35	36		37	38	39		40	41	42		43	44	45		46	47	48	49	

MATCH-UP
Can you find the two pictures below that are identical?
Answer and explanation on page 267

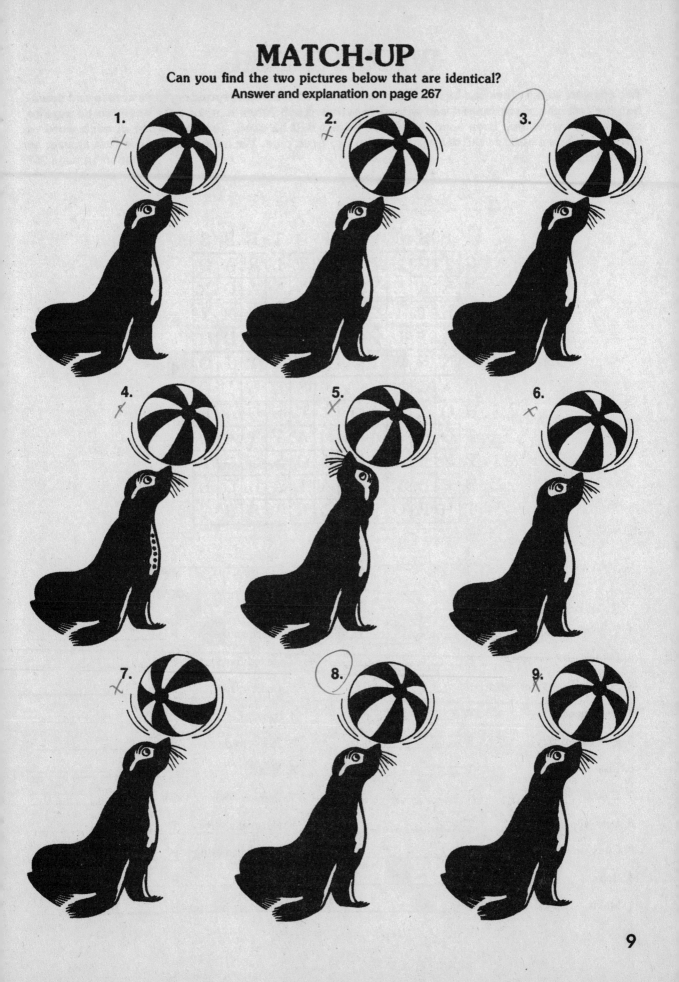

WORDFINDER

The answers to the clues can be found in the diagram in their corresponding rows across and down, but the letters are rearranged and mixed together. Each letter is used only once, so be sure to cross it out when you have used it. All the letters will be used. The first letter of each word or phrase is shown outside the diagram and next to each clue. We have filled in the first answer as an example.

Solution on page 267

```
        P  S  J  V  W  P  C  T  P  B  S
   C  [ T  C  E  T  E  H  T  L  R  A  O ]
   P  [ E  A  E  Y  T  E  N  N  A  O  R ]
   F  [ H  T  I  O  F  T  T  R  E  N  Y ]
   V  [ A  I  L  E  S  S  O  N  N  H  H ]
   S  [ N  N  W  I  E  N  E  E  T  T  O ]
   T  [ A  E  N  U  A  M  S  E  L  I  C ]
   H  [ O  L  U  T  F  T  P  E  G  A  L ]
   T  [ O  O  A  A  E  M  A  T  T  A  O ]
   P  [ Y  R  I  I  E  R  O  S  O  G  T ]
   B  [ R  D  V  E  R  A  I  A  D  G  L ]
   T  [ H  R  O  R  I  O  R  T  S  R  C ]
```

ACROSS			DOWN		
1. Type of needlework	C	ROCHET	1. Large snake	P	YTHON
2. Lying face downward	P	RONE	2. Gazed fixedly	S	TARED
3. Strengthen against attack	F	ORTIFY	3. Light spear	J	AVELIN
4. Disappear	V	ANISH	4. Assortment	V	ARIETY
5. Add sugar to	S	WEETEN	5. Most tired	W	EARIEST
6. Fine powder	T	ALCUM	6. Model	P	ATTERN
7. Useful	H	ELPFUL	7. Comics	C	ARTOONS
8. Love apple	T	OMATO	8. Natural ability	T	ALENT
9. Clergyman	P	RIEST	9. Cost for mailing	P	OSTAGE
10. Span	B	RIDGE	10. A real buy	B	ARGAIN
11. Molar	T	OOTH	11. Learning institute	S	CHOOL

10

FOUR CORNERS

The letters of the four corner crossword puzzles have been alphabetized and listed across the top and bottom and down the sides of the diagram. Thus, the letters of the crossword in the upper left corner have been alphabetized with those of the upper right corner and listed in the four rows across the top. The letters from the upper left corner have also been alphabetized with those of the lower left corner and listed in the four columns on the left. Determine where the letters belong in the squares to create the four crossword puzzles. Every letter is in its proper row and column. We have inserted the letter V in its proper place by way of illustration and to get you started.

Solution on page 267

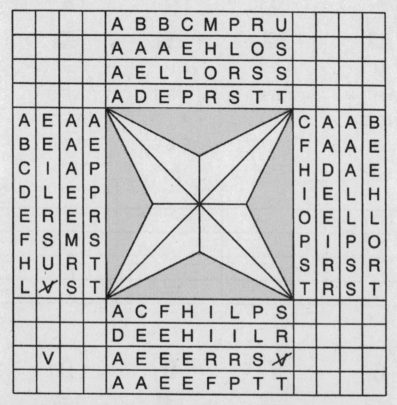

CATEGORIES

For each of the categories listed, can you think of a word or phrase beginning with each letter on the left? Count one point for each correct answer. A score of 15 is good, and 21 is excellent.

Our solutions on page 267

	SIGNS OF THE ZODIAC	ROOMS	EUROPEAN CAPITALS	BEVERAGES	PEOPLE IN THE BIBLE
C	ANCER	CLASS	COPENHAGEN	COCOA	CAIN
L	IBRA	LIBRARY	LONDON	LEMONADE	LAZZARUS
A	QUARIUS	ATTIC	ATHENS	ALE	ANAS
S	AGITTARIUS	STUDIO	STOCKHOLM	SODA	SIMON
P	ICES	PARLOR	PARIS	PUNCH	PILATE

BOWL GAME

To bowl a "strike" (20 points), you must create a 10-letter word using all the letters in each pin below. In each pin, the letter on top is the first letter of the "strike" word. To bowl a "spare" (10 points), use the same 10 letters to form two words. Splits are not allowed: you may not divide the "strike" to form a "spare." For example, SWEETHEART may not become SWEET and HEART.

Our solutions with a perfect score of 300 points on page 267

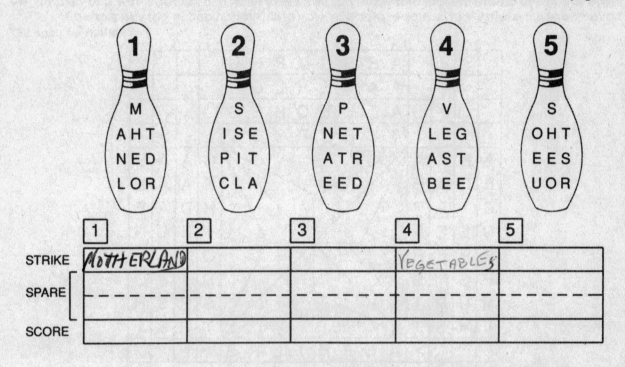

	1	2	3	4	5
STRIKE	MOTHERLAND			VEGETABLES	
SPARE					
SCORE					

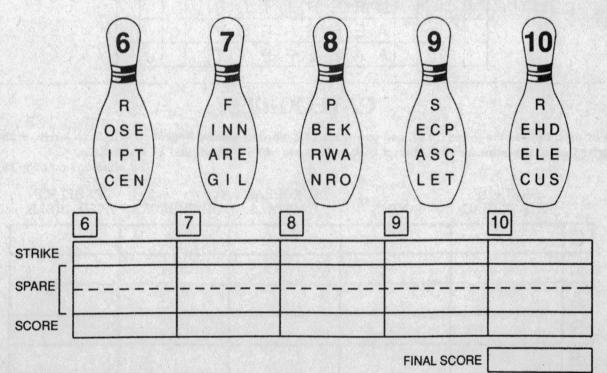

	6	7	8	9	10
STRIKE					
SPARE					
SCORE					

FINAL SCORE

ROULETTE

A guaranteed winner! Fill in the 6-letter answers to clues 1 to 12 radially, from the outside ring to the center. The 3- and 5-letter answers to clues 13 to 24 read in a clockwise direction. When all the clues are answered, add the 12 letters given below to the outermost ring and you will discover a quotation from Eugene Ionesco.   Solution on page 267

B E E I I L M N O S S U

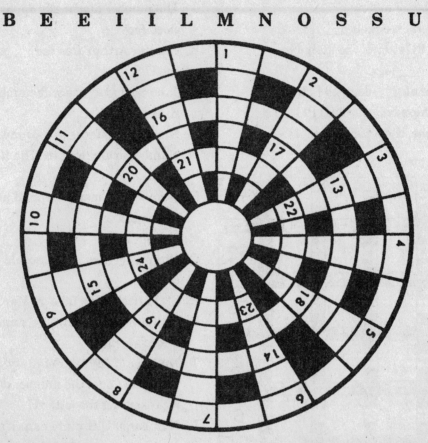

RADIALLY (Out to in)

1. Shaving foam
2. Woods
3. Chant
4. Deer horn
5. Soothes
6. Flat pasta strip
7. Eye part
8. Nab
9. Watch out
10. Try hard
11. Sewing implement
12. Fuse metal

AROUND (Clockwise)

13. Sum
14. Exterior
15. Inferior
16. Metric quart
17. Self
18. In addition
19. Important age
20. Accomplished
21. Causes a tie
22. Poor
23. Yearns
24. Unknit

QUOTATION: __ __ __ __ __   __ __   __ __ __   __ __ __ __ __ __ __   __ __ __ __ __ __.

CROSS NUMBERS

Place the answer to each clue below into the corresponding space in the diagram. The answer for each clue is a number. If you are stuck on an answer, use the equations both across and down to fill in the missing numbers.

Solution on page 267

A. Number of faces on Mt. Rushmore
B. Atomic number of mercury
C. Roman numeral L equals ____.
D. N is the _14_ th letter of the alphabet.
E. A spider has ____ legs.
F. Water freezes at _31_ degrees Fahrenheit.
G. Number of ship's bells for 2:00 PM = 2
H. On a telephone, the letter J is represented by number _5_.

I. Number of stars on a rear admiral's insignia
J. The number diagonally opposite the 4 on a clock face _10_
K. Chester Arthur was the ____st president of the U.S.
L. Jane Seymour was wife number ____ for King Henry VII.
M. Number of ounces in a pound _116_
N. Number of children in "The Brady Bunch" family
O. Number of times a biennial plant blooms in four years _8_
P. Lincoln bill _5_
Q. Number of aces in a pinochle deck of cards
R. St. Patrick's day falls on March _17_ th.
S. Excluding Rudolph, _8_ reindeer pull Santa's sleigh.
T. Number of days in February, 1986
U. In Morse Code, the number of dots representing the letter H
V. Number of U.S. state names ending in "s"
W. Number of years in a decade _100_
X. A hexagon has _8_ sides.
Y. Number of stars in the Big Dipper

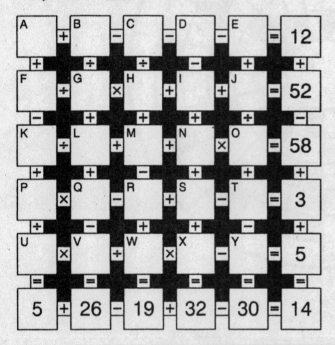

DART GAME

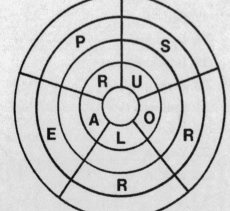

Form five words, reading from the center of the diagram outward, by adding the letters given below to complete the 5-letter words. Each letter will be used only once and each word begins with the center letter. Solution on page 267

A D E G H L O T U V Y

ABACUS

Slide the abacus beads on the wires to form five related words reading down. All the beads will be used. Keep in mind that the beads are on wires and cannot jump over each other. An empty abacus is provided for you to work in.

Solution on page 267

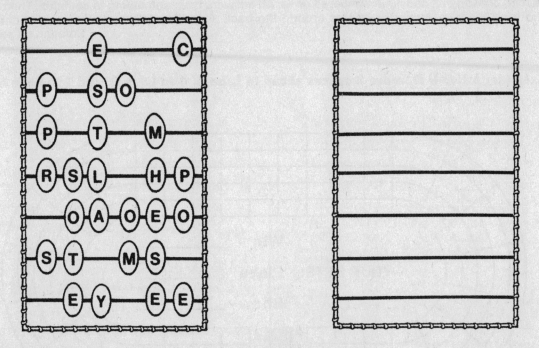

CHIPS

Place the chips of words given below on the blanks, one letter per blank, to discover a saying. When a word contains an even number of letters, it is split in half to form two chips. If it contains an odd number of letters, the extra letter is added to the second chip.

Solution on page 267

| HAR | A | IST | TERY | HING | S | O | NOT | T |
| RES | FLAT | O | IT | TH | I | AN | DER | F | B |

—— —— —— —— —— ——   —— ——   —— —— ——

—— ——   —— —— —— ——   —— —— —— ——

—— ——   —— ——   —— —— —— —— —— .

FINISH THE FOURS

Place letters into the diagram to form a string of overlapping 4-letter words. A 4-letter word begins in each numbered square. If you choose the correct letters, the circled letters will reveal the name of a literary character, reading in order from left to right.

Solution on page 267

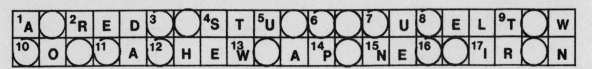

15

PUZZLE DERBY

Ladies and gentlemen, the horses are at the starting gate. Select your favorite vowel (A, E, I, O or U), and the race is on. First fill in the blanks with the answers to the clues. Vowels always go above numbered dashes, and consonants above unnumbered ones. All answers have something in common. Then to find out who wins the race, move the horses around the track according to the number values under the vowels.

Solution on page 267

Example: <u>A</u> <u>L</u> <u>O</u> <u>U</u> <u>D</u>, **move 2 spaces ahead in Lane A, 4 in Lane O, and 1 in Lane U.**
   2   **4 1**

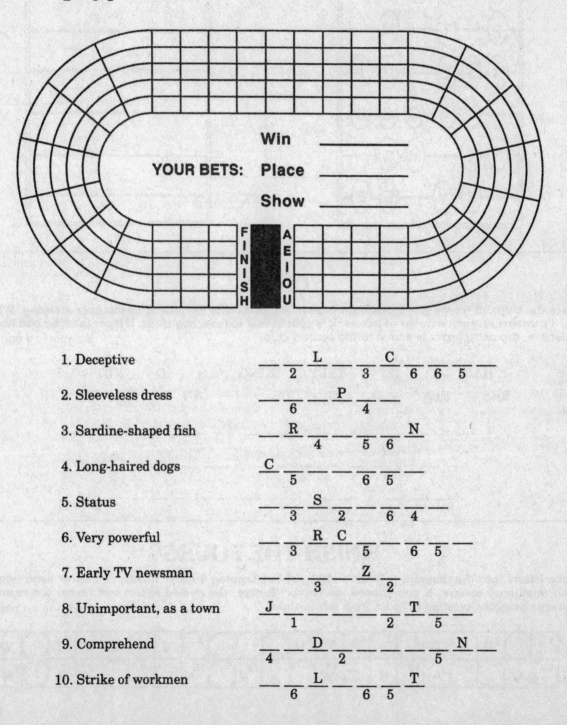

YOUR BETS:
Win _____
Place _____
Show _____

FINISH

A E I O U

1. Deceptive   __ <u>L</u> __ __ <u>C</u> __ __ __
         2   3   6 6 5

2. Sleeveless dress   __ __ <u>P</u> __
         6   4

3. Sardine-shaped fish   __ <u>R</u> __ __ <u>N</u>
         4   5 6

4. Long-haired dogs   <u>C</u> __ __ __ __ __
         5   6 5

5. Status   __ __ <u>S</u> __ __ __
         3   2   6 4

6. Very powerful   __ __ <u>R</u> <u>C</u> __ __ __
         3   5   6 5

7. Early TV newsman   __ __ __ <u>Z</u> __ __
          3   2

8. Unimportant, as a town   <u>J</u> __ __ __ <u>T</u> __
         1   2 5

9. Comprehend   __ __ <u>D</u> __ __ __ <u>N</u> __
         4   2   5

10. Strike of workmen   __ __ <u>L</u> __ __ <u>T</u>
         6   6 5

SYLLASTEPS

The answers to each clue below is a 4-syllable word. All the syllables are given in the SYLLABARY, so cross each one off as you use it. Place the syllables in the diagram, one syllable per box, in the corresponding row. When completed, the diagram will contain two related words reading diagonally downward from numbers 1 and 5, as indicated by the tinted boxes.

Solution on page 267

SYLLABARY

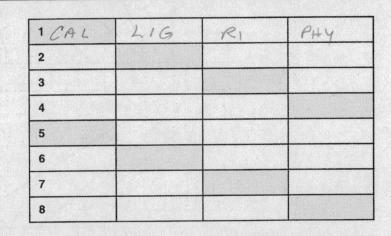

A	A	AD	BLE	CA	CAL	COM	CU	ER	ER	I	IM	IN	LA
LAC	LIG	LO	MIS	PHY	PRO	PU	RA	RE	RI	SCRU	TA
TIES	TION	TION	TOR	TY	U

1. Elegant penmanship

2. Keenness

3. Devoted fan

4. Jagged tear

5. Diplomatic person

6. Foreign particles

7. Mysterious

8. Movement to a new place

1	CAL	LIG	RI	PHY
2				
3				
4				
5				
6				
7				
8				

MARBLES

Place the letters of a common 5-letter word in the empty "marbles" so that when you start at any of the 16 outside "marbles" and read inward along connecting lines to the center, you will read a common 4-letter word. All 16 of the 4-letter words are different.

Solution on page 267

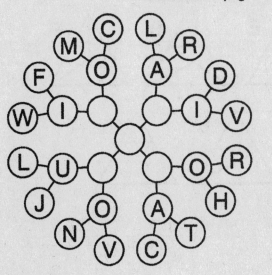

LETTER SCORE

In this game, you seek the lowest score possible. Add a few letters to each side of the letters below to form ten common words. You must add at least one letter to each side. To score, count one point for each letter you add and seven points for each word you cannot form. We added a total of 39 letters.

Our solutions on page 267

1. _____ T W _____
2. _____ W T _____
3. _____ W R _____
4. _____ D F _____
5. _____ E B R _____
6. _____ D F A _____
7. _____ P P O _____
8. _____ X I B _____
9. _____ A U Z _____
10. _____ E T P _____

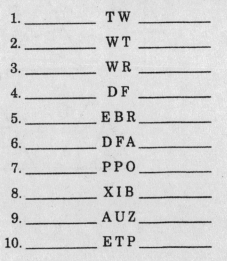

17

PULLING STRINGS

Place the answers to the definitions into the squares. Squares which are connected with lines contain the same letter. Don't get tangled!

Solution on page 267

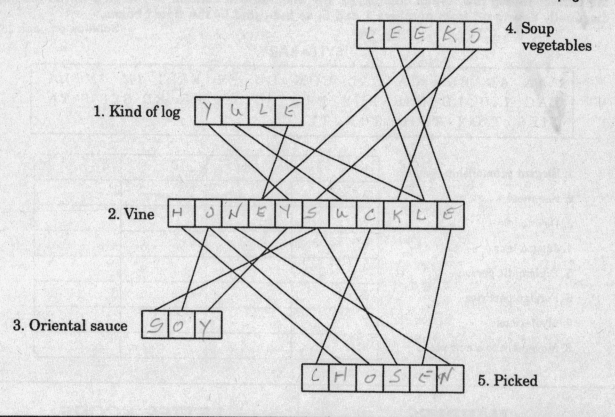

4. Soup vegetables

1. Kind of log

2. Vine

3. Oriental sauce

5. Picked

TRIANGLE QUOTE

Each letter in the quotation is represented by a number. To determine that number, count the number of triangles in the symbol next to the letter. Next, place that letter on the correspondingly numbered blank at the bottom to reveal the Triangle Quote.

Solution on page 267

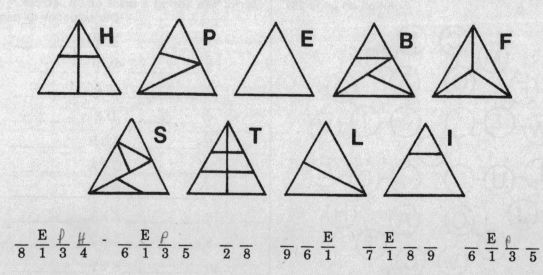

$$\frac{E}{8}\frac{P}{1}\frac{H}{3}\frac{}{4} - \frac{E}{6}\frac{P}{1}\frac{}{3}\frac{}{5} \quad \frac{}{2}\frac{}{8} \quad \frac{}{9}\frac{E}{6}\frac{}{1} \quad \frac{E}{7}\frac{}{1}\frac{}{8}\frac{}{9} \quad \frac{E}{6}\frac{P}{1}\frac{}{3}\frac{}{5}$$

18

BRICK BY BRICK

Rearrange this stack of bricks to form a crossword puzzle. The clues will help you fit the bricks into their correct places. Row 1 has been filled in for you. Use the bricks to fill in the remaining spaces.

Solution on page 267

ACROSS

1. Infant's bed
   Water barriers
   Harbingers
2. Actress Turner
   Exude
   Western show
3. Pismires
   Lunchrooms
4. More timid
   Remote
   Mr. Preminger
5. For each
   Actress Sandra
   Ms. Farrow et al.
6. Myth
   Improves
7. Parable
   Goofy
   Danish coin
8. Wish
   Maui dances
   Ollie's pal
9. Ripen
   Gropes
   Mountain ridge
10. Sculptor's stone
    Butter-colored
11. Boorish
    Aries
    Sugar suffix
12. FDR's mother
    Vetch
    Keg
13. Rhode Island's
    capital
    Miss Kett
14. Ms. Burstyn
    Chilly
    Snapped
15. Activists
    Pairs
    Actress Daly

DOWN

1. Vise
   Fraud
   Zoomed
2. Hindu queen
   Forum fashion
   Singer Guthrie
3. Trespasser
   Stage part
4. Sunbathe
   Before, in verse
   More valiant
5. Jittery
   Winter ailment
   Those elected
6. Fiat
   Listened to
7. Physician's org.
   Follow
   Put up
8. Irk
   Doozy
   Winter forecast
9. Vapor
   Surgical tool
   Murmur
   lovingly
10. Hearings
    Stereotypes
11. Mineral
    March sister
    ____ mater
12. Glum
    B'way sign
    Breather
13. Rewrite
    Outstanding
14. Clean-cut
    Nuts!
    Author Anya
15. Fair: hyph.
    Rational
    Gladden

BRICKS

EGE / RY	MAR / ▮AG	HOP / AGE	▮YE / E▮R	LAN / ANT
MIT / AFE	COO / TWO	A▮E / SC	BAR / EE	ULA / ELS
RS▮ / ENC	▮L / STO	SAR / PRO	NDS / ORA	KER / ▮DE
AME / LY	EN / RS	R▮ / IAS	A▮E / VID	L▮S / SST
REL / TTA	▮RO / TER	LLO / AM▮	TTO / ▮▮	BLE / RUD
S▮S / ▮AR	HOT / YNE	▮FA / EM	TAN / ETE	E▮H / ▮FE
DEO / IAS	ND▮ / SIL	ELL / DOE	W▮ / OSE	MEE / PER

DIAGRAM

	1	2	3	4	5	6	7	8	9	10	11	12	13	14	15
1	C	R	I	B	▮	D	A	M	S	▮	O	M	E	N	S
2															
3															
4															
5															
6															
7															
8															
9															
10															
11															
12															
13															
14															
15															

Blockbuilders

Fit the letter blocks into the diagram to spell out the name of a famous person.

Solution on page 267

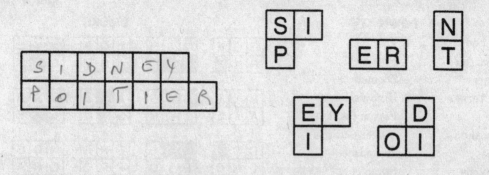

S I D N E Y
P O I T I E R

Rounders

The names of three card games are hidden in these Rounders. For each one, start at one of the letters and read either clockwise or counterclockwise.

Solutions on page 267

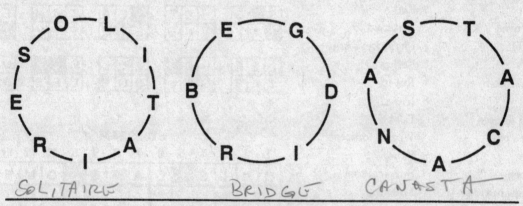

SOLITAIRE   BRIDGE   CANASTA

Guess Who

Change one letter in each word to form the names of famous people.

Solutions on page 267

Example: Clerk Table (**Answer:** Clark Gable)

1. Box Denser   BOB DENVER
2. Dad Father   DAN RATHER
3. Folly Carton   DOLLY PARTON
4. Ray Lend   JAY LENO

5. Fee Margin   LEE MARVIN
6. Man Test   MAE WEST
7. Gel Gibbon   MEL GIBSON
8. Moody Alien   Woody Allen

PLACES, PLEASE

Fill the diagram with all the words in the word list, starting on the matching numbers and reading forward, backward, up, down, and diagonally, always in a straight line. Words from different numbers sometimes overlap; therefore, some letters will be used more than once. The starting letters and the words from number 3 and number 15 have been inserted. When the puzzle is completed, all the squares will be filled.

Solution on page 268

1. EDIT
   ELL
2. BEARDS
   BLESS
   BYPASS
3. ANGLES
   AREAS
4. SLY
   SPA
5. PAR
   PASS
   PAT
   PESOS
   PILL
6. TACT
   TEACH
   TEEN
   THAW
   TIDE
   TOTS
7. SLATE
   SLICK
8. EARMUFFS
   ECHOED
   ENERGY
   ERASER
   ERUPTION
   EUREKA
   EXALTS

9. BEMUSE
   BENEATH
10. RACCOON
    RAPTURE
    RENT
    RESTFUL
    RUNWAYS
11. RAISE
    RECOLOR
    RULES
12. WEARY
    WIDER

WIN
WOO
WROTE
13. DATA
    DEAR
    DEER
    DUST
14. PAPERS
    PAUSE
    PENNY
    PLACE
    PUFFY

15. PANT
    PET
    PRAY
    PURE
    PUT
16. TIGER
    TINY
17. PAN
    PAYS
    POT
    PRIM

1 E	L	L	T	K	S	S	S	A	P	Y	2 B	E
T	D	L	C	S	T	Y	3 A	N	G	L	E	S
A	A	I	A	O	L	A	E	R	E	4 S	A	U
L	L	5 P	6 T	H	A	W	E	S	E	P	R	M
7 S	A	E	E	N	X	N	S	R	I	A	D	E
R	E	S	A	R	8 E	U	R	E	K	A	S	9 B
N	O	O	C	L	A	10 R	A	P	T	U	11 R	E
I	U	S	H	T	R	E	W	A	U	E	N	
12 W	R	O	T	E	M	S	13 D	14 P	L	A	C	E
I	E	R	U	15 P	U	T	U	E	T	M	O	A
D	G	A	A	R	F	F	S	N	E	I	L	T
E	I	N	R	A	F	U	T	N	A	R	O	H
R	16 T	I	N	Y	S	L	S	Y	A	17 P	R	N

21

PHOTO FINISH

Can you find the picture that matches the negative shown?
Answer and explanation on page 268

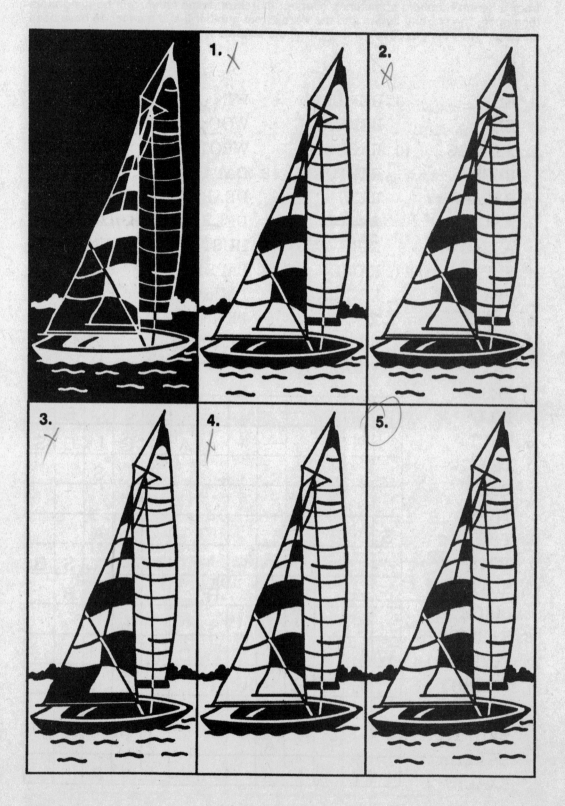

FIRST AND LAST

The answers to each clue can be found in the diagram. You can move up, down, backward, and forward, but not diagonally. Do not skip over any squares. The last letter of each answer is the first letter of the next answer; otherwise, each letter is used only once. The answer to the first clue begins in the outlined box, and the first and last letters of each answer are circled.

Solution on page 268

1. Michael Jordan's game — BASKETBALL
2. The Pelican State — LOUISANA
3. Kind of soup — ALPHABET
4. Record player — TURNTABLE
5. Disastrous tremor — EARTH QUAKE
6. Needlework — EMBROIDERY
7. Standard of measurement — YARD STICK
8. Memento — KEEPSAKE
9. Miss Manners's forte — ETIQUETTE
10. People mover — ESCALATOR
11. New York hockey team — RANGERS
12. Astronomer's subject — STAR
13. Pep club gathering — RALLY
14. Cultured dairy product — YOGURT

I	A	N	A	U	A	K	E	M	B
S	H	P	L	Q	H	T	R	U	R
I	A	R	N	T	T	B	O	G	O
U	B	U	B	A	R	A	Y	L	I
O	E	T	L	E	A	S	A	L	D
L	L	A	B	T	E	K	R	A	E
S	C	A	L	O	R	G	E	T	R
E	T	T	A	T	A	N	R	S	Y
Q	U	E	A	S	E	K	T	S	A
I	T	E	K	P	E	C	I	D	R

23

WHAT'S LEFT?

Following the instructions, cross off words in the diagram. When you are done, the remaining words will form a quotation reading left to right, line by line.

Solution on page 268

A	B	C	D
CHARACTER	CHINA	GOOD	FOR
GOLF	NEVER	THAT	REFLEX
RADIO	ZAIRE	REFEREE	JUST
PERU	DRIVE	DENIM	IS
ROUND	EXPECT	PHASE	QUESTIONS
OUTRANK	FIRST	NANNY	FRO
ROW	PEELS	EASY	HUMBLE
TIDAL	ARIA	TALK	MANE
SAIL	THE	MEXICO	HOUSE
NO	ANSWERS	FUN	FLOW

1. Cross off all words in columns A and D which contain only vowels from the first half of the alphabet.

2. Cross off all words ending in two vowels.

3. Cross off all 6-letter words in columns B and D.

4. Cross off all words immediately above, below, or next to a word containing an X.

5. Cross off all 5-letter words whose middle three letters spell a woman's name.

6. Cross off all words which are the names of countries.

7. Cross off all words which are also words when read backwards.

8. Cross off all words which rhyme with DOUGH.

THREE TO ONE

Starting with each word in Column A, add a word from Column B and then one from Column C to build ten longer words. For example, CORN plus ERST plus ONE is CORNERSTONE. Each small word will be used only once. Solution on page 268

	A	B	C		
1.	HE	HA	LIST	1.	HEAD REST
2.	NOT	IS	CAB	2.	NOTATION
3.	OR	I	A	3.	ORCHESTRATE
4.	DENT	A	BET	4.	DENTISTRY
5.	RE	ILL	ION	5.	REINDEER
6.	FIN	AD	ANT	6.	FINALIST
7.	ALP	AT	TRY	7.	ALPHABET
8.	IN	CHEST	DEER	8.	INFORMANT
9.	VAN	FORM	REST	9.	VANILLA
10.	TAX	IN	RATE	10.	TAXI CAB

Hubcaps

Insert two letters into the center of each circle below to form three 6-letter words reading across and diagonally (top to bottom). When you are finished, the letters you have entered, reading across, will spell a bonus word. Solution on page 268

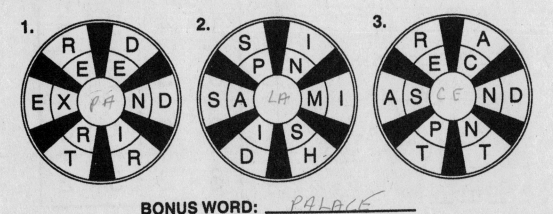

BONUS WORD: _PALACE_

25

Headings

Use the letters in each Heading to fill in the blanks to complete words related to the Heading. Cross out each letter as you use it.   Solutions on page 268

1. TODAY'S TELEPHONES

M __ M __ R __

C _O_ R _D_ L _E_ S S

DIA _L_

__ __ E __ K __ R

__ O U C __ - __ O __ E

2. LET'S PAINT THE HOUSE

B R __ __ __

__ C R __ __ __ R

R _O_ _L_ L _E_ R

__ __ I __ N __ R

__ __ N __

3. SAY IT WITH FLOWERS

_F_ U C _H_ S I A

H _Y_ A C _I_ N _T_ H

_W_ I _S_ T E _R_ I A

_W_ I L D R _O_ S _E_

D _A_ I _S_ Y

_T_ U L _I_ P

Tile Patterns

Place the numbered tiles into the diagram to form the pattern given. The tiles may be placed horizontally, as shown, or vertically, with the number on the left on the top and the number on the right on the bottom.   Solution on page 268

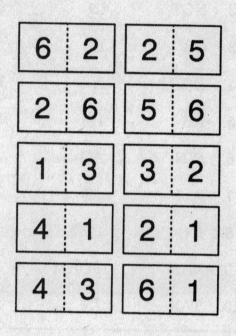

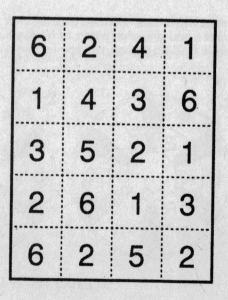

26

SPLIT PERSONALITIES

The names of eight tennis players have been split into 2-letter segments. The letters in each segment are in order, but the segments have been scrambled. For each group can you put the pieces together to identify the tennis player?

Solutions on page 268

1. IE KI BI JE NG AN LL   *BILLIE JEAN KING*

2. EF GR AF FI ST   *STEFFI GRAF*

3. UR AS TH HE AR   *ARTHUR ASHE*

4. ED ST RG AN BE EF   _____

5. TI GA SA BR LA BA NI IE   _____

6. RI RT SE CH VE   _____

7. AV TI RT AN VA LO RA IN MA   _____

8. MM NO ON YC JI RS   _____

Slide-O-Rama

Slide down each column of letters up or down independently to form the names of as many different items of clothing as you can. The word will appear in the middle row where GOWN is now.

Our list of 11 words on page 268

27

MIND BOGGLER

Each of the symbols in the diagram represents one of the numbers given. Replace each of the four symbols with one of the numbers in order to make this subtraction problem work.

Solution on page 268

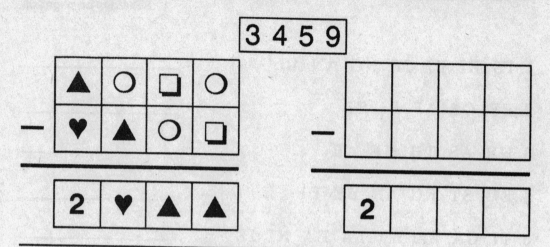

Crypto-Trivia

The interesting bit of trivia below is in a substitution code.

Solution on page 268

```
OYAAM  HLXEZ  NFJF  XDS  DJYAYXLGGM
BLVF  YX  STF  ZTLOF  DK  L  OYA.  YX  STF
BYVVGF  LAFZ,  EYSPTFX  ISFXZYGZ  NFJF
BLVF  KJDB  LX  DJLXAF  PGLM  PLGGFV
''OMAA.''  STYZ  PGLM  NLZ  IZFV  SD  BLEF
PIOZ,  VYZTFZ,  ODSZ,  LXV  QLJZ.  OFDOGF
DKSFX  ZLCFV  BDXFM  YX  STFYJ  ''OMAA
QLJZ.''  FCFX  NTFX  OMAA  NLZ  XD  GDXAFJ
IZFV,  STF  XLBF  JFBLYXFV.
STF  OMAA  QLJZ  HFPLBF
OYA  HLXEZ  NTFX  ODSSFJZ
BLVF  STF  HLXEZ  YX  STF
ZTLOF  DK  STF  LXYBLG,
STF  OYA.
```

WORD DIALS

Each Word Dial below contains a word, but one letter is missing. When you determine the missing letter, enter it into the center of the dial. Then you will be able to spell a word in a clockwise direction. After you have completed the four words, rearrange the four center letters to spell the name of a fish. Solutions on page 268

1.

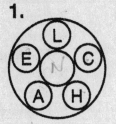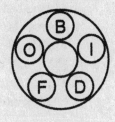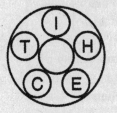

FISH: _____

2.

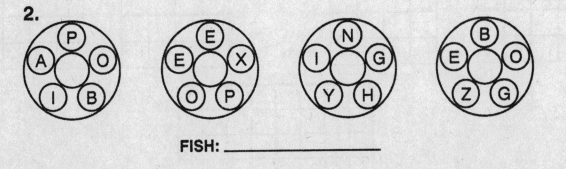

FISH: _____

Guest Star

Unscramble the letters of each group to form a 5-letter word and place the word into the correspondingly numbered column reading from top to bottom. Next, rearrange the top letters to spell the first name and the bottom letters to spell the last name of our Guest Star. Solution on page 268

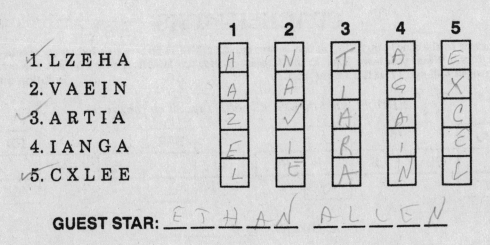

	1	2	3	4	5
1. L Z E H A	H	N	T	A	E
2. V A E I N	A	A	I	G	X
3. A R T I A	Z	V	A	A	C
4. I A N G A	E	I	R	I	E
5. C X L E E	L	E	A	N	L

GUEST STAR: E T H A N   A L L E N

29

FOUR SQUARE

Arrange the 8 answers to the given clues for each small square directly below them so that 4 words read across and 4 words read down. Then transfer the completed diagrams into the 4 sections of the larger diagram so that 4 8-letter words or phrases are formed reading across the top and bottom and down the sides.

Solution on page 268

CLUES

1. Risque
2. Lock openers
3. Labor
4. No longer are
5. BPOE members
6. Pile of hay
7. Great Lake
8. Verbal

1. Camera eye
2. Lofty
3. August babies
4. Sports group
5. Gen. Robert ____: 2 wds.
6. Female singer
7. Like ____ of bricks: 2 wds.
8. Lichen

1. Goulash
2. Close
3. Musical sound
4. Actress Moran
5. Poi source
6. "Exodus" author
7. Mata ____
8. Sagacious

1. Chain segment
2. Small pie
3. Brink
4. Seize
5. Wedding band
6. Opera solo
7. Story
8. Moistureless

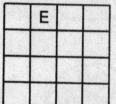

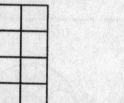

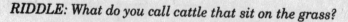

CRACKERJACKS

Find the answer to the riddle by filling in the center boxes with the letters needed to complete the words across and down. When you have filled in the Crackerjacks, the letters reading across the center boxes from left to right will spell out the riddle answer.

Solution on page 268

RIDDLE: *What do you call cattle that sit on the grass?*

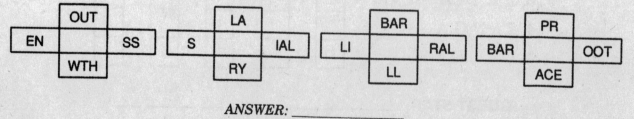

ANSWER: _____

PATCHWORK QUOTE

Fit the eight Patchwork squares into the diagram to reveal a saying reading left to right, line by line. A black square indicates the end of a word.

Solution on page 268

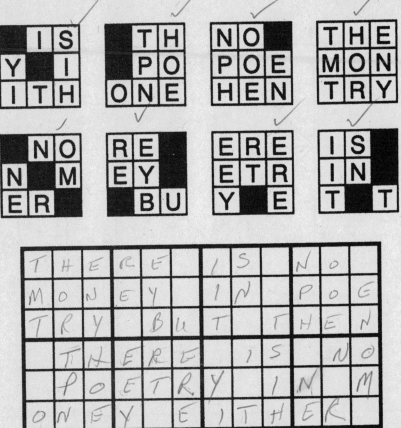

	T	H	E	R	E		I	S		N	O
M	O	N	E	Y		I	N		P	O	E
T	R	Y		B	U	T		T	H	E	N
	T	H	E	R	E		I	S		N	O
P	O	E	T	R	Y		I	N		M	
O	N	E	Y		E	I	T	H	E	R	

Riddle Me This

Here are four riddles and their mixed-up answers! Unscramble each group of letters to form a word. Use those words to fill in the answer blanks.

Solutions on page 268

SNAACV   ISONE   INNE   SANIPHEPS

1. If two is company and three is a crowd, what are four and five?   NINE

2. What increases the more it is shared with others?   HAPPINESS

3. What does every child spend time making, yet no one can see it when it's made?   NOISE

4. What is appropriate material for an artist to wear?   CANVAS

HOW MANY SQUARES?

This diagram is filled with squares small, medium, and large. Try to count them all. There are more than you may think!

Solution on page 268

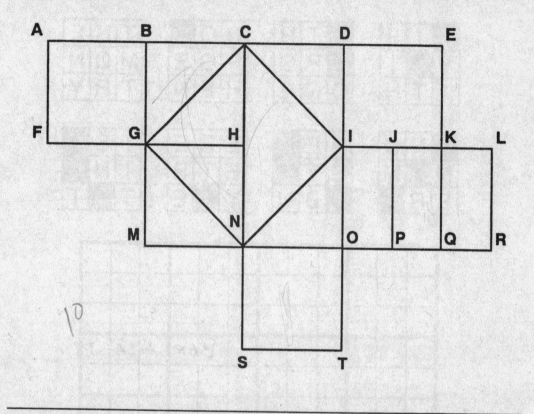

Blips

Place one of the given letters in each circle to form nine 3-letter words reading from top to bottom. Use each letter only as many times as it is listed.

Solution on page 268

A B D E E G G H N U X Y Y

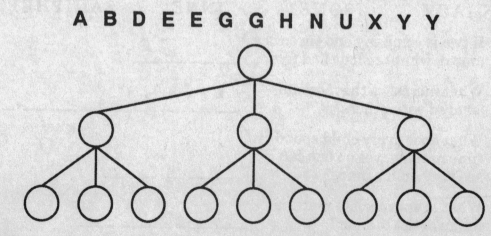

SHUFFLE

Two words with their letters in the correct order are combined in each row of letters. To solve the puzzle separate both words. There are no extra letters, and no letter is used more than once.

A. PRESIDENTS

1. GFEROARDLD   _GERALD FORD_

2. BCILINLTOLN   _BILL CLINTON_

3. JCAIMRTEMYR   _JIMMY CARTER_

4. RORENAGALADN   _RONALD REGAN_

B. FIRST LADIES

1. PNIATXRIOCINA   _PATRICIA NIXON_

2. BETRSUMASN   _BESS TRUMAN_

3. BABRBUARSAH   _BARBARA BUSH_

4. EROLEOASENVEOLRT   _ELENOR ROOSEVELT_

Lucky Clover

Fit the nine words into the four-leaf clover. Each word starts in a circle and may go in either direction. Words sometimes overlap.
Solution on page 268

Anchovy   Furnace

Camel   Orchard

Cedar   Ruffle

Chunk   Unkeyed

Data

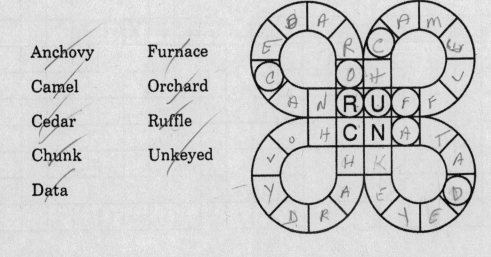

33

Framework 1

These words relating to football are listed in alphabetical order according to length. Fit them into their proper places in the Framework. This puzzle has been started for you with the entry DOWN. Now look for a 6-letter entry starting with N. Continue working this way until the puzzle is completed.

3 Letters
Tie
Win

4 Letters
Down ✓
Fake
Flag
Game
Half
Home
Line
Loss

Play

5 Letters
Clock
Coach
Sacks
Score
Squad
Train

6 Letters
Eleven
Helmet

Huddle
Number
Onside
Screen
Signal
Sprint
Tackle

7 Letters
Defense
Offside
Pigskin
Stadium

8 Letters
Schedule
Split end
Tight end

9 Letters
Bleachers
Goalposts
Officials
Scrimmage

Solution on page 269

34

Framework 2

4 Letters
Brew
Gins
Gong
Knit
Loft
Logs
Mill
Plow
Trap
Tubs
Well

5 Letters
Amber
Cabin
Posts
Strap
Trunk

6 Letters
Cradle
Dirndl
Edging
Fossil
Frocks

Grates
Harrow
Romper
Runner
Scroll
Surrey

7 Letters
Darning
Sampler

8 Letters
Cast iron

Colonial
Love seat

11 Letters
Butter molds
Roll-top desk

12 Letters
Counterpanes
Rocking horse
Stereoscopes

First word across on page 290

Solution on page 269

Framework 3

4 Characters
2G3G
2V2H
ABX2
GH17
H4T3
K55B
Q845
QQ82
V36H

5 Characters
086KY

1D254
338PV
837YG
92HU7
LKV62
MEX58
PRR57
R7H8A

6 Characters
3505HJ
4930DP
829VZL

GLK342
L993K4
NN586W
WV4090
XAT44J
XCV157
YZZL78

7 Characters
0065ABC
687USAF
843287H
G7452XB

XCU9900

8 Characters
029PJKY4
2938HHDM
FFRLP889
GGABKD77
GH55LK66

First word across on page 290

Solution on page 269

36

Friendly Relations

Framework 4

This Framework is solved in the usual manner EXCEPT that the words for the outlined areas are not given in the word list. All of the outlined words are types of roadways. You have to figure out what words they are from the crossing letters.

The list of related words is on page 275

3 Letters
All
Era
Ore
Sag
Sir
You

4 Letters
Boat
Deer
Else
Hoof

5 Letters
Arena
Erase
Keeps
Macaw

Live
Meet
Nine
Rely
Ring
Sign
Volt

Mouse
Noble
Rouge
Shady
Widen

6 Letters
Answer
Grease
Rabbit
Subtle
Wigwam

7 Letters
Cinemas
Perform

8 Letters
Enhances
Referral
Unbutton

9 Letters
Inventory

First word across on page 290

Solution on page 269

Framework 5

Water Supply

3 Letters
Bay
Ria
Sea

4 Letters
Cove
Gulf
Lake
Loch
Moor
Pool
Reef

Rill
Tide
Wash

5 Letters
Basin
Bayou
Canal
Creek
Delta
Fjord
Marsh
Ocean

River
Swamp

6 Letters
Lagoon
Runnel
Seaway
Slough
Strait
Stream

7 Letters
Culvert

Estuary
Freshet
Narrows
Rivulet

8 Letters
Aquarium
Cataract

9 Letters
Reservoir
Streamlet
Tributary

First word across on page 290

Solution on page 269

38

3 Letters
Ado
Eat
Mat
Pie
See
Win

4 Letters
Acts
Calf
Fair
Goat
Line

Sale
Seat
Tent

5 Letters
Cheer
Ducks
Fudge
Music
Prize
Rides
Rodeo
Sheep
Stars

6 Letters
Crafts
Hot dog
Midway
Stalls
Stands

7 Letters
Judging
Visitor

8 Letters
Displays
Drawings

Ring toss

9 Letters
Amusement
Sideshows

10 Letters
Excitement
Hippodrome

12 Letters
Entertainers
Merry-go-round

First word across on page 290   Solution on page 269

M	I	D	W	A	Y		D	R	A	W	I	N	G	S		C	A	L	F
U			I					I				O				H			
S	T	A	N	D	S		E	N	T	E	R	T	A	I	N	E	R	S	
I		M		A			G				T			E			T		
C		U		L			T			D		P	R	I	Z	E			
		S	I	D	E	S	H	O	W	S			I			N			
V		E		I		S		E	X	C	I	T	E	M	E	N	T		
I		M		S	T	A	R	S		A		K							
S	H	E	E	P				A		T		S	T	A	L	L	S		J
I		N		L	I	N	E			C		D							U
T		T		A		M	E	R	R	Y	G	O	R	O	U	N	D		
O				Y		F		A		A			O				G		
R	I	D	E	S		A	C	T	S		F	U	D	G	E		I		
				I			E	A	T				E				N		
H	I	P	P	O	D	R	O	M	E		S		H	O	T	D	O	G	

Framework 7

These entries are listed in numerical order according to length. Fit them into their proper places in the diagram.

3 Digits	5332	64815	744678	8431053
142	8218	88133	764981	8581999
158	8621	94732	809127	
563	9582		843380	**8 Digits**
713		**6 Digits**	861234	21483467
802	**5 Digits**	184732		23459932
	12987	237944	**7 Digits**	45992817
4 Digits	14810	415254	5851432	53488214
1765	16781	478215	6381792	93214682
1899	26834	517712	6775321	
4373	31284	608234	7295343	
5124	33512	614821	8281443	

First word across on page 290

Solution on page 269

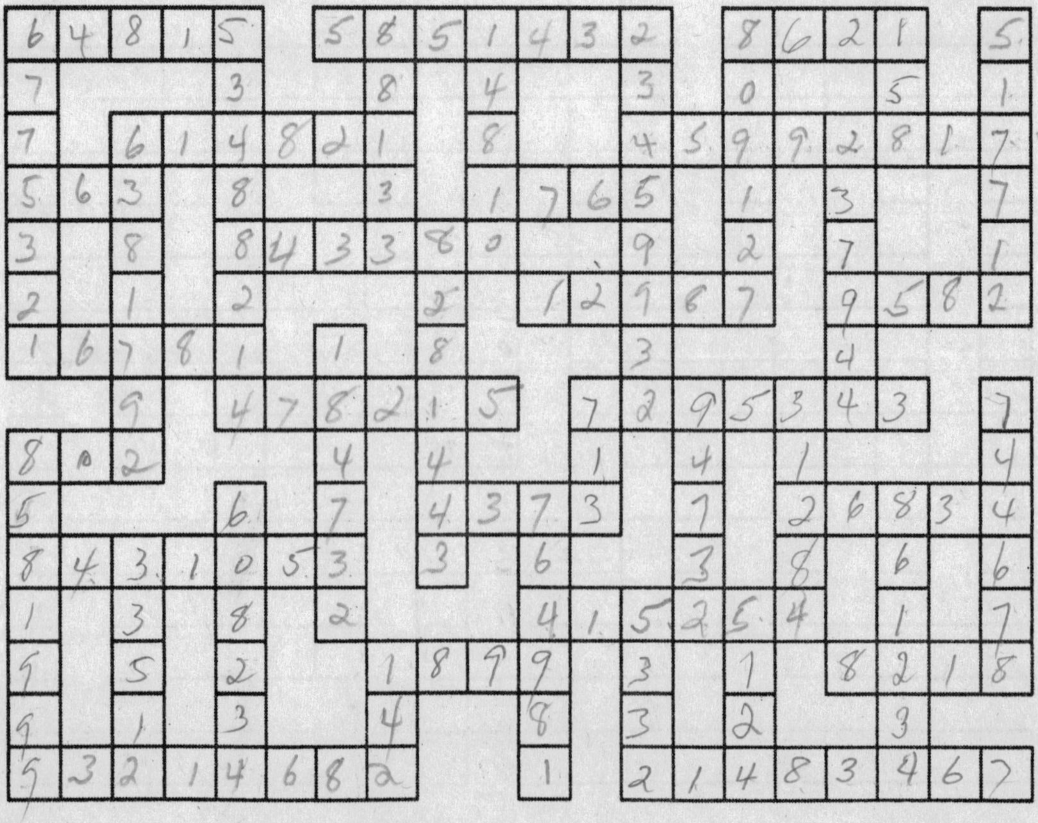

Framework 8

3 Letters
Sir
Sis
Sob
Sow
Spa
Sue

5 Letters
Scrap
Sense
Sepia
Spend
Swami
Swiss

7 Letters
Scholar
Session
Sliding
Stunned
Subside
Suspect
Sustain

Surprise
Suspense

9 Letters
Shipshape
Spearmint
Stormiest

4 Letters
Sash
Save
Sect
Seer

6 Letters
Sacred
Seines
Sparse
Splint
Strain

8 Letters
Sawhorse
Spiteful
Stillest
Suppress

10 Letters
Stammering
Standpoint
Suggestion

First word across on page 290

Solution on page 269

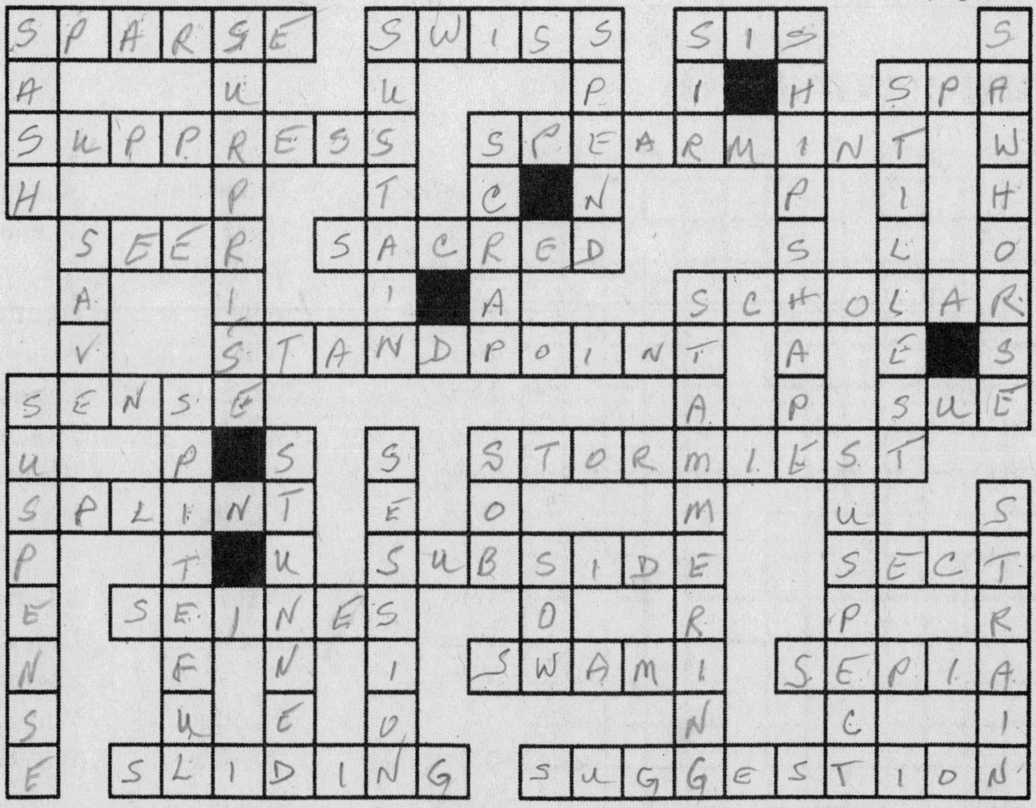

Framework 9

Quest for Fitness

These entries are listed in alphabetical order according to length. Fit them into their proper places in the Framework. This puzzle has been started for you with the word MUSCLE. Now look for an 8-letter entry starting with M. Continue this way until the puzzle is completed.

Solution on page 269

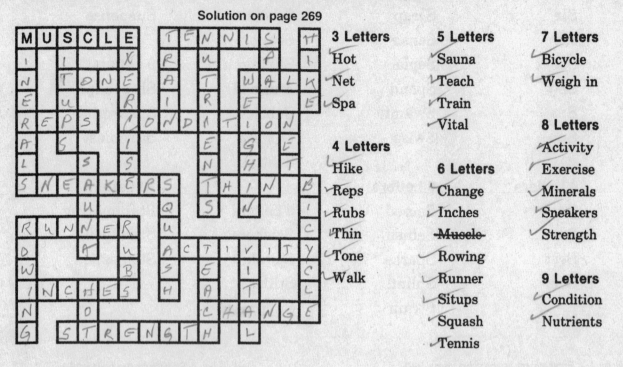

3 Letters
Hot
Net
Spa

4 Letters
Hike
Reps
Rubs
Thin
Tone
Walk

5 Letters
Sauna
Teach
Train
Vital

6 Letters
Change
Inches
Muscle
Rowing
Runner
Situps
Squash
Tennis

7 Letters
Bicycle
Weigh in

8 Letters
Activity
Exercise
Minerals
Sneakers
Strength

9 Letters
Condition
Nutrients

Framework 10

Wild W's

First word on page 290   Solution on page 269

3 Letters
Awl
Dew
Ewe
How
Now
Owl
Row
Wed
Wok
Woo
Wow
Wry

4 Letters
Anew

Draw
Ewer
Wall
Wide
Wilt
Wore
Wren

5 Letters
Known
Whirl
Worth

6 Letters
Warsaw
Willow

Window
Winnow

7 Letters
Awkward
Lowdown
Swallow
Walkway
Wayward

8 Letters
Downtown
Showdown
Williwaw
Woodwork

Number Frame

Framework 11

First number on page 290   Solution on page 269

3 Digits		
055	3130	20713
147	4178	20874
242	4188	21721
314	4296	28549
319	5608	40486
326	6895	42087
435	7057	51077
494	7398	53823
630	7503	57075
763	8062	67359
914	8207	70658
981	8720	72104
	9263	78354
	9530	86347
4 Digits	9897	
0482		**6 Digits**
1430	**5 Digits**	017482
2099	07279	280933
2479	09123	313875
2828	14286	

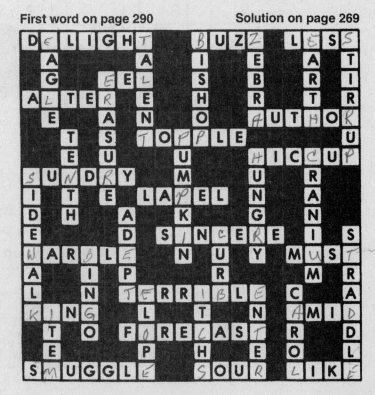

Framelinks

Framework 12

First word on page 290   Solution on page 269

Fill in missing links in this diagram with the letters given below. All the words are common words, but the puzzle is harder than it looks.

AA BBB CCC
D EEEEEEEE
G HH III K
LLL M N O
PPPP RRRRR
SS TTTTT U
W Y Z

"QUOTEFALLS"

The letters in each vertical column go into the squares directly below them, but not necessarily in the order they appear. A black square indicates the end of a word. When you have placed all the letters in their correct squares, you will be able to read a quotation across the diagram from left to right.   **Solutions on page 270**

1.
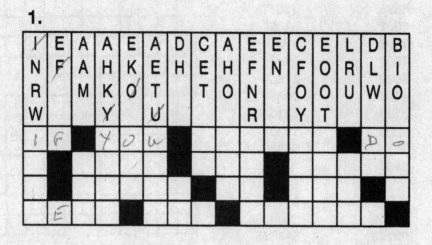

2.
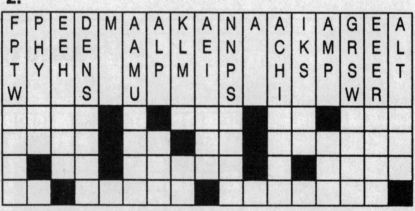

3.

FILL-IN

The entries for this puzzle are given to you, listed alphabetically according to length. Across and Down words are all mixed together, and you are to find their proper places in the diagram.

Solution on page 270

2 Letters
As
He

3 Letters
Ads
Ale
Ape
Arm
Dor
Duo
Ess
Ira
Les
Lie
Moo
Pig
Pow
Rio
Set
Sod
Tar
Tea

4 Letters
Aden
Arab
Asea
Deli
Dine

Even
Ever
Gone
Here
Lads
Mode
Nest
Ogre
Omit
Oral
Pert
Pipe

Rode
Runs
Scat
Teen
Vile

5 Letters
Acres
Alive
Arete
Beats
Dense

Eaten
Enact
Evade
Place
Raise
Reels
Regal
Space
Swede
Taped
Tenet

6 Letters
Appear
Atoned
Indeed
Native
Needle
Tender

7 Letters
Cistern
Pretend

The grid (filled in):

T	A	R			O	M	I	T		S	C	**A**	T
A	L	E		G	O	N	E		P	I	P	**E**	
P	I	G		R	O	D	E		A	S	E	**A**	
E	V	A	D	E		E	N	A	C	T			
D	E	L	I		H	E		R	E	E	L	S	
			N	E	E	D	L	E		R	I	O	
A	P	P	E	A	R		A	T	O	N	E	D	
D	O	R		T	E	N	D	E	R				
S	W	E	D	E		A	S		A	R	A	B	
	T	E	N	E	T		P	L	A	C	E		
A	D	E	N		V	I	L	E		I	R	A	
R	U	N	S		E	V	E	R		S	E	T	
M	O	D	E		N	E	S	T		E	S	S	

45

NINE OF DIAMONDS

Fill the small diamonds in the diagram with the 2-letter pieces in the box to form the answers to the clues. All answer words have eight letters and read clockwise around the corresponding number. Words overlap in the diagram so that a 2-letter piece may be in more than one word. We have set number 5, CONDENSE, for you.

Solution on page 270

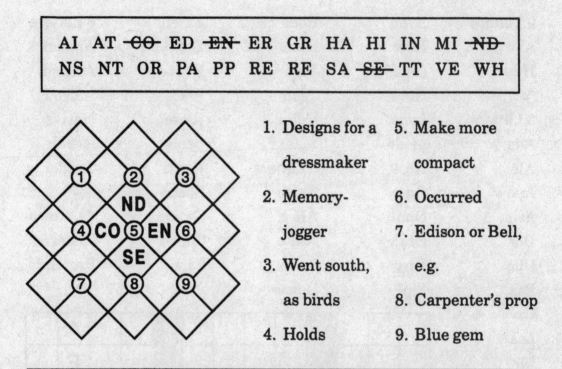

AI	AT	~~CO~~	ED	~~EN~~	ER	GR	HA	HI	IN	MI	~~ND~~
NS	NT	OR	PA	PP	RE	RE	SA	~~SE~~	TT	VE	WH

1. Designs for a dressmaker
2. Memory-jogger
3. Went south, as birds
4. Holds

5. Make more compact
6. Occurred
7. Edison or Bell, e.g.
8. Carpenter's prop
9. Blue gem

Squares

Each of the Squares contains an 8-letter word. It can be found by starting at one of the letters and reading either clockwise or counterclockwise. In the example, the word STANDARD is found by starting at the letter S and reading counterclockwise.

Solutions on page 270

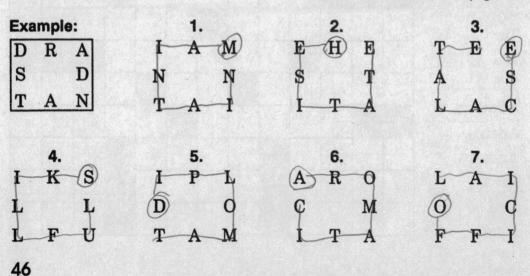

Example:

D	R	A
S		D
T	A	N

1.

I	A	M
N		N
T	A	I

2.

E	H	E
S		T
I	T	A

3.

T	E	E
A		S
L	A	C

4.

I	K	S
L		L
L	F	U

5.

I	P	L
D		O
T	A	M

6.

A	R	O
C		M
I	T	A

7.

L	A	I
O		C
F	F	I

46

Hubcaps

Insert two letters into the center of each circle below to form three 6-letter words reading across and diagonally (top to bottom). When you are finished, the letters you have entered, reading across, will spell a bonus word.

Solution on page 270

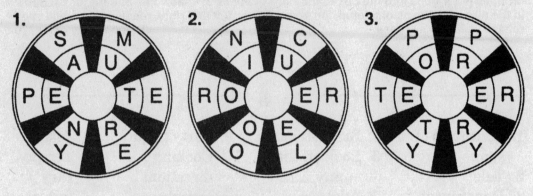

1. 2. 3.

BONUS WORD: _____

Hop, Skip, and Jump

What is the longest word you can find starting with any letter, moving only left to right? You may Hop, Skip, and Jump over any number of letters, but once you choose a letter you may not backtrack. A word with 9 letters is excellent.

Our 9-letter word on page 270

N C A V U E T I Z R O I T P I S K O C N D

Letter Tiles

Form four words reading across and five words reading down by placing the eight Letter Tiles into the diagram. Horizontal tiles go into horizontal spaces, vertical tiles into vertical spaces. In the example, three tiles fit together to form the words SAW, ONE, SO, AN, and WE.

Solution on page 270

Example:

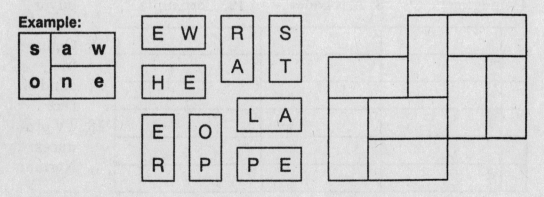

ESCALATORS

Place the answer to clue 1 in the first space, drop a letter, and arrange the remaining letters to answer clue 2. Drop another letter and arrange the remaining letters to answer clue 3. The first dropped letter goes into the box to the left of space 1, and the second dropped letter goes into the box to the right of space 3. Follow this pattern for each row in the diagram. When completed, the letters on the left and right, reading down, will spell related words or a phrase.

Solutions on page 270

1

1. Snowman of song
2. Tale
3. Donahue of films
4. Went by boat
5. Brainstorms
6. Look on the sunny ____
7. Adolescents
8. Opposite of north
9. Party giver
10. Cooking directions
11. Crawl
12. Look searchingly
13. Jets
14. Temporary failure
15. Hit
16. Rubs harshly
17. Gaze fixedly
18. "____ of Eden"

	1 FROSTY	2 STORY	3 TORY	S
F				
S	4 SAILED	5	6	
	7	8	9	
	10	11	12	
	13	14	15	
	16	17	18	

2

1. Endured
2. Directs
3. Snow coaster
4. Judging
5. Behemoth
6. Turner of song
7. Refunded
8. Arrogance
9. Faucet problem
10. Black birds
11. Trap
12. Corn units
13. Shut
14. Lumps of clay
15. Found a buyer for
16. Genuinely
17. Kind of race
18. TV producer Norman

	1	2	3	
	4	5	6	
	7	8	9	
	10	11	12	
	13	14	15	
	16	17	18	

3

1. Brook
2. Rips
3. Night light
4. Cutting
5. Birds' arms
6. Gulp
7. Quick glimpse
8. Not dirty
9. Walking stick
10. Purpose
11. Got up
12. Aching
13. Include
14. Leases
15. Sparrow's home
16. Emulated Arnold Palmer
17. Inn
18. Distribute
19. The world is your ___
20. Market
21. Decays

1	2	3	
4	5	6	
7	8	9	
10	11	12	
13	14	15	
16	17	18	
19	20	21	

4

1. Stations
2. Sat for a portrait
3. Raced
4. Rabbit's treat
5. Performer
6. Jacket
7. Dried grape
8. Downpours
9. Ventilates
10. Fires
11. Not true
12. Ego
13. Boil slowly
14. Stingy person
15. Father
16. Applaud
17. Boscs and Anjous
18. Knocks
19. Court sport
20. Beer mug
21. Location
22. Collect
23. Mars's neighbor
24. Listen to

1	2	3	
4	5	6	
7	8	9	
10	11	12	
13	14	15	
16	17	18	
19	20	21	
22	23	24	

CIRCLES IN THE SQUARE

The twenty 5-letter words all fit in the diagram. All words begin and end in a dark circle. Horizontal words read from left to right; all other words read from top to bottom.

Solution on page 270

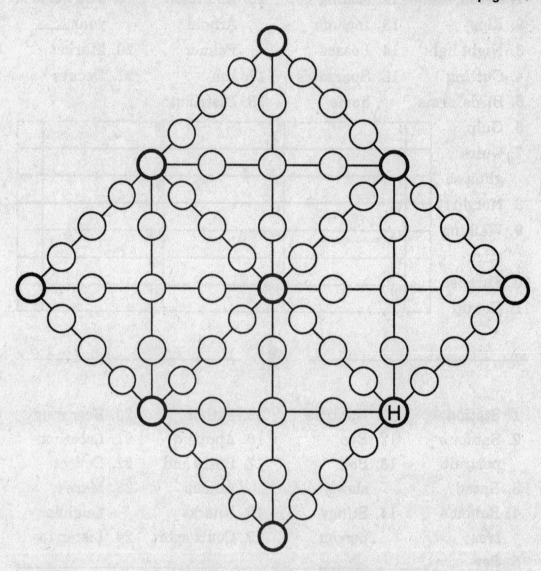

EAGER	EXTOL	LEVEL	REGAL
EAGLE	HORSE	LIGHT	TOUCH
ELITE	LATCH	LITHE	VINYL
EPOCH	LEASH	LOOSE	VITAL
EQUAL	LEAST	RAISE	VOICE

Halftime

Pair off the groups of letters to form twelve 6-letter men's names.

Solutions on page 270

AND	DON	GHT	MAN	REN	TOR
ART	DWI	GOR	MAR	REW	VIC
CAL	EPH	HUR	NIS	ROB	VIN
DEN	ERT	JOS	NOR	TIN	WAR

ANDREW   DWIGHT   WARREN

ARTHUR   JOSEPH   VICTOR

CALVIN   MARTIN   NORMAN

DENNIS   ROBERT   GORDON

Rounders

The names of three board games are hidden in these Rounders. For each one, start at one of the letters and read either clockwise or counterclockwise.

Solutions on page 270

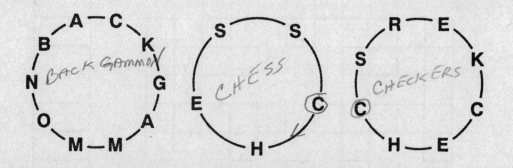

BACK GAMMON   CHESS   CHECKERS

Pairs in Rhyme

Each of these pairs of words is a rhyme for a familiar phrase.

Solutions on page 270

Example: Car and ride (**Answer:** Far and wide)

1. Bees and parrots   PEAS & CARROTS

2. Fat and house   CAT & MOUSE

3. Sand and soot   HAND & FOOT

4. Beer and cow   HERE & NOW

5. Choose and box

MASTERWORDS

Using only the ten letters shown, fill in the diagram by forming words across and down to achieve the highest possible score. Each letter has a given value, so try to use the high-value letters as much as possible. You may repeat letters as often as you wish, even within words. Do not repeat words in the diagram. Foreign words, abbreviations, and words starting with a capital letter are not allowed.

When the diagram is completely filled, add up your score. Count across only, each letter, line by line. Put the total for each line in the boxes at the right.

Our solution with a score of 372 on page 270

A	D	E	H	L	M	P	R	S	T
3	3	5	5	2	1	1	4	2	4

SCORE

TOTAL

52

Daisy

Form five 5-letter words using the letters in each Daisy petal PLUS the letter in the Daisy center, C. The C may not be used as the first letter of these words. Next, form a bonus 6-letter word using the first letters of these words and beginning with the center letter C.

Solution on page 270

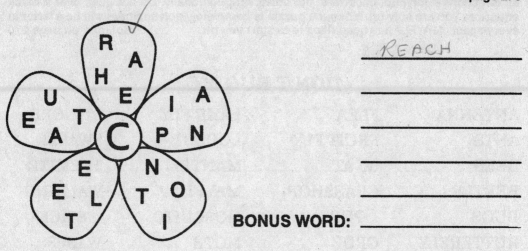

REACH

_____

_____

_____

_____

BONUS WORD: _____

Tiles

Imagine that these tiles are on a table, each showing a 2-letter combination. Can you rearrange these tiles visually to form a 10-letter word?

Solution on page 270

PASSIONATE

Three to One

Starting with each word in Column A, add a word from Column B and then one from Column C to build five longer words. For example, CORN plus ERST plus ONE is CORNERSTONE. Each small word will be used only once.

Solution on page 270

	A	B	C	
1.	DO	SON	ME	1. DOOR STEP
2.	CON	SO	ION	2. CON SON ANT
3.	LONE	US	MAT	3. LONE SO ME
4.	DIP	OR	ANT	4. DIP LO MAS
5.	ILL	LO	STEP	5. ILL USION

LETTERBOXES

Can you find the correct places for the words in the word list? The starting letters for all the words are given in the circled squares. These letters may also be used as parts of other words because of overlapping or crossing. The words read in a straight line and in all directions—forward, backward, up, down, and diagonally. Do not pass over a black square as you are solving. When the puzzle is completely solved, there will be a letter in every space. MAYFLY has been filled in to start you off.   Solution on page 270

DON'T BUG ME

ANTENNA ✓	FLEA ✓	LAKE FLY ✓	STINGER ✓
ANTS ✓	FRUIT FLY ✓	LOCUST ✓	SWARM ✓
BEES ✓	GNAT ✓	MANTIS ✓	TERMITE ✓
BEETLE ✓	GRASSHOP-	MAYFLY ✓	WALKING
BUGS ✓	PER ✓	MOSQUITO ✓	STICK ✓
BUTTERFLY ✓	GRUB ✓	MOTH ✓	WASPS ✓
DRAGONFLY ✓	HATCH ✓	NEST ✓	WATER BUG ✓
DRONE ✓	HIVE ✓	QUEEN ✓	WORM ✓
EARWIG ✓	INSECT ✓	ROACH ✓	
EGGS ✓	KATYDID ✓	SPIDER ✓	

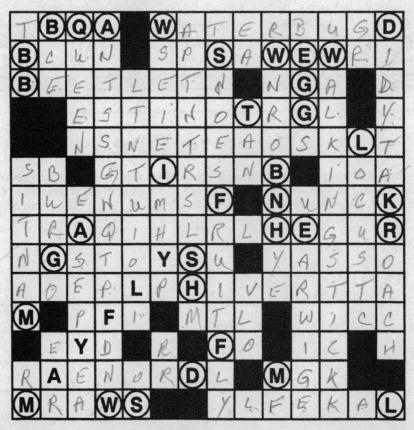

INSERT-A-WORD

Insert a word from Group B into a word from Group A to form a longer word. Each word is used only once. For example, if the word FAR appeared in Group A and THE appeared in Group B, the answer would be FATHER (FA-THE-R).   Solution on page 270

GROUP A	GROUP B	
1. MOW	APER	1. _____
2. REED	RISK	2. _____
3. BOOM	TAT	3. _____
4. DICE	RIB	4. _____
5. WART	INN	5. _____
6. DRIES	SIGN	6. _____
7. TUNE	RED	7. _____
8. BET	LOW	8. _____
9. PANT	RAN	9. _____
10. BOUT	TIE	10. _____

Middle of the Road

Place the correct missing letters into the diagram to form words reading down. Then read the filled-in letters across from left to right to reveal a saying. Be careful—some of the words are tricky!   Solution on page 270

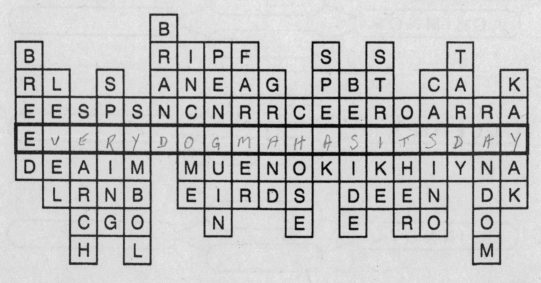

WORD MERGERS

Rearrange the letters in each Word Merger to form two words using all the given letters only once. Then rearrange these same letters and merge them into one long word. You might want to form the long word first and then the pair of words. Score 5 points for each pair of words you form and 10 points for each long word. A score of 70 is good, 80 is very good, and 90 is excellent.

Our answers with a perfect score of 105 points on page 270

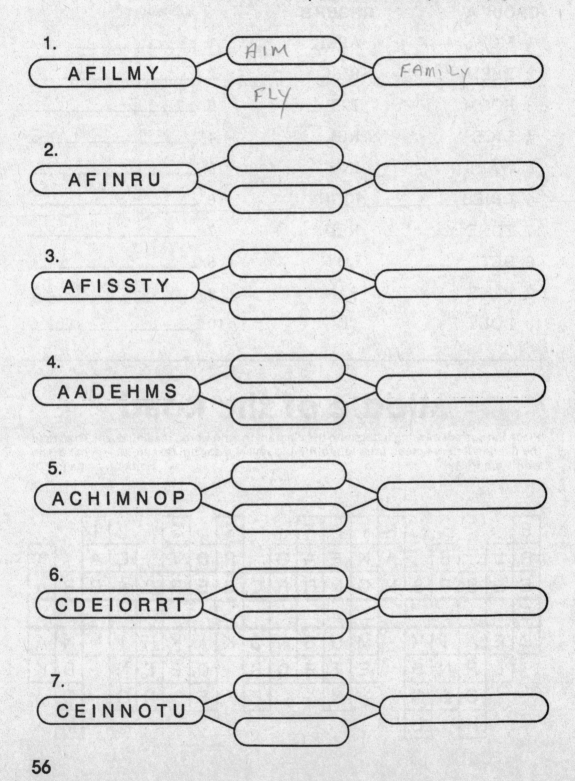

1. AFILMY — AIM / FLY — FAMILY

2. AFINRU

3. AFISSTY

4. AADEHMS

5. ACHIMNOP

6. CDEIORRT

7. CEINNOTU

56

THREE'S COMPANY

This alphabetical list of seemingly unrelated words actually contains 15 groups of three related items. Your job is to sort them out into those 15 groups using each item only once. The trick is that some of the items could be used in more than one list, but only one arrangement of all the items will work. Remember, use each item only once and have exactly three items in each group.

Solution on page 270

Aunt	Creed	June	November	Tenet
Birch	Cutters	Jupiter	Pistons	Thor
Cadillac	Dagger	Kayak	Pop	Toddler
Celtics	Detroit	Knife	Roosevelt	Tot
Child	Dogma	Lansing	Schooners	Uncle
Cleaver	Ewe	Lincoln	September	Vixen
Clippers	Filly	Magnolia	Sister	Ward
Cottonwood	Ford	May	Sloops	Washington
Cow	Jefferson	Mercury	Stiletto	Zeus

1. Months — _MAY_ _NOVEMBER_ _SEPTEMBER_

2. Sharp implements — _STILETTO_ _DAGGER_ _KNIFE_

3. Female animals — _FILLY_ _COW_ _VIXEN_

4. Family members — _AUNT_ _SISTER_ _UNCLE_

5. Car makes — _FORD_ _LINCOLN_ _MERCURY_

6. Trees — _BIRCH_ _COTTONWOOD_ _MAGNOLIA_

7. "Leave It to Beaver" — _CLEAVER_ _JUNE_ _WARD_

8. Sailing vessels — _SCHOONERS_ _SLOOPS_ _CUTTERS_

9. Faces on Mount Rushmore — _JEFFERSON_ _ROOSEVELT_ _WASHINGTON_

10. Mythological deities — _ZEUS_ _JUPITER_ _THOR_

11. Palindromes — ____ ____ ____

12. Michigan cities — _DETROIT_ _LANSING_ _CADILLAC_

13. Youngster — _TOT_ _CHILD_ _TODDLER_

14. Doctrine — _CREED_ _DOGMA_ _TENET_

15. NBA teams — _CELTICS_ _PISTONS_ _CLIPPERS_

57

FLOWER POWER

The answers to this petaled puzzle will go in a curve from the number on the outside to the center of the flower. Each number in the flower will have two 5-letter answers. One goes in a clockwise direction and the second in a counterclockwise direction.

Solution on page 271

CLOCKWISE

1. Sidewalk fault
2. Uniform cloth
3. Twist forcibly
4. Tasteless
5. Singer Patsy ____
6. Shopping center
7. Post-office purchase
8. Shuts with force
9. Ground grain
10. Great fear
11. Cape
12. Pedigree
13. Welcome
14. Threefold
15. Feed on grass
16. Sudden burst
17. Verify
18. Blackboard crayon

COUNTERCLOCKWISE

1. Household task
2. Desire
3. Marine mammal
4. Building block
5. Sharp, ringing sound
6. Town in Texas
7. Hurl
8. Point of view
9. Pottery coating
10. Theatrical piece
11. Hair wave
12. Consecrate
13. Shortstop Dick ____
14. Trample
15. Aristotle, e.g.
16. Cooked in oil
17. Sow
18. Trend

MAZE

Find your way through this maze from the arrow at the top to the one at the bottom.
Solution on page 271

ALPHABET SOUP

Insert a different letter of the alphabet into each of the 26 empty boxes to form words of five or more letters reading across. The letter you insert may be at the beginning, the end, or in the middle of the word. Each letter of the alphabet will be used only once. Cross off each letter in the list as you use it. All the letters in each row are not necessarily used in forming the word.   Our solution on page 271

Example: In the first row across we have inserted the letter H to form the word MOLEHILL.

A B C D E F G H I J K L M N O P Q R S T U V W X Y Z

D	E	M	O	L	E	H	I	L	L	E	N	T
A	G	G	L	O	B		L	A	R	C	O	N
C	O	S	T	R	I		E	N	T	E	E	S
S	H	A	R	L	E		U	I	N	D	L	Y
E	Q	U	A	R	R		B	U	S	I	N	S
G	R	O	U	T	L		N	E	T	E	I	L
S	Q	U	R	A	I		E	N	T	T	L	E
G	R	E	S	C	O		S	E	N	K	E	D
C	O	A	L	E	T		U	C	E	E	T	H
A	F	F	I	N	A		E	T	I	R	N	S
C	O	R	S	T	E		H	O	R	T	H	Y
D	I	S	A	R	B		U	G	H	A	U	D
D	R	O	P	E	A		E	F	U	L	T	H
H	O	U	R	G	L		S	S	T	I	C	A
I	N	A	L	C	O		E	M	E	R	D	S
C	E	H	A	D	R		U	G	U	L	A	R
A	R	O	O	M	A		E	N	T	A	D	A
P	I	N	C	O	R		E	C	T	O	I	N
L	U	E	P	I	T		A	L	L	C	O	N
N	I	P	T	U	K		A	P	S	A	C	K
A	C	Q	U	I	Z		I	C	A	L	P	H
T	H	E	C	O	D		L	U	S	I	O	N
S	C	U	T	R	E		U	S	S	I	E	R
W	U	N	S	P	O		D	E	R	A	G	H
E	L	F	O	C	U		T	O	C	L	I	D
S	E	Q	U	I	C		S	A	N	D	O	L

Enjoy More of the Puzzles You Love!

You get hours of solving fun with these special collections of your favorite puzzles!

Each collection brings you 64 full-sized pages devoted to one kind of puzzle. That means you can spend more time solving your favorites!

These collections are sold only through the mail, and only by Penny Press. Circle the volumes you want on the order form below, and mail it to us with your payment today!

Available only by mail!

PUZZLE TYPE	CODE	VOLUMES AVAILABLE (Circle your choices)						
Alphabet Soup	APH	1	2	*NEW!*				
Anagram Magic Square	ANG	32	33	34	35	36	37	38
Brick by Brick	BRK	184	185	186	187	188	189	190
Codewords	CDW	252	253	254	255	256	257	258
Crostics	CST	177	178	179	180	181	182	183
Crypto-Families	CFY	49	50	51	52	53		
Cryptograms	CGR	102	103	104	105	106	107	108
Diagramless	DGR	42	43	44	45	46	47	48
Double Trouble	DBL	18	21	22	23	24		
Flower Power	FLW	16	17	18	19	20	21	22
Frameworks	FRM	27	28	29	30	31	32	33
Letterboxes	LTB	74	75	76	77	78	79	80
Match-Up	MTU	2	3	4	5			
Missing List Word Seeks	MLW	15	16	17	18	19	20	
Missing Vowels	MSV	233	234	235	236	237	238	239
Patchwords	PAT	29	30	31	32	33	34	35
Places, Please	PLP	194	195	196	197	198	199	200
Quotefalls	QTF	40	41	42	43	44	45	46
Share-A-Letter	SAL	1	2	*NEW!*				
Stretch Letters	STL	1	2	3	4			
Syllacrostics	SYL	81	82	83	84	85	86	87
The Shadow	SHD	1	2	3	4			
Three's Company	TCG	1	*NEW!*					
What's Left?	WTL	1	2	3	4	5	6	
Wizard Words	WWD	2						
Word Games Puzzles	WGP	14	15	16	17	18	19	20
Zigzag	ZGZ	3	4	5	6			

Penny Marketing ™

Dept. G, 6 Prowitt St., Norwalk, CT 06855-1220

Order Toll-Free (M-F 8 a.m.–7 p.m., EST)

1-800-220-7443
Orders only, please!

_____ books at $5.25 each:	
Shipping & handling: ($1.50 per volume; $7.50 total for 5 or more volumes)	
Total amount enclosed (U.S. funds):	

✔**YES!** Send me the ____ volumes I've circled. My check for $ _____ (U.S. funds) is enclosed.

Name _____
(Please Print)

Address _____

City _____

State _____ ZIP _____

AMAZING QUOTE

A quotation is concealed in the diagram. The number of letters in each word is shown under the answer blanks. The letters for each word are in a straight line reading up, down, forward, backward, or diagonally. The last letter of one word adjoins the first letter of the next. The solution is one continuous line through each of the words. Lines will never cross, and a letter may be used only one time. We have started you off with the word HARD. Next, look for a 4-letter word that adjoins the D in HARD.

Solution on page 271

```
        G N D I W H T N T K L S
      R Y S A E W O E R V L G N M
    M T K I N F P C J U Y A T I E Q
  K B H R X O S O F Q P H S D G D E Z
  R U I M N O I T A L U M U C C A H B
  A S N A A E D I K R J S B L Z I N C
  E T G N A M E F S D H A V E F Y T A
  R L S T H A T A Q L P X M Y T T O F
  B I T I C D Y R G U M C L B L S W Z
  C N O F A E O L K O W A O I T W N A
  D T N D I D U R U H Q B X S A A F E
  L O E N V Y P O H S S H I U L Z V N
  H R W H E N Y A N J D S R O E C B C
  S A N D S A D C R I N D O K T E J A
  J W R O L B M S V O M Q F A S G U Z
    W O D O E F Q C G I B P S K T O
      Q O W O R K J E P N C H R X
        D N G K E T H S K G K S
```

HARD
__4__   __4__   __8__   __2__   __2__

__12__   __2__   __4__   __6__   __4__

__3__   __5__   __2__   __4__   __3__

__6__   __4__

AROUND THE BLOCK

Find your way from START to FINISH by passing through all the white squares one time only. You may move up, down, and across, but not diagonally.

Solution on page 271

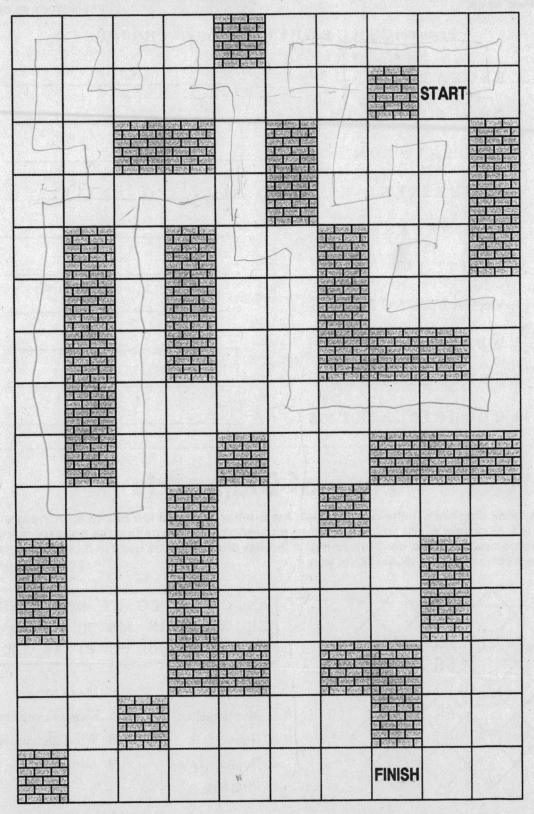

START

FINISH

SHUFFLE

The two-word names of foods with their letters in the correct order are combined in each row of letters. To solve the puzzle, separate both words. There are no extra letters, and no letter is used more than once.

Solutions on page 271

Example: C S H U E O P Y (CsHueOPy) = CHOP SUEY

1. R B O E A S E T F   *Roast Beef*
2. C H G I C U K M E B O N   *Chicken Gumbo*
3. F I M I L G E N T O N   *Filet Mignon*
4. P D U E K I C K N G   *Peking Duck*
5. S W S T I S E A S K   *Swiss Steak*
6. I S R I T E S W H   *Irish Stew*
7. V S C A E L L A O P L I N E   *Veal Scallaopine*
8. W R A E B L S B I H T   *Welsh Rabbit*
9. L O N E B W S T B U R E R G   *Lobster Newburg*
10. Q L O U R I R C A I H E N E   *Quiche Lorraine*

Nine of Diamonds

Fill the small diamonds in the diagram with the 2-letter pieces in the box to form the answers to the clues. All answer words have eight letters and read clockwise around the corresponding number. Words overlap in the diagram so that a 2-letter piece may be used in more than one word. We have set number 5, DISCOVER, for you.

Solution on page 271

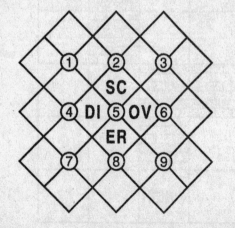

AN	CA	CH	CO	CT	~~DI~~	ED	~~ER~~
ER	IG	IM	IN	MB	LE	OA	~~OV~~
PR	RA	RD	RE	~~SC~~	ST	TE	UR

1. Sieve
2. Mix together
3. Gave a talk
4. Demonstrate
5. Find out
6. Made better
7. Sweater variety
8. Wind instrument
9. Admonish

64

PYRAMID POWER

Fill in the Pyramid with the 6-letter answers to the clues. Each answer fits into a triangle (which consists of six circles connected with lines) either clockwise or counterclockwise. The words in neighboring triangles will share letters. The answer to the first clue is ASPECT; it has been placed into the diagram for you. You must determine where the other answers belong. As a solving aid, you will find that the answers to the clues are in alphabetical order.

Solution on page 271

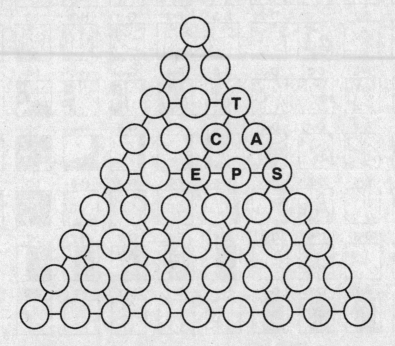

1. Mien	A S P E C T
2. Poplar trees	___ ___ ___ ___ ___ ___
3. Evaluate	___ ___ ___ ___ ___ ___
4. Witches' groups	___ ___ ___ ___ ___ ___
5. Refusal	___ ___ ___ ___ ___ ___
6. Paper wasp	___ ___ ___ ___ ___ ___
7. African antelope	___ ___ ___ ___ ___ ___
8. Sheets, e.g.	___ ___ ___ ___ ___ ___

9. Vivifies	___ ___ ___ ___ ___ ___
10. Drink of the gods	___ ___ ___ ___ ___ ___
11. Sense of taste	___ ___ ___ ___ ___ ___
12. Tea biscuits	___ ___ ___ ___ ___ ___
13. Scampi	___ ___ ___ ___ ___ ___
14. Goal	___ ___ ___ ___ ___ ___
15. Flourish	___ ___ ___ ___ ___ ___
16. Royal seat	___ ___ ___ ___ ___ ___

Changaword

Can you change the top word into the bottom word in each column in the number of steps indicated in parentheses? Change only one letter at a time and do not change the order of the letters. Proper names, slang, and obsolete words are not allowed.

Our solutions on page 271

1. MAKE (3 steps)   2. TURN (4 steps)   3. HOME (5 steps)   4. TAKE (6 steps)

TIME   BACK   SOON   LOOP

PICTURE THIS

You do not need any special art training to produce a picture in the empty grid. Use the letter-number guide above each square and carefully draw what is shown into the corresponding square in the grid.

Solution on page 271

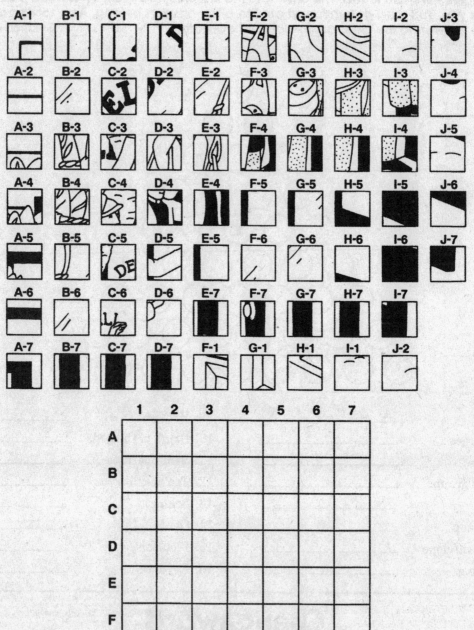

TAKEOUTS

Cross off all the pictures of football players that are one square beneath a pennant, one square to the left of a helmet, or directly between two footballs (horizontally or vertically). How many football players are left?

Solution on page 271

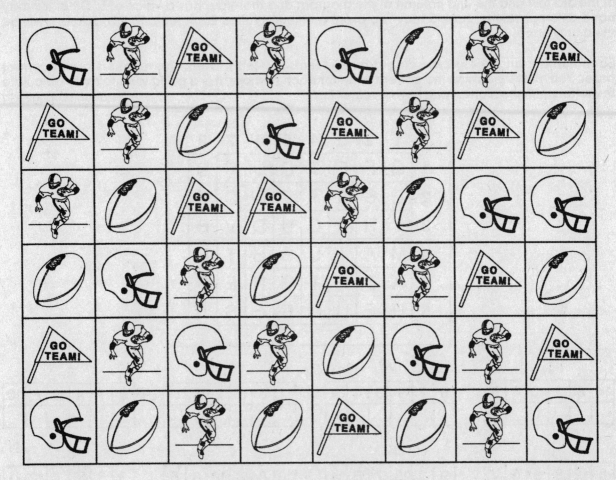

Start and Finish

Form words which start and finish with the same letter. For example, ___ O A S ___ becomes TOAST when a T is placed at the beginning and end of that set of letters. Use a different letter for each set.

Our solutions on page 271

1. ___ U S ___

2. _P_ L U M _P_

3. ___ I N D O ___

4. _B_ U L _B_

5. _N_ A T I O _N_

6. ___ E P E N ___

7. ___ A U R E ___

8. _C_ H I _C_

9. ___ I G O ___

10. ___ E D I U ___

67

WORD CALCULATOR

Each of the letters in the diagram has a numerical value which you can calculate by adding the number of the row (across) and the column (down) in which the letter is shown. For example, R is in the 3rd row and the 2nd column of the diagram and therefore has a value of 5. Other R's may have different values. Each 5 may represent a different letter. Each letter in the diagram will be used only once.

Each number chart below the diagram represents a 6-letter word. The numbers are in correct order. You must determine the correct letter for each number. It is a good idea to try to calculate the letters with the highest and lowest values first.

Solution on page 271

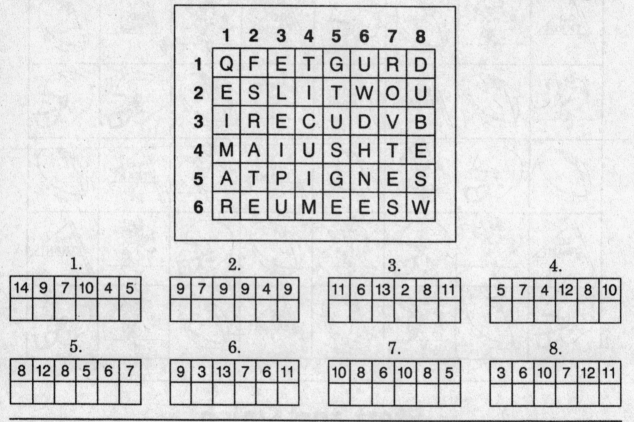

	1	2	3	4	5	6	7	8
1	Q	F	E	T	G	U	R	D
2	E	S	L	I	T	W	O	U
3	I	R	E	C	U	D	V	B
4	M	A	I	U	S	H	T	E
5	A	T	P	I	G	N	E	S
6	R	E	U	M	E	E	S	W

1.

14	9	7	10	4	5

2.

9	7	9	9	4	9

3.

11	6	13	2	8	11

4.

5	7	4	12	8	10

5.

8	12	8	5	6	7

6.

9	3	13	7	6	11

7.

10	8	6	10	8	5

8.

3	6	10	7	12	11

You Know the Odds

Six banking terms are spelled out, but they are missing every other letter. It shouldn't be too difficult to fill in the even letters now that You Know the Odds!

Solutions on page 271

1. C _H_ E _C_ K _I_ N _G_ A _C_ C _O_ U _N_ T
2. D _E_ P _O_ S _I_ T
3. M _O_ N _E_ Y _O_ R _D_ E R
4. B _A_ L _A_ N _C_ E
5. P _R_ O _M_ I _S_ S _O_ R _Y_ N O T _E_
6. L _I_ A B _I_ L _I_ _T_ Y

THE SHADOW

Can you find the picture that matches the silhouette shown?
Solution on page 271

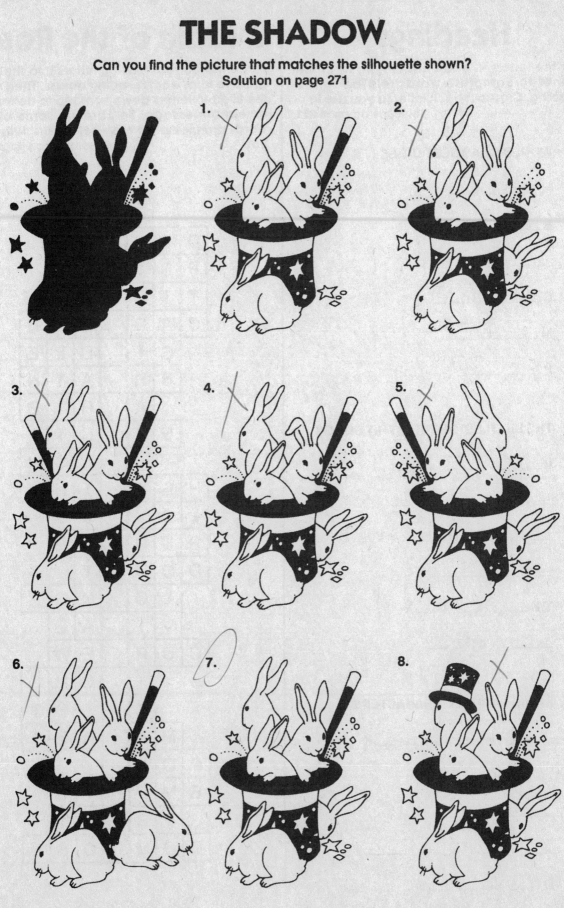

Headings

Use the letters in each Heading to fill in the blanks to complete words related to the Heading. Cross out each letter as you use it.

Solutions on page 271

1. WORLD'S LARGEST CITIES

M __ D __ I __

B __ __ J I N __

__ __ O U __

C A __ __ U __ __ A

M __ __ C O __

P A __ __ __ __

2. THE BEATLES' GREATEST HIT SONGS

L __ __   __ __   B __

__ O M E __ __ I __ __

__ H __   __ O V E __   Y __ U

__ E __   __ __ C K

Y E __ __ E __ D __ Y

__ __ Y   J U D __

3. LEWIS CARROLL CHARACTERS

__ A __ E __ P I __ __ __ R

__ L __ C __

__ A __ __ U __

__ __ E __ H I __ E   __ __ T

D O __ M __ U S __

Middle of the Road

Place the correct missing letters into the diagram to form words reading across. Then read the filled-in letters down from top to bottom to reveal a message. Be careful—some of the words are tricky! We have set the first letter for you.

Solution on page 271

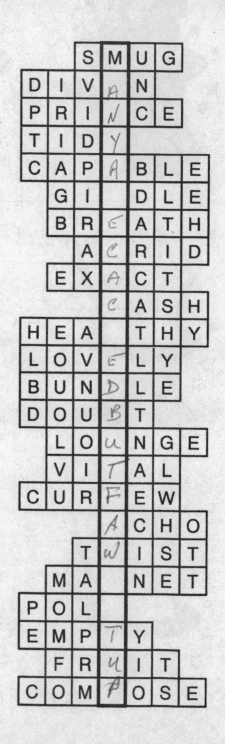

S	M	U	G
D I V	A	N	
P R I	N	C E	
T I D	Y		
C A P	A	B L E	
G I	I	D L E	
B R	E	A T H	
A	C	R I D	
E X	A	C T	
	C	A S H	
H E A		T H Y	
L O V	E	L Y	
B U N	D	L E	
D O U	B	T	
L O	U	N G E	
V I	T	A L	
C U R	F	E W	
	A	C H O	
T	W	I S T	
M A		N E T	
P O L			
E M P	T	Y	
F R	U	I T	
C O M	P	O S E	

70

JIGSAW PUZZLE

When you have put the pieces of the Jigsaw Puzzle into their correct places in the diagram, they will form a crossword puzzle with words reading across and down. Do not turn the pieces. The heavy lines in the diagram will help you locate their proper places. We have set one piece to start you off. Solution on page 271

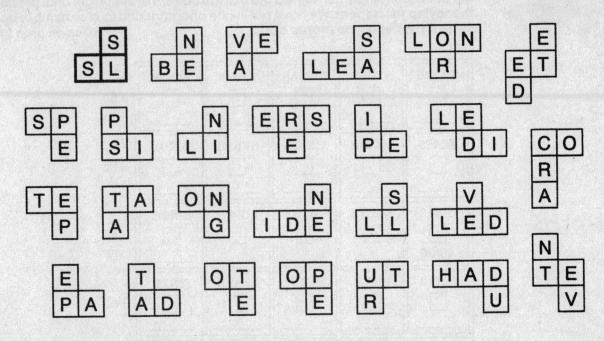

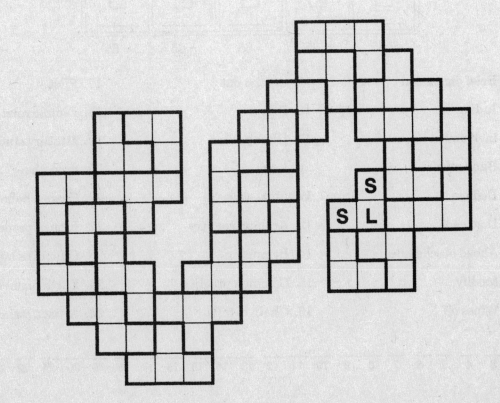

ANAGRAM MAGIC SQUARE

Rearrange the 5-letter word in each box to form another word. The anagrammed word will answer one of the clues. Put the number of that clue into the small square and write the anagram on the dash. The numbers in each row and column will add up to 65. Write the first letter of each anagram on the correspondingly numbered dash at the bottom of the page; and, presto!, the saying will appear. We have put in one anagram and its clue number and set its first letter on the proper dash.

Solution on page 271

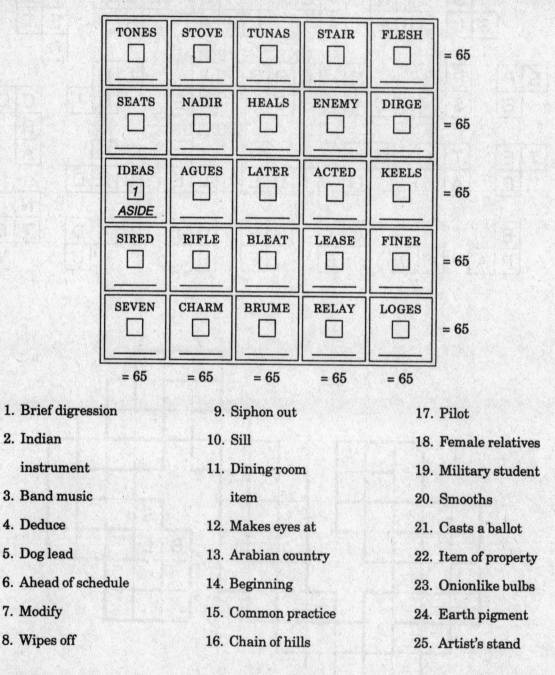

TONES □ ___	STOVE □ ___	TUNAS □ ___	STAIR □ ___	FLESH □ ___	= 65
SEATS □ ___	NADIR □ ___	HEALS □ ___	ENEMY □ ___	DIRGE □ ___	= 65
IDEAS [1] ASIDE	AGUES □ ___	LATER □ ___	ACTED □ ___	KEELS □ ___	= 65
SIRED □ ___	RIFLE □ ___	BLEAT □ ___	LEASE □ ___	FINER □ ___	= 65
SEVEN □ ___	CHARM □ ___	BRUME □ ___	RELAY □ ___	LOGES □ ___	= 65

= 65 = 65 = 65 = 65 = 65

1. Brief digression
2. Indian instrument
3. Band music
4. Deduce
5. Dog lead
6. Ahead of schedule
7. Modify
8. Wipes off

9. Siphon out
10. Sill
11. Dining room item
12. Makes eyes at
13. Arabian country
14. Beginning
15. Common practice
16. Chain of hills

17. Pilot
18. Female relatives
19. Military student
20. Smooths
21. Casts a ballot
22. Item of property
23. Onionlike bulbs
24. Earth pigment
25. Artist's stand

A __
  1 2 3 4 5 6 7 8 9 10 11 12 13 14 15 16 17 18 19 20 21 22 23 24 25

Wizard Words

After you have located and circled all the words in the diagram, read the leftover letters to find the Wizard's Words. Words in the diagram read forward, backward, up, down, and diagonally, and always in a straight line.

Wizard Words on page 273

Solution on page 272

☑ ANDROMEDA ☐ NEBULA ☐ PLUTO ☐ SPACE

☐ ASTEROID ☐ NEPTUNE ☐ POLARIS ☐ STAR

☐ CLOUD ☐ NOVA ☐ SATELLITE ☐ URANUS

☐ COMET ☐ ORBIT ☐ SATURN ☐ VENUS

☐ COSMOS ☐ ORION ☐ SIRIUS ☐ VESTA

☐ CRATER ☐ PLANET ☐ SOLSTICE ☐ ZODIAC

☐ EARTH

☐ ECLIPSE

☐ EQUINOX

☐ GALAXY

☐ GALILEO

☐ JUPITER

☐ MARS

☐ MERCURY

☐ MERIDIAN

☐ METEOR

☐ MILKY WAY

☐ MOON

```
T E C I T S L O S H V E S T A
H T E S A S T R T Z N O N Y O
M I E A A R S R D U O L C X W
P L A N E T A A T S L D A A S
K L E D A E U P S E D P I L Y
N E C R A T E R U G M H X A O
O T M O O N S N N A W O W G C
V A E M S B P U A L N Y C S J
A S T E R O I D R I K S O U I
S N E D L A L E U L D M P N S
S I O A L H C Q I E S I O E E
R Y R U C R E M C O T I R V E
P I B I L I E A C E R D T E H
S E I I U N P G R O S A R E M
N L T O O S R A M K I N G U P
```

Before you can loop these words relating to government, you must first fill in the circles in the diagram with the missing vowels A, E, I, O, and U. We have filled in and circled AMBASSADOR as an example.   Solution on page 272

☑ AMBASSADOR   ☐ DEPUTY   ☐ JUSTICE   ☐ PASS
☐ BILL   ☐ DIPLOMAT   ☐ LEGISLA-   ☐ PENTAGON
☐ BUDGET   ☐ FEDERAL   TURE   ☐ POLICY
☐ CAPITOL   ☐ GOVER-   ☐ MAYOR   ☐ POLITICS
☐ COALITION   NOR   ☐ MINISTER   ☐ PRESIDENT
☐ CONGRESS   ☐ HOUSE   ☐ NOMINEE   ☐ REPEAL
☐ DELEGATE   ☐ JUDICIARY   ☐ PARTY   ☐ REPRE-
                                                SENTATIVE
                                             ☐ SECRE-
                                                TARY

```
D P O L O T O C S P B P O S S
R O P T O M O L P O D Y T O C
O T O V P N P O R T Y C V C M
T P B N G N J O D O C O O R Y
O L O R O A O D L O T L R O W
N M O H F M G O C O L O O T O
O S O G W B O O T O P N O T
S O Y N O A T N B O O P R R O
T N O D O S O R P N L T O Y G
L O Y G O S L R T W J O V R O
J T T J O A T O W O S O O H L
S O O R C D G O T O G Y G C O
C O P O T O L O R O O D W N D
B O O M N R T Y L M R M O C V
R B D L R S L O R O D O F B W
```

☐ SENATE
☐ SENATOR
☐ STATE
☐ TREASURY
☐ VETO
☐ WHIP

Alphabetics

Each of the answer words starts with a different letter of the alphabet. The words are in the diagram reading forward, backward, up, down, and diagonally, and always in a straight line. Words may overlap. Not all the letters in the diagram will be used. The number in parentheses is the number of letters in the word.
Word list on page 273   Solution on page 272

A <u>LLIGATOR</u> (9)   J _____ (7)   S _____ (7)

B _____ (9)   K _____ (9)   T _____ (9)

C _____ (7)   L _____ (8)   U _____ (6)

D _____ (8)   M _____ (8)   V _____ (7)

E _____ (9)   N _____ (6)   W _____ (9)

F _____ (7)   O _____ (8)   X _____ (5)

G _____ (9)   P _____ (7)   Y _____ (9)

H _____ (8)   Q _____ (9)   Z _____ (6)

I _____ (8)   R _____ (8)

```
A U T S A F K A E R B O A V R K Q Q X N
N I Y F S I T A S N D R A O R P U X O O
V I N T A G E U K F A C T O R Y K N Y I
Y L T N E C O N N I U A D W K L E E K T
O W A A I R N I O D G A T A F X S N H A
L R Y N O Z S P W I H B L T P T R I Y T
A C G M G A R E L A T I V E E Z E M S O
B E U A C U H L E I E I N R M J N S K U
Q H S C N P A X D H R S D F T A T A O Q
A R O N E I Q G G O I A Y A L C R J C M
U M M N T O Z M E V Y O T L R F A A K F
G U A R A N T E E I O W X L S T P Z C W
```

Word Seek 4

To solve this puzzle, find two words beginning with the letter B, one in each diagram, in the same location in both diagrams, which combine to form one longer word or phrase. The first half of each answer is in the top diagram; the second half is in the bottom diagram in the same location, reading in the same direction. Words read forward, backward, up, down, and diagonally, and always in a straight line. Not all the letters will be used. For example, BACKBITE is formed by combining BACK from the top diagram with BITE from the bottom diagram, in the same location and reading in the same direction.
Word list on page 275

Solution on page 272

YOUR WORD LIST
(37 entries)

```
B A Y O K K C A B L U E L
A B B C R U N B A K E D I
E R A B U X L I C Y O L A
A L B S B U K G K Y S U B
B E A N E W C B U S H R Y
A U K T W O O D N W O R B
B W N I Y B R O W N E O
I D R K A Y B A B A L E S
E K E Y E B U S K L A K O
S E Y B S D C L B C B C M
A B I B A N K R L B A A N
D R O X B T H B E E T L E
S N M O B O H C A E B B B
```

```
B A H I D E N O B I R D D
I B T R A C E B E A N S N
K C A B R O E E N A N T O
O O B L I L R N D Y D O B
B A G S L K E B A B Y E N
R E E E B R E T S R A E B
E O D T Y L B E T T Y U U
A G U S I E U L B Y O B D
T B U N N B O Y D Y A Y D
H E Y B R O C S K R W R Y
A B O B O O K S Y N A R W
N E O N B Y I B R O W E D
D N S O N B S L L A B B B
```

The word LUCKY appears in the ONE & ONLY diagram one time, but it appears in the HOW MANY? diagram 26 times.

Solutions on page 272

ONE & ONLY

```
K U L L K U C C K Y U L
U L K C L K Y C L U C L
L U L C Y Y K U U C C Y
Y U L Y C U C C U U L
L Y Y Y L U U U C U C C
K C K U L L C Y C C K
U U U U K U Y C U U U Y
C L U L C C U C U K K K
C U L Y Y K Y C L L K U
Y K Y C C C K U K K U C
```

HOW MANY?

```
L L U C K Y K C U L U L
U L U C K Y K Y U Y Y U
C L U C K Y K C K Y K C
K Y U Y Y L K C U C C K
Y L K K U Y U L U L U Y
K L C C L L Y C U L L L
U U K U U C K Y K C U L
L Y C L K L C Y L Y K C
Y K C U L L U C K Y Y Y
Y Y K C U L L Y K C U L
```

Before you can loop these names of gems, you must first fill in the circles in the diagram with the missing vowels A, E, I, O, and U. We have filled in and circled AGATE as an example.

Solution on page 272

GEMS

☑ AGATE
☐ AMBER
☐ AMETHYST
☐ AQUAMARINE
☐ BLOODSTONE
☐ CARNELIAN
☐ CAT'S-EYE

☐ CITRINE
☐ CORAL
☐ DIAMOND
☐ DIOPSIDE
☐ EMERALD
☐ GARNET
☐ GOSHENITE

☐ JADE
☐ JASPER
☐ JET
☐ LAPIS
　 LAZULI
☐ MOON-
　 STONE
☐ MORGAN-
　 ITE
☐ OBSIDIAN
☐ ONYX
☐ OPAL
☐ PEARL
☐ PERIDOT
☐ ROSE
　 QUARTZ
☐ RUBY
☐ SAPPHIRE
☐ SPINEL
☐ SPODU-
　 MENE
☐ TANZA-
　 NITE
☐ TOURMA-
　 LINE
☐ TUR-
　 QUOISE
☐ ZIRCON

```
L J O D O N O T S D O O L B D
O J X B N O O L O N R O C N Y
N O B S O D O O N O R H O H D
O Z Z O R C O N P O Y M X O C
P O T N O M T S C L O P O O O
S T O R M S O O M O M P L M T
Q O O X O J P O D O S O B S S
C N R R O O R O O O Z O Y O O
O O M X Q G Q N D O R H Z P Y
T Z O Y O O S O L O T O O P E
R N L N B T O S S O M O P H T
O O O O O O O O O O M O R O M O A
N T N N G P R O S L R L N R G
O T O J O G O S H O N O T O A
N J D L O R O M O G O R N O T
```

78

Alphabetics

Each of the answer words starts with a different letter of the alphabet. The words are in the diagram reading forward, backward, up, down, and diagonally and always in a straight line. Words may overlap. Not all the letters in the diagram will be used. The number in parentheses is the number of letters in the word.

A _____ (10)

B _____ (10)

C _____ (9)

D _____ (8)

E _____ (7)

F _____ (8)

G _____ (6)

H _____ (9)

I _____ (6)

J _____ (6)

K _____ (5)

L _____ (8)

M _____ (6)

N _____ (5)

O _____ (11)

P _____ (6)

Q _____ (8)

R _____ (6)

S _____ (9)

T _____ (6)

U _____ (9)

V _____ (5)

W _____ (7)

X _____ (7)

Y _____ (7)

Z _____ (5)

Word list on page 273

Solution on page 272

```
S N N A H C I H T N A X G R D O J P A R B E X
R R N Q H O N E Y C O M B N V K L E P O R P A
T E R I U N N O Q U E L T A I F C L Z O O U H
Y T H G S F M U S H C G L B E A L O K L C F S
A N H T L I A P T S M U R D R A E H N T F G H
L I N O A D A R I I E H Q U N N M P I K L J O
P I O Y R E L R E D E S U O H K C O L B E J R
R K I A K N W Y Q D R P G S Z Z N O X S S E T
E N T T Y T A T U I N A V O W E B L T C Y I C
D E J S Z B C S E Y I E M T E A V E K Y M D A
N E F A R M Y A R D O B G R T A R T A N L W K
U D R O P X D N F M I N O R C H E S T R A T E
```

Before you can loop the words about airports given in the word list, you must first fill in the circles in the diagram with the missing vowels A, E, I, O, and U. Words in the diagram read forward, backward, up, down, and diagonally and always in a straight line. Circle each word when you find it and cross it off the list. Words will often overlap, and some letters may be used more than once. Not all of the letters in the diagram will be used. One answer has been filled in as an example.

AIRPORTS

Agents ✓	Copilot	Get lost	Restaurant
Airport	Counter	Guards	Runways
Aisles	Crew	Halls	Seat
Baggage	Departure	Jets	Security
Boarding	Doors	Landings	Signs
Busy	Engineer	Late	Stores
Captain	Flight	Lounge	Suitcases
Cargo	Food	Metal	Takeoff
Cockpit	Fuel	On time	Terminal
Control	Galleys	Passengers	Tickets
Conveyor	Gates	Planes	Waiting

Solution on page 272

```
J Y R O O N O G N O H R O S T O O R O N T S S
R S O C O R O T Y D P S L L O H C O R G O Y O
O O T Q N P T M O O L O G B S N G O S B D O T
Y B N R V O O P S L O N O L N D O N G S W O
O K O S P T O S O L R O C O O G F O L C O N G
V S O K O R O T O X T L R C S O G O O F S O O
N T C L T N O N P W N P O Y Y L N O M F O R O
O O L O G N O D R O O B W V O Z O G G O C T R
C R R O T M M D F R C O P O L O T S O O T N D
T O R O R G N O T O O W L J L S R O O D O N S
M S O O S T O J B S T N E G A K G H L O O F O
N S T O K C O T O K O O F F G G O T L O S T S
```

LOOKING FOR MISSING VOWELS? You'll find them in each of our special collections packed with 55 entertaining Missing Vowels puzzles! To order, see page 61.

Solve this puzzle by seeking numbers instead of letters.

Solution on page 272

☐ 14925 ☐ 62021 ☐ 75069 ☐ 86453 ☐ 92344
☐ 16988 ☐ 63437 ☐ 75491 ☐ 87254 ☐ 92788
☐ 17909 ☐ 69528 ☐ 82622 ☐ 92295 ☐ 96042
☐ 23528
☐ 25663
☐ 33102
☐ 34061
☐ 34773
☐ 40642
☐ 48243
☐ 49521
☐ 53825
☐ 54294
☐ 54767
☐ 58863

```
3 5 2 1 9 2 6 8 7 5 2 3 3 0 1
3 4 4 0 2 6 3 9 2 5 4 6 1 1 0
5 5 8 4 2 1 1 3 5 3 1 7 9 0 9
2 6 5 2 9 1 4 4 3 2 2 2 6 2 8
8 8 6 4 5 2 9 7 0 4 8 0 3 7 9
8 8 5 3 4 0 2 7 9 0 8 5 4 5 9
8 7 9 6 8 2 5 3 2 6 4 5 3 2 3
2 5 2 6 0 6 5 1 4 9 4 8 7 1 4
7 0 4 5 1 5 1 5 5 2 2 8 4 0 0
3 6 1 2 4 5 3 2 9 5 8 8 6 3 2
3 9 2 3 4 4 1 4 8 0 3 4 0 6 1
0 2 6 3 3 1 6 7 1 7 2 4 9 6 1
```

CODEBREAKER

Each group of 5 letters listed below is a word in a simple substitution code (a different letter represents the real one). The same code is used throughout. The clue next to each group gives you one of the real letters. The 10 clues give you the 10 letters used to form all the words. As a starter, we'll tell you that V stands for E in all words.

Decoded words listed on page 271

1. W M H J V — one letter is S
2. X C B F L — one letter is D
3. L F V M X — one letter is N
4. C M B H V — one letter is I
5. B C M J V — one letter is R
6. V M C F H — one letter is A
7. F M L V X — one letter is K
8. J M W B C — one letter is P
9. H M J B F — one letter is T
10. M X V W J — one letter is E

How well do you know your TV stars and their roles? Hidden in the diagram below is the last name of the actor who portrayed each pair of television characters listed. For example, we have circled (Bea) ARTHUR, who portrayed Maude Findlay on the series "Maude" and who starred as Dorothy Zbornak on "The Golden Girls." HINT: The names you are looking for are listed in alphabetical order.

Maude Findlay/
Dorothy Zbornak ✓

Howard Cunningham/
Father Dowling

Perry Mason/
Robert Ironside

Frank Cannon/
Nero Wolfe

Alexander Scott/
Cliff Huxtable

KITT/
Mark Craig

Tony Banta/
Tony Micelli

Maynard G. Krebs/
Gilligan

Jed Clampett/
Barnaby Jones

Bentley Gregg/
Blake Carrington

Fred Mertz/
Bub O'Casey

Bret Maverick/
Jim Rockford

Florence Johnston/
Mary Jenkins

Chris Cagney/
Rosie O'Neill

Andy Taylor/
Benjamin L. Matlock

Francis Muldoon/
Herman Munster

Tony Nelson/
John Ross Ewing

George Jefferson/
Ernest Frye

Dr. Johnny Fever/
Charlie Moore

Opie Taylor/
Richie Cunningham

Sabrina Duncan/
Amanda King

Brenda Morgenstern/
Marge Simpson

Ted Baxter/
Henry Rush

Little Joe Cartwright/
Jonathan Smith

Murray Slaughter/
Merrill Stubing

Steve Austin/
Colt Seavers

Nancy Drew/
Fallon Carrington Colby

Vivian Harmon/
Blanche Devereaux

Laura Petrie/
Mary Richards

Bill Gannon/
Sherman Potter

Bob Hartley/
Dick Loudon

Archie Bunker/
Bill Gillespie

James T. Kirk/
T.J. Hooker

Sally McMillan/
Kate McArdle

Dan Tanna/
Spenser

Sue Ann Niven/
Rose Nylun

Jim Anderson/
Marcus Welby

List of actors on page 273

Solution on page 272

```
M A R T R A H W E N D O S H A T N E R D O T D
O R I N O S K C A J E F F T K A T I E H H D E
G I B B S M T H E R M S L I J A X N A G A E N
D L D A N Z A A R Y T I F F L A V G I N Y H V
O Y O R D N N U R I O H N F O E M N I P E T E
E B E S A V B E L U S U U I R A K E E M L Y M
L S H L R W R Y E A C G N R N A L T S R W S O
C O C O N N O R E N N Y W G A S P L R E A R R
A C I N O R O H T L G D L E B S E N O S R O G
M A R D C O N B I N S E O S B Y M U J O F F A
T R U E M A J O H R S O W N D I A M A R T I N
R E N R A G A R W S K I B H E S S E M A N S O
```

To solve this puzzle, locate and loop in the diagram all those words which are underlined in the poem. Words in the diagram read forward, backward, up, down, and diagonally, always in a straight line.

TREASURES

Down on the beach when the tide is out

Beautiful things lie all about—

Rubies and diamonds and shells and pearls,

Starfish, oysters, and mermaids' curls;

Slabs of black marble cut in the sand,

Veined and smoothed and polished by hand;

And whipped-up foam that I think must be

What mermen use for cream in tea.

These and a million treasures I know

Strew the beach when the tide is low—

But very few people seem to care

For such gems scattered everywhere.

Lots of these jewels I hide away

In an old box I found one day.

And if a beggar asks me for bread

I will give him diamonds instead.

— Mary Dixon Thayer

Solution on page 272

```
C R A G G E B H S M O O T H E D A E T S N I N
D T R B L F G D E R S Q S S O T V Y L O D W E
M L S P O J K R E L P E H T C Y W X I B O X M
N A O D B U M N A N T S R R B B S L D D R Z R
J E O L N A T B J T I H G E F D L T J N K A E
P E A F I O S R H F D E A W H I P P E D U P M
L C W D B K M E R T E U V S M W H A T R L O S
K M S E R U S A E R T R L L G M Y C P S S G F
N N A P L E T D I I S R T L A F U R Q R N T V
I C D N A S V Q F D A V T E B R D S E I B U R
H A N D H W R U G E M S R H L Z B C H V T X W
T D E H S I L O P X W C Y S C A T T E R E D Y
```

CRYPTOGRAMS

Each of these Cryptograms is a message in substitution code. THE SMART CAT might become MRX DGYUM LYM if M is substituted for T, R for H, X for E, etc. One way to break the code is to look for repeated letters. E, T, A, O, N, R, and I are the most often used letters. A single letter is usually A or I; OF, IS, and IT are common 2-letter words; try THE or AND for a 3-letter group. The code is different for each Cryptogram.

Solutions on page 273

1. RS TQCOGOHC CFOSWH CFJ EYRHH OH FRYU
   UDYY; R QJHHOGOHC CFOSWH CFJ EYRHH OH
   FRYU JGQCB. R AJRYOHC WSTVH CFRC OU FJ
   HCOPWH RATDSM, FJ'H JLJSCDRYYB ETOSE CT
   FRLJ CT VRHF CFJ EYRHH.

2. Q SJCWHF BQV OWXXCHP UW QANZO Q KTNCJ TW
   TQF TWQJF OTQO TQF VZHP BCOTNZO QHD
   CHVOJZUWHOQX AQKRCHP. TW WIYXQCHWF, "QHF
   OTWD YWJSNJUWF BCOTNZO UZVCKQX
   QKKNUYXCVTUWHO."

3. BWCDNYG TYECB NY YKRBVNRBY RKQB VGEW
   RBQB VEYVB, ATUCRBWV, EWU BUTSEVNKW —
   YKRBVNRBY NV'Y YGBBQ DTSF, DNFB CBVVNWC
   ESQKYY E YVQBBV.

4. SNOLNOG DL SYGH YG DL XFDU, VL'P D FYL
   ZYGO ETK VE, SNVFO UYT DGO QYVKW LNO YKO,
   UYT QYK'L MYKPLDKLFU EOOF UYT YTWNL LY CO
   QYVKW LNO YLNOG.

5. BUI YAIXGZMI PI SIMLHI JMRF SRLVW JXHRMG
   LG YXMBAO LV BUI JIIALVW LB WLHIG ZG BUXB
   PI XMI VRB XABRWIBUIM PRMBUAIGG.

84

6. XQI XIG DWAABGOAIGXJ BNI JQWNX BGO XW XQI
   HWFGX JFAHCT VIDBEJI XQIT YINI KFUIG XW EJ
   OFNIDXCT, YFXQWEX XQI QICH WS CBYTINJ.

7. GL GR ABWX GADBWLZQL LB CQBS SOXWX KBJ
   ZWX VBGQV LOZQ LB VXL LOXWX IJGUCPK. TB
   QBL AGRLZCX ZULGNGLK MBW ZUOGXNXAXQL.

8. MJXDMVN IMKIWM JXM KUNMD IMKIWM YGK
   GJCTNLJWWP WKKQ KD NGM VMXTKLV VTSM KU
   NGTDAV NGJN GJFM DK VMXTKLV VTSM.

9. WPYIDJI HZQ WZRI QVG XKVH MIPDC FKVDC ZDA
   YVVEPDC XVVYPWL, MGU PU FPYY ZYWV AIOKPRI
   QVG VX ULI OVWWPMPYPUQ VX MIPDC KPCLU.

10. FQA ALOQSYHA DT OQCBMFRSM JCAMAYFM
    DKHQF FD EA CAOBJCDOSG CSFQAC FQSY
    CAFSGBSFDCZ.

11. CNSNG NMAKDZC — HUJG IGZNCRE RU CUF CNNR
    ZF, DCR HUJG NCNTZNE YZKK CUF WNKZNSN ZF
    DCHYDH.

12. WE RKM VKZ'B TDB DJDORBIWZT RKM CQZB,
    BIWZX KE BID BIWZTU RKM VKZ'B TDB BIQB RKM
    VKZ'B CQZB.

13. L KWF PD XBWOR NE OASR AS OLUYD LBWNRV
    JAS ENVVUS.

14. XS'B Q KQMS: Q EJQHHN LXT FQY YJUJE LHAOB
    VXB IYAOB.

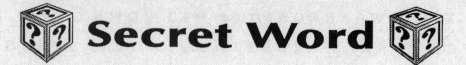

Secret Word

Discover the 5-letter Secret Words by the process of elimination and deduction. Fill in the blanks with the 5-letter answers to the clues. The number in parentheses next to each answer tells you how many of the letters in that word are also in the Secret Word. A zero next to an answer indicates that none of the letters in that word is in the Secret Word. After you have determined the correct five letters, rearrange them to form the Secret Word. No letter is repeated in any Secret Word or within any answer word. The first letters of the answers, reading down, spell out a hint to the Secret Word.

Solutions on page 273

1. Secret Word ☐☐☐☐☐

Hoodlums	_ _ _ _ _ (1)
Beagle	_ _ _ _ _ (2)
Give a speech	_ _ _ _ _ (2)
Perturb	_ _ _ _ _ (0)
Raise the shoulders	_ _ _ _ _ (2)
Famous fabler	_ _ _ _ _ (1)
Hospital worker	_ _ _ _ _ (2)
Hoodwinks	_ _ _ _ _ (1)

2. Secret Word ☐☐☐☐☐

Impel	_ _ _ _ _ (1)
Peruvian natives	_ _ _ _ _ (2)
Coastline	_ _ _ _ _ (2)
Kilns	_ _ _ _ _ (2)
Stretch	_ _ _ _ _ (3)
Dehydrates	_ _ _ _ _ (0)
Cowgirl Dale ___	_ _ _ _ _ (2)
Elevate	_ _ _ _ _ (1)

3. Secret Word ☐☐☐☐☐

Universe	_ _ _ _ _ (0)
Perfect	_ _ _ _ _ (2)
Written reminders	_ _ _ _ _ (3)
Trickles	_ _ _ _ _ (2)
Baby hooter	_ _ _ _ _ (1)
Windshield blade	_ _ _ _ _ (2)
Promise	_ _ _ _ _ (3)

4. Secret Word ☐☐☐☐☐

Convenient	_ _ _ _ _ (2)
Performer	_ _ _ _ _ (3)
Pay	_ _ _ _ _ (1)
Intended	_ _ _ _ _ (0)
Different	_ _ _ _ _ (3)
Lowest point	_ _ _ _ _ (2)
Luxury craft	_ _ _ _ _ (2)

5. Secret Word ☐☐☐☐☐

Leaves out	_ _ _ _ _ (1)
Adobe	_ _ _ _ _ (3)
Play the guitar	_ _ _ _ _ (0)
Labors	_ _ _ _ _ (2)
Actors' parts	_ _ _ _ _ (2)
Brown color	_ _ _ _ _ (1)
Bread morsel	_ _ _ _ _ (2)
Deceive	_ _ _ _ _ (2)

6. Secret Word ☐☐☐☐☐

King of Judea	_ _ _ _ _ (2)
Moslem faith	_ _ _ _ _ (2)
Tardier	_ _ _ _ _ (2)
Directed	_ _ _ _ _ (2)
Regal	_ _ _ _ _ (1)
Thoughts	_ _ _ _ _ (1)
Aromatic herb	_ _ _ _ _ (3)
Swiss song	_ _ _ _ _ (0)

JIGSAW SQUARES

Your goal is to fit the PUZZLE PIECES into their proper places in the diagram to reveal a quotation. Fill the diagram by placing the PUZZLE PIECES horizontally into their corresponding sections of the diagram. There are 16 sections, identified by letter/number combinations (A-1, A-2, A-3, etc.). The quotation reads left to right, line by line. A black square indicates the end of a word. One PUZZLE PIECE has been entered for you.

Solution on page 271

PUZZLE PIECES

A-1	A-2	A-3	A-4	B-1	B-2	B-3	B-4
A	H	N	AND	TO	S	A	WAS
A	S	W	PAR	ING	ON	D	CEED
G	DI	AD	ILLI	SHE	SAI	I	SKED
AM	DY	DI	SRAE	TNER	COMP	TS	THEM
LA	~~JAMI~~	NNER			NIGH	ARE	
LI	LADS	TONE				SUC	
BEN							

C-1	C-2	C-3	C-4	D-1	D-2	D-3	D-4
FAS	E	D	PER	D	I	WAS	D
ONE	ON	GL	UNT	IL	T	CINA	ME
SON	WAS	THE	ADST	NER	FAS	ELIS	MAN
CONV	CINA	ARTH	MOST	THA	ISRA	UADE	THE
	INCE	TING		MOST	PERS		TING

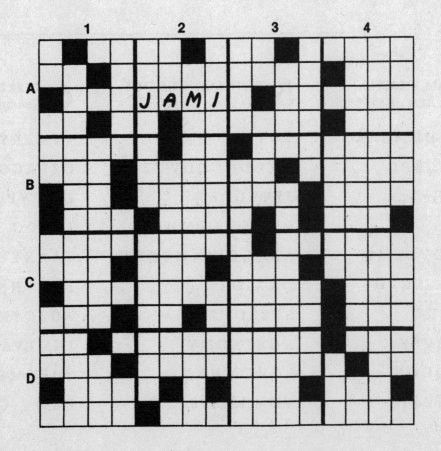

87

CRYPTO-FAMILIES

Each Crypto-Family is a list of related words in code. Each Family has its own code. When you have identified a word, use the known letters to help decode the other words in the Family.

Solutions on page 273

1. FRUIT CUP
Example: Watermelon

GZIJ

LIWBZJNWZ

IGJNMDL

MIWLIXDRGZ

QDWZASZE

DJIWBZ

YNEN

MQZJJA

BJIGZ

GZIMQ

2. COMMUNICATION
Example: Television

QNMESF

ZLXLVJUS

FLIJN

USTMQLQSF

ZSZN

MQSSYA

YLGOSXFLZ

MLESOOJES

ESOSQANUS

OSEESF

3. DOGGONE IT!
Example: Dalmatian

NGUIA

OKYJP

LGMWBIA

LGGSXI

RAIPOGKWS

HGXXMI

CJMBC

NICRXI

SCHOYOKWS

CMAISCXI

4. ICE CREAM, PLEASE!
Example: Rum raisin

CHEMQ   DHMSRK

ARAAMQ   BRC

FHSVMMH

ZJXXQQ

XRIBQ   OVEEMQ

ARKKQO   EQZHS

ZUJZJMHKQ

EQEEQOCVSK

TKOHDAQOON

EVTKHZUVJ

5. STUFF AND NONSENSE
Example: Horsefeathers

TNTDZ   YNTDZ

WZDDGUQOWZZI

JZTTOLZJ

DMGQULQMHK

ABQQGU-AMQQGU

DNXINT

SZSSOVZVI

AGBTAGMT

KZWEMHK

VGMSJLMS

6. DEAL THE CARDS!
Example: Solitaire

VJMJRYJ

OZVACO

ECKWPO

ILHOC

TAKRY

EQJVHNJVH

AOJCYR

IKMLVAQO

VJRKML

PKM   CZFFD

Window Boxes

There is a common 4-letter word hidden in each strip of letters in Column I. Think of the strips in Column II as open and closed windows. Then match each letter strip with its correct Window Box so that the 4-letter word will show. There are different possibilities, but there is only one way in which each letter strip and each window strip are used once. Solution on page 274

Example: P L O D E N T   P O E T

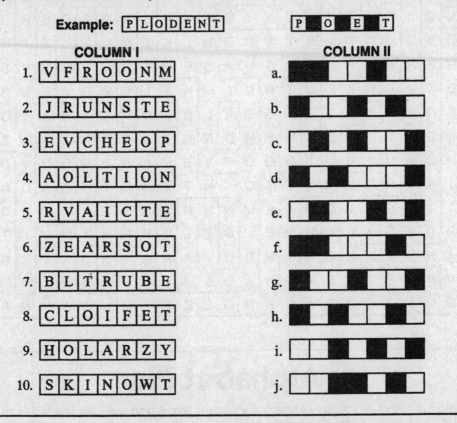

COLUMN I

1. V F R O O N M
2. J R U N S T E
3. E V C H E O P
4. A O L T I O N
5. R V A I C T E
6. Z E A R S O T
7. B L T R U B E
8. C L O I F E T
9. H O L A R Z Y
10. S K I N O W T

COLUMN II

a.
b.
c.
d.
e.
f.
g.
h.
i.
j.

Common Combos

Listed below are groups of four unrelated words. Can you find a word that can either precede or follow each of the words in each group? Solutions on page 274

1. MULE	TRACK	WAGON	MAN	_____
2. WAY	CITY	MUSIC	MARK	_____
3. POLE	BLUE	STONE	SIGNAL	_____
4. RED	DOUBLE	STITCH	WALK	_____
5. BOX	EXPRESS	ORDER	JUNK	_____
6. OVER	AFTER	OUT	ALIKE	_____
7. HOUSE	LIME	NIGHT	PEN	_____
8. SKIP	JUMPING	BLACK	HAMMER	_____

TURN A PHRASE

Find your way through the maze to discover the hidden quotation.

Solution on page 274

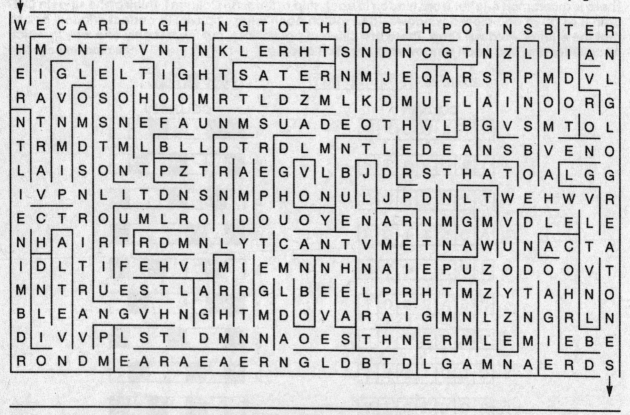

Alphabet Plus

Form common 5-letter words by rearranging each word and adding the letter of the alphabet shown with it. The word CHAIN (the letters of INCH plus the letter A) has been filled in for you.

Our solutions on page 274

A	+	INCH	=	CHAIN		N	+	GOAL	=	
B	+	IDEA	=			O	+	VEIL	=	
C	+	ROAN	=			P	+	DOTE	=	
D	+	SOIL	=			Q	+	MAUL	=	
E	+	FROG	=			R	+	SOFT	=	
F	+	TORN	=			S	+	LOGS	=	
G	+	HINT	=			T	+	CHEF	=	
H	+	TALC	=			U	+	VASE	=	
I	+	TANG	=			V	+	ROTE	=	
J	+	ROAM	=			W	+	BORN	=	
K	+	CRIB	=			X	+	ROBE	=	
L	+	ACED	=			Y	+	DARE	=	
M	+	FARE	=			Z	+	GEAR	=	

CIRCLES IN THE SQUARE

The twenty 5-letter words all fit in the diagram. All words begin and end in a dark circle. Horizontal words read from left to right; all other words read from top to bottom. We have placed one letter in the diagram.

Solution on page 274

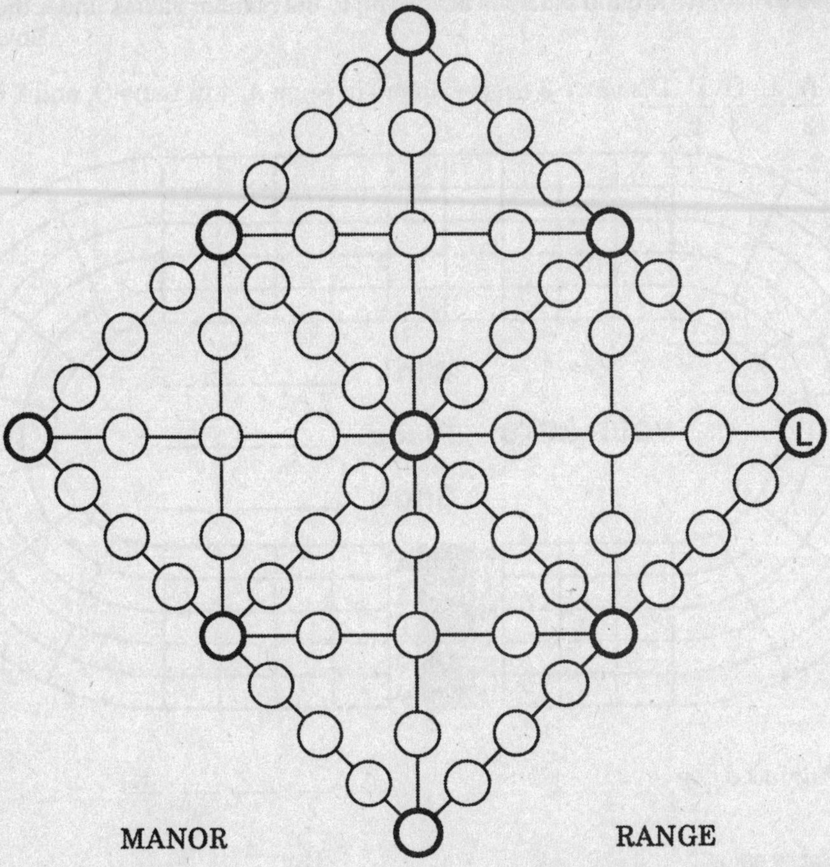

CAROM			SHAPE
CATER			STAIR
CRUST	MANOR	RANGE	TAPER
EBONY	MORAL	RAVEL	TOTEM
EVILS	MOVES	RUSTS	TOURS
LOOKS	RAINY	SHADY	TRADE

A Few Choice Words

Find the 6-letter answers by choosing one letter from each of the letter groups to the right of each clue. For example, the answer to number 1 is COMEDY.

Solutions on page 274

1. Humor	h**b**c	**o**ir	t**m**l	v**e**m	**d**mb	tm**y**
2. Allow	apt	eak	ore	klm	ins	two
3. Agile	lon	ilk	tvm	abe	yul	ren
4. Tusked mammal	wed	lna	oil	rub	guz	mas
5. Intelligent	cab	srl	ite	avg	mhi	dot
6. Charming	pqs	aru	lea	nip	nra	tmy

91

PUZZLE DERBY

Ladies and gentlemen, the horses are at the starting gate. Select your favorite vowel (A, E, I, O, or U), and the race is on. First fill in the blanks with the answers to the clues. Vowels always go above numbered dashes and consonants above the unnumbered ones. All answers have something in common. Then, to find out who wins the race, move the horses around the track according to the number values under the vowels.

Solution on page 274

Example: $\underset{2}{\underline{A}} \ \underline{L} \ \underset{4}{\underline{O}} \ \underset{1}{\underline{U}} \ \underline{D}$: move 2 spaces ahead in Lane A, 4 in Lane O, and 1 in Lane U.

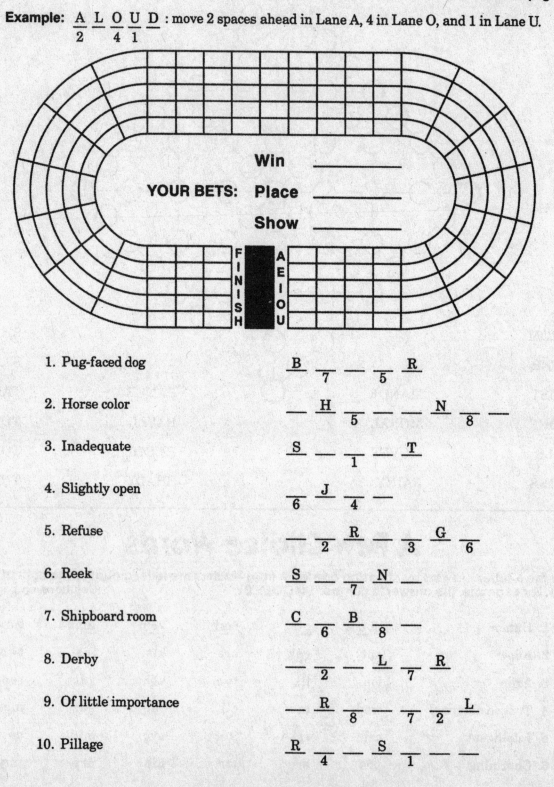

YOUR BETS:

Win _____

Place _____

Show _____

1. Pug-faced dog
   $\underline{B} \ \underset{7}{\underline{\ \ }} \ \underline{\ \ } \ \underset{5}{\underline{\ \ }} \ \underline{R}$

2. Horse color
   $\underline{\ \ } \ \underline{H} \ \underset{5}{\underline{\ \ }} \ \underline{\ \ } \ \underline{\ \ } \ \underline{N} \ \underset{8}{\underline{\ \ }} \ \underline{\ \ }$

3. Inadequate
   $\underline{S} \ \underline{\ \ } \ \underset{1}{\underline{\ \ }} \ \underline{\ \ } \ \underline{T}$

4. Slightly open
   $\underset{6}{\underline{\ \ }} \ \underline{J} \ \underset{4}{\underline{\ \ }} \ \underline{\ \ }$

5. Refuse
   $\underline{\ \ } \ \underset{2}{\underline{\ \ }} \ \underline{R} \ \underline{\ \ } \ \underset{3}{\underline{\ \ }} \ \underline{G} \ \underset{6}{\underline{\ \ }}$

6. Reek
   $\underline{S} \ \underline{\ \ } \ \underset{7}{\underline{\ \ }} \ \underline{N} \ \underline{\ \ }$

7. Shipboard room
   $\underline{C} \ \underset{6}{\underline{\ \ }} \ \underline{B} \ \underset{8}{\underline{\ \ }} \ \underline{\ \ }$

8. Derby
   $\underline{\ \ } \ \underset{2}{\underline{\ \ }} \ \underline{\ \ } \ \underline{L} \ \underset{7}{\underline{\ \ }} \ \underline{R}$

9. Of little importance
   $\underline{\ \ } \ \underline{R} \ \underset{8}{\underline{\ \ }} \ \underline{\ \ } \ \underset{7}{\underline{\ \ }} \ \underset{2}{\underline{\ \ }} \ \underline{L}$

10. Pillage
    $\underline{R} \ \underset{4}{\underline{\ \ }} \ \underline{\ \ } \ \underline{S} \ \underset{1}{\underline{\ \ }} \ \underline{\ \ }$

LUCKY SCORE

Fill in the diagram with words reading across to earn the highest possible score. The basic value of each letter is shown in the LETTER VALUE CHART. However, the value of a letter is doubled if it is used in a square with a circle and tripled if used in a square with a diamond. Add up your score across for each word, then add up your grand total.

Our solution with a grand total of 681 points on page 274

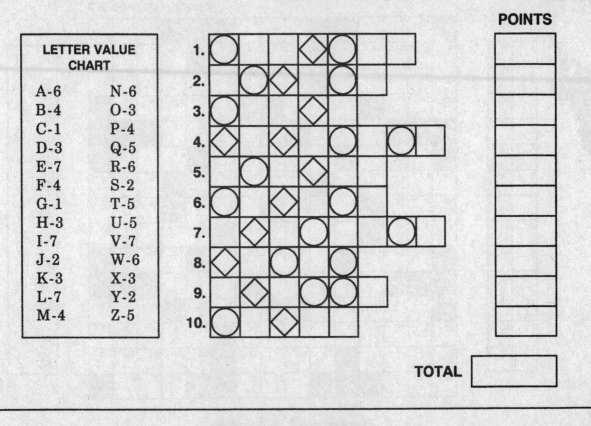

LETTER VALUE CHART	
A-6	N-6
B-4	O-3
C-1	P-4
D-3	Q-5
E-7	R-6
F-4	S-2
G-1	T-5
H-3	U-5
I-7	V-7
J-2	W-6
K-3	X-3
L-7	Y-2
M-4	Z-5

POINTS

TOTAL

Guess Who

Change one letter in each word to form the name of a famous person.
Solutions on page 274

Example: CLERK TABLE (**Answer:** Clark Gable)

1. JOIN PAIL JOKES _____

2. BELL GLASS _____

3. LEND HORSE _____

4. SMILE COLA _____

5. BOW DOLL _____

6. MEAN SUMMONS _____

7. BORNE GREECE _____

8. MANE GREW _____

9. GIANT WORD _____

10. LOBBY UNDER _____

11. TOO CHANCY _____

12. CLING BLOCK _____

CODEWORD

Codeword is a special crossword puzzle in which conventional clues are omitted. Instead, answer words in the diagram are represented by numbers. Each number represents a different letter of the alphabet, and all of the letters of the alphabet are used. When you are sure of a letter, put it in the code key chart and cross it off in the alphabet box. A group of letters has been inserted to start you off.

Solution on page 274

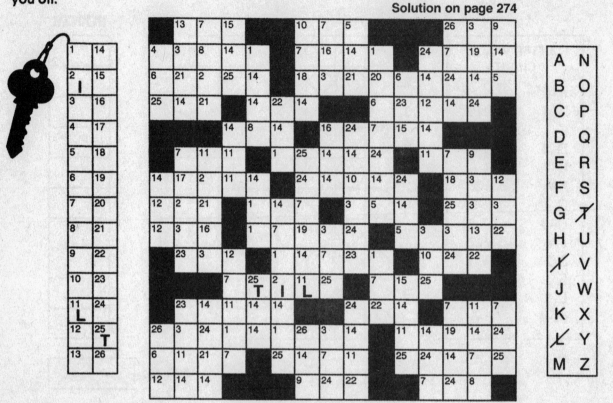

Word Math

In these long-division problems letters are substituted for numbers. Determine the value of each letter. Then arrange the letters in order from 0 to 9, and they will spell a word or phrase.

Solutions on page 274

1 `0 1 2 3 4 5 6 7 8 9`

```
              S I S
       _____
NUNS | BUBBLE
       B E P S
       _____
         U G I L
         P G H E
         _____
           B U L E
           B E P S
           _____
             P S S
```

2 `0 1 2 3 4 5 6 7 8 9`

```
               R U N
        _____
READ | BORDER
        H E T N
        _____
        A B D A E
        A H A T T
        _____
          A U U U R
          A O A B R
          _____
            A O R E
```

3 `0 1 2 3 4 5 6 7 8 9`

```
                Y E T
        _____
NONE | SNEAKY
        K Y S N
        _____
         L Y Y K
         A E A S
         _____
          O M L S Y
          O M A O T
          _____
            O L S
```

POINT THE WAY

The answers to the clues are 4-letter words that are divided in half before being placed in the diagram. Write each answer in the diagram, two letters per square, in the direction indicated by the arrow. The pair of letters in each square will be part of at least two words. The words PIER and ERGS have been given for you.

Solution on page 274

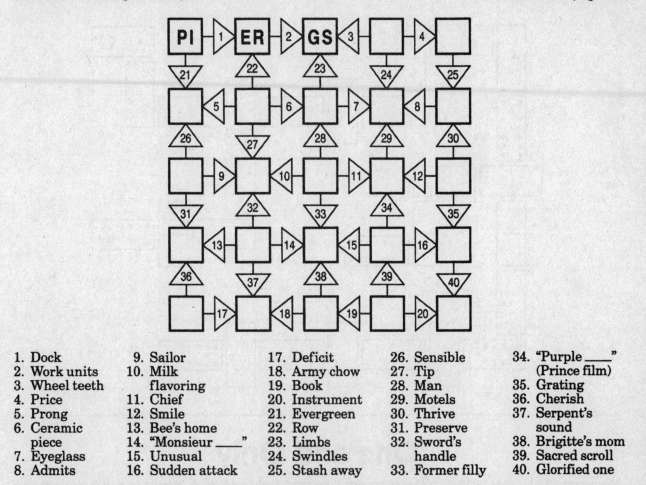

1. Dock	9. Sailor	17. Deficit	26. Sensible
2. Work units	10. Milk	18. Army chow	27. Tip
3. Wheel teeth	flavoring	19. Book	28. Man
4. Price	11. Chief	20. Instrument	29. Motels
5. Prong	12. Smile	21. Evergreen	30. Thrive
6. Ceramic	13. Bee's home	22. Row	31. Preserve
piece	14. "Monsieur ___"	23. Limbs	32. Sword's
7. Eyeglass	15. Unusual	24. Swindles	handle
8. Admits	16. Sudden attack	25. Stash away	33. Former filly

34. "Purple ___"
(Prince film)
35. Grating
36. Cherish
37. Serpent's
sound
38. Brigitte's mom
39. Sacred scroll
40. Glorified one

Categories

For each of the categories listed, can you think of a word or phrase beginning with each letter on the left? Count one point for each correct answer. A score of 15 is good, and 21 is excellent.

Our solutions on page 274

	MUSICAL INSTRUMENTS	WORLD CAPITALS	SPORTS	COMEDIANS	DESSERTS
B					
I					
R					
C					
H					

95

MISSING DOMINOES

In this game you use all 28 dominoes that are in a standard set. Each one has a different combination from 0-0, 0-1, 0-2, to 6-6. Domino halves with the same number of dots lie next to each other. To avoid confusion we have used an open circle to indicate a zero. Can you fill in the Missing Dominoes to complete the board?

Solution on page 274

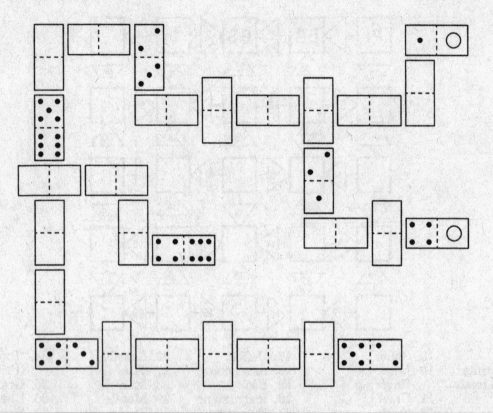

One and Only

The word CLAMOR is hidden in the diagram One and Only one time. It will read in a straight line either forward, backward, up, down, or diagonally.

Solution on page 274

```
A L C O L R A C O L M R A C O L C O A L R C M L A
O C M A C L A R A O R L C R A M L A R C A L A C O
R M A C M A L C O L A M A L C L A O M A R A L R C
C L O R A C M A L O R C O M A L M A R O C L R A A
A O C A L M C A M A M C A O L A C M A R L A C M O
O R A L C A R M A L C R M A L R A O L M A O L R C
R A C M L O C R O A L C A C R M C A C A L R A O R
C L O R A M A C L R O A L M O L A R O L A C M A L
```

ROUNDERS

The names of nine U.S. universities are hidden in these Rounders. For each one, start at one of the letters and read either clockwise or counterclockwise.

Solutions on page 274

1.

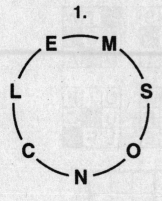

2.

3.

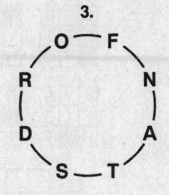

4.

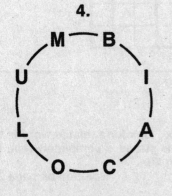

5.

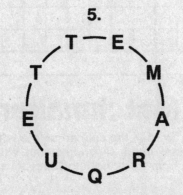

6.

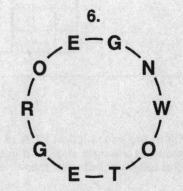

7.

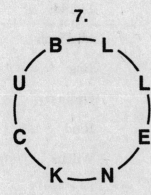

8.

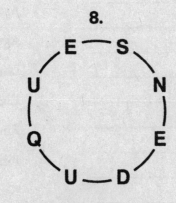

9.

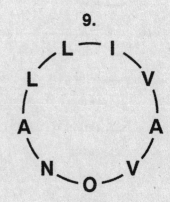

PATCHWORK QUOTE

Place the 12 Patchwork squares into the empty diagram to reveal a message reading left to right, line by line. Copy the squares exactly as they appear, but not necessarily in the order they are given. Black squares indicate the ends of words. Words continue from the right side onto the next line.

Solution on page 274

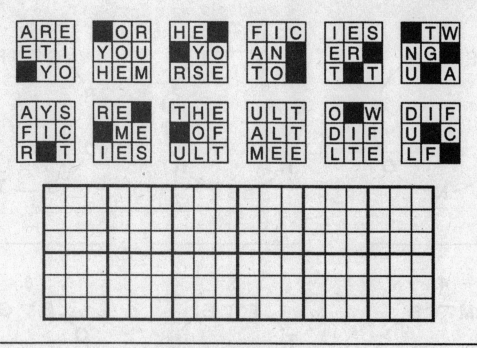

Matchmaker

Fill in the missing first letter of each word in the column on the left. Next, look for a related word in the group at the right and put it in the blank in the second column. When the puzzle is completed, read the first letters of both columns in order, from top to bottom, to reveal a song title.

Solution on page 274

____ ennessee _____

____ ank _____

____ late _____

____ ix _____

____ nding _____

____ anal _____

____ range _____

____ rville _____

____ ravel _____

____ olid _____

____ cute _____

____ aven _____

____ gg _____

Aaron	Liquid
Agent	Michigan
Depress	Nog
Eight	Ordinary
Finale	Rind
Ibis	Wilbur
Keen	

THREE FROM NINE

Place the letters of the 9-letter words on the dashes, one letter per dash, to spell a 7-letter word, a 5-letter word, and a 3-letter word. Each letter of a 9-letter word will be used once.

Solutions on page 274

1. HORSEPLAY

    __ E __ T __ E __ __
    __ R __ X __ __
    __ S __

2. DECATHLON

    __ A __ P __ L __ __
    __ U __ C __ __
    __ R __

3. FORTUNATE

    __ F __ E __ S __ __
    __ O __ S __ __
    __ P __

4. RELUCTANT

    __ P __ I __ O __ __
    __ R __ P __ __
    __ I __

5. VERSATILE

    __ I __ L __ G __ __
    __ P __ N __ __
    __ U __

6. ENJOYMENT

    __ I __ T __ R __ __
    __ A __ S __ __
    __ W __

7. GARDENING

    __ R __ N __ T __ __
    __ I __ E __ __
    __ O __

8. DIPLOMACY

    __ A __ S __ E __ __
    __ L __ U __ __
    __ R __

9. PRAGMATIC

    __ O __ C __ T __ __
    __ R __ S __ __
    __ U __

Ringmaster

Place the letter groups in the diagram to form 24 five-letter words as indicated by arrows. The two-letter groups go in the circles in the outer ring, the three-letter groups in the inner ring. Two words have been given to start you off.

Solution on page 274

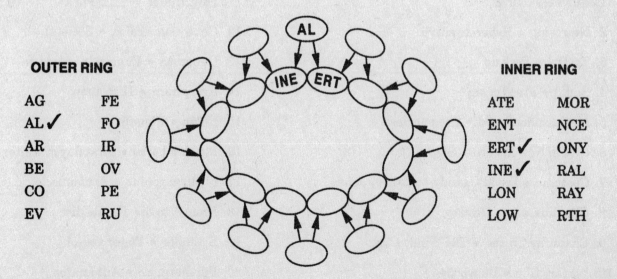

OUTER RING		INNER RING	
AG	FE	ATE	MOR
AL ✓	FO	ENT	NCE
AR	IR	ERT ✓	ONY
BE	OV	INE ✓	RAL
CO	PE	LON	RAY
EV	RU	LOW	RTH

99

SHARE-A-LETTER

Fill in the diagram with answers to the clues. Letters to be filled into the larger areas will be shared by more than one word. All answers read across only. Two clues are given for rows containing two answers. If you can't get an answer, solve the words above and below to discover more letters in the word.

Solution on page 274

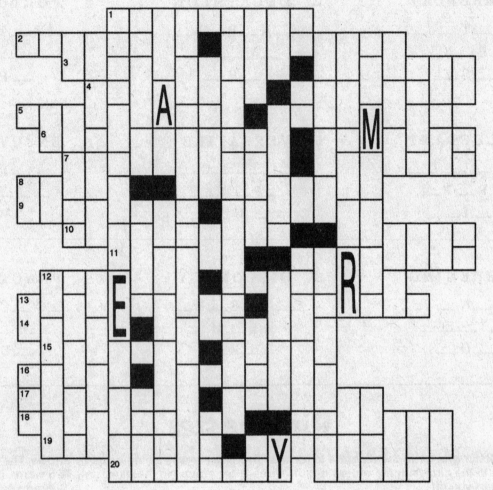

1. Business course

2. New wing • Hypersensitive

3. Tactful • Perk up

4. Squid • Freed of sin

5. Math student's aid • Heinousness

6. City in New Mexico • Sign

7. Costume • David Cassidy, to Shirley Jones

8. Claudius, e.g. • Destroy

9. Castaway Crusoe • The Windy City

10. Library film • Busybody

11. Faultfinder • "____ Park"

12. Get by succession • Societal

13. Generous • Engage in cronyism

14. Army horn • Hire anew

15. Relax • Piquant

16. Mottled horse • First day of winter

17. Musical genius • Arm muscle

18. From A to Z • Fertile dirt

19. Slammer • Water vessel

20. Furthermore • Automaton

"QUOTEFALLS"

The letters in each vertical column go into the squares directly below them, but not necessarily in the order they appear. A black square indicates the end of a word. When you have placed all the letters in their correct squares, you will be able to read a quotation across the diagram from left to right.

Solutions on page 275

1.

D	I	B	C	E	F	O	F	E	L	S	A	E	E	S	A
O	L	C	C	E	E	S	S	E	O	A	H	E	E	S	C
R	U	I	E	W	S	T	H	U	Y	T	M	M	N		F
S	V	L	O			T	R				P	R	R		

2.

A	B	E	E	N	A	H	C	H	E	E	D	E	H	A	R	O	B
A	H	R	N	T	S	I	I	H	I	D	O	I	N	G	S	S	P
A	R	L	N		T		O	N	P	L	R	P	P	I	Y		
W	T	T	Y		W		T	S		T	R			P			

3.

G	D	A	A	E	A	C	A	A	D	C	A	A	R	E	A	C	E	O	H	E	D	N	A
I	R	L	T	H	E	E	D	E	I	A	N	N	S	I	E	E	L	T	O	E	E	N	E
N	T	S	V	R	L	R	O	S	T	O	U	R	T	T	M	L	L	O	S	H	E	R	
T	U			V			R	T		O						R		W	W	P			
S										S													

4.

A	E	B	H	A	A	D	E	S	A	H	A	N	B	A	D	A	D	C	A	I	E	H	A	P	I	A
B	E	S	T	R	I	L	G	W	S	M	E	O	C	S	E	O	V	E	S	M	N	A	A	R	S	H
H	O	U	T	S	R	N	L		T	O	U		E	W	H	R	Y	O		O	S		T	T		P
O	U	U	U			N			Y	Y	S				N			S			T		U			T

101

1. UNDZGQLW TQL KLQI TGLXF TF UVHXQLNLWGDWR
   HVGLQW BFTFDBFDUB. ANLW FNLI BTI,
   ''LKLQIVWL LZBL DB TZZVALG FV,'' DF YBYTZZI
   DB STBLG VW T BYQKLI VP VWL.

2. HAA GHIFPIN PW NPKPNJN PIRZ RBVJJ
   TAHWWJW: RBZWJ SBZ HVJ PGGZKHDAJ; RBZWJ
   SBZ HVJ GZKHDAJ; HIN RBZWJ SBZ GZKJ.
   (DJICHGPI XVHIFAPI)

3. VWUVGW XMW QAKHAKB PRXP X DACVGWM
   GAQWDPFGW VMUTAHWD BMWXPWM
   DXPADQXEPAUK PRXK X MWGWKPGWDD VSMDSAP
   UQ CXPWMAXGADC. (GXSMWKEW D.
   MUEOWQWGGWM)

4. FE B FWXBTPIIBRZI NER HEFBS WVXHIBF EU
   HEDEPPEM. SEC MWZZ XBYI HMIVHS-UECP LECPX
   EU FPIBFWVT HE FE WH, MLWZI LBYWVT
   HMIVHS-UECP LECPX HE XBYEP HLI UIIZWVT
   HLBH HLI NER WX FEVI.

5. CL'V LCNY LT PCYL JBP YGYSZCVY AFYB DTK
   JZZYIL LFY EJZL LFJL DTK ZJB ETTO VTNY TE
   LFY IYTIOY JOO TE LFY LCNY JBP JOO TE LFY
   IYTIOY VTNY TE LFY LCNY — XKL BTL AFCOY
   DTK'SY AYJSCBH J XJLFCBH VKCL.

6. NTCIJWE JW KWHHTIFGTN: ''HZDT ZC JUT
   NTCIJT ZN FTJJZCF JWW KWSVHZKIJTP. ZJ'N
   ZSVWNNZYHT JW NZPTNJTV WCT ZNNGT XZJUWGJ
   NJTVVZCF WC ICWJUTE WCT.''

7. KDX YIQ SGZFV OTGDXUT WDPV MZU UIPV
   YDPBDXQSW. OTZW PICVW ZO VIWZVG LDG
   IQZPIRW OD DMWVGFV TXPIQW ZQ OTVZG
   QIOXGIR TIMZOIO, OTV IXODPDMZRV.

8. KFYM HT G HGD MWOF FWK FTGU FTJU FWCF
   GDU W'JJ KFYM QYL G HGD MFY EGDDYO CTO
   LKTU OY FWK PWNYEGJK.

9. S LESRU LEI PMFL FHLSFGNSRT LESRT S'OI IOIX
   VMRI SF GSJJ MZL PN LHB XILZXR SR XMPHR
   RZPIXHJF.

10. PNIRLMSRME MRIRL OQLEWRLRH GMC
    RMERLKLYUR TQE TC EWR GBGJLYEC DYEW
    DWYJW YE PNE NQE NO YEU DGC.

11. NVR YL E ZEZMJ PYLLOM LS LAEWW NVMC RSO
    OLM YP GSJ RSOJ CSLM, ECX LS WEJQM NVMC YP
    GYCXL YPL NER YCPS PVM NELVYCQ AEKVYCM?

12. UQK T NTP CETVM YUG STNG MUQKM MQNGYURPS
    QA URM LUTHTLYGH; UQK UG EQMGM MUQKM TEE
    QA RY.

13. LFV BFTO WLO TKILWP GOMICJ WKIOA KX CM
    OMNCMIOAON XUOBKOX VLKJO WLO UYMP
    TFXRYKWF QJFYAKXLOX?

FLOWER POWER

The answers to this petaled puzzle will go in a curve from the number on the outside to the center of the flower. Each number has two 5-letter words. One goes in a clockwise direction and the second in a counterclockwise direction. Try working from both sets of clues to fill the flower. Solution on page 275

CLOCKWISE

1. Shadowy
2. Review
3. Carols
4. Work groups
5. Curses
6. Fray
7. Basketball teams
8. Add energy
9. Wish grantor
10. Superman portrayer
11. Tumbler
12. Blockhead
13. Pan-fry
14. Ice
15. Tumble
16. Reared up
17. Gladden
18. Narrow parallel line

COUNTERCLOCKWISE

1. Iron alloy
2. Tatter
3. Way up
4. Dutch delight
5. Singer Moe _____
6. Lank
7. Rattlesnake teeth
8. "Days of Our _____"
9. Presents
10. Enjoy greatly
11. Heredity units
12. Calvin or Anne
13. Bond servant
14. Motive
15. Closes
16. Swimmer Mark _____
17. South American country
18. Decoy

SYL˝LA-CROS´TIC

Fill in the answers to the clues by using all the syllables in the Syllabox. The number of syllables to be used in each answer is shown in parentheses. The number of letters in each answer is indicated by the blank spaces. Each syllable will be used once. When the words are correctly filled in, their first and last letters, reading down, will reveal an epigram preceded by its author's name. Solution on page 275

✳ SYLLABOX ✳

AB AC AL AR BEL BRE CA CA CA CEN DER DI ED ED EEN EM FE
GA HAL IC ING LA ~~LARD~~ LINE LISH LOW LU MA ~~MAL~~ MO NEF O
OC OR OS OUST QUIT SION SORB STAND TA TA TAN TEN THUR TI
TIL TION TION TOR TOW U UN VER VO WA

1. Common wild duck   (2) M A L L A R D

2. Exonerate   (2) __ __ __ __ __ __

3. Decorate   (3) __ __ __ __ __ __ __ __ __

4. African dry riverbed   (2) __ __ __ __ __

5. Schooling   (4) __ __ __ __ __ __ __ __ __

6. Upright   (2) __ __ __ __ __ __ __

7. Doomed ship   (3) __ __ __ __ __ __ __

8. Mexican food   (3) __ __ __ __ __ __ __ __

9. Showy display   (4) __ __ __ __ __ __ __ __ __ __ __

10. Soak up too much of   (4) __ __ __ __ __ __ __ __ __ __

11. Gruesome   (3) __ __ __ __ __ __ __

12. Subsurface current   (3) __ __ __ __ __ __ __ __ __

13. Mexican coin   (3) __ __ __ __ __ __ __

14. Eve of All Saints' Day   (3) __ __ __ __ __ __ __ __ __ __

15. Expelled by force   (2) __ __ __ __ __

16. Catlike   (2) __ __ __ __ __ __

17. King of the Round Table   (2) __ __ __ __ __ __

18. Swindler   (2) __ __ __ __ __

19. Imitation gold   (3) __ __ __ __ __ __ __ __

20. Infrequent   (4) __ __ __ __ __ __ __ __ __ __ __

QUOTAGRAMS

Fill in the answers to the clues. Then transfer the letters to the correspondingly numbered squares in the diagrams. The completed diagrams will contain quotations.

Solutions on page 275

A.

1. Courtroom panel — $\overline{20}\ \overline{13}\ \overline{2}\ \overline{19}$

2. Plunges — $\overline{26}\ \overline{16}\ \overline{29}\ \overline{32}\ \overline{7}$

3. Resilient — $\overline{11}\ \overline{17}\ \overline{34}\ \overline{9}\ \overline{25}\ \overline{33}\ \overline{22}$

4. Tinkered — $\overline{1}\ \overline{35}\ \overline{27}\ \overline{31}\ \overline{14}\ \overline{4}\ \overline{6}$

5. Obtrude — $\overline{30}\ \overline{12}\ \overline{10}\ \overline{21}\ \overline{38}\ \overline{36}$

6. Hammer's target — $\overline{5}\ \overline{24}\ \overline{28}\ \overline{18}$

7. Change position — $\overline{23}\ \overline{8}\ \overline{3}\ \overline{37}\ \overline{15}$

1	2	3	4	5	6	7	8	9	10	11	■	12	13	14
15	16	17	18	19	■	20	21	22	23	■	24	25	26	■
27	28	29	30	31	32	■	33	34	35	36	37	38	■	

B.

1. Gypsy dance — $\overline{30}\ \overline{14}\ \overline{21}\ \overline{39}\ \overline{38}\ \overline{11}\ \overline{4}\ \overline{12}$

2. Dunked — $\overline{29}\ \overline{15}\ \overline{35}\ \overline{8}\ \overline{25}\ \overline{42}$

3. Intimidate — $\overline{16}\ \overline{37}\ \overline{5}\ \overline{24}\ \overline{27}\ \overline{22}\ \overline{7}\ \overline{41}$

4. Ganders — $\overline{32}\ \overline{1}\ \overline{19}\ \overline{9}\ \overline{6}$

5. Made-up story — $\overline{23}\ \overline{40}\ \overline{20}\ \overline{17}\ \overline{10}\ \overline{3}\ \overline{28}$

6. Overeaters — $\overline{2}\ \overline{18}\ \overline{34}\ \overline{36}\ \overline{26}\ \overline{31}\ \overline{13}\ \overline{33}$

1	2	3	■	4	5	6	7	8	9	■	10	11	■	12	13	■	14
15	16	17	18	19	■	20	21	22	■	23	24	25	26	■	27	28	29
■	30	31	32	33	■	34	35	■	36	37	38	■	39	40	41	42	■

C.

1. Deadly — $\overline{14}\ \overline{26}\ \overline{55}\ \overline{6}\ \overline{1}\ \overline{35}$

2. Ridicule — $\overline{32}\ \overline{21}\ \overline{4}\ \overline{24}\ \overline{7}$

3. Interstellar cloud — $\overline{27}\ \overline{53}\ \overline{20}\ \overline{46}\ \overline{36}\ \overline{9}$

4. Complained — $\overline{16}\ \overline{8}\ \overline{23}\ \overline{51}\ \overline{42}\ \overline{15}$

5. Likewise — $\overline{22}\ \overline{41}\ \overline{10}\ \overline{12}\ \overline{45}$

6. Vows — $\overline{13}\ \overline{48}\ \overline{2}\ \overline{38}\ \overline{11}$

7. Voltaic cell — $\overline{29}\ \overline{34}\ \overline{18}\ \overline{25}\ \overline{39}\ \overline{3}\ \overline{44}$

8. Necessary — $\overline{52}\ \overline{17}\ \overline{28}\ \overline{31}\ \overline{40}$

9. Suggestions — $\overline{19}\ \overline{50}\ \overline{49}\ \overline{5}\ \overline{33}$

10. Perfume — $\overline{43}\ \overline{47}\ \overline{30}\ \overline{54}\ \overline{37}$

1	■	2	3	4	5	6	■	7	8	9	10	11	■	12	13	14	15	■	16	17	18	19
■	20	21	22	■	23	24	25	26	27	28	■	29	30	31	32	33	■	34	35	36	■	37
38	39	■	40	41	42	43	■	44	45	46	■	47	48	49	■	50	51	52	53	54	55	■

DIAGRAMLESS FILL-IN

For this fill-in puzzle we have given you all of the E's that appear in the diagram, but none of the black squares. As you solve the puzzle remember to put a black square at the beginning and end of each answer and to balance each black square with its symmetrical counterpart on the opposite side of the diagram.

Solution on page 275

3 Letters	4 Letters		Tact	Lager	Slides
Apt	Avis	Kern	Tate	Lapis	Spoils
Art	Bars	Lady	Then	Lotus	System
Can	Bunt	Lava	Tone	Shiny	
Cat	Cape	Less	Undo	Singe	7 Letters
Dim	Coma	Lion	Vies	Tansy	Anodyne
Dog	Done	Lows	Wigs	Token	Formula
Dye	Dual	Nook		Topic	Oracles
Eli	Edge	Omar	5 Letters	Total	Salerno
Gal	Ergo	Ones	Anise	Trait	
Ler	File	Open	Chose	Trust	8 Letters
Los	Flow	Over	Close	Wares	Standard
Ted	Fret	Sank	Cover		Wintered
Too	Fund	Sent	Dines	6 Letters	
Win	Honk	Shun	Dotes	Agents	9 Letters
	Ides	Silo	Douse	Flakes	Juveniles
	Jail	Snow	Haiti	Method	Northwest
		Sort			

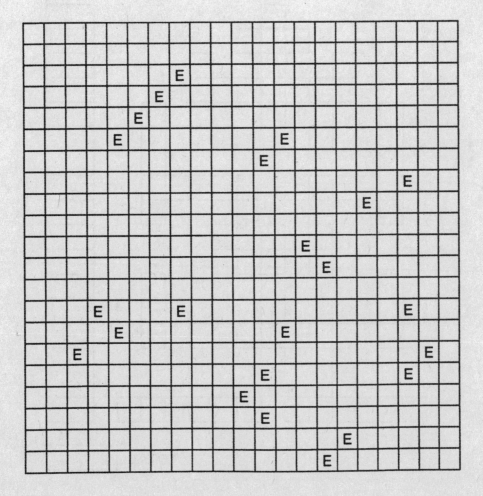

107

MASTERWORDS

Using only the ten letters shown, fill in the diagram by forming words across and down to achieve the highest possible score. Each letter has a given value, so try to use the high-value letters as much as possible. You may repeat letters as often as you wish, even within words. Do not repeat words in the diagram. Foreign words, abbreviations, and words starting with a capital letter are not allowed.

When the diagram is completely filled, add up your score. Count across only, each letter, line by line. Put the total for each line in the boxes at the right.

Our solution with a score of 367 given on page 275

A	E	G	H	L	N	R	S	T	V
1	5	1	3	3	2	4	2	4	5

SCORE

TOTAL

108

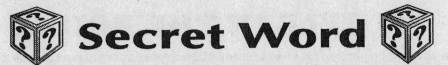

Secret Word

Discover the 5-letter Secret Words by the process of elimination and deduction. Fill in the blanks with the 5-letter answer words to the clues. The number in parentheses next to each answer word tells you how many of the letters in that word are also in the Secret Word. A zero next to an answer word indicates that not one of the letters in that word is in the Secret Word. After you have determined the correct 5 letters, rearrange them to form the Secret Word. No letter is repeated within any Secret Word or within any answer word. The first letters of the answer words, reading down, spell out a hint to the Secret Word.

Solutions on page 275

1. Secret Word ☐ ☐ ☐ ☐ ☐

Doctrine	D O G M A (2)
Black	_ _ _ _ _ (2)
State of oblivion	_ _ _ _ _ (0)
Outfit	_ _ _ _ _ (1)
Dutch cheese	_ _ _ _ _ (2)
Saunter	_ _ _ _ _ (2)
Claw	_ _ _ _ _ (3)
African antelope	_ _ _ _ _ (3)

2. Secret Word ☐ ☐ ☐ ☐ ☐

Rolypoly	_ _ _ _ _ (0)
Grown-up	_ _ _ _ _ (2)
Drench	_ _ _ _ _ (2)
Mature insect	_ _ _ _ _ (2)
Roused	_ _ _ _ _ (3)
Ruff at cards	_ _ _ _ _ (2)
Unlocks	_ _ _ _ _ (2)
Scoundrel	_ _ _ _ _ (1)

3. Secret Word ☐ ☐ ☐ ☐ ☐

Valentine shape	_ _ _ _ _ (2)
Bizarre	_ _ _ _ _ (2)
Mr. Polanski	_ _ _ _ _ (3)
Aversion	_ _ _ _ _ (2)
Javelin	_ _ _ _ _ (0)
Collide	_ _ _ _ _ (1)
Give a speech	_ _ _ _ _ (2)
16 ounces	_ _ _ _ _ (2)
Plant disease	_ _ _ _ _ (2)

4. Secret Word ☐ ☐ ☐ ☐ ☐

Babble	_ _ _ _ _ (1)
Prepared	_ _ _ _ _ (1)
Brilliance	_ _ _ _ _ (2)
Arrow part	_ _ _ _ _ (2)
Perfect	_ _ _ _ _ (2)
Cubes	_ _ _ _ _ (3)
English composer	_ _ _ _ _ (1)
Under, to a poet	_ _ _ _ _ (2)
Vagabond	_ _ _ _ _ (0)

5. Secret Word ☐ ☐ ☐ ☐ ☐

Float	_ _ _ _ _ (1)
Poet Poe	_ _ _ _ _ (3)
Wicked	_ _ _ _ _ (2)
Beginning	_ _ _ _ _ (1)
Brawls	_ _ _ _ _ (0)
Russian cooperative	_ _ _ _ _ (3)
Inclination	_ _ _ _ _ (2)
Western state	_ _ _ _ _ (2)
Predictions	_ _ _ _ _ (2)
Din	_ _ _ _ _ (1)

6. Secret Word ☐ ☐ ☐ ☐ ☐

Robins, e.g.	_ _ _ _ _ (2)
CB or ham	_ _ _ _ _ (1)
Needing a scratch	_ _ _ _ _ (1)
Fact	_ _ _ _ _ (1)
Impede, at law	_ _ _ _ _ (2)
Peevish	_ _ _ _ _ (3)
___ Polo	_ _ _ _ _ (1)
Skillful	_ _ _ _ _ (1)
Thoughts	_ _ _ _ _ (2)
Every 24 hours	_ _ _ _ _ (0)

PUZZLE IN THE ROUND

To solve this challenging puzzle, first fill in as many of the 5-letter answers next to their clues as you can. Next, scramble the order of the letters, look for shared letters, and enter each letter into its correct place in the diagram. Words will share letters as indicated by the lines in the diagram. For example, the letter in the center will be shared by all the answer words. The unshared letters will go into the outer ring and form a common saying, reading from 1 to 24.

Solution on page 275

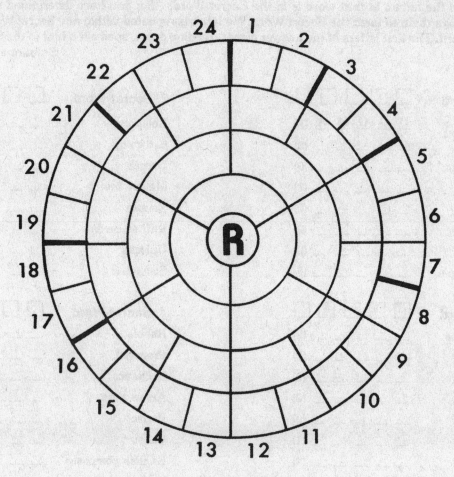

CLUES

1. Furious
2. Trick or ——
3. Kitchen clock
4. Periods of office
5. Outline
6. Attain
7. Frighten
8. Complains
9. Harpoon
10. Clutch
11. Train tracks
12. Entangle
13. Approaches
14. Get up
15. Farm buildings
16. Boasts
17. Worship
18. Managed
19. Rips
20. Stock unit
21. Welcome
22. Heron
23. Bury
24. Attempted

CODEWORD

Codeword is a special crossword in which conventional clues are omitted. Instead, answer words in the diagram are represented by numbers. Each number represents a different letter of the alphabet, and all of the letters of the alphabet are used. When you are sure of a letter, put it in the code key chart and cross it off in the Alphabet Box. A group of letters has been inserted to start you off.

1	2	3	4 E	5	6	7	8	9	10	11	12 I	13
14	15	16	17	18	19	20	21 V	22	23 D	24	25	26

Solution on page 276

	11	22	20			26	4	4	17		11	22	3	
10	25	12	8	11		25	14	1	4		7	1	4	4
22	16	23	12	7		10	25	22	1		1	4	22	1
7	1	4	24	25	1				11	9	16	22	1	4
		22	21	4		11	20	25	16	7				
19	8	4	15	4	23		5	25	18	4	11	7	2	
8	22	15			17	4	23	22	8		5	25	14	
25	17	7		11	25	8		4	8	8		4	13	4
17	4	1		7	1	22	17	11			24	4	18	
	8	22	11	22	14	18	22		23	12	21	4	11	7
		22	21	22	11	7			22	1	4			
5	22	1	23	4	18				24	22	1	1	25	3
22	21	12	23		12	20	25	18		7	12	22	1	22
7	25	8	8		6	25	18	4		4	8	21	4	11
	3	4	4		4	17	4	4		2	4	11		

(D I V E at positions 23 12 21 4 in the grid)

Alphabet Box

A B C D̸ E̸ F G H I̸ J K L M N O P Q R S T U V̸ W X Y Z

111

Each of these cryptograms is a sentence in a substitution code. One letter of the alphabet is substituted for the correct letter. THE SMART CAT might become MRX DGYUM LYM. M is substituted for T, R for H, X for E, etc. One way to break the code is to look for repeated letters. E, T, A, O, N, R, and I are the most often used letters. A single letter is usually A or I; OF, IS, and IT are common two-letter words; try THE or AND for a three-letter group. The code is different for each cryptogram.

Solutions on page 276

1. YCF PMJY EIIEYUYEZV GFIJMZ UY U
   ROUJJ IFWZEMZ EJ YCF VWL SCM CUJ
   TMYC CUEI UZQ PMZFL.

2. XW HXK WJTWIBE QKBXFQL HFNN QWCWG
   OW YFEPTTKFQBWY.

3. AINOMOSR, BQ RHHYR QI QOWH LODJ OR
   DIAK QI KHQ BAQI MHGQ OAM QNBUH OR
   DIAK QI KHQ ITQ.

4. LMHS XHHONSYU LJOHS DHBHPV P VLO LJ
   IVLUHK XNSKU.

5. NYC ODVYA QC IEE PYNQ IMNTO ODC
   JRCCW NX EVADO VJ ODIO VO ACOJ DCLC
   ONN CILES VY ODC UNLYVYA.

6. TNBX BN HOYYXJ SFQFBUNTXJH: ICXT
   RNO'JX FKSUHXK BN BJFSXM MUACB,
   BCXR YXFT RNOJ HOUBQFHX, TNB RNOJ
   IFMMXB.

7. RMD REZVIFD NURM RDFFUOP C PZZB
   LRZEH UL RMCR UR EDQUOBL RMD ZRMDE
   PVH ZX C BVFF ZOD.

8. ART OWTJATVA XCHTWHTKTYIMTH
   ATWWNAIWG IC TJWAR NV ART JWTJ
   YGNCO PTAZTTC RXLJC TJWV.

112

9. YIX BSHBXFY SK HGYWSHT IGT XGBI
   BSJHYFP TWHNWHN WH G OWKKXFXHY VXP.

10. W IJKNEDKK NK QMM INF SADE NQ QWODK
    W SDDO HML FMKKNG QM FM HLMY MED
    DET MH QAD MHHNVD QM QAD MQADL.

11. ZG VWF QUCX U TZJRD DFTO GTWQ DRX
    YXGD YUOX, VWF'TX HTWNUNYV LFMD
    PUTXYXMM, UOB OWD TXUYYV ARUD DRX
    JFV NXRZOB VWF PUYYXB VWF.

12. JW'L ZPCULW JCBULLJNPR WU LRR WKR
    LJPHRV PJTJTO GKRT AUY'VR PJHJTO JT
    Z QUO.

13. FE GVLLTB QEZ GDHQ JED LBJ LE
    OGMBEUT EF GELQTB FVLDBT, JED'BT FEL
    ROIIOFA WVLQTB LOGT.

14. GOT NSBGTQ EGVGTE PFNXQ ZT ZTGGTC
    FRR BR PT OVQ XTEE LFSYTCEVGBFS VSQ
    HFCT LFSETCYVGBFS.

15. ZXC IDYJPZ YS UMCCG ECWJRECF NL ZXC
    ITCEIKC GCEUYP RU JUJIMML ZCP
    DRPJZCU DYEC.

16. XQUC ZIVU NUINHU EOHY OSIAE EQUWB
    POVWHR EBUU, EQUR AZAOHHR EBWV IPP
    O SBOCFQ QUBU OCK EQUBU.

17. YONGNAGBL AOXJAIAGZB GN I HZA
    OINGOY STOB SO ATGBE SO'HH JYZRIRHP
    LOA IBZATOY UTIBUO HIAOY ZB MZSB ATO
    HGBO.

Crostic 1

Use the CLUES on the left to fill in the WORDS column. Then transfer each letter to the correspondingly numbered square in the diagram. (We have inserted WORD A as an example.) It is not necessary to know all the words to start solving. Work back and forth from the diagram to the WORDS column until both are filled. A black square indicates the end of a word. The completed diagram will contain a quotation, and the first letter of each word in the WORDS column, reading down, will spell the author's name and the source of the quotation.

CLUES **WORDS**

A. "King Lear," e.g.
T R A G E D Y
125 47 16 116 56 119 105

B. Grapple
___ ___ ___ ___ ___ ___ ___
1 113 33 111 12 73 121

C. Degas, for one
___ ___ ___ ___ ___ ___
99 138 35 114 50 108

D. Catching
___ ___ ___ ___ ___ ___ ___ ___ ___ ___
11 124 72 69 34 143 79 97 22 131

E. Meridian
___ ___ ___ ___ ___ ___ ___
86 137 13 100 95 7 74

F. Small gray bird
___ ___ ___ ___ ___ ___ ___
31 85 93 142 58 140 70

G. Vanity
___ ___ ___ ___ ___ ___ ___
19 60 106 96 51 84 42

H. Lump of gold
___ ___ ___ ___ ___ ___
144 30 147 101 24 80

I. Average man: 2 wds.
___ ___ ___ ___ ___ ___ ___
32 126 98 20 55 123 28

J. Believer
___ ___ ___ ___ ___ ___ ___ ___
102 15 132 43 57 91 115 122

K. Monastic
___ ___ ___ ___ ___ ___ ___
44 36 146 78 46 29 109

L. Protest strongly
___ ___ ___ ___ ___ ___ ___
130 6 18 128 145 141 75

M. Of course, for short
___ ___ ___ ___ ___
52 5 112 64 90

N. Paternal
___ ___ ___ ___ ___ ___ ___ ___
136 3 38 65 110 9 139 89

O. Hurried
___ ___ ___ ___ ___ ___
54 92 77 2 81 87

P. Insult
___ ___ ___ ___ ___ ___ ___
66 37 129 25 53 134 62

Q. Heroine of "War and Peace"
___ ___ ___ ___ ___ ___ ___
118 49 21 88 41 27 63

R. Board imperfection
___ ___ ___ ___ ___ ___ ___ ___
103 67 10 26 39 71 120 104

S. Medieval weapon
___ ___ ___ ___ ___ ___ ___
14 59 107 135 127 45 48

T. Senseless
___ ___ ___ ___ ___ ___
133 17 76 82 4 40 68

U. Approached
___ ___ ___ ___ ___ ___
83 61 117 23 94 8

Solution on page 276

1 B	2 O	3 N	4 T		5 M	6 L		7 E	8 U	9 N	10 R	11 D	12 B		13 E	14 S	15 J
16 A	17 T	18 L	19 G	20 I	21 Q	22 D	23 U	24 H	25 P		26 R	27 Q	28 I		29 K	30 H	31 F	32 I
33 B	34 D	35 C		36 K	37 P		38 N	39 R	40 T	41 Q		42 G	43 J	44 K	45 S	46 K	47 A		48 S	49 Q	50 C
	51 G	52 M		53 P	54 O	55 I	56 A	57 J		58 F	59 S		60 G	61 U	62 P		63 Q		64 M	65 N	66 P
67 R	68 T	69 D		70 F	71 R		72 D	73 B	74 E		75 L	76 T	77 O		78 K	79 D	80 H	81 O		82 T	83 U
	84 G	85 F	86 E	87 O	88 Q	89 N		90 M	91 J		92 O	93 F	94 U	95 E		96 G	97 D		98 I	99 C	100 E
101 H		102 J		103 R	104 R	105 A		106 G	107 S		108 C	109 K	110 N		111 B	112 M	113 B	114 C	115 J	116 A	
	117 U	118 Q	119 A		120 R	121 B	122 J		123 I	124 D		125 A	126 I		127 S	128 L		129 P	130 L	131 D
	132 J	133 T	134 P	135 S		136 N	137 E	138 C		139 N	140 F	141 L	142 F	143 D	144 H	145 L	146 K	147 H

114

Crostic 2

A. Longitudinally $\overline{95}\ \overline{180}\ \overline{149}\ \overline{73}\ \overline{10}\ \overline{129}\ \overline{31}\ \overline{120}\ \overline{142}\ \overline{178}$

B. Clark Kent's changing room: 2 wds. $\overline{4}\ \overline{111}\ \overline{3}\ \overline{42}\ \overline{21}\ \overline{184}\ \overline{55}\ \overline{11}\ \overline{103}\ \overline{199}$

C. Lucky item? $\overline{88}\ \overline{159}\ \overline{40}\ \overline{83}\ \overline{189}\ \overline{23}\ \overline{173}\ \overline{125}\ \overline{67}$

D. Person's printed protest: 2 wds. $\overline{108}\ \overline{7}\ \overline{117}\ \overline{134}\ \overline{185}\ \overline{127}\ \overline{80}\ \overline{193}\ \overline{112}\ \overline{68}$

E. Restriction $\overline{150}\ \overline{167}\ \overline{126}\ \overline{138}\ \overline{78}\ \overline{147}\ \overline{49}\ \overline{59}\ \overline{30}\ \overline{62}$

F. Pinocchio, for one $\overline{70}\ \overline{119}\ \overline{145}\ \overline{45}\ \overline{156}\ \overline{197}\ \overline{102}\ \overline{27}\ \overline{33}\ \overline{163}$

G. Tied: hyph. $\overline{86}\ \overline{93}\ \overline{74}\ \overline{139}\ \overline{181}\ \overline{16}\ \overline{153}\ \overline{116}\ \overline{9}\ \overline{179}$

H. "Dombey and ___" $\overline{15}\ \overline{34}\ \overline{32}$

I. Incessant talking $\overline{162}\ \overline{91}\ \overline{115}\ \overline{136}\ \overline{198}\ \overline{195}\ \overline{54}\ \overline{41}\ \overline{121}\ \overline{35}$

J. Moderate in eating $\overline{161}\ \overline{191}\ \overline{44}\ \overline{146}\ \overline{5}\ \overline{85}\ \overline{130}\ \overline{170}\ \overline{76}\ \overline{187}$

K. "People" for Barbra Streisand: 2 wds. $\overline{1}\ \overline{114}\ \overline{79}\ \overline{201}\ \overline{39}\ \overline{124}\ \overline{51}\ \overline{158}\ \overline{20}$

L. Dairy animal $\overline{143}\ \overline{6}\ \overline{194}$

M. Alfred Noyes subject $\overline{58}\ \overline{141}\ \overline{140}\ \overline{66}\ \overline{2}\ \overline{84}\ \overline{90}\ \overline{101}\ \overline{24}\ \overline{52}$

N. Under least favorable conditions: 3 wds. $\overline{43}\ \overline{65}\ \overline{37}\ \overline{137}\ \overline{69}\ \overline{57}\ \overline{100}\ \overline{25}\ \overline{97}\ \overline{12}$

O. Man's sleeping garment $\overline{131}\ \overline{154}\ \overline{107}\ \overline{28}\ \overline{160}\ \overline{175}\ \overline{38}\ \overline{151}\ \overline{157}\ \overline{182}$

P. Done on purpose $\overline{172}\ \overline{71}\ \overline{8}\ \overline{105}\ \overline{176}\ \overline{36}\ \overline{17}\ \overline{174}\ \overline{46}\ \overline{82}$

Q. Put into a scabbard $\overline{99}\ \overline{188}\ \overline{94}\ \overline{166}\ \overline{87}\ \overline{81}\ \overline{177}$

R. Simple mathematics $\overline{92}\ \overline{109}\ \overline{148}\ \overline{98}\ \overline{104}\ \overline{56}\ \overline{89}\ \overline{155}\ \overline{186}\ \overline{60}$

S. Crumble $\overline{123}\ \overline{63}\ \overline{132}\ \overline{200}\ \overline{171}\ \overline{26}\ \overline{22}\ \overline{183}\ \overline{110}\ \overline{196}$

T. Explanation $\overline{190}\ \overline{122}\ \overline{53}\ \overline{77}\ \overline{106}\ \overline{50}\ \overline{128}\ \overline{64}\ \overline{133}\ \overline{168}$

U. Bramble fruit $\overline{14}\ \overline{96}\ \overline{118}\ \overline{48}\ \overline{19}\ \overline{169}\ \overline{192}\ \overline{164}\ \overline{72}\ \overline{113}$

V. Seismic event $\overline{135}\ \overline{13}\ \overline{29}\ \overline{165}\ \overline{61}\ \overline{75}\ \overline{47}\ \overline{18}\ \overline{152}\ \overline{144}$

Solution on page 276

1 K	2 M	3 B		4 B	5 J	6 L	7 D	8 P	9 G		10 A	11 B	12 N	13 V	14 U		15 H	16 G	17 P	18 V	19 U
20 K	21 B	22 S	23 C		24 M	25 N	26 S		27 F	28 O	29 V	30 E	31 A	32 H		33 F	34 H	35 I	36 P	37 N	38 O
39 K	40 C		41 I	42 B		43 N		44 J	45 F	46 P	47 V	48 U	49 E	50 T	51 K	52 M		53 T	54 I	55 B	56 R
	57 N	58 M	59 E	60 R	61 V		62 E	63 S	64 T	65 N	66 M	67 C	68 D		69 N	70 F	71 P	72 U	73 A	74 G
75 V	76 J	77 T	78 E	79 K		80 D	81 Q	82 P		83 C	84 M	85 J	86 G		87 Q	88 C	89 R	90 M		91 I	92 R
93 G	94 Q		95 A	96 U	97 N	98 R		99 Q	100 N	101 M	102 F	103 B	104 R	105 P	106 T	107 O		108 D	109 R		110 S
111 B	112 D	113 U		114 K	115 I	116 G	117 D		118 U	119 F	120 A	121 I	122 T	123 S		124 K	125 C	126 E	127 D	128 T	129 A
130 J	131 O	132 S		133 T	134 D	135 V		136 I	137 N	138 E	139 G	140 M		141 M	142 A		143 L	144 V	145 F	146 J	147 E
148 R	149 A		150 E	151 O	152 V	153 G		154 O	155 R		156 F	157 O		158 K	159 C	160 O		161 J		162 I	163 F
164 U	165 V	166 Q	167 E	168 T		169 U	170 J	171 S	172 P		173 C	174 P	175 O		176 P	177 Q	178 A	179 G		180 A	181 G
182 O	183 S	184 B	185 D	186 R	187 J	188 Q	189 C	190 T		191 J	192 U	193 D	194 L	195 I	196 S	197 F		198 I	199 B	200 S	201 K

Crostic 3

A. Romance language
___ ___ ___ ___ ___ ___
123 182 166 131 11 38

B. Storybook tug: 2 wds.
___ ___ ___ ___ ___ ___ ___ ___ ___ ___
90 149 174 141 3 41 100 71 15 80

C. Intermittently: 3 wds.
___ ___ ___ ___ ___ ___ ___ ___
32 170 83 54 195 77 96 36

D. In one's salad days
___ ___ ___ ___ ___
169 31 135 48 52

E. 34th president: 2 wds.
___ ___ ___ ___ ___ ___ ___ ___ ___
26 107 67 14 101 78 44 198 187
___ ___ ___ ___ ___ ___ ___
194 140 81 85 160 62 9

F. Vessels of commerce: 2 wds.
___ ___ ___ ___ ___ ___ ___ ___ ___
200 161 53 129 144 184 68 196 33
___ ___ ___ ___ ___
24 75 111 92 60

G. Instant
___ ___ ___ ___ ___ ___ ___ ___ ___
171 50 7 22 105 115 91 65 183

H. Coats
___ ___ ___ ___ ___ ___ ___ ___ ___
29 1 97 87 208 35 168 137 23

I. Shining
___ ___ ___ ___ ___ ___ ___ ___
2 152 203 47 58 134 19 34

J. Ancient people of Tuscany
___ ___ ___ ___ ___ ___ ___ ___ ___
82 43 136 177 197 70 205 148 20

K. Open shelter
___ ___ ___ ___ ___ ___
158 130 72 12 138 192

L. Submariner's fish
___ ___ ___ ___ ___ ___ ___
110 207 127 133 159 88 95

M. Minced
___ ___ ___ ___ ___ ___
21 124 121 156 102 93

N. Enables
___ ___ ___ ___ ___ ___ ___ ___
186 103 73 119 165 209 18 178

O. Aliments
___ ___ ___ ___ ___ ___ ___
173 181 28 30 16 191 151

P. Subcontinent
___ ___ ___ ___ ___
10 63 46 118 202

Q. TV's "My ___": 2 wds.
___ ___ ___ ___ ___ ___ ___ ___ ___
99 45 172 4 162 204 155 8 114
___ ___ ___ ___ ___ ___
179 61 143 139 189 150

R. Puts one over on
___ ___ ___ ___ ___
5 64 79 185 113

S. Teary
___ ___ ___ ___ ___ ___ ___ ___ ___
112 40 122 190 56 98 167 89 206

T. Unintentional tax breaks
___ ___ ___ ___ ___ ___ ___ ___ ___
116 57 142 146 66 27 84 108 13

U. Temporary abodes
___ ___ ___ ___ ___
164 147 120 55 42

V. Debt
___ ___ ___ ___ ___ ___ ___ ___ ___ ___
39 94 117 128 69 154 188 201 176 109

W. 1936 Kay Francis film, with "The": 2 wds.
___ ___ ___ ___ ___ ___ ___ ___ ___ ___
59 175 51 106 126 6 199 49 145 153

X. Conclusions
___ ___ ___ ___ ___ ___ ___
76 180 37 104 25 193 132

Y. Did over
___ ___ ___ ___ ___ ___
86 157 125 74 17 163

Solution on page 276

1 H	2 I	3 B		4 Q	5 R		6 W	7 G	8 Q	9 E	10 P	11 A	12 K
13 T		14 E	15 B	16 O	17 Y		18 N	19 I	20 J	21 M	22 G	23 H		24 F	25 X	26 E		27 T	28 O	29 H
30 O	31 D	32 C	33 F	34 I		35 H	36 C	37 X		38 A	39 V	40 S	41 B	42 U	43 J	44 E	45 Q	46 P	47 I	48 D	49 W
	50 G	51 W	52 D	53 F	54 C	55 U	56 S	57 T	58 I		59 W	60 F	61 Q	62 E		63 P	64 R	65 G	66 T	67 E	68 F
69 V		70 J	71 B	72 K	73 N	74 Y	75 F	76 X	77 C		78 E	79 R		80 B	81 E	82 J		83 C	84 T	85 E	86 Y
87 H	88 L	89 S		90 B	91 G	92 F	93 M		94 V	95 L	96 C	97 H		98 S	99 Q		100B	101E	102M		103N
104X	105G	—	106W	107E	108T	109V	110L	111F	112S	113R		114Q	115G	116T	117V	118P	119N	120U	121M		122S
123A		124M	125Y	126W	127L	128V	129F	130K	131A	132X		133L	134I	135D	136J	137H	138K		139Q	140E	141B
142T		143Q	144F	145W		146T	147U	148J	149B	150Q	151O	152I	153W	154V		155Q	156M	157Y	158K	159L
160E	161F	162Q	163Y		164U	165N	166A	167S	168H	169D	—	170C	171G	172Q	173O		174B	175W	176V	177J	178N
179Q	180X	181O		182A	183G	184F	185R		186N	187E	188V	189Q	190S	191O		192K	193X	194E	195C	196F	197J
	198E	199W		200F	201V	202P	203I	204Q		205J	206S	207L	208H	209N	

Crostic 4

A. Dull voice
— 57 168 39 192 133 171 206 149

B. Derogatory remark
— 28 164 198 200 86 189 47 35

C. Flightless bird
— 121 80 111 56

D. Former
— 53 172 108 118 184 125 167 93 20

E. Word endings
— 52 23 18 46 163 77 2 9

F. Storm-ridden Cape
— 185 65 41 138 73 155 110 98

G. Kingdoms
— 84 64 142 156 139 96 69

H. Pitcher's injury area: 2 wds.
— 103 129 135 40 124 186 193 24 180
— 92 19

I. Anterior tooth
— 42 32 7 113 22 94 144

J. Convincing
— 152 104 54 38 201 31 177 141

K. Unyielding
— 127 159 120 36 26 11 115

L. Saw
— 100 43 102 178 88 12 61

M. Ship's rope
— 25 205 3 106 76 14

N. Major league team: 2 wds.
— 165 15 182 143 72 204 99 37 21
— 137 49 60 123

O. 1949 Cagney movie: 2 wds.
— 187 16 114 166 122 116 105 131 59

P. Consented
— 153 68 78 140 48 158 91 70 136 179

Q. Nearly here
— 147 157 119 176 44 50 151 83

R. Pointer
— 173 30 146 82 34 203 66 45 51

S. U.S. Revolutionary War hero: 2 wds.
— 174 63 202 130 150 29 196 107 5 160

T. Flooded
— 117 27 197 81 109

U. Pacific island invaded in 1943
— 195 134 74 13 95 188

V. Name of eight popes
— 79 97 85 6 169

W. Indian chiefs
— 62 58 199 112 89 161

X. Disturbed
— 145 33 67 162 87 190 126 101

Y. Cut: 2 wds.
— 128 17 4 154 90 175 10 1 170

Z. Tenant
— 55 71 183 132 8 194

a. Part of a Thanksgiving menu
— 75 181 191 148

Solution on page 277

1 Y	2 E	3 M		4 Y	5 S	6 V	7 I	8 Z	9 E		10 Y	11 K		12 L	13 U	14 M	15 N
16 O		17 Y	18 E	19 H	20 D	21 N		22 I	23 E	24 H	25 M		26 K			27 T	28 B	29 S
30 R	31 J	32 I	33 X		34 R	35 B	36 K	37 N	38 J	39 A	40 H	41 F	42 I	43 L	44 Q		45 R	46 E		47 B	48 P
49 N	50 Q	51 R	52 E	53 D		54 J	55 Z	56 C	57 A	58 W	59 O	60 N		61 L	62 W	63 S	64 G	65 F	66 R	67 X	68 P
	69 G	70 P	71 Z	72 N	73 F	74 U	75 a		76 M	77 E	78 P	79 V	80 C	81 T	82 R	83 Q	84 G		85 V	86 B	87 X
88 L	89 W	90 Y	91 P		92 H	93 D	94 I	95 U	96 G	97 V	98 F		99 N	100 L	101 X		102 L	103 H	104 J	105 O	106 M
	107 S	108 D		109 T	110 F	111 C	112 W	113 I	114 O		115 K	116 O	117 T	118 D		119 Q	120 K	121 C	122 O	123 N
124 H	125 D	126 X		127 K	128 Y	129 H	130 S	131 O		132 Z	133 A	134 U	135 H	136 P		137 N		138 F	139 G	140 P	141 J
	142 G	143 N	144 I	145 X	146 R	147 Q	148 a	149 A		150 S	151 Q	152 J		153 P		154 Y	155 F	156 G	157 Q	158 P
159 K	160 S	161 W	162 X	163 E	164 B	165 N	166 O	167 D	168 A	169 V		170 Y	171 A	172 D		173 R	174 S	175 Y	176 Q	177 J	178 L
	179 P	180 H	181 a	182 N	183 Z		184 D	185 F	186 H		187 O	188 U	189 B	190 X		191 a	192 A	193 H
	194 Z		195 U	196 S	197 T	198 B		199 W	200 B	201 J	202 S		203 R		204 N	205 M	206 A	

117

Crostic 5

A. Betray
$\overline{117}\ \overline{10}\ \overline{186}\ \overline{157}\ \overline{162}\ \overline{62}\ \overline{149}$

B. Pertaining to Britain
$\overline{77}\ \overline{26}\ \overline{46}\ \overline{41}\ \overline{61}\ \overline{177}\ \overline{69}$

C. Perplexed
$\overline{113}\ \overline{18}\ \overline{153}\ \overline{179}\ \overline{51}\ \overline{122}\ \overline{74}$

D. Term for a spouse: 2 wds.
$\overline{66}\ \overline{57}\ \overline{126}\ \overline{180}\ \overline{144}\ \overline{13}\ \overline{5}\ \overline{188}\ \overline{75}\ \overline{165}$

E. Pleasure boater
$\overline{102}\ \overline{131}\ \overline{79}\ \overline{12}\ \overline{8}\ \overline{143}\ \overline{183}\ \overline{150}\ \overline{37}$

F. Neck injury
$\overline{43}\ \overline{109}\ \overline{145}\ \overline{24}\ \overline{119}\ \overline{6}\ \overline{103}\ \overline{80}$

G. Trial-lawyer's cry
$\overline{32}\ \overline{95}\ \overline{158}\ \overline{70}\ \overline{47}\ \overline{7}\ \overline{191}\ \overline{178}\ \overline{156}$

H. Timely
$\overline{129}\ \overline{138}\ \overline{23}\ \overline{105}\ \overline{166}\ \overline{90}\ \overline{99}\ \overline{163}\ \overline{115}$

I. "Around the World in 80 Days" star: 2 wds.
$\overline{81}\ \overline{48}\ \overline{96}\ \overline{25}\ \overline{125}\ \overline{73}\ \overline{34}\ \overline{111}\ \overline{29}\ \overline{189}$

J. Finish a paint job: 2 wds.
$\overline{4}\ \overline{141}\ \overline{39}\ \overline{11}\ \overline{104}\ \overline{159}\ \overline{172}$

K. Confined: 2 wds.
$\overline{140}\ \overline{92}\ \overline{168}\ \overline{154}\ \overline{112}\ \overline{151}\ \overline{97}\ \overline{45}$

L. All people
$\overline{171}\ \overline{121}\ \overline{193}\ \overline{135}\ \overline{87}\ \overline{71}\ \overline{52}\ \overline{128}\ \overline{83}$

M. Rough estimate
$\overline{164}\ \overline{142}\ \overline{182}\ \overline{139}\ \overline{28}$

N. South Korean port
$\overline{63}\ \overline{130}\ \overline{175}\ \overline{187}\ \overline{2}\ \overline{116}$

O. Confute
$\overline{38}\ \overline{55}\ \overline{101}\ \overline{19}\ \overline{120}\ \overline{89}\ \overline{67}$

P. Finished
$\overline{148}\ \overline{181}\ \overline{123}\ \overline{88}\ \overline{106}\ \overline{65}\ \overline{170}$

Q. Pagan images
$\overline{14}\ \overline{160}\ \overline{94}\ \overline{40}\ \overline{42}$

R. Type of whiskey: 2 wds.
$\overline{20}\ \overline{127}\ \overline{136}\ \overline{56}\ \overline{17}\ \overline{30}\ \overline{35}\ \overline{91}$

S. Unlearned
$\overline{174}\ \overline{161}\ \overline{86}\ \overline{22}\ \overline{59}\ \overline{110}\ \overline{146}\ \overline{49}$

T. Nil
$\overline{1}\ \overline{152}\ \overline{169}\ \overline{21}\ \overline{44}\ \overline{64}\ \overline{53}$

U. Tipsters
$\overline{68}\ \overline{98}\ \overline{72}\ \overline{16}\ \overline{54}$

V. Beset
$\overline{9}\ \overline{78}\ \overline{173}\ \overline{58}\ \overline{100}\ \overline{15}\ \overline{118}\ \overline{190}$

W. Sea birds
$\overline{76}\ \overline{27}\ \overline{185}\ \overline{124}\ \overline{134}\ \overline{31}$

X. Golden king
$\overline{137}\ \overline{155}\ \overline{133}\ \overline{82}\ \overline{192}$

Y. Cognizant
$\overline{50}\ \overline{3}\ \overline{85}\ \overline{60}\ \overline{114}$

Z. Runs in neutral
$\overline{36}\ \overline{108}\ \overline{132}\ \overline{176}\ \overline{147}$

a. "Odd Couple" actor
$\overline{107}\ \overline{184}\ \overline{93}\ \overline{84}\ \overline{167}\ \overline{33}$

Solution on page 277

1 T	2 N	3 Y		4 J	5 D	6 F	7 G		8 E	9 V	10 A		11 J	12 E	13 D
14 Q	15 V	16 U	17 R	18 C	19 O		20 R	21 T	22 S	23 H	24 F	25 I	26 B	27 W		28 M	29 I
30 R	31 W	32 G	33 a		34 I	35 R		36 Z	37 E		38 O	39 J	40 Q	41 B		42 Q	43 F	44 T	45 K	46 B
47 G	48 I	49 S	50 Y	51 C	52 L	53 T	54 U		55 O	56 R	57 D		58 V	59 S	60 Y	61 B	62 A	63 N	64 T	65 P
66 D	67 O		68 U	69 B	70 G		71 L	72 U	73 I	74 C	75 D	76 W		77 B	78 V	79 E	80 F		81 I	82 X	83 L
	84 a	85 Y	86 S	87 L		88 P	89 O		90 H	91 R	92 K	93 a		94 Q	95 G	96 I	97 K	98 U	99 H	100 V	101 O
102 E		103 F	104 J	105 H	106 P	107 a	108 Z		109 F	110 S	111 I	112 K		113 C	114 Y	115 H	116 N		117 A	118 V	119 F
120 O	121 L	122 C	123 P	124 W	125 I		126 D	127 R		128 L	129 H	130 N	131 E	132 Z	133 X		134 W	135 L	136 R	137 X	138 H
139 M		140 K	141 J	142 M	143 E	144 D		145 F	146 S	147 Z	148 P	149 A	150 E	151 K		152 T	153 C		154 K	155 X	156 G
157 A		158 G	159 J	160 Q	161 S	162 A	163 H	164 M		165 D	166 H	167 a	168 K		169 T	170 P	171 L		172 J	173 V	174 S
175 N	176 Z	177 B		178 G	179 C		180 D	181 P	182 M		183 E	184 a	185 W	186 A	187 N	188 D	189 I	190 V	191 G	192 X	193 L

Crostic 6

A. Remunerative
163 144 94 125 159 122 56 80 111 67

B. Monstrous creature
152 101 66 180 183 32 174 45

C. Oscar Madison, to Felix Unger
29 165 115 95 25 178 65 53

D. Agave roots
131 61 41 52 46 181

E. Toothy gear
141 50 161 133 10 64 28 189

F. The Bluegrass State
27 98 38 116 149 158 2 69

G. Highly charged
49 79 4 99 36 104 12 26 169

H. Goddess of divine retribution
160 191 102 176 150 58 19

I. Take back, as a law
42 110 48 21 96 59

J. Parisian tower
73 91 121 173 108 33

K. Tapless tap dance: hyph.
192 70 40 44 136 117 106 17

L. In the wings
126 156 103 171 90 62 13 147

M. The Pelican State
132 153 34 1 92 113 157 107 81

N. Raring to go: 3 wds.
154 75 166 54 179 11 164

O. Most tenacious
9 24 71 146 175 184 39 93

P. Question-asking meeting
172 140 85 74 105 129 89 30 5

Q. The Buckeye State
185 77 14 120

R. The Corn-husker State
88 78 137 127 134 16 97 18

S. Two-person chair
82 187 35 155 123 139

T. The Bear State
167 47 63 151 55 84 87 119

U. Widely and unfavorably known
57 182 170 43 22 128 6 143 31

V. Juvenile
177 142 168 23 86 112 162 60

W. Translucent paper
37 186 83 148 3 190 72 118 7

X. Most strapped
124 138 130 114 20 8 109 76

Y. Ability to relate vicariously
188 68 51 145 15 100 135

Solution on page 277

1 M		2 F	3 W	4 G	5 P		6 U	7 W	8 X		9 O	10 E	11 N	12 G	13 L		14 Q	15 Y	16 R
	17 K	18 R	19 H	20 X	21 I	22 U		23 V	24 O		25 C	26 G	27 F	28 E		29 C	30 P	31 U	32 B	33 J	34 M
35 S	36 G	37 W	38 F	39 O		40 K	41 D	42 I		43 U	44 K	45 B	46 D	47 T		48 I	49 G	50 E	51 Y	52 D	53 C
	54 N	55 T		56 A	57 U		58 H	59 I	60 V	—	61 D	62 L	63 T	64 E		65 C	66 B	67 A	68 Y	—	69 F
70 K	71 O	—	72 W	73 J	74 P	75 N	—	76 X	77 Q	78 R	79 G		80 A	81 M	82 S	83 W	84 T		85 P	86 V	87 T
88 R		89 P	90 L		91 J	92 M		93 O	94 A		95 C	96 I	97 R	98 F		99 G	100 Y	101 B	102 H		103 L
104 G	105 P		106 K	107 M	108 J	109 X	110 I	111 A	112 V		113 M		114 X	115 C		116 F	117 K	118 W	119 T		120 Q
121 J	122 A	123 S	124 X		125 A	126 L	127 R		128 U	129 P	130 X		131 D	132 M	133 E	134 R	135 Y	136 K		137 R	138 X
139 S	140 P		141 E	142 V	143 U	144 A	145 Y	146 O	147 L	148 W	149 F	150 H		151 T	152 B	153 M	154 N	155 S		156 L	157 M
158 F	159 A	160 H	161 E		162 V	163 A		164 N	165 C		166 N	167 T	168 V	169 G	170 U	171 L		172 P	173 J		174 B
175 O	176 H	177 V		178 C	179 N	180 B		181 D	182 U	183 B	184 O	185 Q	186 W	187 S		188 Y	189 E	190 W	191 H	192 K

CRAVING CROSTICS? *Satisfy your appetite with our many special collections of Crostics; each features loads of challenging puzzles. To order, see page 61.*

Crostic 7

Use the CLUES on the left to fill in the WORDS column. Then transfer each letter to the correspondingly numbered square in the diagram. (We have inserted WORD A as an example.) It is not necessary to know all the words to start solving. Work back and forth from the diagram to the WORDS column until both are filled. A black square indicates the end of a word. The completed diagram will contain a quotation, and the first letter of each word in the WORDS column, reading down, will spell the author's name and the source of the quotation.

CLUES / WORDS

A. Strict
A(74) U(70) S(35) T(61) E(9) R(4) E(16)

B. River in Jordan
_(21) _(97) _(60) _(52) _(134) _(131)

C. Style of jazz
_(15) _(23) _(145) _(99) _(111) _(116) _(51)

D. Add nutrients to
_(29) _(44) _(75) _(63) _(6) _(126)

E. Restrained
_(109) _(105) _(3) _(13) _(26) _(10) _(86)

F. Occurrence
_(119) _(110) _(5) _(133) _(27) _(11) _(103)

G. Ship's main pole
_(93) _(62) _(142) _(139)

H. Magician's word
_(32) _(95) _(66) _(47) _(73) _(42)

I. Seeks
_(81) _(121) _(39) _(128) _(92)

J. Goat or cat variety
_(7) _(67) _(40) _(94) _(28) _(137)

K. Congressional body
_(55) _(113) _(8) _(1) _(125) _(30)

L. Disclose
_(123) _(31) _(19) _(127) _(112) _(22)

M. Glisten
_(135) _(33) _(143) _(48) _(65) _(82) _(118)

N. Depressed at the poles
_(84) _(69) _(102) _(34) _(80) _(59)

O. Trifling
_(144) _(76) _(129) _(36) _(90) _(53) _(72)

P. Folklore beings
_(91) _(108) _(85) _(2) _(56) _(122)

Q. Pertaining to the supernatural
_(49) _(124) _(101) _(77) _(24) _(68)

R. Threatening
_(38) _(120) _(71) _(57) _(14) _(114) _(37)

S. Twist out of shape
_(43) _(107) _(115) _(87) _(117) _(50) _(140)

T. Fine cotton fabric
_(64) _(130) _(100) _(78) _(12) _(41) _(106) _(25)

U. Ornamental centerpiece
_(132) _(20) _(45) _(98) _(83) _(138) _(96)

V. Card game
_(46) _(17) _(89) _(54) _(58)

W. Tail
_(104) _(88) _(18) _(79) _(141) _(136)

Solution on page 277

1 K	2 P	3 E	4 A R	5 F	6 D	7 J		8 K	9 A E	10 E	11 F	12 T		13 E	14 R	15 C	16 A E		17 V	18 W	19 L
20 U	21 B		22 L	23 C	24 Q	25 T		26 E	27 F	28 J	29 D		30 K	31 L	32 H	33 M	34 N	35 A	36 O	37 R
38 R	39 I		40 J	41 T	42 H	43 S		44 D	45 U	46 V	47 H		48 M	49 Q	50 S	51 C		52 B	53 O	54 V	55 K
	56 P	57 R	58 V	59 N	60 B	61 A T	62 G	63 D	64 T	65 M	66 H	67 J	68 Q		69 N	70 A U	71 R	72 O	73 H		74 A A
75 D	76 O	77 Q	78 T	79 W		80 N	81 I	82 M		83 U	84 N	85 P	86 E		87 S	88 W	89 V	90 O	91 P	92 I
93 G	94 J	95 H	96 U		97 B	98 U	99 C	100T	101Q	102N	103F	104W		105E	106T		107S	108P	109E	110F	111C
112L	113K		114R	115S		116C	117S	118M	119F		120R	121I	122P	123L	124Q		125K	126D	127L	128I
129O	130T	131B	132U	133F		134B	135M		136W	137J	138U	139G		140S	141W		142G	143M	144O	145C

120

Crostic 8

A. Speechless: hyph.
104 4 143 81 138 113 182 46 170 41

B. Bee's bank
161 137 92 32 146 163 94 171 53

C. Accepting bribes: 3 wds.
178 165 70 90 37 56 145 123 150

D. Foolishly wasted
47 82 116 98 151 9 181 160

E. Gymnast
88 119 157 76 169 14 135

F. Wrap-around garments
67 132 22 167 124 154 35

G. Sissy, informally
36 172 133 111 110 126 142 153 50 72

H. Apportionment
164 100 109 49 8 24 152 20 156 30

I. Reduce to ashes
34 83 17 73 108 59 5 114 89 55

J. Citizen of a particular country
118 158 168 66 78 23 21 39

K. Submerged
128 166 139 18 85 122 117 134

L. Italian painter
79 6 15 140 180 60 54

M. Not erasable
175 3 33 99 65 91 147 19 174

N. Chicken-gravy ingredients
93 52 64 38 28 97 11

O. Child's toy: hyph.
136 107 115 102 87 112 121 58 45 131

P. Become air-borne: 2 wds.
62 84 149 120 125 95 13

Q. Enter quietly: 2 wds.
74 127 10 48 42 155

R. Days of yore: 2 wds.
29 86 173 40 177 77 44 141 16 106

S. Pugilism
101 71 130 68 25 69 159 176

T. Truman's home
144 80 61 51 12 103 27 1

U. Engaged in debate
63 179 2 26 148 129

V. Tobacco ingredient
7 96 31 57 43 105 75 162

Solution on page 277

1 T	2 U	3 M	4 A	5 I	6 L	7 V	8 H	9 D		10 Q	11 N		12 T	13 P		
14 E		15 L	16 R	17 I	18 K	19 M	20 H	21 J	22 F		23 J	24 H	25 S	26 U	27 T	28 N
29 R	30 H	31 V	32 B		33 M	34 I	35 F	36 G	37 C	38 N	39 J	40 R	41 A		42 Q	43 V	44 R	45 O		46 A
47 D	48 Q	49 H	50 G	51 T	52 N	53 B	54 L	55 I		56 C	57 V		58 O	59 I	60 L	61 T	62 P	63 U	64 N	65 M	66 J
67 F	68 S		69 S	70 C		71 S	72 G		73 I	74 Q		75 V	76 E	77 R		78 J	79 L	80 T	81 A	82 D	83 I
84 P	85 K	86 R	87 O		88 E		89 I	90 C	91 M	92 B	93 N		94 B	95 P		96 V	97 N	98 D	99 M	100 H	101 S
	102 O	103 T	104 A		105 V	106 R		107 O	108 I	109 H	110 G		111 G	112 O	113 A		114 I	115 O	116 D	117 K	118 J
119 E	120 P		121 O	122 K		123 C	124 F	125 P	126 G	127 Q	128 K	129 U	130 S	131 O		132 F	133 G	134 K		135 E	136 O
137 B	138 A	139 K	140 L		141 R	142 G	143 A		144 T	145 C	146 B		147 M	148 U		149 P	150 C	151 D	152 H		153 G
	154 F	155 Q	156 H	157 E	158 J	159 S	160 D		161 B	162 V		163 B	164 H	165 C	166 K	167 F	168 J			
	169 E	170 A		171 B	172 G	173 R	174 M		175 M	176 S	177 R	178 C	179 U	180 L	181 D	182 A			

Crostic 9

A. Feeling of
   horror: 2 wds. `10 154 18 84 132 126 43 56 4`

B. Attack: 2 wds. `51 11 152 138 83 32`

C. Detach `147 19 113 75 50 25 140`

D. Erase: 2 wds. `109 131 86 7 145 64`

E. Infantile `81 115 108 9 2 46 54`

F. Imitative in
   sound `99 100 123 29 117 72`

G. Rather coarse `125 130 12 5 37 73 97 24`

H. Unattractive `119 26 136 158 103 42`

I. Joseph's
   younger son `17 91 14 6 80 38 27`

J. Conglomeration `142 47 20 137 92 118`

K. Grovel: 2 wds. `57 60 120 105 31 39 160`

L. Lures: 2 wds. `102 52 151 156 148 78 35`

M. Acting as boss:
   2 wds. `106 66 69 98 44 89 112 153`

N. Pleasant to
   view `62 129 135 30 58 16 128`

O. Heavy; dull `23 36 49 90 13 143`

P. Lunatics `134 101 96 1 76 63`

Q. Because: 2 wds. `33 79 121 157 155 114`

R. Dogwood `94 71 146 88 67`

S. Looks after:
   2 wds. `3 141 104 53 107 34`

T. Deteriorate:
   3 wds. `48 110 15 161 61 124 95 77`

U. Expression of
   censure `70 133 28 45 144 87 59`

V. Certainly:
   3 wds. `162 74 55 149 139 111 40 150`

W. Invoice clerk `8 22 82 116 65 93`

X. Country
   bumpkins,
   collectively `41 122 85 68 21 159 127`

Solution on page 277

1 P	2 E	3 S	4 A		5 G	6 I	7 D	8 W	9 E		10 A	11 B	12 G	13 O	14 I	15 T		16 N	17 I		18 A
19 C	20 J	21 X	22 W	23 O	24 G		25 C	26 H	27 I	28 U	29 F	30 N	31 K	32 B	33 Q	34 S	35 L		36 O	37 G	38 I
39 K	40 V	41 X		42 H	43 A	44 M	45 U	46 E		47 J	48 T	49 O		50 C	51 B	52 L		53 S	54 E	55 V	56 A
57 K		58 N	59 U		60 K		61 T	62 N	63 P	64 D	65 W	66 M	67 R	68 X		69 M	70 U	71 R	72 F	73 G	74 V
75 C	76 P	77 T		78 L	79 Q		80 I		81 E	82 W	83 B	84 A	85 X	86 D	87 U	88 R	89 M	90 O		91 I	92 J
93 W	94 R	95 T	96 P		97 G	98 M	99 F		100F	101P	102L	103H	104S	105K		106M	107S		108E	109D	110T
111V	112M	113C	114Q		115E		116W	117F	118J	119H	120K		121Q	122X		123F	124T	125G		126A	127X
128N		129N	130G	131D		132A	133U	134P	135N	136H	137J	138B	139V		140C	141S	142J		143O	144U	145D
	146R	147C	148L	149V		150V	151L	152B	153M		154A	155Q	156L		157Q	158H	159X		160K	161T	162V

Window Boxes

There is a common 4-letter word hidden in each strip of letters in Column I. Think of the strips in Column II as open and closed windows. Then match each letter strip with its correct Window Box so that the 4-letter word will show. There are different possibilities, but there is only one way in which each letter strip and each window strip are used once.

Solution on page 278

Example: P L O D E N T   P O E T

COLUMN I

1. F E U A R O M
2. C H O U A R P
3. L S T E M A P
4. G T R A I N M
5. A C H L O Y E
6. O M U T S I T
7. D I D E N A R
8. S M P O I U R
9. A L O S E I T
10. T H O A W I N

COLUMN II

a.
b.
c.
d.
e.
f.
g.
h.
i.
j.

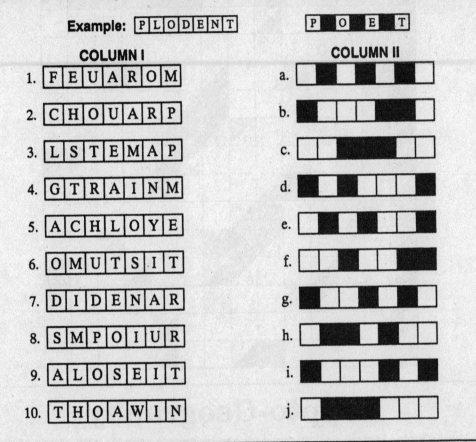

CATEGORIES

For each of the categories listed, can you think of a word or phrase beginning with each letter on the left? Count one point for each correct answer. A score of 15 is good, and 21 is excellent.

Our solutions on page 278

	CANADIAN CAPITALS	MONOPOLY	SHAKESPEARE CHARACTERS	MYTHICAL GODS	ARTISTS
H					
O					
V					
E					
R					

123

SUM TOTALS

Place one digit (1 to 9, no zeros) in each square so that the sum of the numbers in each group of squares across or down is the number given. The number below a diagonal is the sum of the numbers below it. The number to the right of a diagonal is the sum of the numbers to the right of it. IMPORTANT: No digit is used more than once in any group of squares leading to a sum. One group of digits has been given for you.

Solution on page 278

Crypto-Geography

One of the United States is pictured with a question mark showing the location of one of its cities. Some interesting information about the city is in a substitution code.

Solution on page 278

IGP SYGPXLIXK, XGTLSKYPLG
(city)   (state)

YQHUGYH FLCTLPB TGWAPEAH, "IGP SYGPXLIXK

MGI KPTU KPA HYGRDGXF — 'ELI MGYH EK

TAGNA." EMLI LWCKYEGPE XAPEAY SKY

LPHQIEYU, XKWWAYXA, EKQYLIW, GPH SLPGPXA

LI GTIK FPKRP SKY LEI XKPIEGPE XTLWGEA

GPH MLTTILHA NLARI.

ALPHABET PLUS

Form common 5-letter words by rearranging each word and adding the letter of the alphabet shown with it. The word CANAL (the letters of CLAN plus the letter A) has been filled in for you.

Our solution on page 278

A + CLAN = <u>CANAL</u>

B + ORAL = _____

C + OVAL = _____

D + FOOL = _____

E + NICE = _____

F + FIST = _____

G + NEAR = _____

H + SURE = _____

I + ROAD = _____

J + TUNA = _____

K + NOTE = _____

L + POSE = _____

M + SLAP = _____

N + CLUE = _____

O + RICH = _____

P + DATE = _____

Q + SUIT = _____

R + RACY = _____

S + DUTY = _____

T + HERO = _____

U + TINE = _____

V + WEAR = _____

W + LOVE = _____

X + EARL = _____

Y + ARID = _____

Z + ROAR = _____

Numberboxes

Using the hints below, correctly place the numbers 1 through 9 into the diagram.

Solution on page 278

1. 1 is bottom center.

2. 3 is two squares directly above 7.

3. 8 is directly below 4.

4. 2 is two squares left of 5.

5. 4 is two squares above 1.

6. 9 is directly left of 4.

7. 6 is two squares below 9.

TO PLAY:

1. Enter the first seven LETTERBOX letters onto the first DRAWLINE and cross them off in the LETTERBOX.

2. Form a word of at least two letters across or down on the GAMEBOARD. One letter of the first word must go into the starred square.

3. Tally your score in the SCORE column.

4. Carry down all unused letters onto the next DRAWLINE. Transfer enough letters from the LETTERBOX, in the given order, so that you have seven letters to work with.

5. Build a new word or words by:
   a. adding one or more letters before and/or after words on the GAMEBOARD.
   b. adding one or more letters at right angles to words on the GAMEBOARD.
   c. adding a word parallel to one on the GAME-BOARD.

IMPORTANT: All adjoining letters must spell out complete words.

6. Continue working this way until all the letters from the LETTERBOX have been used.

7. Asterisks (✱) are "wild" letters and may represent any letter you choose, but once used they cannot be changed.

NOTE: Proper names, foreign words, and abbreviations are not allowed. No word may appear twice on the GAMEBOARD.

TO SCORE:

Score every letter in each new word as follows:
1. Letters in unnumbered squares count 1 point.
2. Letters in numbered squares count the given value of the square.
3. Double the score of a word containing a circle.
4. Triple the score of a word containing two circles.
5. Add 20 points if all seven letters from a DRAW-LINE are used in one play.

Can you beat our game of 242 points given on page 278?

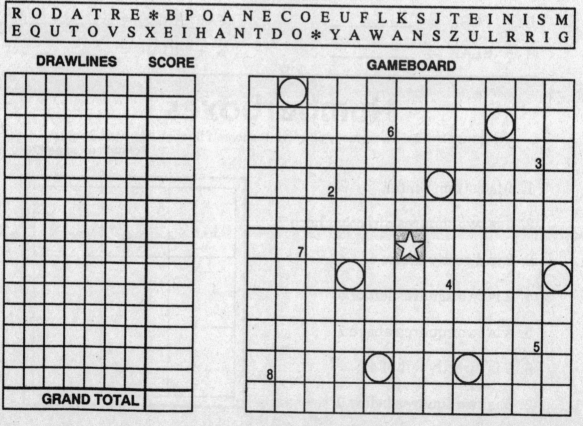

LETTERBOX

```
R O D A T R E * B P O A N E C O E U F L K S J T E I N I S M
E Q U T O V S X E I H A N T D O * Y A W A N S Z U L R R I G
```

DRAWLINES   SCORE   GAMEBOARD

GRAND TOTAL

126

SIMON SAYS

Start with LADY'S-SLIPPER and follow the directions carefully to discover a phrase that is apropos.

Solution on page 278

1. Print the letters in LADY'S-SLIPPER.

1. _____

2. Double each L and each Y.

2. _____

3. Change the PP to TH.

3. _____

4. Reverse the order of the first four letters.

4. _____

5. Move the fifth letter to the left of the R.

5. _____

6. Change the SS to OF.

6. _____

7. Move LLI to the right of the D.

7. _____

8. Move the second and fourth consonants to the left of the next-to-last letter.

8. _____

9. Insert VA to the right of the E.

9. _____

10. Delete the first, fourth, and final letters, and insert an E before the last Y.

10. _____

11. Change each L to a U, and delete the Y's and the V.

11. _____

12. Reverse the order of all the letters.

12. _____

13. Double the seventh letter.

13. _____

14. Change the F to a B and make it the first letter.

14. _____

15. Eliminate the first, third, and sixth vowels.

15. _____

16. Reverse the order of the last nine letters.

16. _____

17. Change the A to a C and add a P at the end.

17. _____

18. Delete the second and third letters.

18. _____

19. Replace the H with an R and move it to the left of the C.

19. _____

ESCALATORS

Write the answer to clue 1 in the first space. Drop one letter and rearrange the remaining letters to answer clue 2. Put the dropped letter into Column A. Drop another letter and rearrange the remaining letters to answer clue 3. Put the dropped letter into Column B. Follow this pattern for each row in the diagram. When completed, the letters in Column A and Column B, reading down, will spell related words or a phrase.

Solutions on page 278

1

1. Moisten
2. Appointed
3. Patch
4. Butter or gallery
5. Eucharistic plate
6. Adhesive strip
7. Building for horses
8. Swipe
9. Meadows
10. Place of worship
11. Fuzzy fruit
12. Headland
13. Final-year student
14. Saw wood?
15. Sea eagles
16. Figured out
17. Cherished
18. Bird of peace
19. Coiffure
20. Boom box
21. Sudden invasion
22. Jeopardy
23. Magnificent
24. Fix with stitches
25. Offered devout petition
26. Settle
27. Peel

	A			B	
1		2		3	
4		5		6	
7		8		9	
10		11		12	
13		14		15	
16		17		18	
19		20		21	
22		23		24	
25		26		27	

2

1. Woven container
2. T-bone
3. Well-being
4. Geronimo, for one
5. Inexpensive
6. Gait
7. Most tragic
8. Begat
9. Frees (of)
10. Novelist Willa ____
11. Attain
12. Worry
13. Spring holiday
14. Rubberneck
15. Interlude
16. Zealous
17. Swap
18. Expensive
19. Separate
20. Defraud
21. Detest
22. On the beach
23. Be generous
24. Char
25. Dally
26. Mix up
27. Alan or Cheryl
28. Reply
29. Vow
30. Item of merchandise

	A			B	
1		2		3	
4		5		6	
7		8		9	
10		11		12	
13		14		15	
16		17		18	
19		20		21	
22		23		24	
25		26		27	
28		29		30	

BOWL GAME

To bowl a strike (20 points) you must create a 10-letter word using all the letters in each pin. The letter on top in the pin is the first letter of the strike word. To bowl a spare (10 points) use the same 10 letters to form two words. Splits are not allowed: you may not divide the strike to form a spare. For example, SWEETHEART may not become SWEET and HEART.

Our solutions with a perfect score of 300 points given on page 278

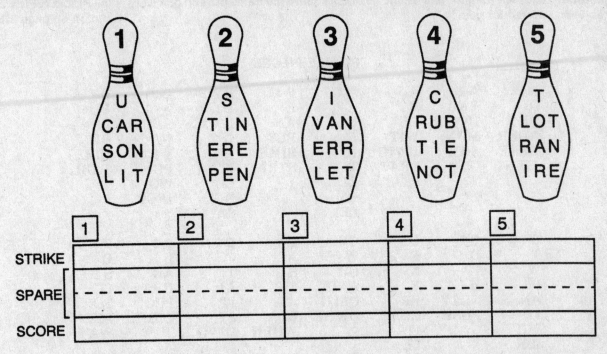

	1	2	3	4	5
STRIKE					
SPARE	- - -	- - -	- - -	- - -	- - -
SCORE					

Pin 1: U CAR SON LIT
Pin 2: S TIN ERE PEN
Pin 3: I VAN ERR LET
Pin 4: C RUB TIE NOT
Pin 5: T LOT RAN IRE

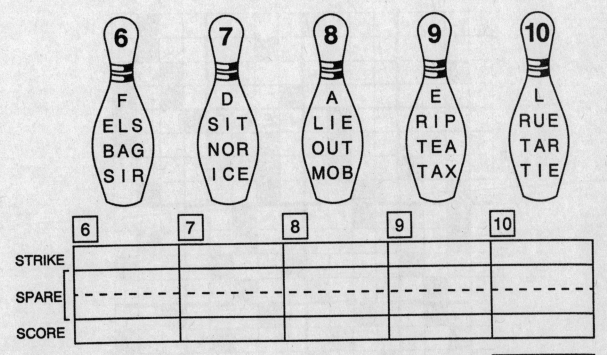

	6	7	8	9	10
STRIKE					
SPARE	- - -	- - -	- - -	- - -	- - -
SCORE					

Pin 6: F ELS BAG SIR
Pin 7: D SIT NOR ICE
Pin 8: A LIE OUT MOB
Pin 9: E RIP TEA TAX
Pin 10: L RUE TAR TIE

FINAL SCORE [ ]

JIGSAW SQUARES

Your goal is to fit the PUZZLE PIECES into their proper places in the diagram to reveal a quotation. Fill the diagram by placing the PUZZLE PIECES horizontally into their corresponding sections of the diagram. There are 16 sections, identified by letter/number combinations (A-1, A-2, A-3, etc.). The quotation reads left to right, line by line. A black square indicates the end of a word. One PUZZLE PIECE has been entered for you.

Solution on page 278

PUZZLE PIECES

A-1	A-2	A-3	A-4	B-1	B-2	B-3	B-4
O	RAL	R	A	E	D	A	I
DE	HOWE	US	E	AN	H	E	LL
ADER	MONS	WIT	E	PUT	O	N	OF
GENE	SHIP	DWIG	H	SIMP	P	Y	ULD
ISEN		TRAT	T	STRI	IT	PU	TABL
			ED		LE	WO	
			HT		NG	~~IECE~~	
			LE		SA		

C-1	C-2	C-3	C-4	D-1	D-2	D-3	D-4
T	D	F	W	A	T	L	D
W	IT	N	OU	S	T	AN	S
W	ILL	Y	AND	JU	AL	HAT	IT
AN	EREV	ER	OLLO	RE	IT	PEO	TO
IT	PUSH	GO	OWHE	LEA	ST	COME	PLE
WH		IT		WHEN	DING		WAY
ISH		LL					

	1	2	3	4

(grid diagram with rows A, B, C, D and columns 1, 2, 3, 4; one piece "IECE" entered)

ANAGRAM MAGIC SQUARE

Find an anagram for the 5-letter word in each box. The anagram will answer one of the clues. Put the number of that clue into the small square and write the anagram on the dash. The numbers in each row and column will add up to 65. Write the first letter of each anagram on the correspondingly numbered dash at the bottom of the page; and, presto!, the Anagram Magic quote will appear. To start you off, we have put in one anagram and set its first letter on the proper dash at the bottom of the page.

Solution on page 278

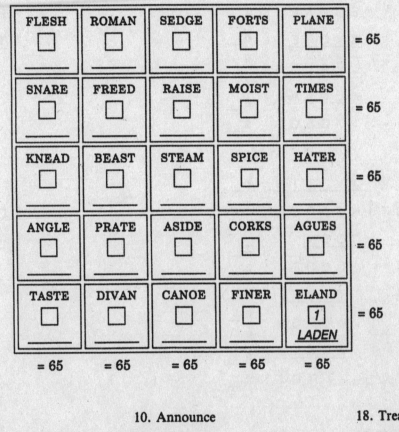

FLESH □ ___	ROMAN □ ___	SEDGE □ ___	FORTS □ ___	PLANE □ ___	= 65
SNARE □ ___	FREED □ ___	RAISE □ ___	MOIST □ ___	TIMES □ ___	= 65
KNEAD □ ___	BEAST □ ___	STEAM □ ___	SPICE □ ___	HATER □ ___	= 65
ANGLE □ ___	PRATE □ ___	ASIDE □ ___	CORKS □ ___	AGUES □ ___	= 65
TASTE □ ___	DIVAN □ ___	CANOE □ ___	FINER □ ___	ELAND [1] *LADEN*	= 65
= 65	= 65	= 65	= 65	= 65	

1. Burdened
2. Ignores
3. Ledge
4. Candle
5. Subdues
6. Thoughts
7. Estate
8. Poems
9. Articles

10. Announce
11. Approaches
12. Ground
13. Food provision
14. Borders
15. Sways
16. Jack ____
17. Pacific ____

18. Treatment
19. Unclad
20. Postpone
21. Assists
22. Reap
23. Ascent
24. Imply
25. Home of Mt. Everest

L ___
1 2 3 4 5 6 7 8 9 10 11 12 13 14 15 16 17 18 19 20 21 22 23 24 25

WORD MATH

In these long-division problems letters are substituted for numbers. Determine the value of each letter. Then arrange the letters in order from 0 to 9, and they will spell a word or phrase.

Solutions on page 278

1.

```
                PAY
PEAR | COLLARS
        RACLF
        ECFAR
        CYCFE
        EALYS
        ECAAL
         CSOC
```

0 __
1 __
2 __
3 __
4 __
5 __
6 __
7 __
8 __
9 __

2.

```
                 ILL
NILE | LEATHER
        HLSEE
        HRTHE
        TGRLE
        HESER
        TGRLE
         RILR
```

0 __
1 __
2 __
3 __
4 __
5 __
6 __
7 __
8 __
9 __

3.

```
               TIN
WEST | HIDDEN
       COSN
       CEOE
       TISE
       WCOSN
       WCCID
         TOI
```

0 __
1 __
2 __
3 __
4 __
5 __
6 __
7 __
8 __
9 __

4.

```
               SUN
DON | FLEECY
      FSEC
      FCEC
      NLUL
      NONY
      OUNU
       DCS
```

0 __
1 __
2 __
3 __
4 __
5 __
6 __
7 __
8 __
9 __

5.

```
              CAN
LAD | COFFEE
      EADS
      HNFE
      HECD
      OHHE
      ODSS
       EHE
```

0 __
1 __
2 __
3 __
4 __
5 __
6 __
7 __
8 __
9 __

6.

```
                GAS
CRIB | NOTION
       OBGB
       IOAIO
       IABAB
       CCOON
       CIRSB
        GINN
```

0 __
1 __
2 __
3 __
4 __
5 __
6 __
7 __
8 __
9 __

ABACUS

Slide the abacus beads across the wires to form five related words reading down. All the beads will be used. Keep in mind that the beads are on wires and cannot jump over one another. An empty abacus is provided for you to work in.

Solution on page 278

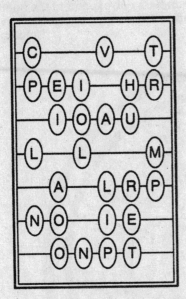

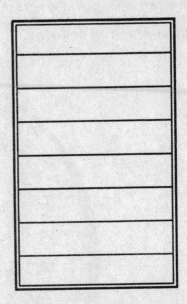

COMMON DENOMINATOR

Only one letter of the alphabet appears in all the words of each line. Transfer that letter to the correspondingly numbered blank at the bottom to spell the bonus word.

Solution on page 278

1. Reindeer, Panda, Kinkajou, Baboon, Skunk

2. Giraffe, Bandicoot, Porcupine, Wapiti, Guinea pig

3. Armadillo, Caribou, Leopard, Springbok, Sloth

4. Woodchuck, Shrew, Wart hog, Cheetah, Bighorn

5. Coati, Chinchilla, Wildcat, Raccoon, Fitchew

6. Zebu, Lemming, Hyena, Elephant, Antelope

7. Wombat, Pangolin, Donkey, Dingo, Gray wolf

8. Gopher, Jaguar, Kangaroo, Dromedary, Panther

9. Chamois, Mongoose, Muskrat, Marmoset, Sable

10. Zebra, Wolverine, Burro, Jerboa, Sambar

Bonus word: ___ ___ ___ ___ ___ ___ ___ ___ ___ ___
          8 4 2 1 3 5 6 10 7 9

What do all the words have in common?

This is a new target for those who can think in circles. The game works two ways, outward and inward. If you're outward bound, guess the word that fits clues 1-6 (the numbers correspond to the numbers of letters in the answer). Then go on to clue 7-12 and so on. If you're stuck with an outward clue, try the inward clues. Work both ways to hit the Bull's-Eye.

Solution on page 278

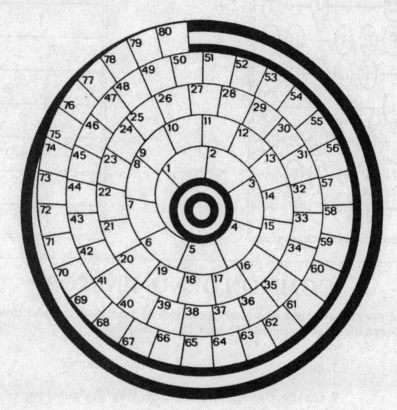

OUTWARD

1-6. Baby's wear

7-12. Unagitated

13-16. Saudi resident

17-23. Warm-blooded animals

24-29. Set on fire

30-36. Prohibition of trade

37-43. Tropical disease

44-52. Stick to the job

53-58. Weasellike animal

59-64. Reddish-brown horse

65-70. Alphabet member

71-75. Has a temper tantrum

76-80. Executive's woe

INWARD

80-74. Hermit

73-68. Artist's workplace, perhaps

67-62. Bank employee

61-56. List

55-51. Allude (to)

50-47. Actress Arden et al.

46-41. Fix

40-36. Remember the ____!

35-32. Seize

31-25. Rendezvous

24-20. Moslem religion

19-15. African poisonous snake

14-8. Politically uncompromising

7-1. Purchased ahead of time

PICTURE THIS

You do not need any special art training to produce a picture in the empty grid. Use the letter-number guide above each square and carefully draw what is shown into the corresponding square in the grid.

Solution on page 279

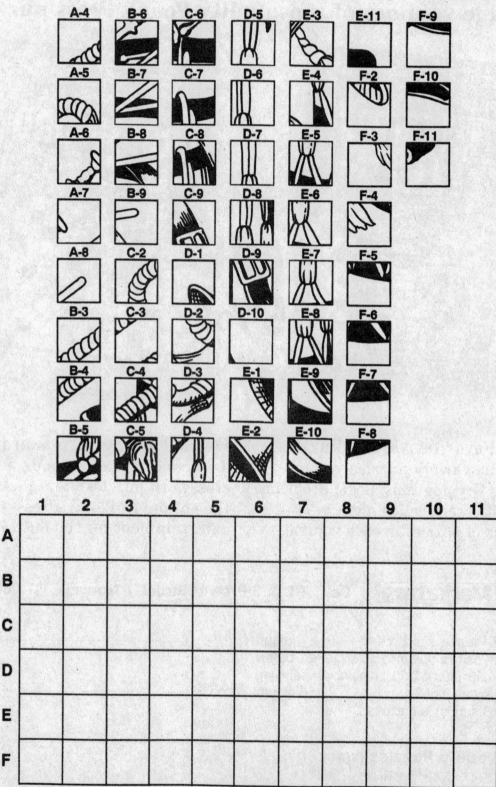

LOGIC PROBLEM

CASH GIVEAWAY

To celebrate its 100th year in business, Boomingsales Department Store held a secret cash giveaway. Each of five cash prizes was presented to the first shopper of the day at each of Boomingsales's five stores. The prizes totaled $100,000. The winners included two women—Gina and Karen—and three men—Henry, Paul, and Robert. Each store is located in a different town's mall. From the information provided, determine the first and last names (one last name is Dunne) of each winner, the town mall (one is Southtown Mall) in which he or she entered Boomingsales, and the amount each won.

1. The winner at the Westdale Mall (who isn't surnamed Crawford) won twice as much money as did Ms. Weber (who had gone to Boomingsales that morning in order to buy a hat).

2. Gina won the $25,000 prize.

3. The Northport Mall winner had driven to Boomingsales expressly for the purpose of buying a wedding gift.

4. The winner surnamed McNeily won more money than Henry, but less money than Robert.

5. The winner surnamed Baldwin won twice as much money as Paul, but not as much money as the Eastville Mall winner.

6. The Center City Mall winner (who isn't Henry) had gone to Boomingsales with the intention of buying a sofa.

This chart is to help you record information from the clues as well as the facts you deduce by combining information from different clues. We suggest you use an "X" for a "no" and a "•" for a "yes."

		LAST NAME					MALL					AMOUNT				
		BALDWIN	CRAWFORD	DUNNE	MCNEILY	WEBER	CENTER CITY	EASTVILLE	NORTHPORT	SOUTHTOWN	WESTDALE	$10,000	$15,000	$20,000	$25,000	$30,000
FIRST NAME	GINA															
	HENRY															
	KAREN															
	PAUL															
	ROBERT															
AMOUNT	$10,000															
	$15,000															
	$20,000															
	$25,000															
	$30,000															
MALL	CENTER CITY															
	EASTVILLE															
	NORTHPORT															
	SOUTHTOWN															
	WESTDALE															

Solution on page 279

HEADINGS

Use the letters in each Heading to fill in the blanks to complete words related to the Heading. Cross out each letter as you use it.

Solutions on page 279

1. UNDER THE TREE ON CHRISTMAS DAY

__R__M

S__I__T

__AR__S

__R__I__

____AD__ET

__A__DY

T__U__P__T

__R__C__CL__

__K__T__B__A__D

2. TRAINING AT OBEDIENCE SCHOOL

__OLL__E

M__ST__FF

__OX__R

C____W

__ER____ER

P__I__T__R

__R__YH__UND

D____H__HU__D

__A__MA__IA__

3. ON SAFARI WITH CAMERA IN HAND

EL__N__

__YE__A

Z__BR__

J____K__L

L__O__

G__R__F__E

C__A__ELEO__

O__T____CH

__A____H__G

THREESOMES

Locate in the diagram all the letters that appear exactly alike three times. A letter may appear many times in different styles, but you want only those that are exact triplicates. Rearrange the Threesomes letters to spell a common word.

Solution on page 279

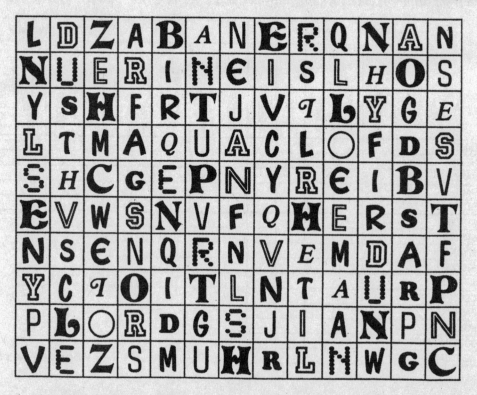

THREESOMES WORD: _____

138

SYL''LA-CROS'TIC

The directions for solving are given on page 105. Solution on page 279

✳ SYLLABOX ✳

A A A A A AB AGE AH AL AP ATE AV BEK BEN BI BLE
CEN COUR DAPH DE DER DI DO E E EC EN ER FAC GARD
GEN GLOT GRAPH HES I IM IN ING KEEP KO LAG LESS MAT
MEN MENT MO MON MORPH MUS NI NO O O O OUS POR
PRAIS RA RA RAB RE RE REG RICE SEIS SIR STI TANT TATE
THOS TION TION TOR TOW TRIC TU U UN UN UP YO

1. Knowing only one language   (3) __ __ __ __ __ __ __
2. Opposing subsurface current   (3) __ __ __ __ __ __ __
3. Wife of Isaac   (3) __ __ __ __ __ __
4. Shine   (3) __ __ __ __ __ __
5. Belly   (3) __ __ __ __ __ __
6. Ms. Ono   (2) __ __ __ __
7. Growth   (4) __ __ __ __ __ __ __ __
8. Greed for riches   (3) __ __ __ __ __ __ __ __
9. Despite   (3) __ __ __ __ __ __ __ __
10. Synagogue official   (2) __ __ __ __
11. Fixture   (4) __ __ __ __ __ __ __ __
12. Droll   (3) __ __ __ __ __ __
13. Liberal   (3) __ __ __ __ __ __
14. Support   (4) __ __ __ __ __ __ __ __ __ __ __
15. Earthquake recorder   (3) __ __ __ __ __ __ __ __
16. Pause   (3) __ __ __ __ __ __ __
17. Mint family herb   (4) __ __ __ __ __ __ __ __
18. Irrelevant   (4) __ __ __ __ __ __ __ __
19. Hare or pika   (3) __ __ __ __ __ __ __
20. Pleasing   (4) __ __ __ __ __ __ __ __
21. Donor   (4) __ __ __ __ __ __ __ __
22. Quirky   (3) __ __ __ __ __ __ __
23. Valuation   (3) __ __ __ __ __ __ __
24. Tiny freshwater crustacean   (3) __ __ __ __ __ __
25. Maintenance   (2) __ __ __ __ __
26. Spirit of a culture   (2) __ __ __ __ __

ROUNDABOUT

Go round and roundabout in clockwise order using the clues to fill in the curving 6-letter words. When the diagram is complete, fill in the numbered boxes below the diagram with the correspondingly numbered letters to discover the answer to the riddle.

Solution on page 279

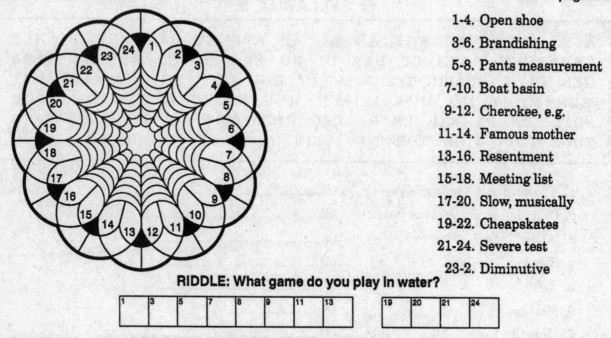

1-4. Open shoe

3-6. Brandishing

5-8. Pants measurement

7-10. Boat basin

9-12. Cherokee, e.g.

11-14. Famous mother

13-16. Resentment

15-18. Meeting list

17-20. Slow, musically

19-22. Cheapskates

21-24. Severe test

23-2. Diminutive

RIDDLE: What game do you play in water?

1	3	5	7	8	9	11	13		19	20	21	24

Quick Quote

Fill in the answers to the clues and transfer the letters to the correspondingly numbered dashes to reveal the Quick Quote. Some letters from the quote may be used in more than one word.

Solution on page 279

CLUES

1. Doris Day movie

2. Notion that if one falls, all fall

3. Rex Harrison musical

4. Romberg operetta, with "The"

5. King of Thebes

6. Chayefsky play

7. Michael Bennett musical, with "A"

WORDS

1. $\overline{27}\ \overline{12}\ \overline{20}\ \overline{32}\ \overline{9}\ \overline{38}\ \overline{14}\ \overline{7}\ \overline{23}\ \overline{5}\ \overline{28}\ \overline{15}$

2. $\overline{4}\ \overline{39}\ \overline{34}\ \overline{53}\ \overline{25}\ \overline{35}\ \overline{13}\ \overline{46}\ \overline{55}\ \overline{31}\ \overline{33}\ \overline{19}$

3. $\overline{54}\ \overline{30}\ \overline{6}\ \overline{43}\ \overline{1}\ \overline{22}\ \overline{11}\ \overline{49}\ \overline{29}\ \overline{19}$

4. $\overline{48}\ \overline{2}\ \overline{10}\ \overline{26}\ \overline{16}\ \overline{42}\ \overline{45}\ \overline{40}\ \overline{22}\ \overline{8}\ \overline{25}\ \overline{9}\ \overline{17}$

5. $\overline{20}\ \overline{41}\ \overline{26}\ \overline{24}\ \overline{18}\ \overline{21}\ \overline{3}$

6. $\overline{37}\ \overline{46}\ \overline{51}\ \overline{44}\ \overline{47}\ \overline{25}\ \overline{52}\ \overline{46}\ \overline{50}\ \overline{43}\ \overline{25}$

7. $\overline{9}\ \overline{38}\ \overline{14}\ \overline{33}\ \overline{36}\ \overline{48}\ \overline{11}\ \overline{53}\ \overline{25}\ \overline{17}$

QUICK QUOTE:

$\overline{1}\ \overline{2}\ \overline{3}\quad \overline{4}\ \overline{5}\ \overline{6}\ \overline{7}\ \overline{8}\ \overline{9}\ \overline{10}\ \overline{11}\ \overline{12}\quad \overline{13}\ \overline{14}\quad \overline{15}\ \overline{16}\ \overline{17}\ \overline{18}\quad \overline{19}\ \overline{20}\ \overline{21}\ \overline{22}$

$\overline{23}\ \overline{24}\ \overline{25}\ \overline{26}\quad \overline{27}\ \overline{28}\ \overline{29}\quad \overline{30}\ \overline{31}\ \overline{32}\ \overline{33}\quad \overline{34}\ \overline{35}\ \overline{36}\ \overline{37}\ \overline{38}\quad \overline{39}\ \overline{40}\ \overline{41}\ \overline{42}\quad \overline{43}\ \overline{44}$

$\overline{45}\ \overline{46}\ \overline{47}\quad \overline{48}\ \overline{49}\ \overline{50}\ \overline{51}\quad \overline{52}\ \overline{53}\ \overline{54}\ \overline{55}$

JIGSAW PUZZLE

When you have put the pieces of the Jigsaw Puzzle into their correct places in the diagram, they will form a crossword puzzle with words reading across and down. Do not turn the pieces. The heavy lines in the diagram will help you locate their proper places. Solution on page 279

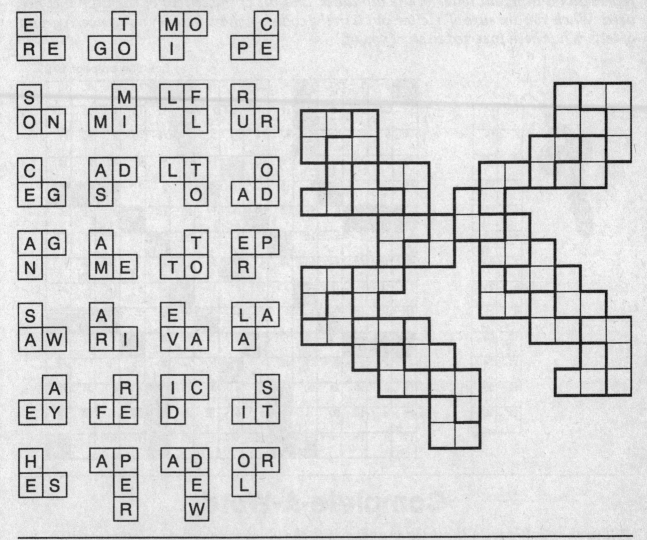

Changaword

Can you change the top word into the bottom word in each column in the number of steps indicated in parentheses? Change only one letter at a time and do not change the order of the letters. Proper names, slang, and obsolete words are not allowed. Our solutions on page 279

1. DROP (5 steps)   2. HEAD (5 steps)   3. GAIN (6 steps)   4. SHOW (7 steps)

HOLD   FOOT   LOSE   HIDE

CODEWORD

Codeword is a special crossword puzzle in which conventional clues are omitted. Instead, answer words in the diagram are represented by numbers. Each number represents a different letter of the alphabet, and all of the letters of the alphabet are used. When you are sure of a letter, put it in the code key chart for easy reference. A group of letters has been inserted to start you off.

Solution on page 279

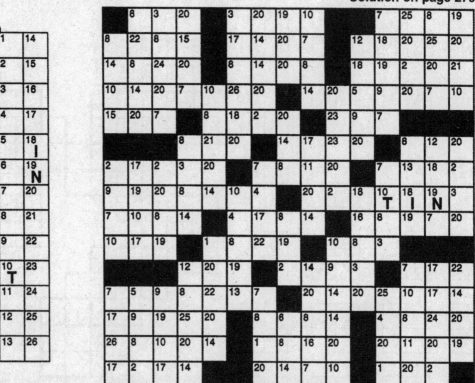

Complete-A-Word

Fill in the dashes with the 4-letter answers to the clues to complete 7-letter words.

Solutions on page 279

1. Warble — L I __ T __ __ __
2. Not any — __ __ M I __ E __
3. Complicated — C __ __ __ A __ E
4. Manufacture — __ I S T __ __ __
5. Related — P __ R __ __ __ G
6. Destiny — __ E __ __ H __ R
7. Depend — O __ D __ R __ __
8. Large town — S O __ __ E __ __

BOOKWORMS

Bookworms have been eating entire words in this diagram. The words they have eaten are listed alphabetically according to length. Each word will fit into a set of circles connected by lines, but you must decide at which end each word begins. When the words are correctly placed, a message will be revealed, reading left to right, line by line.

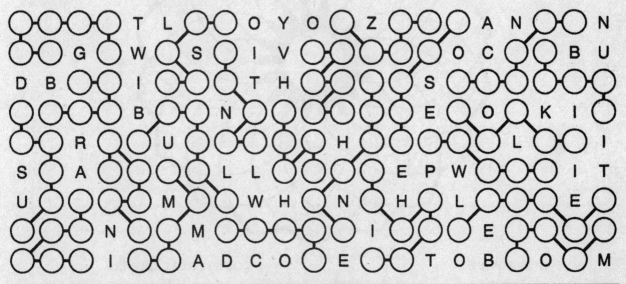

5 Letters	NOVEL	WASHY	HONING	7 Letters
BEAMS	SHIRT		HOOKED	INTENSE
FACES	SIGHT	6 Letters	INTACT	REALITY
FLOAT	SMITH	DELUDE	RELISH	
GODLY	SNAIL	FOULED	SERENE	
METAL	THIEF	HARDEN		

Solution on page 279

SHUFFLE

Two words with their letters in the correct order are combined in each row of letters. To solve the puzzle, separate both words. There are no extra letters, and no letter is used more than once. Helpful hint: the two words are related.

Solutions on page 279

Example: SMYESTTHEMOD (SmYeStThEMod) = SYSTEM, METHOD

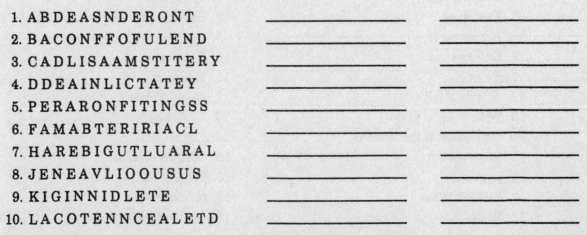

1. ABDEASNDERONT
2. BACONFFOFULEND
3. CADLISAAMSTITERY
4. DDEAINLICTATEY
5. PERARONFITINGSS
6. FAMABTERIRIACL
7. HAREBIGUTLUARAL
8. JENEAVLIOOUSUS
9. KIGINNIDLETE
10. LACOTENNCEALETD

FLOWER POWER

The answers to this petaled puzzle will go in a curve from the number on the outside to the center of the flower. Each number has two 5-letter words. One goes in a clockwise direction and the second in a counterclockwise direction. Try working from both sets of clues to fill the flower.　　Solution on page 279

CLOCKWISE

1. Dwell
2. Breathing
3. Wear away
4. Hog sound
5. Ordinary writing
6. Break an egg
7. Cook an egg
8. Pamphlet
9. Hiking path
10. Lachrymose
11. Swap
12. Article of faith
13. With window glass
14. Goddesses of the seasons
15. River mouth
16. Sew loosely
17. Wait on table
18. Wares

COUNTERCLOCKWISE

1. Main artery
2. Over
3. Slur over
4. Networks
5. Verify
6. Unrefined
7. Lying flat
8. Browned bread
9. Copy through thin paper
10. Raceway
11. Educate
12. Characteristic
13. Oyster gem
14. Convenient
15. Charity receiver
16. French cap
17. Mixed greens
18. Heroic exploit

144

SIMON SAYS

Start with CANDY STRIPER and follow the directions carefully to discover a phrase that is apropos.

Solution on page 279

1. Print the words CANDY STRIPER.

    1. _____

2. Change the Y to H.

    2. _____

3. Double each vowel.

    3. _____

4. Insert an F to the left of the S.

    4. _____

5. Switch the D and the H.

    5. _____

6. Make each I an S.

    6. _____

7. Change the 1st letter from the left to O.

    7. _____

8. Replace the 5th consonant from the right with an L.

    8. _____

9. Move the 8th letter from the left to the 1st place from the right.

    9. _____

10. Insert an O to the left of the N.

    10. _____

11. Move the 2nd consonant from the left to the left of the P.

    11. _____

12. Reverse the order of the 4th and 5th letters from the right.

    12. _____

13. Change the D to an E.

    13. _____

14. Move the 1st vowel from the left to the left of the F.

    14. _____

15. Move the 9th letter from the left to the right of the 2nd E.

    15. _____

16. Insert an N between the A's.

    16. _____

17. Move the 1st three letters from the left, keeping them in order, to the right of the T.

    17. _____

18. Reverse the order of the letters 6 through 10 from the left.

    18. _____

19. Switch the 5th consonant from the left and the 3rd vowel from the right.

    19. _____

WORD MATH

In these long-division problems letters are substituted for numbers. Determine the value of each letter. Then arrange the letters in order from 0 to 9, and they will spell a word or phrase.

Solutions on page 279

1.

```
              A I R        0 __
  A I D E | I N J U R E    1 __
                           2 __
            J K R C        3 __
            R E N C R      4 __
            R C E U N      5 __
              K R C E      6 __
              A I D E      7 __
                           8 __
              R K C D      9 __
```

2.

```
                C A R      0 __
  A R E A | R A S H E R S  1 __
                           2 __
            R H E L S       3 __
            T S R E R       4 __
            R L R B A       5 __
              O S H B S     6 __
                           7 __
              H E H L L     8 __
                E L O       9 __
```

3.

```
              T A P        0 __
  N O O N | I N S T A N T   1 __
                           2 __
            I S H A U       3 __
            P S S E N       4 __
            E N I H N       5 __
              E A E H T     6 __
                           7 __
              E H P T H     8 __
                P N O T     9 __
```

4.

```
                R O E      0 __
  O O Z E | O I L M E N    1 __
                           2 __
            O O Z E         3 __
              N N O E       4 __
              E E M L       5 __
              R F N M N     6 __
                           7 __
              L K Z M       8 __
                R M O K     9 __
```

5.

```
              O U T        0 __
  C O Y | R O U S T S      1 __
                           2 __
            P S U O         3 __
            D B D T         4 __
            O O O U         5 __
              U Y P S       6 __
                           7 __
              D S P T       8 __
                P B Y       9 __
```

6.

```
                A D D      0 __
  P I L E | L E A T H E R  1 __
                           2 __
            L D A R E       3 __
            I B A L E       4 __
            R T A D E       5 __
              I B R B R     6 __
                           7 __
              R T A D E     8 __
                R D P P     9 __
```

Framework 13

These words are listed in alphabetical order according to length. Fit them into their proper places in the Framework. This puzzle has been started for you with the entry WITS. Now look for a 9-letter entry starting with W. Continue working this way until the puzzle is completed.

3 Letters
Bet
Car
End
Fun
Lot
Run
Tie
Yes

4 Letters
Best
Grab
Host
Luck
Most
Race

Shop
Song
Star
Tape
Time
Wits ✓

5 Letters
Block
Board
Exact
Games
Match
Meter
Noise
Oh, boy!
Prize

Score
Shock
Shout
Shows
Teams
Yells
Yield

6 Letters
Choice
Emcees
Guests
Scream
Second
Squeal
Trivia
Trophy

Winner
You win

7 Letters
Answers
Contest
Embrace
Fidgety
New show
Players
Problem

8 Letters
Big money
Eligible
Lose some
Question

Reacting
Roll dice
Surprise
Time is up

9 Letters
Bells ring
Delighted
Don't faint
Wonderful

10 Letters
Contestant
Excitement

Solution on page 280

BULL'S-EYE SPIRAL

This is a new target for those who can think in circles. The game works two ways, outward and inward. If you're outward-bound, guess the word that fits clue 1-7. Then go on to clue 8-12 and so on. If you're stuck on an outward-bound word, try the inward clues. Work both ways to hit the Bull's-Eye.

Solution on page 279

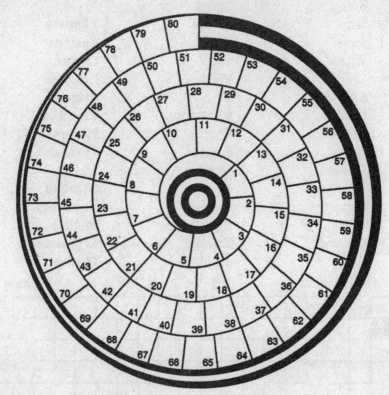

OUTWARD

1-7. Cancel a statement
8-12. Fragment
13-20. Distantly
21-24. Russian king
25-29. Residence
30-35. Continue after a pause
36-39. Alaska city
40-43. Moniker
44-48. Music drama
49-52. Tire mishap
53-56. Netman Lendl
57-61. Hindu statesman
62-65. Ajar
66-70. Speak
71-74. Amphibian
75-77. Wrath
78-80. Label

INWARD

80-77. Movable barrier
76-72. Severity
71-68. Guitar ridge
67-64. Melody
63-60. Serve tea
59-55. Hair tint
54-50. Essential
49-46. Transportation charge
45-42. Verse
41-35. Windflower
34-31. Ponder
30-27. Change the decor
26-23. Vamp Theda _____
22-18. Fashion
17-14. Heavy volume
13-7. Record of payment
6-1. Ford's successor

Mystery Guest

Framework 14

When the words are all entered, the name of the mystery guest will be revealed, reading across the center of the diagram. Mystery guest solution given on page 281.

Solution on page 280

3 Letters
All
Auk
Ear
Emu
End
Irk
Mil
Orb
See
Soy
Spa
Tan
Tea
Win

4 Letters
Chic
Epic

Gene
Kick
Kite
Magi
Node
Only
Over
Sled
Sync
Wear
Yolk

5 Letters
Among
Apron
Champ
Cycle
Ennui
Haste

Imbed
Kayak
Libra
Livid
Match
Omega
Onion
Oxide
Ratio
Rusty
Think
Track
Valid

6 Letters
Circus
Rabbit
Resume
Tomato

Framelinks

Framework 15

First word across on page 290   Solution on page 280

Fill in the empty squares in the diagram with the given letters to form common words.

AAAA CC DDD EEEE

FFF G HHH I J

K LLLLL MM NN

OOO PP Q RRRR SS

TTTTT U W YYY

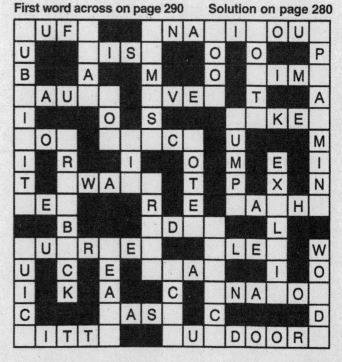

149

Framework 16

Solution on page 280

Fiddler's Frame

It will take a little fiddling to solve this special Framework. Two or three letters will go in each box. The words are listed according to the number of boxes they will fill. We have filled in one example.

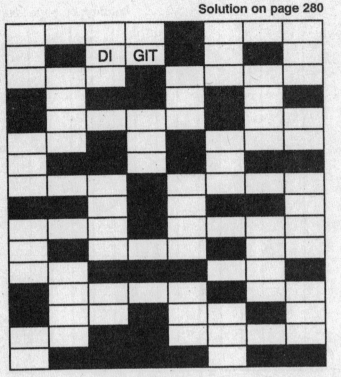

2 Boxes
Bleat
Camel
Cider
Cite
Deck
Diced
Digit ✓
Fates
Ingest
Legit
Melts
Order
Sere
Sick

3 Boxes
Atelier

Attests
Calories
Dervish
Edition
Enclose
Endanger
Endorser
Estonian
Failure
Gasoline
Incense
Install
Ourselves
Provencal
Realist
Sentries
Tidies

4 Boxes
Alteration
Alternator
Atonement
Condescend
Eradicates
Galleries
Medicating
Orientates
Projectile
Reconsider
Serviceman
Staggered
Tambourine
Tormented

Framework 17

Animated Films

First word across on page 290   Solution on page 280

3 Letters
Ali
Ink
See

4 Letters
Deer
Duck
Kids
Lady
Love

5 Letters
Alice
Bambi

Dwarf
Honey
Magic
Pluto
Queen
Tramp
Wendy

6 Letters
Beauty
Mickey
Minnie

7 Letters
Cricket

Studios

8 Letters
Fantasia
Pooh Bear
Treasure

9 Letters
Adventure
Snow White

Framework 18

3 Letters
Cup
Ear
Fan
Fry
Ice
Oil
Rug
Urn

4 Letters
Area
Bone
Chef
Eats
Eggs
Fork
Nuts
Oven
Plug
Rare
Salt
Sink
Soap
Soda
Stew
Tray
Work

5 Letters
Alarm
Anise
Apple
Award
Blade
Board
Broom
Carve
Clamp
Clock
Glass
Ladle
Mixer
Pasta

Phone
Puree
Radio
Range
Roast
Salad
Tongs
Tools
Whisk

6 Letters
Aprons
Chairs
Pantry
Pencil

Ricers
Saucer
Steaks
Teapot

7 Letters
Baskets
Blender
Gadgets
Kettles
Measure
Notepad
Pitcher
Scraper
Spatula

8 Letters
Canister
Colander
Curtains
Disposal
Espresso

9 Letters
Can opener
Cookie jar
Meatballs
Place mats
Spice rack
Toothpick

10 Letters
Dishwasher
Mixing bowl
Pepper mill
Yeast rolls

11 Letters
Paper towels
Tenderizers

12 Letters
Grocery lists
Refrigerator

First word across on page 290

Solution on page 280

Framework 19

3 Letters
Abe
Log
May
Not
Old

4 Letters
Ages
Copy
Days
Dear
Debt
Dual

Ends
Eves
June
Keep
Lent
List
Plus
Read
Rely
Spot
Tell
Term
Time
Torn

5 Letters
April
Class
Clear
Erase
Names
Ninth
Pages
Paper
Print
Put up
Santa
Small
Solar

Space
Third
Today
Types

6 Letters
Affair
Chores
Easter
Errand
Events
Extend
Inside
Recall

Record
Romans
Spring
Styles
Sunday

7 Letters
Another
Catalog
Compose
Driving
Holiday
January
October
Planned
Touched
Yearend

8 Letters
December
Labor Day
Leap year
Memorial
Register
Reminder
Veterans
Weekends

9 Letters
September
Valentine
Yesterday
Yom Kippur

10 Letters
Father's Day
Recreation

11 Letters
Appointment
Rosh Hashana

12 Letters
Independence
Thanksgiving

First word across on page 290

Solution on page 280

3 Letters
Arm
Guy
Hod
Leg
Nut
Rig
Rod
Tie

4 Letters
Arch
Axle
Base
Belt
Cash
Edge
Heel
Lift
Pins
Post
Rein
Rest
Ribs
Rope
Sole
Span
Tees

5 Letters
Anvil
Atlas
Cable
Canes
Chair
Easel
Epoxy
Flare
Float

Frame
Front
Irons
Level
Piers
Poles
Props
Pylon
Rails
Scout
Shore
Stake
Strap
Strut

Truss
Wires

6 Letters
Advise
Column
Corset
Crutch
Greats
Halter
Lintel
Litter
Pillar
Shroud

Shrubs
Splint
Stands
Stilts
Tendon
Tripod
Turret

7 Letters
Bolster
Bracket
Bridges
Centers
Experts

Holster
Ignites
Rafters
Ratline
Trellis
Trestle

8 Letters
Abutment
Buttress
Doorjamb
Mattress
Mullions
Pedestal

Pilaster
Platform
Scaffold
Umbrella

9 Letters
Attention
Stretcher

10 Letters
Substratum
Suspenders

First word across on page 290

Solution on page 280

Framework 21

Our Framework expert needed 19 minutes to complete this puzzle. Your solving time: _____.

3 Letters
Coo
Fee
Inn
Odd
See
Tee
Too

4 Letters
Deep
Door
Ebbs
Eggs
Epee

Gull
Ills
Lass
Loot
Olla
Ooze
Puff
Reed
Room
Sass
Toss
Tree

5 Letters
Adder

Aloof
Apple
Asset
Eerie
Ennui
Error
Igloo
Lasso
Passe
Roost
Sheer
Spree
Tooth
Tress

6 Letters
Allude
Appeal
Efface
Effort
Fossil
Frappe
Looser
Mallet
Muffin
Needle
Noodle
Office
Oolong
Pellet

Rebuff
Reeled
Rolled
Russet
Starry
Suffer
Taller
Tattle
Tycoon
Vessel
Yelled

7 Letters
Cuddled
Effendi
Erratic
Express
Flatter
Lettuce
Mission
Narrate
Rookery
Session
Streets
Usually
Vamoose

8 Letters
Applying
Cassette
Expelled
Fritters
Schooner
Telltale
Tireless
Torrents

9 Letters
Affection
Apportion
Classical
Dolefully
Incurring
Lotteries
Offensive

First word across on page 290

Solution on page 280

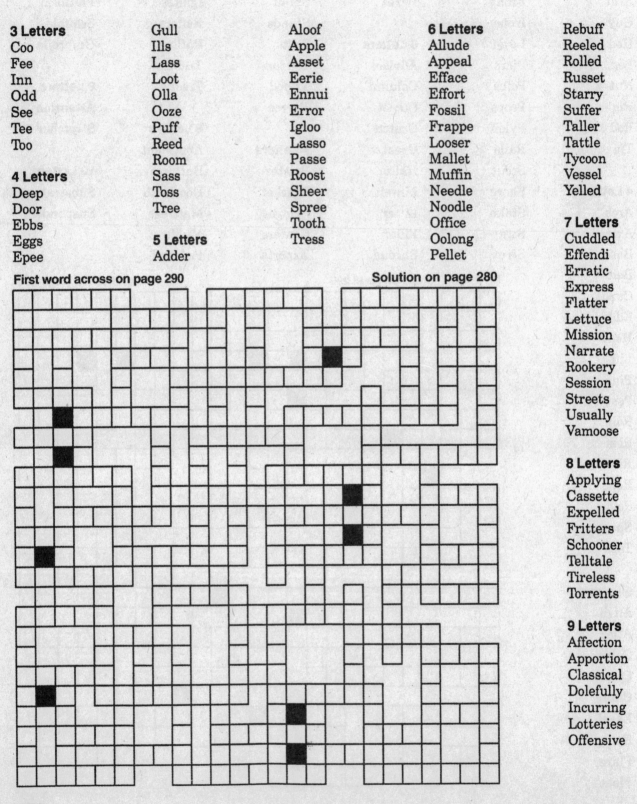

154

Framework 22

4 Letters
Abri
Acer
Aria
Bail
Come
Desi
Eric
Erie
Grid
Haul
Imam
Imps
Mame
Mesa
Mure
Murl
Murr
Napa
Pupa
Pure
Purr
Rift
Rima
Roam
Ruer
Sims
Stem
Unit
Urge

5 Letters
Abaci
Album
Easel
Eerie
Hours
Image
Impar
Moran
Nurls
Nurse
Ourie
Purim
Riems
Rings
Usury

6 Letters
Amurca
Curdle
Erinys
Erring
Gimmer
Gossip
Imamah
Imbrue
Impair
Impure
Limmer
Mimers
Oriole
Purism

Purist
Rimers
Rimmed
Rimmer
Rimmon
Ringer
Riprap
Risked
Rumors
Scampi
Simmer
String
Timber
Untrim
Ursine

7 Letters
Appulse
Arrival
Burster
Glimmer
Imitate
Immerge
Mariner
Rimming
Sodding
Trigger
Trimmed
Uralite

8 Letters
Empurple
Inrigged
Inrigger
Punisher
Rimiform
Simoniac
Urrhodin

9 Letters
Burtonize
Eliminate
Immediacy
Immediate
Nourished

First word across on page 290

Solution on page 280

Framework 23

Border Line

After you have completed this Framework, read the letters in the squares around the outside of the diagram. Start in the top-left square and read clockwise to discover a message. The message is given on page 281.

First word across on page 290   Solution on page 280

3 Letters	5 Letters	Murmur
Lot	Aisle	Outbid
Met	Anise	Scrawl
Rah	Doyen	Triple
Rut	Drive	
Use	Gaped	7 Letters
Was	Liege	Caution
	Title	Laughed
4 Letters	Twang	Lectern
Alma		Samurai
Ends	6 Letters	
Ewer	Canned	9 Letters
Hint	Crates	Antipasto
Seal	Hawaii	Ytterbium
	Limits	

Framework 24

Getting Around

First word across on page 290   Solution on page 280

3 Letters	Kayak	7 Letters
Cab	Ketch	Lorries
Gas	Rides	Scooter
Leg	Stage	Steamer
Map	Yacht	Tractor
Row		
	6 Letters	8 Letters
4 Letters	Hot rod	Rickshaw
OPEC	Rocket	Seaplane
Semi	Saddle	
Skis	Sampan	10 Letters
Tram	Skiffs	Automobile
	Trucks	Catamarans
5 Letters	Wagons	Paddleboat
Canoe		

Tennis, Anyone?

Framework 25

First word across on page 290   Solution on page 280

3 Letters
Ace
Arm
Cut
Let
Net
Tie
Win

4 Letters
Ball
Club
Love
Sets
Team
Toss

5 Letters
Court
Games

Judge
Match
Serve
Train
Upset
White

6 Letters
Center
Player
Tennis
Volley

7 Letters
Driving
Receive
Topspin

8 Letters
Base line

Forehand
Sidespin

9 Letters
Backcourt
Placement

Number Frame

Framework 26

First number across on page 290 Solution on page 280

3 Digits
165
240
349
413
455
528
683
786
791
831

4 Digits
1426
1658
5248
5611
6942
7020

7139
7158
7823
8097
8104
8926

5 Digits
17063
26980
28324
31246
46147
52619
69675
72468
76561
83379
89762

90352
91856

6 Digits
165082
245830
363487
462478
593442
691753
708654
722736
871312
910561

FRAMEWORKS FANS! *Enjoy hours of solving fun with our Special Collections of Selected Frame-works. Each 64-page volume is loaded with your favorite puzzles. To order, see page 61.*

157

THE SHADOW

Can you find the picture that matches the silhouette shown?
Solution on page 281

1.

2.

3.

4.

5.

6.

7.

8.

FLOWER POWER

The answers to this petaled puzzle will go in a curve from the number on the outside to the center of the flower. Each number in the flower will have two 5-letter answers. One goes in a clockwise direction and the second in a counterclockwise direction.

Solution on page 281

CLOCKWISE

1. Custom
2. Float
3. Make merry
4. Settee's kin
5. Furnish food
6. Auto type
7. Masculine ones
8. Defeated person
9. Tendon
10. Semisynthetic fabric
11. Propelled a gondola
12. High body temperature
13. Curved
14. Intimidated
15. Indian tribal emblem
16. Holy plate
17. Warning signal
18. Quibble

COUNTERCLOCKWISE

1. Seraglio
2. Refuge
3. Batman's sidekick
4. Satan
5. African cat
6. Hoarder
7. Iron or tin
8. Burdened
9. Energy type
10. Increased
11. Glass sections
12. Entryway
13. Underneath
14. Assembly of witches
15. Hauled
16. Strength
17. Satisfied
18. Quoted

Window Boxes

There is a 4-letter word hidden in each strip of letters in Column I. Think of the strips in Column II as open and closed windows. Then match each letter strip with its correct Window Box so that the 4-letter word will show. There are different possibilities, but there is only one way in which each letter strip and each window strip are used once.

Solution on page 281

Example: P L O D E N T   P O E T

COLUMN I		COLUMN II
1. G F O V A W L	a.	
2. E C A R G H O	b.	
3. T P J O W O L	c.	
4. W A K H I L M	d.	
5. A W R I C C H	e.	
6. E D U O M P T	f.	
7. G R O E X A M	g.	
8. P O R L K E W	h.	
9. O B L E A Y T	i.	
10. Y H A U N G E	j.	

Picture Pairs

Some of these designs match up as pairs, and some designs have no mates. Can you discover the designs that do not match in three minutes or less?

Solution on page 281

160

Lucky Star

Fill in the 5-letter words which follow the first given words and precede the second to form common words or phrases. Next, enter them into the correspondingly numbered spaces in the Lucky Star diagram. For example, if the two words were KELLY and HOUSE, the answer would be GREEN (Kelly green, Greenhouse).

Solution on page 281

1-2. KITCHEN   _____   TENNIS

3-4. SQUEAKY   _____   CUT

5-6. NO   _____   FINDER

7-8. FLOOD   _____   JANE

9-10. GOOD   _____   SCHOOL

11-12. DIRT   _____   SKATE

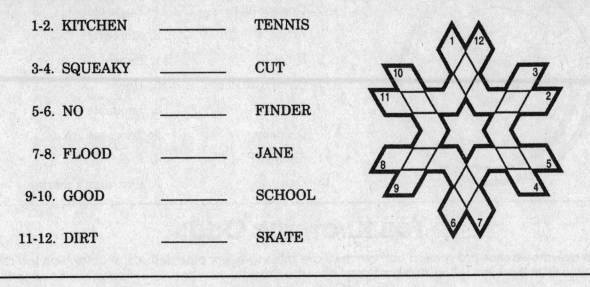

Mind Tickler

A pieman was selling 3 ounce tarts for 20 cents each and 5 ounce tarts for 24 cents each. Simon showed the pieman that he had only $1.50. Then, he told the pieman that his diet would not allow him to have more than 29 ounces of tart per day. The pieman was interested in getting as much of Simon's $1.50 as possible, so what did he offer to sell him? Simon wanted to get as much of his allotted 29 ounces of tart as he could for $1.50, so what did he buy?

Solution on page 281

Across and Down

Place the answers to the clues into their correct places in the diagrams so that the same words read both Across and Down.

Solutions on page 281

A

1. Conclusive

2. Boise's state

3. Consumer advocate

4. In advance

5. Some noblemen

B

1. Our planet

2. Cognizant

3. "M*A*S*H" role

4. Characteristic

5. Unit of frequency

Spinwheel

This puzzle works two ways, outward and inward. Place the answers to the clues in the diagram beginning at the corresponding numbers.

Solution on page 281

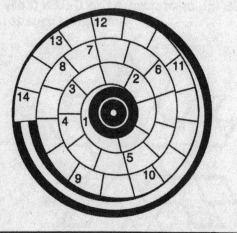

OUTWARD

1. Dresser feature
3. Attire
6. Huge
7. Church officer
9. Fortified residence
11. Footwear
13. Dab

INWARD

14. Bugle call
12. Moreover
11. Punch
10. Holy
8. Readable
5. Talk session
4. Peel
2. Guardian's charge

You Know the Odds

Five downtown sites are spelled out, but they are missing every other letter. It shouldn't be too difficult to fill in the even letters now that You Know the Odds!

Solutions on page 281

1. G _ F _   S _ O _
2. S _ P _ R _ A _ K _ T
3. M _ V _ E _   _ H A _ E _
4. B _ O _ S _ O _ E
5. B _ U _ I _ U _

Anagrams Plus

Find the names of ten sports by adding one of the given letters to each word and rearranging all the letters. Each letter will be used only once.

Solution on page 281

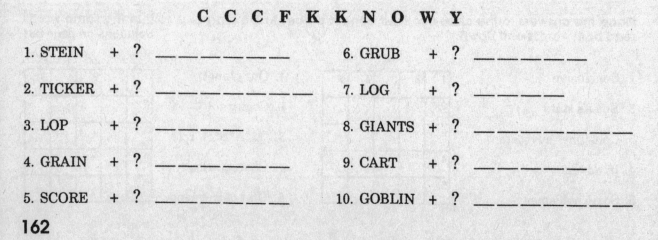

C C C F K K N O W Y

1. STEIN + ? _ _ _ _ _ _
2. TICKER + ? _ _ _ _ _ _ _
3. LOP + ? _ _ _ _
4. GRAIN + ? _ _ _ _ _ _
5. SCORE + ? _ _ _ _ _ _

6. GRUB + ? _ _ _ _ _
7. LOG + ? _ _ _ _
8. GIANTS + ? _ _ _ _ _ _ _
9. CART + ? _ _ _ _ _
10. GOBLIN + ? _ _ _ _ _ _ _

SIMON SAYS

Start with GRATITUDE and follow the directions carefully to discover a phrase that is apropos.

Solution on page 281

1. Print the word GRATITUDE.

1. _____

2. Replace RAT with SIT.

2. _____

3. Change the fifth consonant to a P.

3. _____

4. Drop the first consonant.

4. _____

5. Replace the second T with a V.

5. _____

6. Move the last vowel to the sixth position.

6. _____

7. Delete UP.

7. _____

8. Put the letters THIN at the front.

8. _____

9. Change the first vowel to an A.

9. _____

10. Replace the last E with KING.

10. _____

11. Move the S to the left of the first T.

11. _____

12. Tack POSE on the end.

12. _____

13. Move IT to the right of the last S.

13. _____

14. Drop the first and last letters.

14. _____

15. Insert an E before the K.

15. _____

16. Swap IVE and KING.

16. _____

17. Swap IVE and POSIT.

17. _____

18. Move the first eight letters to the end.

18. _____

CIRCLES IN THE SQUARE

The twenty 5-letter words all fit in the diagram. All words begin and end in a dark circle. Horizontal words read from left to right; all other words read from top to bottom.

Solution on page 281

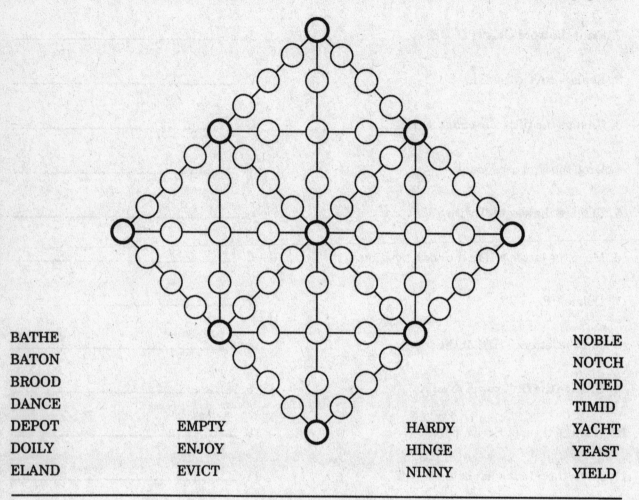

BATHE
BATON
BROOD
DANCE
DEPOT
DOILY
ELAND

EMPTY
ENJOY
EVICT

HARDY
HINGE
NINNY

NOBLE
NOTCH
NOTED
TIMID
YACHT
YEAST
YIELD

Squares

Each of the Squares contains an 8-letter word. It can be found by starting at one of the letters and reading either clockwise or counterclockwise. In the example the word STANDARD is found by starting at the letter S and reading counterclockwise.

Solutions on page 281

Example:

```
D R A
S   D
T A N
```

1.
```
O T R
O   E
K O V
```

2.
```
U L S
P   E
E R D
```

3.
```
O T N
I   E
N T M
```

4.
```
D E X
E   T
D N E
```

5.
```
N A B
E   L
M A E
```

6.
```
C N U
T   F
I O N
```

7.
```
B U B
B   G
L I N
```

8.
```
O R P
C   O
L A R
```

9.
```
V E R
O   Y
C E R
```

164

DOUBLE TROUBLE

Not really double trouble, but double fun! Solve this puzzle as you would a regular crossword, except place one, two, or three letters in each box. The number of letters in each answer is shown in parentheses after its clue.

ACROSS

1. Nurture (6)
4. Minstrel show instrument (5)
7. Pack down (4)
9. Encounters (5)
11. Sullen (4)
12. Pod vegetable (3)
13. Portal (8)
15. Fond of physical pleasures (7)
17. Small sword (6)
19. Everything (3)
20. Companions (7)
22. Gold fabric (4)
24. Snarl (6)
27. Writer Buchwald (3)
28. Affront (6)
29. Nation (4)
30. Warning horn (5)
32. Broad smile (4)
33. AWOL (7)
34. Baking chamber (4)
36. Mild oath (5)
38. Attorney's assistant (9)
41. Picnic dish (11)
44. Lease payment (4)
45. Jointly promoted item (5)
47. Cinema (5)
48. Newsman Koppel (3)
49. Clothing, of old (7)
50. Royal rulers (5)

DOWN

1. Instigate (6)
2. Maneuver (5)
3. Slows down (7)
4. Naughty (3)
5. Snout (4)
6. Diary (7)
7. Florida city (5)
8. Ring (4)
10. Ginger cookie (4)
14. Room top (7)
16. Islamic sovereign (6)
18. Deletion (7)
20. Religious brothers (6)
21. Complete (6)
23. Crucible (10)
25. Window pane material (5)
26. Granting temporary use (7)
31. Work of fiction (5)
33. Thought was someone else (7)
35. Reverse photo (8)
37. First man (4)
38. Natural guardian (6)
39. Graded (5)
40. For fear that (4)
42. Economizing (6)
43. Lords' wives (6)
46. Harden (5)

Solution on page 281

Categories

For each of the categories listed, can you think of a word or phrase beginning with each letter on the left? Count one point for each correct answer. A score of 15 is good, and 21 is excellent.

Our solutions on page 281

	EUROPEAN COUNTRIES	THEATER PEOPLE	ORGANIZATIONS	CAR PARTS	IMPRACTICAL PEOPLE
C					
U					
P					
I					
D					

WHEELS

Answer the clues for the 6-letter words, which go clockwise around the inner Wheels. Three letters of each are given. Then place the three letters you added in the adjoining spaces in the outer Wheel so that a message can be read starting at the arrow and proceeding clockwise.

Solutions on page 281

A. CLUES

1. Large cat

2. Passionate

3. Notable

4. Fellow

5. Outlaw

6. Synthetic fiber

7. Pileup

8. Park bird

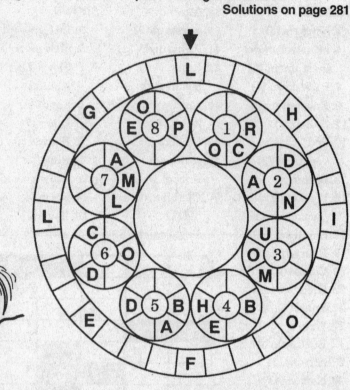

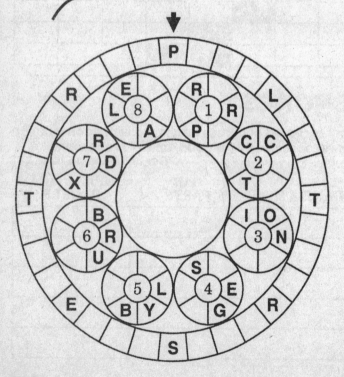

B. CLUES

1. Appropriate

2. Receive

3. Choice

4. Conceit

5. Just

6. Steep

7. English school

8. Aerie dweller

PATCHWORK QUOTE

Place the 12 Patchwork squares into the empty diagram to reveal a message reading left to right, line by line. Copy the squares exactly as they appear, but not necessarily in the order they are given. Black squares indicate the ends of words. Words continue from the right side onto the next line.

CODEWORD

Codeword is a special crossword puzzle in which conventional clues are omitted. Instead, answer words in the diagram are represented by numbers. Each number represents a different letter of the alphabet, and all of the letters of the alphabet are used. When you are sure of a letter, put it in the code key chart and cross it off in the alphabet box. A group of letters has been inserted to start you off.

Solution on page 282

Matchmaker

Fill in the missing first letter of each word in the column on the left. Next look for a related word in the group at the right and put it in the second column. When the puzzle is completed, read the first letters of both columns in order, from top to bottom, to reveal a saying.　　Solution on page 282

___utcast   _____

___otion   _____

___xpert   _____

___illy   _____

___iger   _____   Anew, Coffee, Divergent,

___arly   _____   Dog, Eagle, Exile,

___arallel   _____   Goose, Idea, Implement,

___gain   _____   Ocelot, Overdue,

___op   _____   Skilled, Violet.

___frican   _____

___ool   _____

___nstant   _____

___ockingbird   _____

MISSING DOMINOES

In this game you use all 28 dominoes that are in a standard set. Each one has a different combination from 0-0, 0-1, 0-2, to 6-6. Domino halves with the same number of dots lie next to each other. To avoid confusion we have used an open circle to indicate a zero. Can you fill in the Missing Dominoes to complete the board?   Solution on page 282

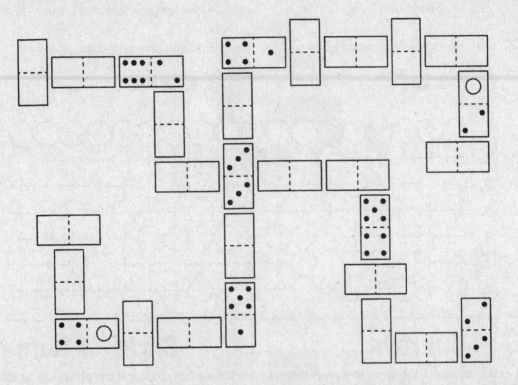

Rhyme Time

The answers to the clues below are pairs of rhyming words. For example: Plump feline would be FAT CAT.   Solutions on page 282

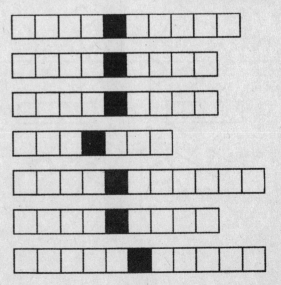

1. Wet winner

2. Ill-mannered fellow

3. Daring grasp

4. Supreme officer

5. Solitary seat

6. Hip slipper

7. Wonderful condition

SPECULATION

Write the answer to each clue in the correspondingly numbered line across—one letter per circle. Next transfer the answer letters to the circles at the top to reveal a saying. Note: Circles in the same vertical column contain the same letter.

Solution on page 282

1. Stumbles

2. Bridge's forerunner

3. Goad

4. Surveyor's tool

5. Explosive liquid, for short

6. Small dams

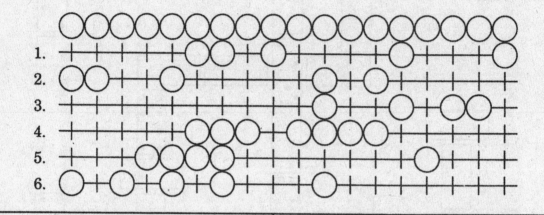

Sunrays

Form 4-letter words using only the nine letters in the center of the diagram. Do not repeat a letter within a word. Place your words into the rays of the diagram so that no two words which are next to each other share a letter.

Our solution on page 282

Slide-O-Rama

Slide each column of letters up or down independently to form as many different words pertaining to units of measure as you can. The word will appear in the middle row where YARD is now.

Our list of 13 words on page 282

170

Anacross

There are three clues for each 7-letter answer word to be entered across in the diagram: a definition, a pair of words that are an anagram of the answer, and the letter A already in its correct place in the diagram. When all the answers have been filled in correctly, the center column reading down will reveal the name of a geometric shape.

Solution on page 282

	DEFINITIONS	ANAGRAMS
1	1. Tumbler	COAT + BAR
2	2. Liked	FACE + DIN
3	3. Indulge	GAIT + FRY
4	4. Chafed	BEAR + ADD
5	5. Refined	GALE + TEN
6	6. Footstool	MOAN + TOT
7	7. Italian matron	SOAR + GIN

Changaword

Can you change the top word into the bottom word in each column in the number of steps indicated in parentheses? Change only one letter at a time and do not change the order of the letters. Proper names, slang, and obsolete words are not allowed.

Our solutions on page 282

1. CARD (3 steps) 2. TAKE (4 steps) 3. FOLD (4 steps) 4. PLAY (4 steps)

GAME   FIVE   HAND   CHIP

Crossblocks

Insert the letters and letter groups into each diagram to form words reading across which answer the clues on the left. A bonus word will read diagonally down in the tinted blocks.

Solutions on page 282

1.   AC CA D E ER
K LA LE M N P
RN S SI UN V

Grotto

Munch

Wash

Easy

2.   AL C D D E EC
G H I IN LA M
ME R RE SP

Coil

Proclaim

Ring

Reward

171

TAKE A LETTER

The names of 12 authors are hidden in the 4-letter words. In the first row across Take a Letter from each word from left to right to spell one author; choose a different letter from each word to spell another; and choose one more to spell a third. One letter of each 4-letter word will be left unused. Do the same for the other rows, spelling the names of three authors in each one.

Solutions on page 282

1. ALUM	FLIP	COLD	IDOL	KITE	REST
2. FAIR	RULE	REVS	BAIT	BEEN	RANG
3. CHEW	IOTA	POLL	DOME	FEET	SURE
4. BLAH	YOUR	OXEN	LAND	VETO	DENY

1. _____ _____ _____

2. _____ _____ _____

3. _____ _____ _____

4. _____ _____ _____

PHRASAGRAMS

Idiomatic phrases can be found by placing letters over the numbered dashes. A recurring letter will appear over the same number every time.

Solution on page 282

CLUES | PHRASES

1. Propose marriage

___ ___ ___ THE ___ ___ ___ ___ ___ ___ ___ ___
19 5 19   9 15 14 11 20 1 5 17

2. Frozen

___ ___ ___ ___ AS ___ ___ ___
7 5 13 2   1 7 14

3. Relax

___ ___ ___ ___ IT ___ ___ ___ ___
20 10 8 14   14 10 11 4

4. Reveal a secret

___ ___ ___ ___ ___ THE ___ ___ ___ ___ ___
11 19 1 13 13   18 14 10 17 11

5. Vent one's anger

___ ___ ___ OFF ___ ___ ___ ___ ___
13 14 20   11 20 14 10 3

6. Become reconciled

___ ___ ___ ___ THE ___ ___ ___ ___ ___ ___ ___
18 15 6 4   16 10 20 7 16 14 20

7. Cause trouble

___ ___ ___ ___ THE ___ ___ ___ ___
6 5 7 8   18 5 10 20

8. Upstage everyone

___ ___ ___ ___ ___ THE ___ ___ ___ ___
11 20 14 10 13   11 16 5 12

172

FANCY FIVES

Each answer in this puzzle is a 5-letter word! Place the answers to the Lettered Clues into the protruding outside squares of the diagram. The answers to the Across and Down Clues are placed in only those boxes which contain numbers (1-21 Down is entered into the squares numbered 1, 6, 11, 16, 21). The answers to the Cube Words are entered in scrambled order into the squares containing the corresponding numbers and the four squares surrounding those squares.

Solution on page 282

LETTERED CLUES

a-b. Pursue

c-d. Rental contract

f-e. Aquatic animal

h-g. Sound reasoning

ACROSS CLUES

1-5. Neckerchief

6-10. Containing fewer flaws

11-15. Irregularly notched

16-20. Restrict

21-25. Lends

DOWN CLUES

1-21. Brief period

2-22. Objet d'art

3-23. Scent

4-24. Varnish ingredient

5-25. Guitar parts

CUBE WORDS

1. Union _____ (minimum wage)
2. Wreck
3. Wake-up call
4. Tempest
5. Musical instrument
6. Feel (one's way)
7. Surmise
8. Russian currency
9. Orb
10. Mean
11. Article of makeup
12. Bush
13. Yell
14. Sod covering
15. Finest part
16. Sheer fabric
17. Social group
18. Entice
19. Very fast
20. Stylish
21. Spice
22. Composed
23. Irrigate
24. Roadside eatery
25. Elevate

ANAGRAM MAGIC SQUARE

Find an anagram for the 5-letter word in each box. The anagram will answer one of the clues. Put the number of that clue into the small square and write the anagram on the dash. The numbers in each row and column will add up to 65. Write the first letter of each anagram on the correspondingly numbered dash at the bottom of the page; and, presto!, the Anagram Magic saying will appear. To start you off, we have put in one anagram and its clue number and set its first letter on the proper dash at the bottom of the page.

Solution on page 282

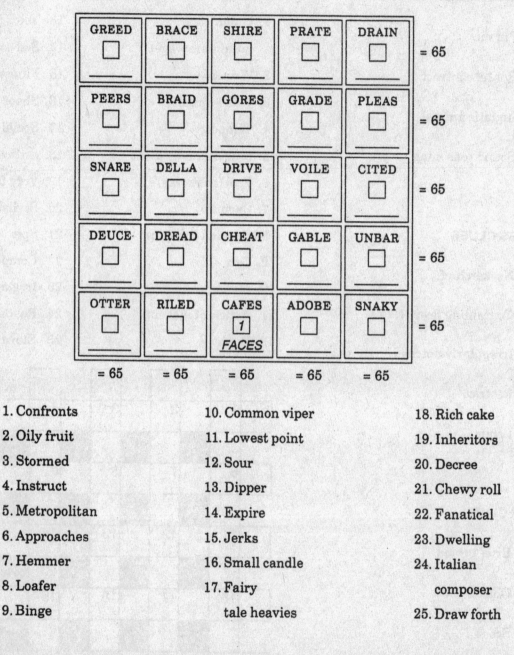

GREED ☐ ___	BRACE ☐ ___	SHIRE ☐ ___	PRATE ☐ ___	DRAIN ☐ ___	= 65
PEERS ☐ ___	BRAID ☐ ___	GORES ☐ ___	GRADE ☐ ___	PLEAS ☐ ___	= 65
SNARE ☐ ___	DELLA ☐ ___	DRIVE ☐ ___	VOILE ☐ ___	CITED ☐ ___	= 65
DEUCE ☐ ___	DREAD ☐ ___	CHEAT ☐ ___	GABLE ☐ ___	UNBAR ☐ ___	= 65
OTTER ☐ ___	RILED ☐ ___	CAFES 1 *FACES*	ADOBE ☐ ___	SNAKY ☐ ___	= 65

= 65   = 65   = 65   = 65   = 65

1. Confronts
2. Oily fruit
3. Stormed
4. Instruct
5. Metropolitan
6. Approaches
7. Hemmer
8. Loafer
9. Binge
10. Common viper
11. Lowest point
12. Sour
13. Dipper
14. Expire
15. Jerks
16. Small candle
17. Fairy
    tale heavies
18. Rich cake
19. Inheritors
20. Decree
21. Chewy roll
22. Fanatical
23. Dwelling
24. Italian
    composer
25. Draw forth

F ___ ___
  1 2 3 4 5 6 7 8 9 10 11 12 13 14 15 16 17 18 19 20 21 22 23 24 25

ANAGRAM MAGIC SQUARE SOLVERS! Enjoy more puzzle magic! Each special collection of Anagram Magic Square is packed with loads of delightful puzzles. To order, see page 61.

BIG QUESTION

Start at the arrow and put the answers to the clues into the diagram in the order in which they are given. Every answer word overlaps the previous answer word by one letter or more. The first letters of all the answer words are shown in the diagram. When the Big Question is filled, place the eight numbered letters into their corresponding spaces in the square at the bottom to reveal the answer to the riddle.

Solution on page 282

Riddle: How did the driver feel upon discovering he had a flat tire?

CLUES

1. Big ape
2. Activate
3. Private room
4. Position
5. Dissertation
6. Sibling
7. Fantastic
8. Flighty
9. Clark's partner
10. Emilio Estevez film
11. Realm
12. Basically
13. Pious
14. Exit
15. Belated
16. "_____ of the Dragon"
17. Klimt or Klee
18. Kind of jam?
19. Advent-wreath feature
20. Camera eye
21. Massachusetts town
22. Appear
23. Equipment
24. Surrender

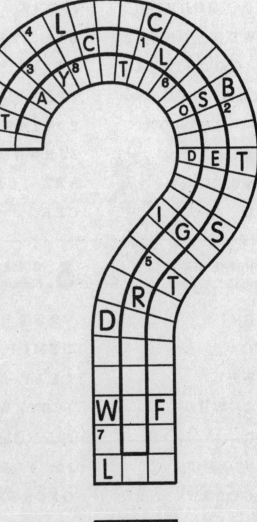

175

CRYPTO-FAMILIES

Each Crypto-Family is a list of related words in code. Each Family has its own code. When you have identified a word, use the known letters to help decode the other words in the Family.

Solutions on page 282

1. **AT THE RACETRACK**
Example: Backstretch

MGSLWR

IAGOGKVAJOWQ

DKULR   QOHBWO

ANOZWDD   ONSHZV

TGDI   TGDHIHGZ

DINOIHZV   VNIW

TAGIG   EHZHDA

AGXWDIOWISA

VONZQDINZQ

DHULD

2. **2-WORD U.S. CITIES**
Example: Fort Worth

MPF   APZY

YPVVP   SRWYP

IPTRV   VRCJTZ

LPA   FHVM

QRYHL   VHWDP

TPZ   OHJLPZ

BJYYBP   VHIM

ZJHWN   ERBBZ

BRZ   GPDRZ

CRBO   QPRIS

3. **IT'S ALL RELATIVE**
Example: Nephew

VRWX

AHXZTN

ZRUOVWM

ULUXTN

GLKT

KVXZTN

RWSYT

ONHXZTN

SHRULW

MVRJZXTN

4. **AT THE THEATER**
Example: Scenery

EWTJBVI

WPCTO

JQAUWPV

EWJZCUWHO

XPVHC

EBR   COWU

BAJMOCUAW   NPU

WNABV

NABNC

KBBUTPHMUC

5. **GEESE**
Example: V-formation

VQWT

OYMPF

EMBF

ICBTXW

UXV-OMMSXT

IMJYQBI

OXCSEXW

UCSXWOMUY

XIIJ

YMBI-BXPFXT

6. **SIGNS OF THE TIMES**
Example: Keep Off Grass

BIFA   AFLY   PE

LYHL   YKL

ZPB   BZ   NPKTI

LZK'B   GHNX

ZKY   GHW

ATIZZN   MZKY

QHJHQY   AHNY

GYB   EHFKB

KZ   P-BPJK

RJHQFNY

CRYPTO-FAMILIES FANS! Meet our family of special collections, each with hundreds of intriguing Crypto-Family puzzles! See page 61 for details.

RINGERS

Each of the five Ringers is composed of five rings. Use your imagination to rotate the rings so that you spell four 5-letter words reading from the outside to the inside when all five rings are aligned correctly.

Solutions on page 282

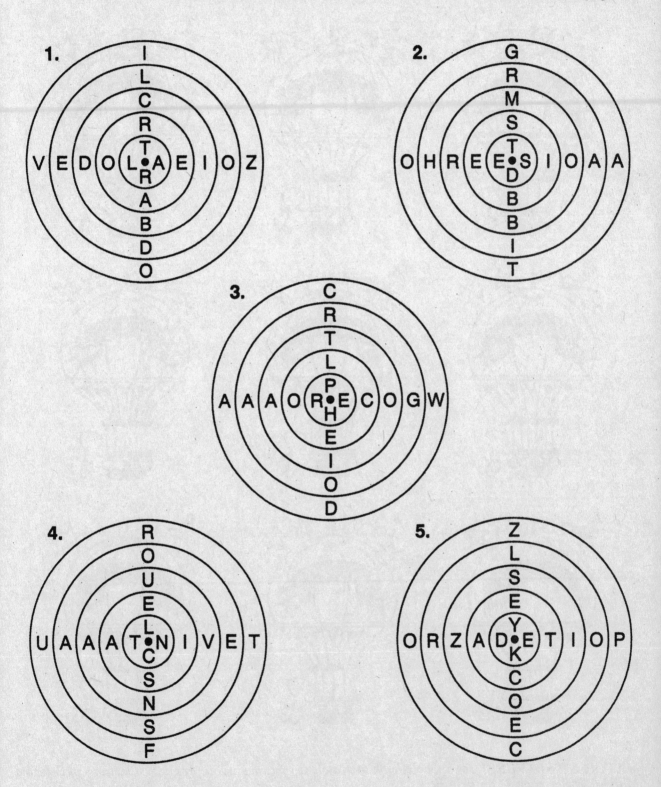

1.

2.

3.

4.

5.

MATCH-UP

Can you find the two pictures that are identical?
Solution on page 282

MATCH-UP SOLVERS! *Get a whole book of Match-Up puzzles in our special collections of Selected Match-Up. See page 61 for details.*

WHICH WAY WORDS

Starting with the correspondingly numbered circles, fit the answer to each clue into the connected circles, one letter in each. The five horizontal lines with the heavily outlined circles will contain related 9-letter entries.

Solution on page 282

1. Pier
2. Threshold
3. Surly
4. False face
5. Light musical drama
6. Harmony
7. Courageous
8. Riding whips
9. Wolflike
10. Without hesitation
11. Alter
12. Synthetic fabric
13. The world around us

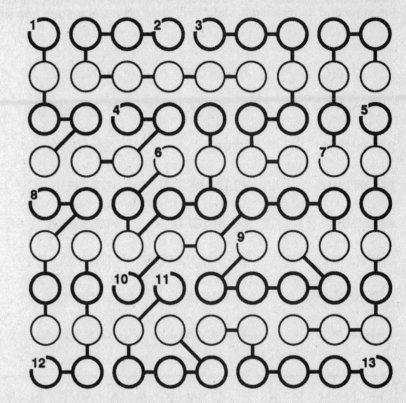

Unscramblers

Rearrange the pairs of letters in the left-hand column to form the names of twelve cities. Then match them with their countries in the right-hand column.

Solution on page 282

CITIES					COUNTRIES
1. AN	AI	SH	GH		A. India
2. PL	ES	NA			B. Australia
3. RA	KA	AN			C. Canada
4. KO	MA	HA	YO		D. Spain
5. IA	EX	AL	AN	DR	E. Greece
6. EY	SY	DN			F. Colombia
7. PE	DA	ST	BU		G. Turkey
8. NS	HE	AT			H. Italy
9. TA	BO	GO			I. Egypt
10. AL	NT	RE	MO		J. Hungary
11. ID	MA	DR			K. China
12. TA	LC	CA	UT		L. Japan

179

The cities and towns from our Mystery State can be found in the diagram reading forward, backward, up, down, and diagonally. After you loop all the cities and towns, the remaining letters will reveal the name of the state and its nickname, state bird, state flower, and state tree which are given on page 284.

Solution on page 283

ATLANTIC	CHESTER	LINDEN	PARAMUS	TRENTON
CITY	CLIFTON	MEDFORD	PASSAIC	UNION
BAYONNE	EDISON	MENDHAM	PATERSON	VINELAND
BOONTON	ELIZABETH	NEPTUNE	PITMAN	WATCHUNG
CAMDEN	GARFIELD	NEWARK	PRINCETON	WAYNE
CAPE MAY	HACKENSACK	NEW EGYPT	RAHWAY	WILDWOOD
CHERRY	HOBOKEN	NEWTON	RAMSEY	
HILL	HOPEWELL	ORADELL	TEANECK	

```
N N M P K E C W K R A W E N Y N O T N E R T D
O C A A J C E L R C S E R E T S E H C A P L C
I Y H T E B A Z I L E T E D I S O N M Y E R A
N H D E E G A S R F D N E N C S T S G I N A M
U A N R R T E V N E T A A S C T E E F D N H D
M N E S P R I N C E T O N E I Y W R O E O W E
E E M O N N Y I N R K O N N T E A O G B Y A N
D P O N E E A H W A T C H U N G W M O L A Y E
F T D L F S D I I N M N A Y A D C K E H B P W
O U A U S R P N O L L T A H L L E W E P O H T
R N E A V I O O I L L W I I T N L L E D A R O
D E P E T R B E D L O A W P A R A M U S K C N
```

Alphabetics

Each of the answer words starts with a different letter of the alphabet. The words are in the diagram reading forward, backward, up, down, diagonally, and always in a straight line. Words may overlap. Not all the letters in the diagram will be used. The number in parentheses is the number of letters in the word.
Word list on page 284   Solution on page 283

A _ _ _ _ _ _ _ _ _ (10)   N _ _ _ _ _ _ _ _ _ (10)
B _ _ _ _ _ _ _ _ _ _ (11)   O _ _ _ _ _ _ _ (8)
C _ _ _ _ _ _ (7)   P _ _ _ _ _ _ _ (8)
D _ _ _ _ _ _ _ (8)   Q _ _ _ _ (5)
E _ _ _ _ (5)   R _ _ _ _ _ (6)
F _ _ _ _ _ _ _ (8)   S _ _ _ _ _ _ _ _ _ _ (11)
G _ _ _ _ _ _ (7)   T _ _ _ _ _ _ (7)
H _ _ _ _ _ (6)   U _ _ _ _ _ _ _ _ (9)
I _ _ _ _ _ _ _ _ (9)   V _ _ _ _ _ _ _ (8)
J _ _ _ _ _ _ _ _ (9)   W _ _ _ _ _ _ _ _ _ _ (11)
K _ _ _ _ _ _ _ _ _ (10)   X _ _ _ _ _ _ _ _ (9)
L _ _ _ _ _ _ _ (8)   Y _ _ _ _ _ _ _ _ (9)
M _ _ _ _ _ _ _ _ (9)   Z _ _ _ _ (5)

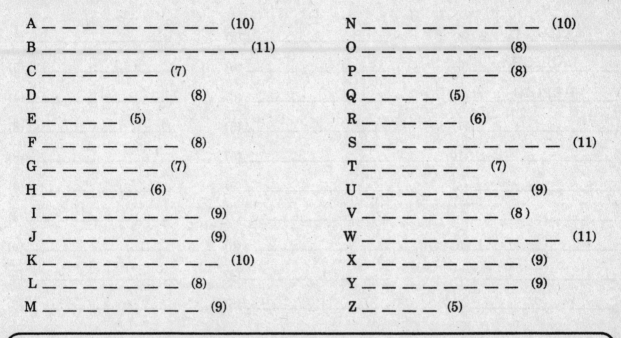

```
K N I G H T R U S T E D S O R R O W F U L L Y
N L T M I G E K A T R E D N U O O S E D I L J
I E N A M E N U C O P S Y V V F L Y E N L C I
G N Y O I G N I N I F E D T F I L T O U Y N T
H O L E T A V I T C T E B I C E S I F C S E T
T H D L A L R A S N E S C D T E T I L T Y E E
H P N O T L H I R Y I I D U R A T I T A V U R
O O E I I A U U L B A A L R G U S N S I M Q B
O L I D O N V O R L E O P I A T Y S S S N L U
D Y R Y N T I N D T S Z V E L Y E M P O T G G
P X F X Y D M A E B L A B L O N E S O M E T R
N S U O I C I L A M N E Y L L A C I S M I H W
```

In this special Word Seek, form a continuous chain of looped words. The last letter of each word will be the first letter of the next. The number of letters in each word is given in parentheses. We have started you off with the first three words.

Word list on page 284   Solution on page 283

RATIONAL (8)	_____ (5)	_____ (6)
LAUNCH (6)	_____ (6)	_____ (5)
HEROIC (6)	_____ (6)	_____ (4)
_____ (7)	_____ (5)	_____ (8)
_____ (10)	_____ (5)	_____ (5)
_____ (8)	_____ (5)	_____ (4)
_____ (5)	_____ (7)	_____ (6)
_____ (5)	_____ (6)	_____ (8)
_____ (6)	_____ (4)	_____ (5)
_____ (6)	_____ (5)	_____ (5)

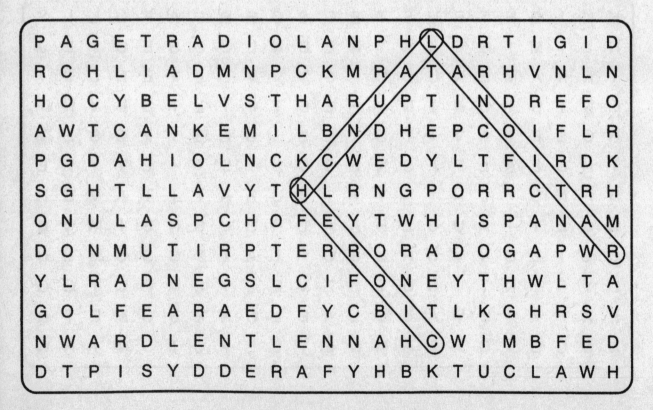

```
P A G E T R A D I O L A N P H L D R T I G I D
R C H L I A D M N P C K M R A T A R H V N L N
H O C Y B E L V S T H A R U P T I N D R E F O
A W T C A N K E M I L B N D H E P C O I F L R
P G D A H I O L N C K C W E D Y L T F I R D K
S G H T L L A V Y T H L R N G P O R R C T R H
O N U L A S P C H O F E Y T W H I S P A N A M
D O N M U T I R P T E R R O R A D O G A P W R
Y L R A D N E G S L C I F O N E Y T H W L T A
G O L F E A R A E D F Y C B I T L K G H R S V
N W A R D L E N T L E N N A H C W I M B F E D
D T P I S Y D D E R A F Y H B K T U C L A W H
```

V-Words

The 5-letter words below are found in the diagram in a V shape pointing left, right, up, and down. The key to finding them all is just around the corner!

Solution on page 283

ATTIC ✓	FAVOR	LABEL	ROUTE
AUDIO	FLARE	LIONS	SAUCE
BAYOU	GLIDE	MAINE	SPAIN
BONGO	GYPSY	MEDIA	STAKE
BROOK	HINGE	NOBLE	TEETH
CAMEO	HOUND	NOISE	THROW
CLUBS	IMPLY	OAKEN	UNITY
DIALS	INLET	OZONE	VENUS
DUTCH	JUDGE	PULSE	VERSE
EAGLE	JUMPY	PUMPS	WAVES
EARTH	KARAT	READY	WORLD

```
J L A X E E D J E V H I J T H G D O R P M U J
U I I L D M S N E O I M U R H I O E N K U A L
D B G O S O I R U L E Z A X A R A E M B V L J
E Y N A C E L A Y O C K J C O T T D S W S E C
P S V H E J T K M S Y U N W Z U E V Y E J I N
L S I T U E U H E A E W A O C L O X E C T U H
K O Y J L I O K B O U V I D B V Y R J A S T D
N X V F W N A Z I B M D E M W L A N C B R L A
M I A Y E X I T O N I C U H P C Z L E J R D C
U V A N V L Y D S L U J Y T M Y D X F K N O B
J P O Z G I A I E B V A C P Z U J G A G O I W
S B X R P O Y B C W M H S O J L P O E K U J H
```

183

Word Seek 16

The entries in this Zigzag puzzle will be found in the diagram in an unusual way. They do not read in straight lines; rather, each entry has one bend in it. Circle each word when you find it in the diagram and cross it off the list. Words often overlap, and some letters may be used more than once. All the letters in the diagram will be used.   Solution on page 283

ABILITY	DECORATION	MYSTIQUE	STATEMENT
ANKLE	DECREASED	NATIONAL	SUBTLE
ANTICS	EFFICIENT	NOONTIDE	THEATER
APPETIZERS	FRIENDS	OPTION	UNDERSTANDING
CALENDAR	GENERICS	PARTITION	VISION
CANDID	GUILTY	PULSATION	WASTEFUL
CAPITAL	HAUNTED	RASPBERRY	WAVER
CHARACTER	HAZARD	REGISTRATION	WICKET
CITIZEN	IDYLLIC	RENDEZVOUS	ZITHER
CONTAINER	LACQUER	SAVANNA	
CUBICLE	LEDGE	SILENT	
DEBUT	LOZENGES	SPIGOT	

```
C H A R A S L O Z E W I C K Y R R E L I P A C
S A E R C E D G N I D N A E W E B U T T Z I T
E N N I T O G G O C S D N T A P F A T N U A H
D O R D E Y E I A N Q U E R S E L F T E R M E
O E I A R S T L P C A E I A T R H A I I D Y R
N D Z O D A E I A S S L R N O I E A E C T S C
T E C V N N T L S U B T F A T H Z D A L T S I
I E G I O C C I T I S W A P T A S T N I K I L
D T A S L U P B O I Z A O T R I N R Q U N L L
E I I T U B S A G N V E V D E O O U E G A E Y
A O E L C I E E R E A N N A C M E N T Z N D R
N N T I C S R D R T I T I O N A P P E T I G E
```

ZIGZAG FANS! *You'll enjoy our special collection packed with dozens of engaging Zigzag puzzles. See page 61 to order.*

Missing Vowels

Before you can loop these words naming herbs, spices, and condiments, you must first fill in the circles in the diagram with the missing vowels A, E, I, O, and U. Words in the diagram read forward, backward, up, down, and diagonally, and always in a straight line. Circle each word when you find it and cross it off the list. Words will often overlap, and some letters may be used more than once. Not all of the letters in the diagram will be used. We have filled in and circled ALLSPICE as an example.

Solution on page 283

HERBS, SPICES, ETC.

ALLSPICE ✓	CILANTRO	HYSSOP	PARSLEY
ANGELICA	CINNAMON	LAVENDER	ROSEMARY
ANISE	CLOVES	LEMON GRASS	SAFFRON
BASIL	CORIANDER	LICORICE	SAGE
BAY LEAF	DILL	MACE	SAVORY
BORAGE	FENNEL	MARJORAM	SORREL
CARDAMOM	GARLIC	NETTLE	TARRAGON
CATNIP	GINGER	NUTMEG	THYME
CHAMOMILE	HOREHOUND	OREGANO	WATERCRESS
CHERVIL	HORSERADISH	PAPRIKA	

```
C P O S S Y H G D B O Y L O O F J M S W B R C
O O C L O V O S M C P O K T D N O M O N N O C
R N O R S S O C O O L O N N O F B T F T D J C
O T O N V W O L P D R O O O K Y O W O F L O O W
O O L J O S O R T V O O M W S R P O R S L O Y
N C O C O G O C R T H R J O C O O F O O L F R
D O M V N K O B O O O Y O R N B W S N H G N O
O L O O O T F R R R L N O S O G O T O V D O G
R R M B C D H O O T O S D S R M R G O M T O N
Y O O J M O H Y K L S C O C N O G O R R O T O
Y G H C O R D O M O M L O V R O H C S G H R G
K V C W D R O D N O V (A L L S P I C E) S N F Y
```

Word Seek 18

The entries in this Horseshoes puzzle will be found in the diagram in an unusual way. They do not read in straight lines; rather each entry is in the shape of a horseshoe in the diagram. We have looped the word APPALOOSA as an example.

Solution on page 283

```
S M N U I G H C A O I O A Y M A I A G J C
T T U P H N N E G E C N P E T N N N D L Y
E I H O X I B I S R E S S E S R I S E E B
E N N I O S S T A G Z R R C L A L H B R A
P G S F F A P I N G E D O A I C B I O S T
E L B S H O M J A K N I H R R K Z P Y D S
V C E C L T L L A G N R O D C A C I I S L
A M O A N V S K C Q I C H D L R H N N T E
S L P O X T C T Y J W O E X E G A G G O G
S B R M A U S A F D H W E R P I R R I E Y
E E E L N T U K H E S Y S N A R L R K T O
N V A E G N M E B R O N F C G E C A C R Y
X K H B R E D S M B B O C J E S F C W O J
L G D A G K C L R Y B P Y O O S Q N N T W
R U Q T R O A T K D U S G B P B O U W W Z
E T O R O H T V A C Y G U T E W E G O M Z
O Z G P I R T H R E T S F M N L L G A X A
A L L G N I Y E A I D E M A I I N A P Y S
P E R P B W T G R X R L R C O V Y T P W O
U W C B E T C A B K E E U O N Y O S A Z O
H O K R O W N U S S Q B L X W B Z W Z L X
```

Appaloosa
Belmont Stakes
Betting
Blinders
Bridle
Broncobuster
Buggy
Carriage
Cavalry
Chariots
Cowboy
Dressage
Fox hunting
Galloping
Gelding
Grazing
Hoofs
Horsemanship
Jockey
Kentucky Derby
Mares
Mount
Mustang
Opening gun
Place
Pony Express
Preakness
Race track
Reins
Rodeo
Shoes
Stableboy
Stagecoach
Stallion
Steeplechasing
Thoroughbred
Triple Crown
Trotting
Winner's circle

Wizard Words

The Wizard is wise and humorous. To complete his words first loop all the words in the word list, then read the leftover letters to reveal the missing words that will complete the Wizard's Words. Words in the diagram read forward, backward, up, down, and diagonally, and always in a straight line. Loop each word when you find it and cross it off the list. Words often overlap, and some letters may be used more than once.

Wizard Words on page 284

Solution on page 283

A BRUTAL ASPECT OF FOOTBALL IS THE

——— ——— ——— ——— ——— ——— ——— ——— ——— ———

ATTACK	HUDDLE	SLANT	TACKLE	TRAIN
BACKFIELD	KICKOFF	SNEAK	TEAM	VARSITY
BALL	OFFENSE	SPRAIN	TIME-OUT	YARDAGE
BENCH	OFFSIDE	STRATEGY	TOUCHDOWN	
BLOCK	PASS			
BRUISES	PLAYS			
CARRY	POINTS			
CLOCK	PUNT			
COACH	QUARTERBACK			
CONVERSION	RECEIVER			
DEFEND	REFEREE			
END RUN	REVERSE			
FAKE	RULE			
GOAL LINE	RUSH			
GRIDIRON	SAFETY			
GUARDS	SCHEDULE			
HOLD	SCORE			

```
Q E G A D R A Y G E T A R T S
U E L K C A T T R A I N R T C
A N P R S E S I U R B E N C H
R D O F F E N S E I C A I C E
T R C A R R Y R M E L C A P D
E U S C O R E A I S O O R L U
R N O I S R E V N O C D P A L
B U I E E T E O E F K N S Y E
A A S L M R E F E R E E F S S
C K L H L I K A E N S F A T E
K C A L T A T S R U L E K N P
C A K I C K O F F S I D E I U
O T S D R A U G R I D I R O N
L T O U C H D O W N S S A P T
B A C K F I E L D D U H O L D
```

WIZARD WORDS WIZARDS! *You'll be enchanted by our special collections packed with dozens of engaging Wizard Words puzzles. See page 61 to order.*

Word Seek 20

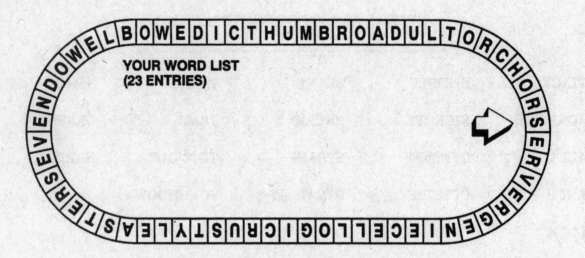

Searchword

We have given you the words for this puzzle, but you must search for them. There are 23 different words of five letters in the oval. Read the letters clockwise only. Words often overlap. You should not skip over or rearrange any letters. Then locate and loop these words in the diagram. We have looped the first two words for you.

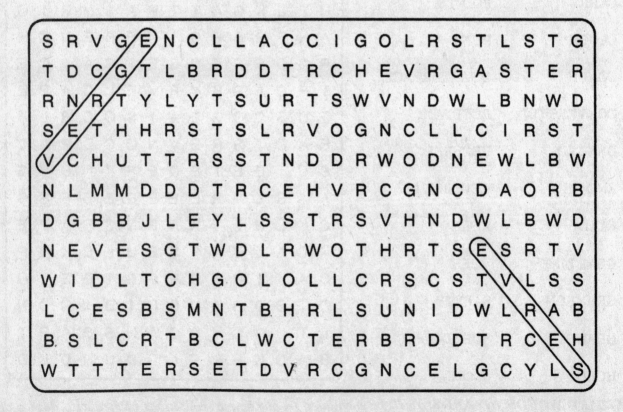

Word list on page 284

Solution on page 283

YOUR WORD LIST (23 ENTRIES)

```
S R V G E N C L L A C C I G O L R S T L S T G
T D C G T L B R D D T R C H E V R G A S T E R
R N R T Y L Y T S U R T S W V N D W L B N W D
S E T H H R S T S L R V O G N C L L C I R S T
V C H U T T R S S T N D D R W O D N E W L B W
N L M M D D D T R C E H V R C G N C D A O R B
D G B B J L E Y L S S T R S V H N D W L B W D
N E V E S G T W D L R W O T H R T S E S R T V
W I D L T C H G O L O L L C R S C S T V L S S
L C E S B S M N T B H R L S U N I D W L R A B
B S L C R T B C L W C T E R B R D D T R C E H
W T T T E R S E T D V R C G N C E L G C Y L S
```

188

Heads & Tails

In this special Word Seek, form a continuous chain of looped words. The last letter of each word will be the first letter of the next. The number of letters in each word is given in parentheses. We have started you off with the first three words.

Word list on page 284   Solution on page 283

JUNGLE	(6)	_____	(8)	_____	(6)
ELEGANT	(7)	_____	(8)	_____	(6)
TANGENT	(7)	_____	(7)	_____	(6)
_____	(10)	_____	(6)	_____	(6)
_____	(6)	_____	(7)	_____	(6)
_____	(6)	_____	(6)	_____	(7)
_____	(6)	_____	(5)	_____	(4)
_____	(10)	_____	(6)	_____	(6)
_____	(7)	_____	(6)	_____	(8)
_____	(6)	_____	(8)	_____	(6)

```
R G L H N L U F T H G U O H T Y L T C A X E Q
U U R M I V D E P E N D S N I E F M A O V B R
O K S M F E W A Y B W G E O L L K G N I E Q C
T S P T S R S U Q X A G V J L L F J D P P D S
E I U A I E O D P H N S K U E O R N A T E T A
D T R C J C A N T A L O U P E W E L I A O L R
G E E L E G A N T B Z M L D I C O T R P L D C
E Z L L I N C M X Y Z E A N O M L N A I H U H
X C J D G B B H C N W C K N X I I T U S G I
D W H E E N A T L A D H U M A N E R P R T V V
Y F L V I E U M E Z R A Y T G X O Q F S W I E
G S O L E M N J E R U T U S U T P M E X E K S
```

189

Word Seek 22

Missing Vowels

Before you can loop these words about vehicles, you must first fill in the circles in the diagram with the missing vowels A, E, I, O, and U. Words in the diagram read forward, backward, up, down, and diagonally, and always in a straight line. Circle each word when you find it and cross it off the list. Words will often overlap, and some letters may be used more than once. Not all of the letters in the diagram will be used. We have filled in and circled BATTERY as an example.

Solution on page 283

VEHICLES

Battery ✓	Gas	Seats	Taxi
Brakes	Gauges	Sedan	Tractor
Bus	Ignition	Snowplow	Trailers
Clutch	Jeep	Spark plugs	Travel
Convertible	Limousine	Speedometer	Truck
Coupe	Motor	Sports car	Van
Designs	Oil	Starter	Wheels
Diesel	Pedals	Station wagon	Windows
Exhaust	Police car	Steer	
Fire engine	Racing car	Stock car	
Gadgets	Radiator	Tanker	

W	P	S	○	○	T	S	○	○	H	X	○	N	○	G	N	○	○	R	○	F	B	F
○	V	○	○	V	S	T	T	T	M	S	R	○	C	G	N	○	C	○	R	L	C	R
N	W	○	L	G	S	N	R	○	L	B	S	T	○	N	K	○	R	X	S	○	R	○
D	○	R	N	○	○	○	G	○	R	A	W	○	D	L	○	○	D	R	Z	M	○	T
○	L	○	S	○	C	○	D	○	J	T	○	L	B	○	T	R	○	V	N	○	C	○
W	P	G	T	K	D	○	G	H	S	T	○	W	C	○	○	L	G	C	K	○	S	M
S	W	N	○	G	P	○	C	P	○	E	J	R	○	N	○	S	L	L	T	S	T	○
○	○	○	○	M	G	L	S	○	K	R	D	D	B	○	C	○	○	M	R	○	R	D
K	N	T	R	○	C	T	○	R	R	Y	○	C	R	D	T	T	H	L	○	N	○	○
○	S	○	S	N	○	P	○	○	C	R	S	T	○	C	K	C	○	R	V	○	P	○
R	M	○	T	○	R	C	R	C	○	X	○	T	H	F	G	W	H	○	○	L	S	P
B	P	N	○	G	○	W	N	○	○	T	○	T	S	P	○	R	K	P	L	○	G	S

Create Your Words

There are 52 words of six or more letters hidden in the diagram. They are all formed by using only the eight letters shown. You may repeat a letter as often as needed in each word. To start you off we have circled the word BETTER.

Word list on page 284

Solution on page 283

YOUR WORD LIST
(52 ENTRIES)

```
B T E L B I R R E T T E L B I T S I S E R R I
E R E B M E M E S I L L I E S T E E M B E M E
L E I B R E B T M T R E B L E I R R E B M I L
I M I B L I R T T M S M T I R I M B M E I L T
R B I B E E S I B B I I S E E S B I R E S L S
E L M S E R R T B L T S I S T E T S L S S E E
T E B T T B I L L E T E S S T T E B E E B T R
S R E B M E M E R E E R E I I T M T B I B E T
L I T T L E R B S B R I R S L E T B T R B L B
B B T B E L T T E S S E L T S E R T B R B L B
T S E M M I L S B L I S T E R R E T S E T E I
I E R I T E R E L I E S R R I R I I I B I R I
```

191

Boxes

All the entries in the list are titles of books. An entry can begin at any point and will read either clockwise or counterclockwise around the edges of a box (sometimes a square and sometimes a rectangle). ALICE ADAMS is boxed in the diagram.

Solution on page 283

ALICE ADAMS ✓	INFORMER, The	SOURCE, The
ARROWSMITH	JANE EYRE	STELLA
BACK STREET	KING COAL	DALLAS
CIMARRON	KITTY FOYLE	THE BIBLE
COVENANT, The	LAST HURRAH, The	THE CITADEL
EGOIST, The	LOLITA	THE FIXER
ETHAN FROME	MAIN STREET	THE GROUP
EXODUS	MOBY DICK	THE MAN
GRAND HOTEL	ONION FIELD, The	THE PIT
HAWAII	RAMONA	YEARLING, The
ICEBOUND	SHOW BOAT	

```
B A D A L O M O N E E K R E H T R O L E L Y O
A L M I L H A R A N Y O N F I X E A L K O R F
Y L J T A K E R J E R I N T E O S O W I T T Y
E E T S S T H U R M A N O D L D U C G N E V E
R L B R Z A T O R R O F R R O Z E T H A V O C
T H A O B E A D A R N E A P W E E K I N T C E
S K C U B C A L M I C E H A S I M O R F Y R S
G R A N D I L A S T I N T I M E R T S U P U O
O G U S H S T I L A D E L R A E N O N T T E R
B L E T O T A L O N K V I F E T M A I I H E G
I S T O W B O M K I M A N G Y K N W I P E G O
B E H I N Y D I C H E H T R A K E A H O T S I
```

Mystery State

Word Seek 25

The cities and towns from our Mystery State can be found in the diagram reading forward, backward, up, down, and diagonally. After you loop all the cities and towns, the remaining letters will reveal the name of the state, its nickname, state flower, state bird, and state tree.

Mystery State on page 284

Solution on page 283

ACTON	BRAINTREE	FALMOUTH	LOWELL	SALEM
ADAMS	BROOKLINE	FRAMINGHAM	LYNN	SAUGUS
AGAWAM	CAMBRIDGE	GLOUCESTER	MARBLEHEAD	SHIRLEY
AMHERST	CHELSEA	HARVARD	MAYNARD	SOMERVILLE
ANDOVER	CHICOPEE	HULL	NEWTON	STOW
AVON	CONCORD	LAWRENCE	OXFORD	SUDBURY
BEVERLY	DANVERS	LEXINGTON	PEABODY	WELLESLEY
BILLERICA	DEDHAM	LINCOLN	READING	WESTON

```
M M M A W A G A N A P L H S S A C A C T O N H
B A Y U A N D O V E R Y I A D E D H A M S D F
O R E R I T T A A O N T E N R S B A M Y S R T
X B A D U G L B M C N I L L C V A T B E A O S
F L A I N B O L H S E M L H S O A A R M Y C R
O E F I N D D E E L W O I K Y E L R I H S N E
R H X W Y T L U R W T C V E O L L N D R U O V
D E C H L S R I S T O W R C U O G L G K G C N
L A W R E N C E T P N L E H A H R D E E U E A
A D R A N Y A M E L A S M M A E R B I W A C D
A N Y L R E V E B H T U O M L A F N O T S E W
E L R E T S E C U O L G S B I L L E R I C A M
```

WORD MATH

In these long-division problems letters are substituted for numbers. Determine the value of each letter. Then arrange the letters in order from 0 to 9, and they will spell a word or phrase.

Solutions on page 284

1.

```
                    TOY      0 __
      YOU | DETOUR           1 __
                             2 __
            DRRC             3 __
            OEOU             4 __
             YOU             5 __
             YCCR            6 __
                             7 __
             ELDU            8 __
              KKO            9 __
```

2.

```
                    POT      0 __
      OTTO | PRINTER         1 __
                             2 __
             MUUMR           3 __
             IMPTE           4 __
             TNUMM           5 __
                             6 __
             PSEIR           7 __
             PSRRO           8 __
               ETS           9 __
```

3.

```
                    TEA      0 __
      PEAR | REPORT          1 __
                             2 __
             OOOC            3 __
             CCLR            4 __
             ELCO            5 __
                             6 __
             OEPT            7 __
             TAPU            8 __
              ASC            9 __
```

4.

```
                    ELM      0 __
      CHUM | MUSCLES         1 __
                             2 __
             MICUW           3 __
             EMILE           4 __
             EWSMM           5 __
                             6 __
             HKSIS           7 __
             HHMKL           8 __
              EUIL           9 __
```

5.

```
                    TEA      0 __
      TORN | DONATES         1 __
                             2 __
             NTTOA           3 __
             DETAE           4 __
             DUEUO           5 __
                             6 __
             DKTTS           7 __
             DAAUD           8 __
              ADO            9 __
```

6.

```
                    SET      0 __
      LAID | STUBBLE         1 __
                             2 __
             IBSSD           3 __
             LSTBL           4 __
             BBUED           5 __
                             6 __
             TDLLE           7 __
             UPDTD           8 __
              BLPE           9 __
```

Secret Word

Discover the 5-letter Secret Words by the process of elimination and deduction. Fill in the blanks with the 5-letter answer words to the clues. The number in parentheses next to each answer word tells you how many of the letters in that word are also in the Secret Word. A zero next to an answer word indicates that not one of the letters in that word is also in the Secret Word. After you have determined the correct 5 letters, rearrange them to form the Secret Word. No letter is repeated in any Secret Word or within any answer word. The first letters of the answer words, reading down, spell out a hint to the Secret Word.

Solutions on page 284

1. Secret Word ☐ ☐ ☐ ☐ ☐

Broad comedy	_ _ _ _ _	(0)
Subsequently	_ _ _ _ _	(1)
Prods	_ _ _ _ _	(2)
Is a match for	_ _ _ _ _	(3)
Spew forth	_ _ _ _ _	(3)
Robes of office	_ _ _ _ _	(3)

2. Secret Word ☐ ☐ ☐ ☐ ☐

Data	_ _ _ _ _	(3)
Frequently	_ _ _ _ _	(2)
Farther down	_ _ _ _ _	(2)
Shoestrings	_ _ _ _ _	(3)
Proprietor	_ _ _ _ _	(2)
Eats greedily	_ _ _ _ _	(0)

3. Secret Word ☐ ☐ ☐ ☐ ☐

Unites	_ _ _ _ _	(1)
Harden	_ _ _ _ _	(1)
Quartet member	_ _ _ _ _	(0)
Winning card	_ _ _ _ _	(3)
Take pleasure in	_ _ _ _ _	(2)
Sloping walks	_ _ _ _ _	(2)
Desire greatly	_ _ _ _ _	(1)

4. Secret Word ☐ ☐ ☐ ☐ ☐

Songstress Lena	_ _ _ _ _	(0)
___ acid	_ _ _ _ _	(3)
Destroys	_ _ _ _ _	(1)
Cash	_ _ _ _ _	(2)
Vows	_ _ _ _ _	(2)
Yankeedom	_ _ _ _ _	(1)
Salad days	_ _ _ _ _	(2)

5. Secret Word ☐ ☐ ☐ ☐ ☐

Vine fruit	_ _ _ _ _	(2)
Cheek cosmetic	_ _ _ _ _	(0)
Got up	_ _ _ _ _	(1)
Grin	_ _ _ _ _	(2)
Backbone	_ _ _ _ _	(3)
Enormous	_ _ _ _ _	(2)
Change a law	_ _ _ _ _	(2)
Poke	_ _ _ _ _	(1)
Trash heaps	_ _ _ _ _	(1)

6. Secret Word ☐ ☐ ☐ ☐ ☐

Wireless set	_ _ _ _ _	(1)
Revises copy	_ _ _ _ _	(3)
Pine Tree State	_ _ _ _ _	(2)
Permeate	_ _ _ _ _	(1)
Hospital worker	_ _ _ _ _	(3)
Asset balance	_ _ _ _ _	(2)
Arab princes	_ _ _ _ _	(2)
Mad, as a dog	_ _ _ _ _	(0)
Not drunk	_ _ _ _ _	(3)

MASTERWORDS

Using only the 10 letters given below, fill in the diagram by forming words across and down to achieve the highest possible score. Each letter has a given value, so try to use the high-value letters as much as possible. You may repeat letters as often as you wish, even within words. Do not repeat words in the diagram. Foreign words, abbreviations, and words starting with a capital letter are not allowed.

When the diagram is completely filled, add up your score. Count across only, each letter, line by line. Put the total for each line in the boxes at the right.

Our solution with a score of 354 on page 284

A	E	G	I	K	L	N	O	R	Y
4	2	5	3	1	1	5	3	4	2

SCORE

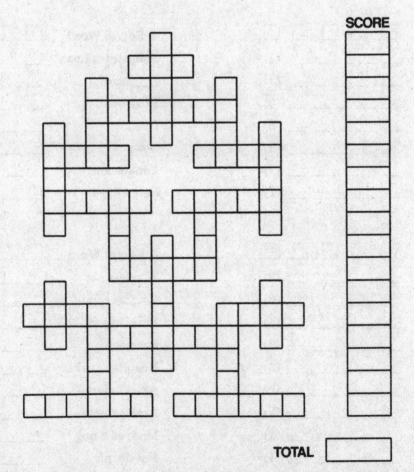

TOTAL

ALPHABET SOUP

Insert a different letter of the alphabet into each of the 26 empty boxes to form words of five or more letters reading across. The letter you insert may be at the beginning, the end, or in the middle of the word. Each letter of the alphabet will be used only once. Cross off each letter in the list as you use it. All the letters in each row are not necessarily used in forming the word.

Our solution on page 284

Example: In the first row across we have inserted the letter W to form the word ANSWER.

| A B C D E F G H I J K L M N O P Q R S T U V W X Y Z |

```
C A L A N S W E R   A S K S
C H O R R I     L E A C N S
U L C H O W     E R O S E S
A T E T O R     O R R E C T
N E D A I L     M P A D E S
D A U T H O     R S O U T H
A D I R E C     M A N A G E
E A N G E E     G E R A T E
F A I R E F     I C I E N T
F R I D A E     E N T T N E
G N E R V O     S C I E N C
M I S T A E     C I T I N G
H A P P F O     G Y E L L O
P R O F O O     T R A W G S
G E N E R A     W H E N E V
S K I E S S     O D I A C E
C O L O R E     A I N T R E
C O N P E R     A N E N T T
T I G E R S     U I C K I N
A C O R E S     I N G L E X
A S I M P L     P L A I N E
N E W S M O     Y A U N A J
S T R A I G     T U M M Y S
R U E S F R     S T I P M O
W I N D W O     D E R U M S
A D E L I C     O U S T E N
```

PUZZLE IN THE ROUND

To solve this challenging puzzle, first fill in as many of the five-letter answers next to their clues as you can. Next, scramble the order of the letters, look for shared letters, and enter each letter into its correct place in the diagram. Words will share letters as indicated by the lines in the diagram. For example, the letter in the center will be shared by all the answer words. The unshared letters will go in the outer ring and form a tourist attraction, reading from 1 to 24.   Solution on page 284

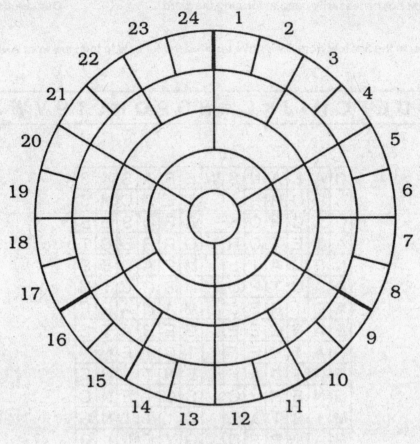

CLUES

1. Shut   _ _ _ _ _

2. Untethered   _ _ _ _ _

3. Chimes   _ _ _ _ _

4. Tree trunks   _ _ _ _ _

5. Memento   _ _ _ _ _

6. Wonderland girl   _ _ _ _ _

7. Wrinkled   _ _ _ _ _

8. Liquid part of fat   _ _ _ _ _

9. Eatery   _ _ _ _ _

10. Made public   _ _ _ _ _

11. Instant   _ _ _ _ _

12. More frigid   _ _ _ _ _

13. Waken   _ _ _ _ _

14. Hospital worker   _ _ _ _ _

15. Get up   _ _ _ _ _

16. Foxier   _ _ _ _ _

17. Lion trainer   _ _ _ _ _

18. Horse opera   _ _ _ _ _

19. Male singer   _ _ _ _ _

20. Course traveled   _ _ _ _ _

21. Solid element   _ _ _ _ _

22. Gladden   _ _ _ _ _

23. Tilts   _ _ _ _ _

24. Unfresh   _ _ _ _ _

MIXMASTER

A quotation is concealed in this Mixmaster diagram. To reveal it, first write the 5-letter answers next to their clues. Next, locate the answers in the diagram and cross off their letters, crossing off one letter from each square Across or Down as indicated. The clues are not given in the order they appear in the diagram. The leftover letters (there will be one in each square) will spell out a phrase, reading left to right, line by line.

Solution on page 284

A.

ACROSS
a. Happen _ _ _ _ _
b. Send a note _ _ _ _ _
c. Damp _ _ _ _ _
d. Pointed _ _ _ _ _
e. Beneath _ _ _ _ _

DOWN
a. Pleasure craft _ _ _ _ _
b. European country _ _ _ _ _
c. Quit _ _ _ _ _
d. Wash _ _ _ _ _
e. Subject _ _ _ _ _

	1	2	3	4	5
1	C S	H T A	C I N	C A R	S T Y P
	C	H	C	C	S
1	S T A I N	A R T Y P			
2	M O	T E O	T E I	H L E	T S E A
3	W O	C P O	E A C	D O A	C U R F
4	I O	R U N	D L A	S T H	R E H E
5	T W	R C Y	N R E	T I E	S E E T

(Grid A, top letter over each square, bottom row of 5-letter rows:)

Row 1: C H C C S / S T A I N A R T Y P
Row 2: M T T H T / O E O E I L E S E A
Row 3: W C E D C / O P O A C O A U R F
Row 4: I R D S R / O U N L A T H E H E
Row 5: T R N T S / W C Y R E I E E E T

B.

ACROSS
a. Rap _ _ _ _ _
b. Watch's place _ _ _ _ _
c. Adult _ _ _ _ _
d. African animal _ _ _ _ _
e. Thickest finger _ _ _ _ _

DOWN
a. Ogle _ _ _ _ _
b. Strumming instrument _ _ _ _ _
c. Express, for one _ _ _ _ _
d. Picture _ _ _ _ _
e. Take the car _ _ _ _ _

	1	2	3	4	5

Row 1: T R I T D / B G A S K O W E T N
Row 2: W E W S T / A H T R M I I R R N
Row 3: D A A R I / Z N O E U B A T A O
Row 4: F N N C K / J K R O G O I E S V
Row 5: S H E N B / T O A E U I M L S E

COMMON COMBOS

The answer for each group can either precede or follow each of the given words.

Solutions on page 284

1. Cart	Course	Ball	Miniature	_____
2. Typing	Term	Back	Clip	_____
3. Camp	Squash	School	Indian	_____
4. Cage	Jail	Bath	Blue	_____
5. Chuck	Fire	Alcohol	Work	_____

LOGIC PROBLEM

IN THE CARDS

Belinda received many cards for her birthday, and she lined them up on the top two shelves of her bookcase, as pictured below. Each card was from a different person and had a different picture on the front. From the information provided, can you determine the person (one was Foster and another was Ida) who sent the card in each position (A through N) and the picture on the front of it (one was a ship and another was irises)?

1. The identification letter of each card, the initial of its sender, and the initial of the picture on it are three different letters of the alphabet.

2. Noelle's card is directly below the one with the picture of balloons, which has the card with parrots to its immediate left.

3. Eddie's card (with a picture of children playing) is to the immediate right of the one of geese and directly above Jill's, which has Olive's (which is not of bells) to its immediate left.

4. Betty's card is to the immediate right of Vicki's, which has a picture of trees, and directly below Rita's.

5. Peter's card has a rainbow on it. Alan's is farther left than George's.

6. Martin's card is K. Card E has a picture of peacocks on it.

7. The roses are directly above the tiger. The one of dogs is in the top row.

8. Wendy's card is directly above the one with the mouse on it.

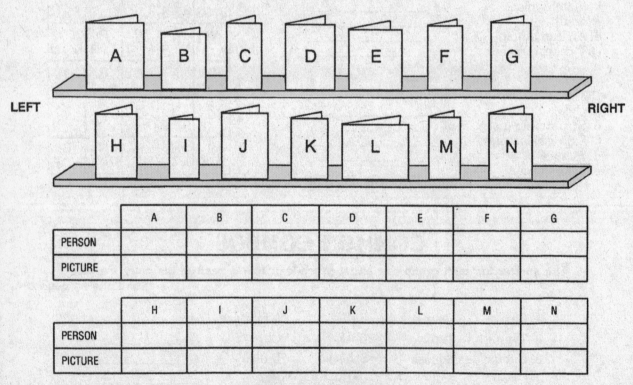

	A	B	C	D	E	F	G
PERSON							
PICTURE							

	H	I	J	K	L	M	N
PERSON							
PICTURE							

Solution on page 284

"QUOTEFALLS"

The letters in each vertical column go into the squares directly below them, but not necessarily in the order they appear. A black square indicates the end of a word. When you have placed all the letters in their correct squares, you will be able to read a quotation across the diagram from left to right.

Solutions on page 285

1.

U	M	B	L	D	O	I	N	N	J	C	R	E	A	R	E
U	O	O	R	E		N	O	T	O	F	S	H	E	S	E
Y	T	U	U	E		O	T	U		U	T	T	U	T	F
	Y	U		R		Y	W				U				T

2.

A	A	E	H	E	A	E	L	A	A	G	H	C	A	N	D	M
A	I	S	M	I	L	E	N	H	O	L	I	O	A	N	G	
D	K	T		W	O	R	T	Y	U	U	L	V	I	S	Y	
W		Y			V				U				U			

3.

P	E	O	B	A	B	E	A	R	N	H	A	E	F	T	A	E	D	E	E	F	A	E
S	F	F	H	L	D	H	O	U	O	O	H	F	I	N	G	O	I	F	I	I	H	L
	R	O	R	O	P	L	S	O	R	S	N	I	S	G	H	I	R	I	R	R	S	T
	W		U	R			Y		T	U	O			M				N		T		

4.

D	A	A	A	C	A	L	C	D	N	F	M	A	E	E	F	L	E	E	A	E	I	E	A
I	L	L	T	G	A	O	O	H	N	M	O	F	K	O	N	H	E	F	F	R	T	H	N
N	S	R			S	P	R	O	S		O	L		V	I	N	G	N	N	R	Y		W
T					W	T	R	O			U	R					I	O	S				

SUNRAYS

Form 4-letter words using only the nine letters in the center of the diagram. Do not repeat a letter within a word. Place your words into the rays of the diagram so that no two words which are next to each other share a letter.

Our solution on page 285

TAKE A LETTER

The names of 12 Christmas terms are hidden in the 4-letter words. In the first row across Take a Letter from each word from left to right to spell one Christmas term; choose a different letter from each word to spell another; and choose one more to spell a third. One letter of each 4-letter word will be left unused. Do the same for the other rows, spelling the names of three Christmas terms in each one.

Solutions on page 285

1.	COWS	RASP	RICE	ROAD	TILT	SHUT
2.	SLIP	PICK	GRIN	MUCH	COLT	SEED
3.	RIMS	BAIT	BRAN	GLIB	TONE	RANG
4.	HOST	LINE	RENT	SAIL	GALE	HOLD

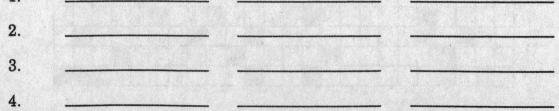

1. _____   _____   _____

2. _____   _____   _____

3. _____   _____   _____

4. _____   _____   _____

SPANNERS

Place each of the 4-letter groups into the diagram between two of the given letters to form a 6-letter word. Form one 6-letter word in each line. Words read across only. Not all the given letters in the diagram will be used in forming words.

Solution on page 285

Groups		Grid (letters read across)
ADIO		R . . . D . . . S
AILO		. I . . . E . . C
AISI		. A . . I . . I .
ANCI		H . . F . . T . .
AUCE		C . . I . S . . .
AVIN		. . T . . I . . H
DIOM		. N . . R . . S .
ENUR		. E . . E . U . .
GUAN		D . . T . . R . .
HERU		I . . C . B . . .
LAPS		. . A . . T . . E
LKAL		. R . . N . . C .
MPIS		. A . . I . A . .
RCHE		H . . A . . R . .
THNI		C . . P . G . . .

IN OTHER WORDS

First, place the answers to the clues into the boxes next to them. Next, rearrange all the letters in all the boxes with the number 1 to form the first word of the phrase on the right; rearrange all the letters with the number 2 to form the second word. The answers to the clues, reading from top to bottom, form an appropriate message about the phrase.

Solution on page 285

Myself — [1]

Observe — [2][2][1]

Science of government — [1][2][1][2][1][1][2][1]

Come in — [2][1][2][1][1]

Country — [2][1][2][1]

1 — [ ][ ][ ][ ][ ][ ][ ][ ][ ][ ][ ][ ][ ]

2 — [ ][ ][ ][ ][ ][ ][ ][ ][ ][ ]

203

STRETCH LETTERS

These words, listed alphabetically by length, are to be entered in the diagram across only. Words do not read down. When writing in a blank taller than a square, stretch the letter to the full height of the blank. The stretched letters are part of more than one entry.   Solution on page 285

• MYTHOLOGICAL CREATURES •

4 Letters
Ares
Eros
Isis
Juno
Loki
Odin
Zeus

5 Letters
Assur
Coeus
Crius
Freya
Pluto
Woden

6 Letters
Apollo
Cronus
Gudrun
Helios
Hermes
Saturn

Sigurd
Themis
Uranus
Vulcan

7 Letters
Artemis
Astarte
Cyclops
Jupiter
Minerva
Nycteus

8 Letters
Brynhild
Dionysus
Hyperion
Poseidon

9 Letters
Aphrodite
Ashtoreth
Mnemosyne

SPELL & SCORE

Choose letters from the LETTERBOX moving only from left to right to complete words of three to six letters starting with the given letters. Use the LETTERBOX only for the letters you add, not the given letters. Cross off each letter as you use it. Only common English words are allowed. For example, the first word could be GET, GLOW, GLAND, and many others, but it cannot be GHOUL.

TO SCORE: When you have formed all your words, score 10 points for each completed word, then subtract 2 points for each letter in the LETTERBOX which you have not used. Not all words will be six letters long to achieve a perfect score. A score of 60-69 is fair, 70-79 is average, 80-89 is good, and 90-100 is excellent.   Our solution with a perfect score of 100 on page 285

LETTERBOX

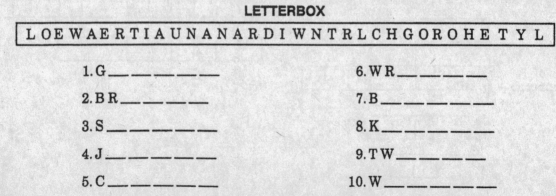

L O E W A E R T I A U N A N A R D I W N T R L C H G O R O H E T Y L

1. G __ __ __ __   6. W R __ __ __ __

2. B R __ __ __ __   7. B __ __ __ __ __

3. S __ __ __ __ __   8. K __ __ __ __ __

4. J __ __ __ __   9. T W __ __ __ __

5. C __ __ __ __ __   10. W __ __ __ __ __

PICTURE THIS

You do not need any special art training to produce a picture in the empty grid. Use the letter-number guide above each square and carefully draw what is shown into the corresponding square in the grid.

Solution on page 285

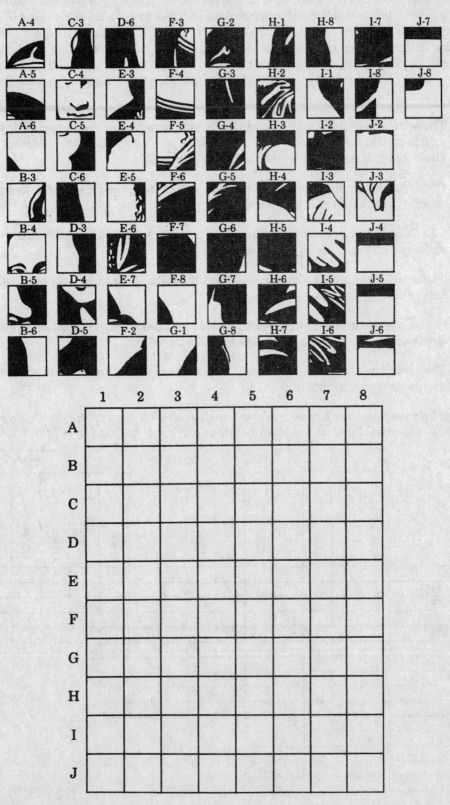

LOGIC PROBLEM

FAR AND WIDE

The staff of *Far and Wide* travel magazine is in the process of planning next year's editorial calendar. The calendar will list the three feature stories that will appear in each monthly issue of *Far and Wide*. Each issue will contain a story on a different U.S. state, a different foreign country, and a different outdoor activity. So far, feature stories have been planned for the issues being published in August, September, October, November, and December. From the information provided, determine the state (one is Texas), country, and activity to be featured in each of the monthly issues from August to December.

1. The article on Maine will appear in an earlier issue than the one containing both the article on Ohio and the one on hiking (which won't appear in the same issue as either the article on Italy or the article on Greece).

2. Of the August and September issues, one will contain the article on Britain and the other will contain the article on skiing.

3. The December issue (which will contain the article on France) will include the article on either camping or horseback riding.

4. The article on Italy and the article on sailing will appear in different issues. Neither will appear in the October issue.

5. Of the issues containing articles on Florida and Iowa, one will contain the article on Spain and the other will contain the article on sailing.

6. The issue containing the article on Florida won't include the article on Greece or the article on horseback riding.

This chart is to help you record information from the clues as well as the facts you deduce by combining information from different clues. We suggest you use an "X" for a "no" and a "•" for a "yes."

		STATE					COUNTRY					ACTIVITY				
		FLORIDA	IOWA	MAINE	OHIO	TEXAS	BRITAIN	FRANCE	GREECE	ITALY	SPAIN	CAMPING	HIKING	RIDING	SAILING	SKIING
MONTH	AUGUST															
	SEPTEMBER															
	OCTOBER															
	NOVEMBER															
	DECEMBER															
ACTIVITY	CAMPING															
	HIKING															
	RIDING															
	SAILING															
	SKIING															
COUNTRY	BRITAIN															
	FRANCE															
	GREECE															
	ITALY															
	SPAIN															

Solution on page 285

ALPHABET SOUP

Insert a different letter of the alphabet into each of the 26 empty boxes to form words of five or more letters reading across. The letter you insert may be at the beginning, the end, or in the middle of the word. Each letter of the alphabet will be used only once. Cross off each letter in the list as you use it. All the letters in each row are not necessarily used in forming the word.

Our solution on page 285

Example: In the first row across insert the letter H and form the word DELIGHT.

A B C D E F G H I J K L M N O P Q R S T U V W X Y Z

A	D	E	L	I	G		T	I	G	R	E	S
E	V	E	E	R	E		U	S	E	I	N	G
K	O	R	E	L	A		S	E	T	A	B	E
R	E	J	E	N	T		I	R	L	D	E	R
B	R	O	W	R	E		U	I	R	E	V	E
I	N	T	E	R	V		E	W	A	T	L	E
C	E	N	P	I	E		C	E	N	T	A	L
A	M	E	N	D	O		O	I	S	T	X	T
W	R	A	B	I	M		R	O	V	I	S	E
L	A	B	R	E	A		F	A	S	T	K	E
R	I	V	P	I	T		H	E	R	M	E	O
Y	O	Z	O	N	V		I	C	E	T	E	N
O	B	E	A	F	A		I	L	I	E	S	Y
S	C	H	N	A	U		E	R	Q	U	I	K
O	P	E	L	O	Y		L	D	R	I	N	G
J	U	S	D	I	N		E	R	N	A	P	E
A	X	E	X	P	E		S	E	O	Y	A	L
T	W	E	N	S	T		E	W	E	L	D	R
V	I	O	L	E	H		N	G	R	Y	T	S
E	X	P	E	R	N		F	F	O	R	T	Y
L	A	S	C	H	E		U	L	E	V	E	D
N	E	O	D	O	F		O	U	N	D	E	R
H	E	A	R	R	E		A	I	N	T	E	A
L	O	A	R	S	U		P	E	N	S	E	Y
H	O	L	I	D	A		S	T	A	M	Y	L
F	L	O	S	O	L		E	W	E	R	I	N

CRYPTO-FAMILIES

Each Crypto-Family is a list of related words in code. Each family has its own code. When you have identified a word, use the known letters to help decode the other words in the family.

Solutions on page 285

1. IN THE CLASSROOM
Example: Table

FDOJPBZE

BZUFSZE

GBPHZVBG

GZUBG

NMUFYNDUEH

ZEUGZE

NDDYG

HZGY

OUJG

FSUMY

2. WORK
Example: Perform

AFCNQ

FCTLV

KLDF

HVYHOQ

AKVDNQ

AKVYOOFQ

LIQVCKQ

ABQCK

IVLHYMQ

QZHQCNLV

3. JOBS TODAY
Example: Electrician

BZETKPD

TPHRSLMH

HZPDI

PCMFWD

KSDKPD

SDHRMFPHF

HSDBPLFPD

TSVWL

JPZCPD

FDEHIPD

4. SCHOOL SUBJECTS
Example: Geometry

KSADLJC

CLJVWZI

OZLVCTKVLU

UCKTLJVZI

DOVLS

AKWAZOXCI

ULFLUJ

ODAKEZO

XCIJLUJ

JWULWDWAI

5. ARTS AND CRAFTS
Example: Woodworking

ICFHMDOQ

YCGOCYM

TBEKDEZJ

WMGNBRCJM

GMOCYEGF

MYIONEWMOQ

NOEJCYE

ZMMWKMRNEZD

GCKKEJOCRXQ

ICDEH

6. JOBS OF OLD
Example: Crofter

HKCESGIL

LIRLCDIL

NMLLWIL

HKCZFCE

HCFJWAD

NGIDHKIL

AGMJJIL

TCWETLWRKD

CLFBLIL

ACSSGIL

FILL-IN

The entries for this puzzle are given to you, listed alphabetically according to length. Across and Down words are all mixed together, and you are to find their proper places in the diagram.

Solution on page 285

3 Letters
Ace
Ail
Ale
Ave
Die
Duo
Erg
Lie
Men
Nor
Pre
War

4 Letters
Abas
Ante
Eria
Errs
Heel
Lace
Lave
Mete
Miss
Oven
Over
Seer
Sess
Slap
Sled ✓
Star

5 Letters
Abide
Aired

Alert
Aping
Arete
Arrow
Aside
Asset
Beats
Bergs
Class
Death
Drank
Eager
Eagle
Edits
Elect
Emits
Evert
Gates
Gnats
Hails
Hairs
Ideal
Ideas
Lairs
Likes
Marks
Moist
Naive
Nines
Niter
Notes
Octet
Olive
Orate
Ounce

Pease
Pulls
Reset
Riled
Rives
Robes
Scent
Sepal
Serge
Shale
Shiva
Slash

Smote
State
Stere
Sties
Swain
Taker
Trend
Truce
Twine
Twist
Wails
Waist

Weave
Worst
Wrest

6 Letters
Arrest
Casino
Chewed
Deeded
Egress
Plants
Plates

Resist
Rooted
Senses
Stress
Teases

7 Letters
Aerates
Antenna
Avarice
Detests
Elaters

Etamine
Evasion
Labored
Ledgers
Parades
Reasons
Resides
Secrete
Serrate
Steward
Triplet

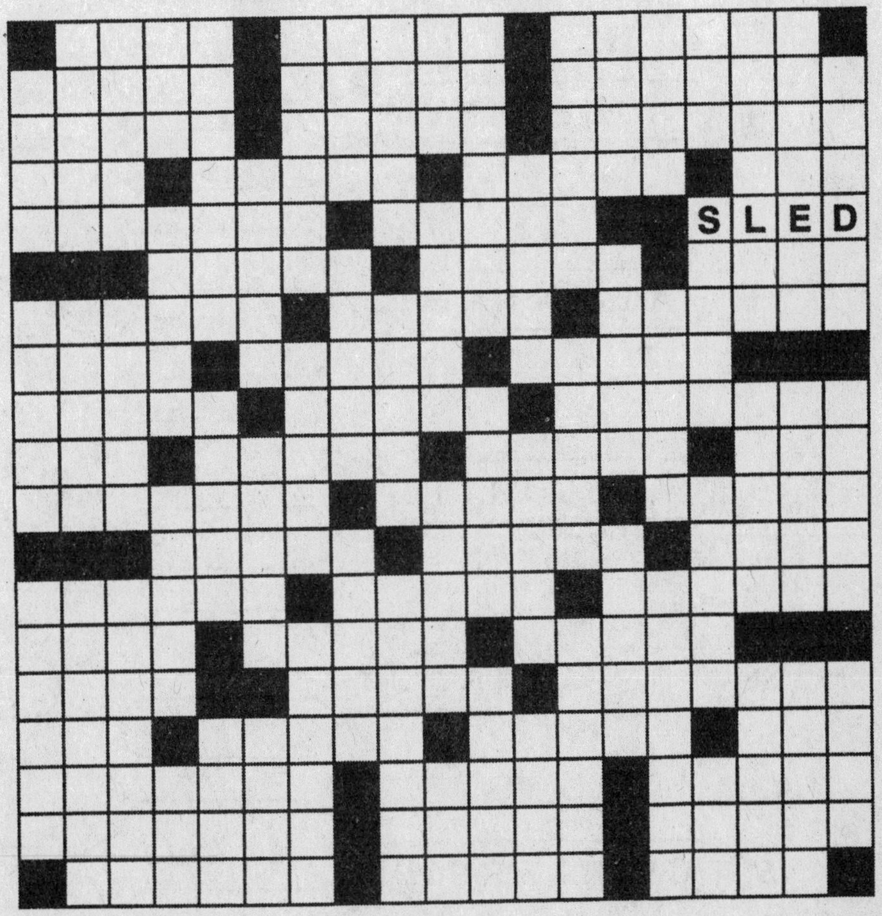

(Grid showing "SLED" filled in)

WORD MERGERS

Rearrange the letters in each Word Merger to form two words using all the given letters only once. Then rearrange the same letters and merge them into one long word. You might want to form the long word first and then the pair of words. Score 5 points for each pair of words you form and 10 points for each long word. A score of 85 is good, 95 is very good, and 105 is excellent.

Our solutions with a perfect score of 120 points on page 285

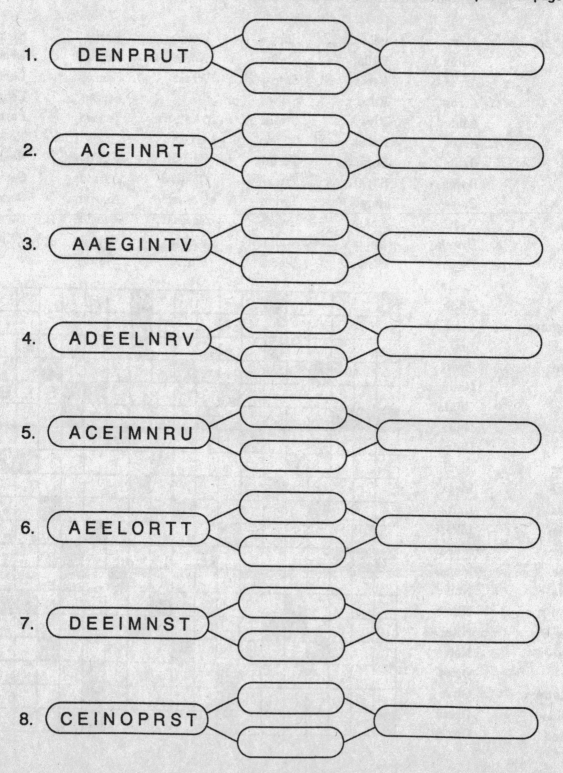

1. DENPRUT

2. ACEINRT

3. AAEGINTV

4. ADEELNRV

5. ACEIMNRU

6. AEELORTT

7. DEEIMNST

8. CEINOPRST

SYL˝LA-CROS´TIC

The directions for solving are given on page 105. Solution on page 285

✳ SYLLABOX ✳

A A AL AR CAS CAS CI CON COT DEN DER DIC ~~DOW~~ EN EN ~~EN~~
EP EX FIED FIL GIOT GUAY GULF I I I IN LEM LIEF LIP LIST
MAKE ME MENT NEG NOR NU NUN O O ON OR OT PER RE REN
RO SOR SUS TA TAGE TAR TER THET TI TIVE TO TO TOR TRO U
U UP UR WA Y YON

1. Bequeath — (2) E N D O W
2. Florentine painter — (2) __ __ __ __ __ __
3. Citrus fruit — (2) __ __ __ __ __ __
4. Descriptive phrase — (3) __ __ __ __ __
5. Turkish city — (2) __ __ __ __ __
6. Test — (4) __ __ __ __ __ __ __ __ __
7. Juliet's love — (3) __ __ __ __ __
8. Cosmetics — (2) __ __ __ __ __ __
9. Blood vessel — (3) __ __ __ __ __
10. Papal messenger — (3) __ __ __ __ __
11. Fresh-water trout — (3) __ __ __ __ __
12. Gesture of the hand — (2) __ __ __ __ __ __
13. Farther — (2) __ __ __ __ __
14. Canadian capital — (3) __ __ __ __ __
15. South American nation — (3) __ __ __ __ __
16. Respite — (2) __ __ __ __ __
17. Cuban ruler — (2) __ __ __ __ __
18. Public speaker — (3) __ __ __ __ __
19. Scandinavian — (2) __ __ __ __ __
20. Italian seaport — (3) __ __ __ __ __ __
21. Informal — (3) __ __ __ __ __
22. Recognized — (4) __ __ __ __ __ __ __ __ __
23. Surround — (2) __ __ __ __ __
24. Expressing a denial — (3) __ __ __ __ __ __
25. Small dwelling — (2) __ __ __ __ __ __
26. Sign up for service — (2) __ __ __ __ __ __

SYLLACROSTICS SOLVERS! *Enjoy loads of entertaining puzzles in each special collection of Selected Syllacrostics. See page 61 for details.*

ANAGRAM MAGIC SQUARE

Find an anagram for the 5-letter word in each box. The anagram will answer one of the clues. Put the number of that clue into the small square and write the anagram on the dash. The numbers in each row and column will add up to 65. Write the first letter of each anagram on the correspondingly numbered dash at the bottom of the page; and, presto!, the Anagram Magic saying will appear. To start you off, we have put in one anagram and its clue number and set its first letter on the proper dash at the bottom of the page.

Solution on page 285

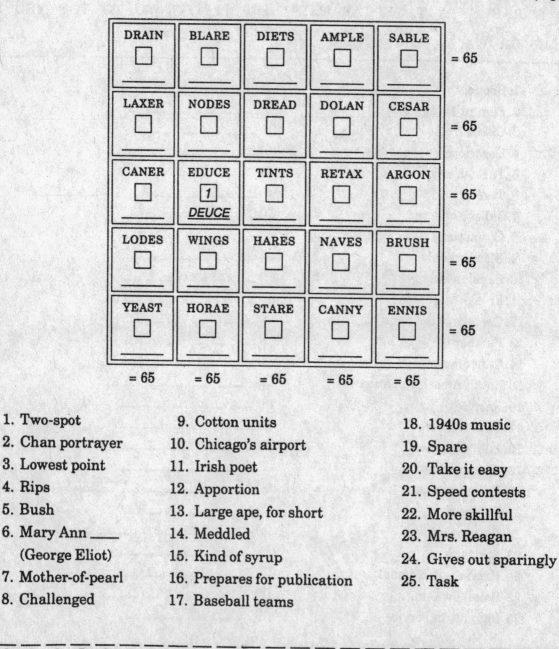

DRAIN ☐	BLARE ☐	DIETS ☐	AMPLE ☐	SABLE ☐	= 65
LAXER ☐	NODES ☐	DREAD ☐	DOLAN ☐	CESAR ☐	= 65
CANER ☐	EDUCE ☐ 1 *DEUCE*	TINTS ☐	RETAX ☐	ARGON ☐	= 65
LODES ☐	WINGS ☐	HARES ☐	NAVES ☐	BRUSH ☐	= 65
YEAST ☐	HORAE ☐	STARE ☐	CANNY ☐	ENNIS ☐	= 65

= 65 = 65 = 65 = 65 = 65

1. Two-spot
2. Chan portrayer
3. Lowest point
4. Rips
5. Bush
6. Mary Ann _____ (George Eliot)
7. Mother-of-pearl
8. Challenged
9. Cotton units
10. Chicago's airport
11. Irish poet
12. Apportion
13. Large ape, for short
14. Meddled
15. Kind of syrup
16. Prepares for publication
17. Baseball teams
18. 1940s music
19. Spare
20. Take it easy
21. Speed contests
22. More skillful
23. Mrs. Reagan
24. Gives out sparingly
25. Task

D __
  1 2 3 4 5 6 7 8 9 10 11 12 13 14 15 16 17 18 19 20 21 22 23 24 25

CIRCLES IN THE SQUARE

The twenty 5-letter words all fit in the diagram. All words begin and end in a dark circle. Horizontal words read from left to right; all other words read from top to bottom.

Solution on page 285

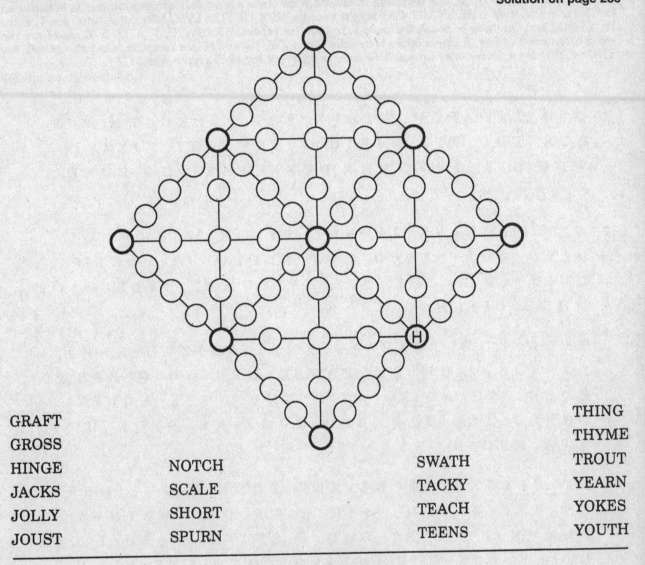

GRAFT			THING
GROSS			THYME
HINGE	NOTCH	SWATH	TROUT
JACKS	SCALE	TACKY	YEARN
JOLLY	SHORT	TEACH	YOKES
JOUST	SPURN	TEENS	YOUTH

Letterdrop

Discover the sayings concealed in these lines. Drop one letter in each pair and decide where words begin and end.

Solutions on page 285

1. VA OW RA ET LC HY EK DU PA LO AT UN RE VR ME RO AB GO IB AL SY.

2. OL TE AW OV DE WY ME OL LA GE NY AO UM NG HO PA LU OM IN DE.

Each of these cryptograms is a message in substitution code. One letter of the alphabet is substituted for the correct letter. THE SMART CAT might become MRX DGYUM LYM. M is substituted for T, R for H, X for E, etc. One way to break the code is to look for repeated letters. E, T, A, O, N, R, and I are the most often used letters. A single letter is usually A or I; OF, IS, and IT are common two-letter words; try THE or AND for a three-letter group. The code is different for each cryptogram.

Solutions on page 286

1. G T K   X J W A P C U   W T D P X   F D I   P C L K C G K N   S J X
   G T K   E D C   F T J   N J K I C ' G   C K K N   G J   F J X A ,
   W D C ' G   I P G   I G P H H ,   D C N   H P A K I   G J   E D A K
   C J P I K .

2. W ' P   S H M L A Y X   I A   O U L   B I M J E   W   E H F ,   O I
   D L L C   O U L P   E I A O   H V J   E B L L O .   W   V L G L M
   D V I B   A M I P   J H F   O I   J H F   B U W S U   I V L E   W ' X X
   U H G L   O I   L H O .

3. T N B G   K U W   T Q Z H   A G   X N B   J Q S H   A G   X N B
   D J S A G E ,   K U W   S B Q Z A V B   Z U P B   A D   Q   E S B Q X
   E Q L B .   A G   R Q I X ,   A X ' D   X N B   U G Z K   E Q L B
   T N B S B   X N B   J Z Q K B S D   T Q G X   X U   D X Q K   U G
   X N B   F B G I N .

4. R F   O I K C F G K   T C K Z   K Z F   P C N H   T Z S   T I H B V
   K S   K Z F   Q N S G K   V F I K   H I K F   Q S N   W Z Y N W Z   C G
   S N M F N   K S   V Z S T   S Q Q   I   G F T   Z I K .   C G   I   Q F T
   L F I N V   V Z F   T C H H   M N S O   C G K S   K Z F   R I W B
   V F I K   K S   P F K   S Y K   J Y C W B H L   C Q   K Z F   R I R L
   W N C F V .

5. D   B F E C W   Z S L Z X V   M Y K X   F Y G Z   D S W   G D H Z V
   V Y   G K B F   S Y E V Z   P Y X   L N Z S L M   M Z D X V   M Y K
   B D S   F D X W C M   V L D S W   E L — L F Z S   W Z O D X L V ,
   C Z D Q E S J   L F Z   F Y K V Z   V Y   V E C Z S L   M Y K
   L F E S H   M Y K   N E C C   J Y   G D W .

6. ZC BIVRRX ILTCX ZWI OIZZIB ZWSLAG SL
   RSUI, CLI DJGZ USBGZ WVHI INMIBSILQIP
   ZWI ZWSLAG ZWIX VBI OIZZIB ZWVL.

7. NPVPVDPN JRF RJTS FR WUS FLP NBOLF
   FLBJO BJ FLP NBOLF ZTUAP, DIF KUN
   VRNP XBKKBAITF WFBTT, FR TPUYP
   IJWUBX FLP CNRJO FLBJO UF FLP
   FPVZFBJO VRVPJF.

8. QT UPBT GA HTPFE GA CT ADF AQE CTIG
   KFZTENI CTSPDIT QT KPHH GAA TPIZHR
   ZEGA GUT GFPW AK CTZEV ADF AQE QAFIG
   TETOZTI.

9. POYOD EDAKO ES SVO QGPPOD SEWNO,
   TBD SVO BPO FVB GR PBS VKPADX ENFEXR
   AOSR SVO WORS BT SVO EDAKLOPS.

10. WIGLXA YZT RTSLBLQX YQ ZICT I SZLPR——
    LY'B WQWTXYQHB. LY LB YQ RTSLRT
    JQMTCTM YQ ZICT UQHM ZTIMY AQ
    EIPGLXA IMQHXR QHYBLRT UQHM OQRU.

11. K FYGZ LQB LFQ QYJZB YH KH LKW; UVZ
    NLEZ VZ GKF UVZ QZGG VZ GDLWZ; UVZ
    QZGG VZ GDLWZ UVZ NLEZ VZ VZKEB: FVT
    PKH'U FZ KQQ SZ QYWZ UVKU SYEB?

12. ZIMIW FSLL HZ KRRKWXVZSXU XK FHJI
    KXNIWL NHRRU——IMIZ SY UKV NHMI XK
    QIHMI XNIF HQKZI XK OK SX.

13. XZD'S PB UZDUBKSBX. QLGS PBUMLGB
    IZL'TB GKSSKDO KD SVB YTZDS GBMS
    XZBGD'S NBMD IZL'TB XTKCKDO SVB UMT.

JIGSAW SQUARES

Your goal is to fit the PUZZLE PIECES into their proper places in the diagram to reveal a quotation. Fill the diagram by placing the PUZZLE PIECES horizontally into their corresponding sections of the diagram. There are 16 sections, identified by letter-number combinations (A-1, A-2, A-3, etc.). The quotation reads left to right, line by line. A black square indicates the end of a word. One PUZZLE PIECE has been entered for you.

Solution on page 286

PUZZLE PIECES

A-1	A-2	A-3	A-4	B-1	B-2	B-3	B-4
G	A	Y	C	M	A	B	O
T	H	FT	C	HE	G	Y	T
AN	T	COST	S	NLY	IT	IT	ES
IN	GI	ECTI	HO	DELI	MO	OF	IT
BES	HE	HEAD	NO	THIN	VER	TAK	TO
LIDA ✓	YS		OU		EMOR	MENT	UT
	IVE		THE				

C-1	C-2	C-3	C-4	D-1	D-2	D-3	D-4
CAN	G	A	CAN	A	O	A	E
IME	R	L	ONE	S	S	S	IT
WEA	PE	N	EVER	CA	ND	S	IZE
THIN	TH	AT	IFET	LE	OU	T	STY
	ITS	THE		GOE	EVE	NE	MILE
	LAST	OPLE		FITS	LLED	OF	
						RYON	

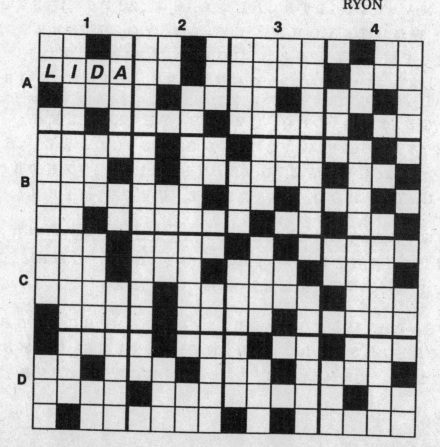

216

ANAGRAM MAGIC SQUARE

Find an anagram for the 5-letter word in each box. The anagram will answer one of the clues. Put the number of that clue into the small square and write the anagram on the dash. The numbers in each row and column will add up to 65. Write the first letter of each anagram on the correspondingly numbered dash at the bottom of the page; and, presto!, the Anagram Magic saying will appear. To start you off, we have put in one anagram and set its first letter on the proper dash at the bottom of the page.   Solution on page 286

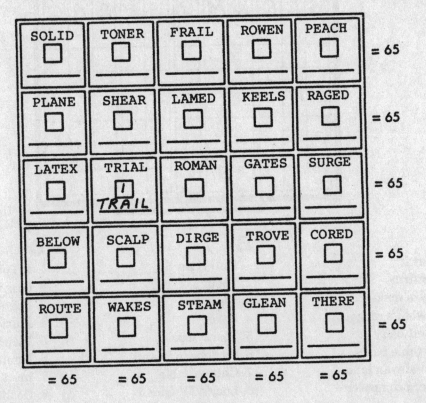

SOLID ☐ ___	TONER ☐ ___	FRAIL ☐ ___	ROWEN ☐ ___	PEACH ☐ ___	= 65
PLANE ☐ ___	SHEAR ☐ ___	LAMED ☐ ___	KEELS ☐ ___	RAGED ☐ ___	= 65
LATEX ☐ ___	TRIAL [1] *TRAIL*	ROMAN ☐ ___	GATES ☐ ___	SURGE ☐ ___	= 65
BELOW ☐ ___	SCALP ☐ ___	DIRGE ☐ ___	TROVE ☐ ___	CORED ☐ ___	= 65
ROUTE ☐ ___	WAKES ☐ ___	STEAM ☐ ___	GLEAN ☐ ___	THERE ☐ ___	= 65

= 65   = 65   = 65   = 65   = 65

1. Beaten path
2. Leverets
3. Arm joint
4. Inexpensive
5. Master
6. Spouses
7. Estate house
8. Grown-up cherub
9. Himalayan kingdom

10. Ornamentation
11. Exterior
12. Natural talent
13. Embrace
14. Impulses
15. Smooth and glossy
16. Number
17. Open
18. Reward for bravery

19. Revered ones
20. Platform
21. Rank
22. Chain of hills
23. Elevate
24. Lopsided
25. Male voice

T
1 2 3 4 5 6 7 8 9 10 11 12 13 14 15 16 17 18 19 20 21 22 23 24 25

TRIPLEX

Place the five-letter answers for A, B, and C clues in the matching sections in the diagram. The answer words overlap: the last two letters in the A word become the first two letters in the B word, and the last two letters in the B word become the first two letters in the C word. When you have completed the diagram, put the letters directly under A, B, and C, reading down consecutively, on the dashes below to spell out a city and state. We have given you the first A, B, and C words and started the answer.

Solution on page 286

A   **B**   **C**

1	S	C	R	A	M	U	S	E	R	A	C
2											
3											
4											
5											
6											
7											
8											

A
1. Beat it!
2. Confirm
3. Violin maker
4. Cowboy's rope
5. Giant deity
6. Perfume base
7. Himalayan land
8. Opera composer

B
1. Entertain
2. Poem
3. Big cat
4. Savor
5. Positive pole
6. Caribbean island
7. Church table
8. Lucy's TV friend

C
1. Ice pinnacle
2. Grayish brown
3. Mistake
4. Musical beat
5. Fiend
6. Iranian religion
7. Inert gas
8. Doolittle

CITY AND STATE: S _ _ _ _ _ _ _ _ _ _ _ , _ _ _ _ _ _
_ _ _ _ _ _ _ _

CHAIN WORDS

Join the 12 words given below into a chain. Pick one word to start; the word that follows will do one of the following: 1. rhyme with it, 2. have the same meaning, 3. be an anagram of it (same letters in a different order), or 4. have one different letter. Work forward and backward to complete the chain. The first and last words will not connect. For example, the following is a chain: State, Great, Large, Lager, Later.

Our solution on page 286

Bribe	Ketch	Tripe	Bring
Gripe	Grape	Shale	Fetch
Brine	Tribe	Leash	Shape

Jumbo Sudoku Puzzle Books!

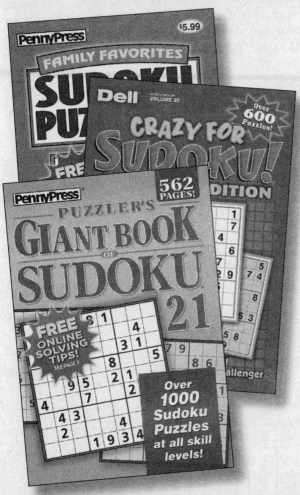

Family Favorites Sudoku

Each oversized volume delivers hundreds and hundreds of Sudoku puzzles handpicked by the editors at *Penny Press*. The puzzles range in difficulty from easy to challenger. Discover why our **Family Favorites** series is such a crowd pleaser! $4.95 each.

Crazy For Sudoku! Maximum Edition

Get **MAXIMUM** enjoyment with over 600 Sudoku puzzles ranging from easy to super-challenger. As an added bonus, nearly 200 puzzles feature the special "X" Factor – where each of the nine or sixteen boxes in the highlighted diagonals must also contain unique numbers. $7.95 each.

Puzzler's Giant Book of Sudoku

Created for the Sudoku puzzle lover who just can't get enough! At **562 pages**, this is our biggest book of Sudoku. You'll get over 1,000 puzzles progressing in difficulty from easy to challenger. **A great value!** Only $7.95.

LOGIC PROBLEM

FOOTBALL FANS

Troy and four other football fans each follow different teams, one of which is the Raiders. Last week, each team played a game that was televised on a different day (Sunday, Monday, Thursday, Friday, or Saturday) at a different time. From the information provided, determine each fan's team, the day each game was televised, and the time each game started (12 p.m., 2:30 p.m., 5:30 p.m., 6 p.m., or 8:30 p.m.). (NOTE: The week begins on Sunday.)

1. The game John watched was televised earlier in the week but later in the day than the Broncos game.

2. The Friday game was shown three hours later in the day than the Cowboys game.

3. The 49ers game started at noon.

4. Steve is a Seahawks fan.

5. George watched his team on Sunday.

6. The game televised at 2:30 p.m. on Saturday involved neither the Seahawks nor the Broncos.

7. Ed's team started its game at 6 p.m.

This chart is to help you record information from the clues as well as the facts you deduce by combining information from different clues. We suggest you use an "X" for a "no" and a "•" for a "yes."

		TEAM					DAY					TIME				
		BRONCOS	COWBOYS	49ers	RAIDERS	SEAHAWKS	SUNDAY	MONDAY	THURSDAY	FRIDAY	SATURDAY	12:00	2:30	5:30	6:00	8:30
FAN	ED															
	GEORGE															
	JOHN															
	STEVE															
	TROY															
TIME	12:00															
	2:30															
	5:30															
	6:00															
	8:30															
DAY	SUNDAY															
	MONDAY															
	THURSDAY															
	FRIDAY															
	SATURDAY															

Solution on page 286

CRYPTO-FAMILIES

Each Crypto-Family is a list of related words in code. (One set of letters has been substituted for the correct letters.) Each "Family" has its own code. When you have identified a word, use the known letters to help decode other words within the group.

Solutions on page 286

1. OILS
Example: Vegetable

IPLMQX

OLOJ

ALWWFRNPK

RFBEP

TLMRFL

TRXXRMAPPV

APALDP

FBMAPPV

ARJOPLM

TRKM

2. CITY STREETS
Example: Traffic light

QZDOBIAYK

MIKHZWE

QWIPXIDE

VZP HZUE

QIHIEPWOYKE

ERGJYNE

PYCOBYG

ESNEBWYQIW

KIJEEPYKH

GZRPOTRIE

3. TREES IN CITY NAMES
Example: Ashland

YLKNSXDQG

ZCDTSEFKG

FCBZCKH

TNHCD DCYLHQ

ECYZNJFFH

YCZE QYDLKMQ

WLDTS DXK

JCZKXG TDNNB

WNNTS MDFON

ILDTDNQG

4. INSECTS
Example: Locust

RPTT DBBQWT

YJWYLBE

FJVAAOPXXBJ

OPMBKRBB

LVEKUWU

TVUKRIF

ZPANIWEP

DVAX

FKXAK ZPEO

EBJZWEB

5. COLORFUL THINGS
Example: Purple mountains

HBO WBHHUIX

XHBBIWZHI

PKLB HUPPZI

UMZHF VZTBH

ZHSIXB QVUYJ

TWUVB TSVBH

HZQB TUIOZT

QUKMBH QCZZI

YZHSK HBBE

CUIJ BKBCWSIV

6. U.S. 5-LETTER CITIES
Example: Ogden

QHOQH

FNIWO

UIHKF

SGHWP

UOTVG

WHFYO

SNFFP

EGAPT

WPIQO

GQORO

MIXED BAG

Rearrange the letters on the left to spell nautical words and place them in the corresponding rows in the diagram. Rearrange all the letters of the squares with the number 1 to form the first word of a line from an old sea chantey, those with the number 2 to form the second word, and so on for all eleven words in the quotation.

Solution on page 286

OWB

ROFE

TRENS

GRIBED

REMATES

LOTHPORE

PAGGNKLAN

MOTORTESSA

BARROTADS

FILETOBA

RESHSAW

ORLIAS

TACHY

YUBO

FAT

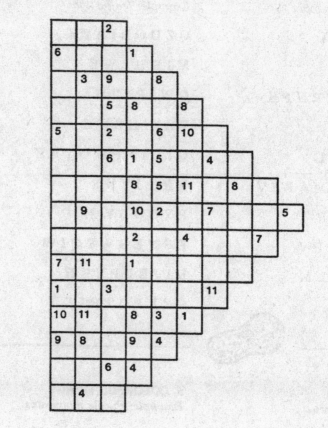

QUOTE:

1. [ ][ ][ ][ ][ ][ ]   2. [ ][ ][ ][ ][ ]   3. [ ][ ][ ][ ]   4. [ ][ ][ ][ ][ ][ ]

5. [ ][ ][ ][ ][ ][ ]   6. [ ][ ][ ][ ][ ]   7. [ ][ ][ ]

8. [ ][ ][ ][ ][ ][ ][ ]   9. [ ][ ][ ][ ][ ]   10. [ ][ ][ ][ ]   11. [ ][ ][ ][ ]

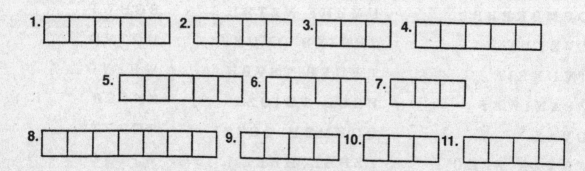

THREE'S COMPANY

This alphabetical list of seemingly unrelated words actually contains twelve groups of three related items. Your job is to sort them out into those twelve groups using each item only once. The trick is that some of the items could be used in more than one list, but only one arrangement of all the items will work. Remember, use each item only once and have exactly three items in each group.   Solution on page 286

Alberta	Elizabeth	Meeting	Sinker
Anne	Emerald	Olive	Soprano
Antonio	Engagement	Ontario	Superior
Banana	Francisco	Orange	Supreme
Baritone	Hook	Plum	Tahoe
Bolero	Jitterbug	Quebec	Tenor
Collie	Lime	Reel	Topmost
Date	Mary	Rod	Unsurpassed
Diego	Mastiff	Rottweiler	Victoria

1. Choir members   _____   _____   _____

2. Excellent   _____   _____   _____

3. British queens   _____   _____   _____

4. Fruit   _____   _____   _____

5. Fishing gear   _____   _____   _____

6. Major lakes   _____   _____   _____

7. Appointment   _____   _____   _____

8. Canadian provinces   _____   _____   _____

9. "San" cities   _____   _____   _____

10. Shades of green   _____   _____   _____

11. Dances   _____   _____   _____

12. Dog breeds   _____   _____   _____

QUICK QUOTES

Fill in the answers to the clues and transfer the letters to the correspondingly numbered dashes to reveal the Quick Quotes. Some letters from a quote may be used in more than one word. We have entered the first answer to get you started.

Solutions on page 286

1.

CLUES	WORDS
A. Cold season	W I N T E R
	25 37 13 30 24 3
B. Timepiece	
	20 12 5 43 41
C. ____ the deck (cheat)	
	21 30 44 7 17
D. Agreement; peace	
	15 1 36 11 19 33 27
E. Enjoy a cigar	
	9 11 16 17 24
F. Computer input	
	35 26 5 32
G. Halley's ____	
	2 19 11 39 34
H. Enchant	
	28 39 14 4 40 31 23
I. Grape plant	
	38 8 18 42
J. Drinking tube	
	21 22 45 10 25
K. Apparent; plain	
	19 28 38 6 16 29 9

QUICK QUOTE:

```
___  ___ R ___ ___ ___ ___   ___ ___  ___   ___ ___ N
 1    2  3  4   5   6   7     8   9    10    11  12 13

___ ___ ___   ___ ___ ___ ___ ___   ___ ___ E   W ___ ___
14  15  16    17  18  19  20  21     22  23 24   25 26 27

___ ___ T   ___ ___ ___ ___ '   ___ ___ I ___ ___   ___ ___ ___
28  29  30   31  32  33  34      35  36 37 38 39    40  41  42

___ ___ ___ .
43  44  45
```

2.

CLUES	WORDS
A. Purple flower	$\overline{15}$ $\overline{24}$ $\overline{30}$ $\overline{6}$ $\overline{21}$ $\overline{1}$
B. Aesop's tale	$\overline{18}$ $\overline{9}$ $\overline{28}$ $\overline{6}$ $\overline{32}$
C. Give to charity	$\overline{23}$ $\overline{12}$ $\overline{31}$ $\overline{14}$ $\overline{26}$ $\overline{3}$
D. Champion	$\overline{8}$ $\overline{20}$ $\overline{5}$ $\overline{31}$ $\overline{29}$ $\overline{19}$
E. Sweet insect?	$\overline{2}$ $\overline{27}$ $\overline{22}$ $\overline{16}$ $\overline{10}$ $\overline{28}$ $\overline{3}$ $\overline{32}$
F. Bread leavening	$\overline{7}$ $\overline{16}$ $\overline{17}$ $\overline{25}$ $\overline{11}$
G. Honorable; deserving	$\overline{8}$ $\overline{4}$ $\overline{19}$ $\overline{26}$ $\overline{13}$ $\overline{10}$

QUICK QUOTE:

$\overline{1}$ $\overline{2}$ $\overline{3}$ $\quad$ $\overline{4}$ $\overline{5}$ $\overline{6}$ $\overline{7}$ $\quad$ $\overline{8}$ $\overline{9}$ $\overline{10}$ $\quad$ $\overline{11}$ $\overline{12}$

$\overline{13}$ $\overline{14}$ $\overline{15}$ $\overline{16}$ $\quad$ $\overline{17}$ $\quad$ $\overline{18}$ $\overline{19}$ $\overline{20}$ $\overline{21}$ $\overline{22}$ $\overline{23}$ $\quad$ $\overline{24}$ $\overline{25}$ $\quad$ $\overline{26}$ $\overline{27}$

$\overline{28}$ $\overline{29}$ $\quad$ $\overline{30}$ $\overline{31}$ $\overline{32}$.

3.

CLUES	WORDS
A. More elevated	$\overline{30}$ $\overline{25}$ $\overline{20}$ $\overline{2}$ $\overline{38}$ $\overline{9}$
B. Motel opening	$\overline{32}$ $\overline{36}$ $\overline{6}$ $\overline{3}$ $\overline{19}$ $\overline{1}$ $\overline{21}$
C. Vacationing traveler	$\overline{26}$ $\overline{13}$ $\overline{23}$ $\overline{4}$ $\overline{10}$ $\overline{12}$ $\overline{16}$
D. Practice a play	$\overline{37}$ $\overline{8}$ $\overline{17}$ $\overline{28}$ $\overline{5}$ $\overline{35}$ $\overline{12}$ $\overline{33}$
E. Employ again	$\overline{29}$ $\overline{15}$ $\overline{27}$ $\overline{18}$ $\overline{37}$ $\overline{24}$
F. "Fried Green ____"	$\overline{7}$ $\overline{34}$ $\overline{14}$ $\overline{31}$ $\overline{26}$ $\overline{22}$ $\overline{38}$ $\overline{11}$

QUICK QUOTE:

$\overline{1}$ $\overline{2}$ $\overline{3}$ $\overline{4}$ $\overline{5}$ $\overline{6}$ $\overline{7}$ $\overline{8}$ $\overline{9}$ $\quad$ $\overline{10}$ $\overline{11}$

$\overline{12}$ $\overline{13}$ $\overline{14}$ $\overline{15}$ $\overline{16}$ $\overline{17}$ $\overline{18}$ $\overline{19}$ $\overline{20}$ $\quad$ $\overline{21}$ $\overline{22}$ $\overline{23}$

$\overline{24}$ $\overline{25}$ $\overline{26}$ $\overline{27}$ $\overline{28}$ $\overline{29}$ $\quad$ $\overline{30}$ $\overline{31}$ $\overline{32}$ $\overline{33}$ $\quad$ $\overline{34}$ $\overline{35}$ $\quad$ $\overline{36}$ $\overline{37}$ $\overline{38}$.

JIGSAW PUZZLE

When you have put the pieces of the Jigsaw Puzzle into their correct places in the diagram, they will form a crossword puzzle with words reading across and down. Do not turn the pieces. The heavy lines in the diagram will help you locate their proper places. We have set one piece to start you off.

Solution on page 286

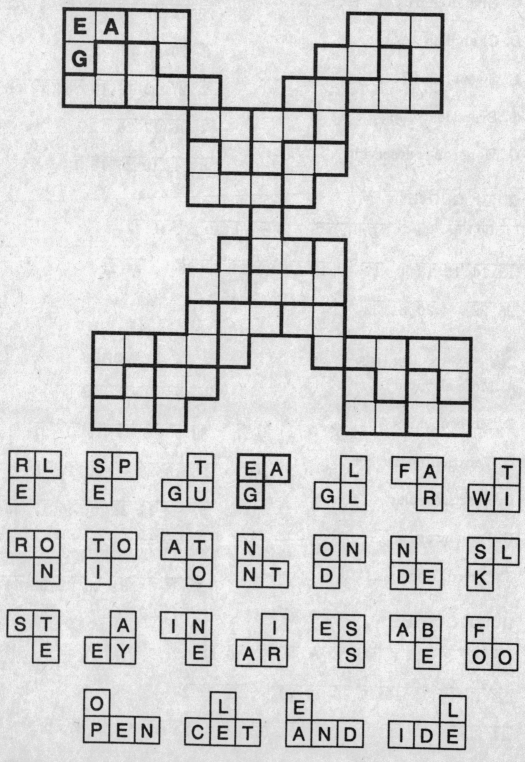

CODEWORD

The directions for solving are given on page 168. Solution on page 287

SPLIT PERSONALITIES

The names of eight tennis players have been split into 2-letter segments. The letters in each segment are in order, but the segments have been scrambled. For each group can you put the pieces together to identify the tennis players?

Solutions on page 287

1. NO YC MM RS ON JI _____

2. AM KR JA ER CK _____

3. VE CH SE RI RT _____

4. HA LC MI NG AE CH _____

5. ER AV DL RO _____

6. GI TH ON BS EA AL _____

7. FI AF EF GR ST _____

8. TI NN CA JE PR ER IF IA _____

WORD MERGERS

Rearrange the letters in each Word Merger to form two words using all the given letters only once. Then rearrange these same letters and merge them into one long word. You might want to form the long word first and then the pair of words. Score 5 points for each pair of words you form and 10 points for each long word. A score of 70 is good, 80 is very good, and 90 is excellent.

Our solutions with a perfect score of 105 points on page 287

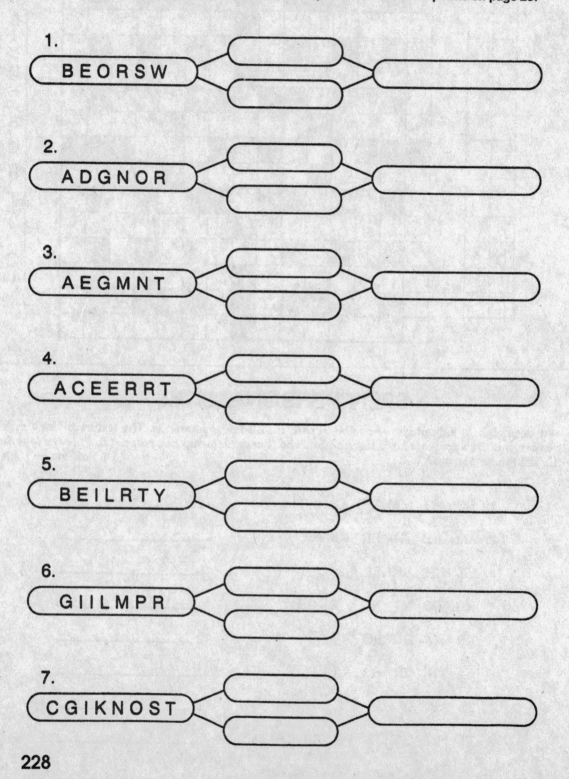

1. BEORSW

2. ADGNOR

3. AEGMNT

4. ACEERRT

5. BEILRTY

6. GIILMPR

7. CGIKNOST

UPS AND DOWNS

Two-word types of sandwich ingredients are hidden in the five groups below. Find them by choosing the correct letter from each vertical pair of letters. For instance, to find EGG SALAD, choose the E from the BE pair, the G from the AG pair, and G from the GN pair, etc.

Solution on page 287

| EXAMPLE: | B A G | S M R A R | EGG SALAD |
| | E G N | T A L I D | |

1.   S L A M U T   B L O T M R
     P E O N D S   D U T A E B

2.   T E N G   O I S E
     L U H A   F V A H

3.   G I N A A   C A L E S I
     M E L O N   S H E A M E

4.   A M O U I T A P   C A W E Y E
     D L E R S C Y N   R H E T S D

5.   L O E S R   B E L F
     R K A N T   P A E N

Triangle Quote

Each letter in the quotation is represented by a number which you can determine by counting the number of triangles in the symbol next to the letter. Place the letters on the correspondingly numbered blanks to reveal the Triangle Quote.

Solution on page 287

$\overline{9}\ \overline{4}\ \overline{2}\ \overline{8}\ \overline{9}\ \overline{5}$ $\overline{2}\ \overline{4}\ \overline{8}\ \overline{1}$ $\overline{6}\ \overline{3}\ \overline{4}\ \overline{10}$ $\overline{1}\ \overline{7}\ \overline{10}\ \overline{9}$.

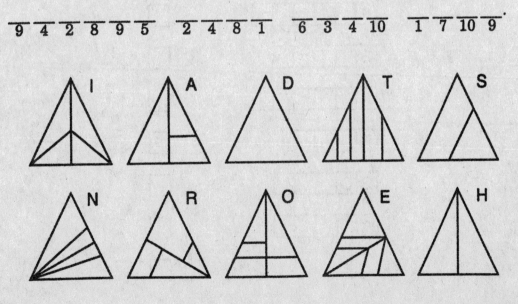

SPELLBOUND

HOW TO SOLVE: Fill in as many boxes as you can to form eleven words starting with the given letters. No letter may be repeated in the word itself, in the word above, or in the word below. For each word the number of letters needed to earn the maximum score is indicated by the number of boxes.

HOW TO SCORE: Each letter used is worth one point. If you use all 26 letters of the alphabet, give yourself a bonus of ten points. Include the given letters in all scoring.

Our solution with a maximum score of 66 on page 287

Sample: S A M P L E   6

      R I N G   4

      C L O U D Y   6

In this sample the word RING cannot be RINGER because the letter R would be repeated in that word and because the letter E appears above in SAMPLE. It cannot be RUNG because U is below in CLOUDY.

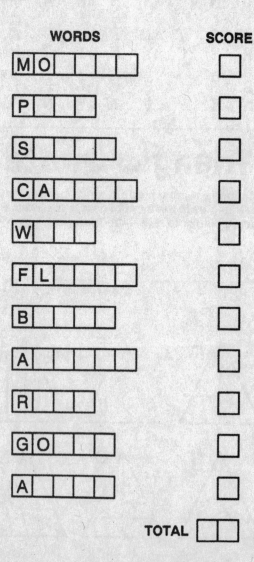

WORDS   SCORE

M O □ □ □ □   □

P □ □ □ □   □

S □ □ □ □   □

C A □ □ □ □   □

W □ □ □   □

F L □ □ □ □   □

B □ □ □ □ □   □

A □ □ □ □ □   □

R □ □ □   □

G O □ □ □   □

A □ □ □ □   □

TOTAL □ □

SIMON SAYS

Start with WATER COOLER and follow the directions carefully to discover a phrase that is apropos.

1. Print the words WATER COOLER.

   1. _____

2. Change the O's to I's.

   2. _____

3. Change the first and last consonants to T's.

   3. _____

4. Insert a D to the left of the L.

   4. _____

5. Move the 3rd vowel from the left to the right of the D.

   5. _____

6. Reverse the order of all the letters.

   6. _____

7. Change each E to an S.

   7. _____

8. Move the 5th letter from the left to the next-to-last position.

   8. _____

9. Delete the 2nd and 4th consonants from the left.

   9. _____

10. Insert an H to the left of the L.

    10. _____

11. Move the 4th letter from the left to the right of the A.

    11. _____

12. Insert an I to the right of the D.

    12. _____

13. Change the 3rd consonant from the left to K.

    13. _____

14. Move the 3rd letter from the left to the right of the D.

    14. _____

Star Words

Place five of the eight words given below into the diagram in the direction of the arrows so that the words share letters as indicated.   Our solution on page 287

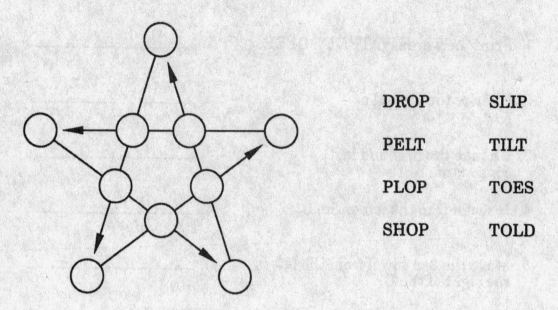

DROP   SLIP

PELT   TILT

PLOP   TOES

SHOP   TOLD

Three from Nine

Place the letters of the 9-letter words on the dashes, one letter per dash, to spell a 7-letter word, a 5-letter word, and a 3-letter word. Each letter of the 9-letter word will be used once.   Solutions on page 287

1. T E L E P H O N E   2. W H O L E S A L E   3. S C R A P B O O K

__R__V__N__   __W__L__O__   __R__C__E__

__U__C__   __O__S__   __T__O__

__W__   __O__   __O__

Tiles

Imagine that these tiles are on a table, each showing a 2-letter combination. Can you rearrange these tiles visually to form a 10-letter word?

Solution on page 287

IS   OC   AL   NO   CA

FILL-IN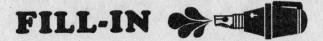

The entries for this puzzle are given to you, listed alphabetically according to length. Across and Down words are all mixed together, and you are to find their proper places in the diagram.   Solution on page 287

2 Letters
As
Pa
To
We

3 Letters
Are
Cad
Era
Eta
Fun
Hah
Ire
Lit
Mea
Nap
Oro
Per
Rag
Red
Rel.
Sag
See
Sip
Tap ✓
Tot
Ups
Uva
Vat
Win

4 Letters
Area
Asti
Bars
Firs
Harp
Leap
Mint
Mort
Need
Newt
Olio
Urge

5 Letters
Aisle
Blast
Capes
Eosin
Metal
Pairs
Pewee
Ripen
Sewer
Sleep
Steer
Tepid

Treat
Wader

6 Letters
Elided
Emerge
Morose
Patted
Resort
Senora

7 Letters
Nominal

Reposed

8 Letters
Hesitate
Potatoes
Serenest
Tempered

233

DART GAME

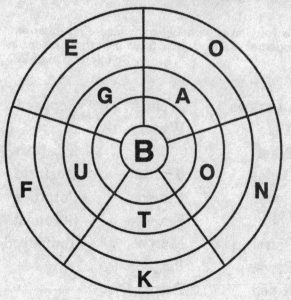

Complete the 5-letter words reading outward from the center by placing the given letters correctly in the diagram blanks. Each letter will be used only once. All five words begin with the center letter, B.

Solution on page 287

A F I L L R R U V W

Crypto-Limerick

This humorous verse is in a substitution code. Solution on page 287

ZUBPB CIYB VQD Q XWDLYLQI IQXBA DKCQI,

VUC VQIZBA ZC JKQT ZUB ZPCXHCIB.

HWZ CIB AQT VUBI UB ZPLBA,

LZ FWDZ VCWKAI'Z DKLAB,

QIA UB NIBV ZUQZ ULD

YUQIYB VQD HKCVI.

234

COMMON COMBOS

Listed below are groups of three unrelated words. Find a word that either precedes all the words in the group or follows all the words in the group.

Solutions on page 287

1. CUTTER   JAW   BLOWING   _____

2. MAN   HAND   STEAK   _____

3. CARPET   LANTERN   FLUTE   _____

4. NAME   HOME   FASHION   _____

5. DOG   BAND   TOWER   _____

6. BLACK   ROOF   HILL   _____

7. TIME   GAME   COFFEE   _____

8. BALL   CUT   SPRAY   _____

9. FACE   MARK   GOOSE   _____

10. PLAY   NEGATIVE   TAKE   _____

Crossout Quote

Cross out one letter in each box so that the remaining letters spell out a quotation reading across from left to right.

Solution on page 287

I/A	N/T	S/D	■	S/O	O/F	■	P/S	I/R	M/U	M/P	L/E	
E/Y	■	T/I	O/N	■	W/B	E/Y	■	R/W	I/H	S/A	T/E	
■	M/J	O	U/S	V/T	T/E	■	T/S	H/W	A/I	N/L	K/L	■
I/O	F/N	■	S/C	O/H	A/M	E/V	E/T	J/H	I/O	N/U	S/G	
■	S/I	T/F	U	P/A	X/I	T/D	■	A/T	T/O	■	S/L	
O/A	Y/W	■	T/C	H/R	A/E	T/N	■	S/P	A/H	N/Y	■	
A/T	H/N	Y/E	■	O/S	P/R	N/P	O/A	S/Q	U/I	T/N	T/E	

BUILDING BLOCKS

Using only the letters in the word SON, complete the words in the Building Blocks. Words read across only. Every word contains each letter of SON at least once.

Solution on page 287

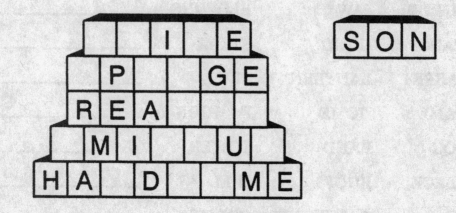

Anagram Quotes

Unscramble each set of letters below the dashes to complete the humorous quotations.

Solutions on page 287

1. The _____ with being on _____ is that _____ is
    BORTUEL   ITEM   OBOYDN

    _____ to _____ it.
    HEETR   EPAPCRITAE

2. A person _____ of _____ must be _____ _____
            AADFIR   KORW   ABERV   EGHNOU

    to _____ _____ .
       ACEF   EPORTVY

3. It _____ a _____ of _____ to make a _____
       AEKST   AEHP   AEMNPSTY   EHOSU

    your _____ .
         EHMO

236

SCRAMBLE ACROSS

Unscramble each group of letters in the diagram on the top to form a word and put it into the corresponding group of squares in the diagram on the bottom. Do this for ACROSS WORDS ONLY. The completed diagram on the bottom will be a crossword puzzle with words reading across and down. For groups of letters that can make more than one word across, solve across and down together.

Solution on page 287

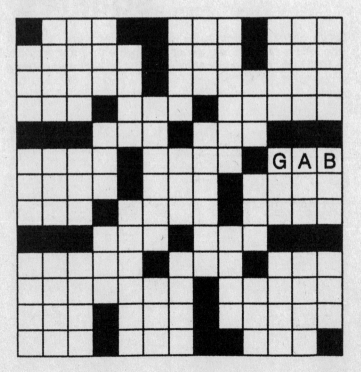

TAKE A LETTER

The names of twelve animals are hidden in the 4-letter words. In the first row across, take a letter from each word from left to right to spell one animal; choose a different letter from each word to spell another; and choose one more to spell a third. One letter of each 4-letter word will be left unused. Do the same for the other rows, spelling the names of three animals in each one.

Solutions on page 287

1.	TWIG	COME	PAPS	SHAG	FEEL	ORAL
2.	JOGS	CAGE	RICE	BULK	IOTA	TALL
3.	CARD	POOL	PUNT	GAWK	CAVE	ARMY
4.	CRAM	OONA	BONY	KNOB	DIET	TYPE

1. _____ _____ _____

2. _____ _____ _____

3. _____ _____ _____

4. _____ _____ _____

Squares

Each of the Squares contains an 8-letter word. It can be found by starting at one of the letters and reading either clockwise or counterclockwise. In the example the word STANDARD is found by starting at the letter S and reading counterclockwise.

Solutions on page 287

Example:

```
D R A
S   D
T A N
```

1.
```
O L B
S   S
S O M
```

2.
```
L E D
I   I
T Y F
```

3.
```
F F I
A   N
Y T I
```

4.
```
C A T
I   H
T E L
```

5.
```
J O U
S   R
Y E N
```

6.
```
L L U
E   B
T I N
```

7.
```
M N I
O   A
U N T
```

238

SATELLITES

Form eight words by placing one syllable in each circle. The center circle contains the first syllable for each of the eight words. All the syllables will be used once. Words read outward from the center.

Solution on page 287

DA FA I

IST LIL

LO LU NA

NAR O

QUY ROR

~~SO~~ TA

TION TY

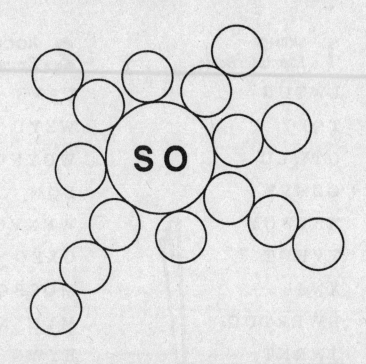

Linkwords

Add a Linkword to the end of the word on the left and the beginning of the word on the right to form two compound words or phrases. The dashes indicate the number of letters in the Linkword. For example, if the words were PEANUT _ _ _ _ _ _ FLY, the Linkword would be BUTTER (Peanut butter, Butterfly).

Solutions on page 287

1. FLAT _ _ _ ROOM

2. WIND _ _ _ _ POND

3. SKIM _ _ _ _ MAN

4. CARE _ _ _ RIDE

5. TEA _ _ _ CAKE

6. WORD _ _ _ _ PEN

7. PASS _ _ _ HOLE

8. ART _ _ _ _ SHOP

9. SUN _ _ _ _ POST

10. SPLIT _ _ _ NUT

CRYPTO-FAMILIES

Each Crypto-Family is a list of related words in code. Each Family has its own code. When you have identified a word, use the known letters to help decode the other words in the Family.

Solutions on page 287

1. SKIING
Example: Boots

LWTUG

TQEY

GTWLU

GZHVE

XHZBUY

YVHQT

XNJL

RWRRTUG

JWRNT

2. HOCKEY
Example: Goalie

UAVG

WZYU WMTN

WGYNQW

EQN

WNXVG

OXEG

MQZBQN

MYN NOXVG

BYWG

3. SNOW____
Example: Shoe

RVKK

RVJD

XKVDN

MKLS

RKLSNH

QHUXB

BUHN

ZLRUKN

ZVJ

4. WHITE____
Example: Bread

CNJJ

AJAZRNYL

TNZ

QJNK

MNJA

MZNTA

WYEKRL

JEA

CNMR

DAISY

Form five 5-letter words using the letters in each Daisy petal PLUS the letter in the Daisy center, F. The F may not be used as the first letter of these words. Next, form a bonus 6-letter word using the first letters of these words and beginning with the center letter, F.

Solution on page 287

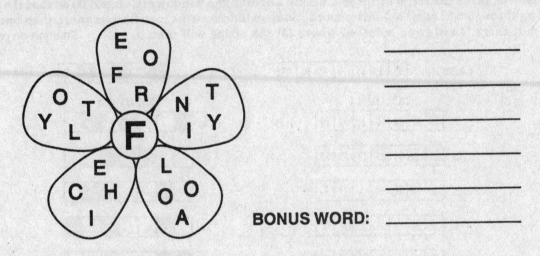

_____

_____

_____

_____

_____

BONUS WORD: _____

How Many Squares?

This diagram is filled with squares small, medium, and large. Try to count them all. There may be more than you think!

Solution on page 287

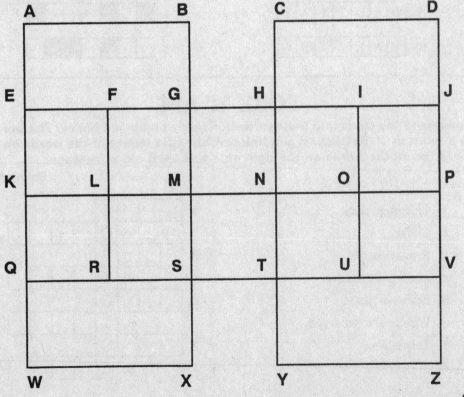

Window Boxes

There is a 4-letter word hidden in each of the ten strips in Column I. Column II has ten window patterns with open windows (white boxes) and closed windows (black boxes). Using your imagination, place the letter strips in Column I behind the windows (Column II) so that the letters showing through will spell a 4-letter word. Some window strips may fit over more than one letter strip, but there is only one solution where all the strips will match.   Solution on page 289

Example: P L O D E N T   P O E T

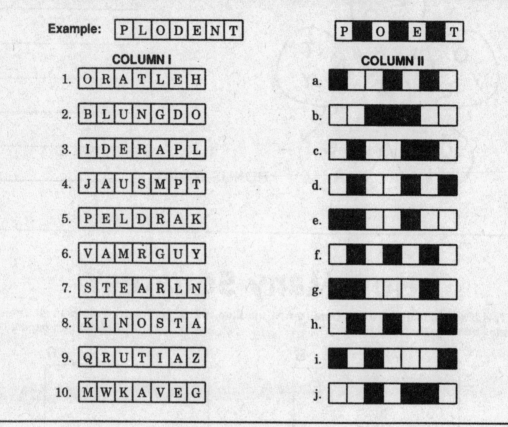

COLUMN I

1. O R A T L E H
2. B L U N G D O
3. I D E R A P L
4. J A U S M P T
5. P E L D R A K
6. V A M R G U Y
7. S T E A R L N
8. K I N O S T A
9. Q R U T I A Z
10. M W K A V E G

COLUMN II

a.
b.
c.
d.
e.
f.
g.
h.
i.
j.

FORE 'N' AFT

Enter the answers to the clues into their correspondingly numbered boxes. The words will begin or end with a letter in TORTOISE. When finished, the first letters of the words on the left side and the last letters of the words on the right side will spell out a message.

Solution on page 287

1. Chimney black
2. Chose
3. Prevaricator
4. Main body section
5. Buckeye State
6. Wife's relative: hyph.
7. Takes first
8. Spritely

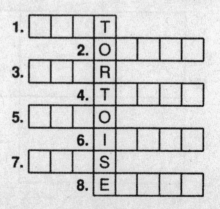

242

OBSERVATION POST

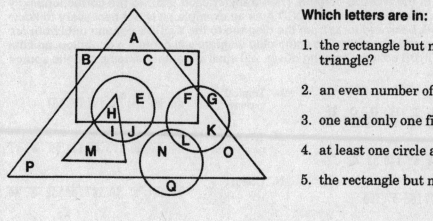

Which letters are in:

1. the rectangle but not in a triangle? _____

2. an even number of figures? _____

3. one and only one figure? _____

4. at least one circle and a triangle? _____

5. the rectangle but not in a circle? _____

Solutions on page 287

TRADE-OFF

The answers to the two clues in each line below are 6-letter words which differ by only one letter, which we have given you. In the example, if you trade off the P from STRIPE with the letter K, in the same position, you get STRIKE. The order of the letters will not change. Solutions on page 287

Example: Chevron S T R I P E   S T R I K E Hit

1. Tersely _ _ _ _ L _   _ _ _ _ S _ Bow

2. Army _ _ G _ _ _   _ _ S _ _ _ Injury

3. Exchange B _ _ _ _ _   C _ _ _ _ _ U.S. President

4. Arrange _ _ _ O _ _   _ _ _ E _ _ Declare

5. GI's lodging _ I _ _ _ _   _ U _ _ _ _ Projectile

CROSSED NAMES

Fill in the squares of each diagram to form the name of a famous person. The first name may appear in either the across or down boxes. Use only the letters given above the diagram. The letter shown in each diagram is shared by both the first and last names. Solutions on page 287

1. A D E I L N O P U

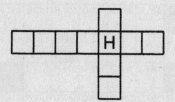

2. A A D E L N R S

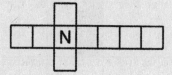

3. B E E G G N O S U

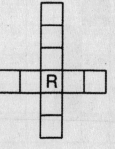

243

Crostic 10

Use the CLUES on the left to fill in the WORDS column. Then transfer each letter to the correspondingly numbered square in the diagram. (We have inserted WORD A as an example.) It is not necessary to know all the words to start solving. Work back and forth from the diagram to the WORDS column until both are filled. A black square indicates the end of a word. The completed diagram will contain a quotation, and the first letter of each word in the WORDS column, reading down, will spell the author's name and the source of the quotation.

CLUES   **WORDS**

A. Royal honor   K N I G H T H O O D
30 111 81 61 103 133 17 120 169 72

B. Stimulate
38 35 80 124 64 97 148 33 55

C. Family member
173 137 93 108 177 150 37 126

D. Igneous rock
79 27 113 165 92 117 73 42

E. Obstacle
15 70 82 159 142 29 115 67 166 123

F. Inundate
63 109 9 160 129 68 11 43

G. Keeper of late hours: 2 wds.
152 136 112 19 168 114 116 85

H. Honest
118 105 5 51 158 10 83 122

I. Basic
139 95 107 54 155 41 76 172 12 62

J. Toad or frog
75 77 135 6 161 21 110 57 125

K. Chewy candy
98 59 69 144 14 128

L. Tropical cyclone
23 90 164 74 151 175 131

M. Trip for newlyweds
49 34 60 170 40 147 99 4 71

N. Useful
18 141 2 28 157 102 132 8 46

O. WWI U.S. infantryman
127 53 176 100 88 94 140 3

P. Money for a child
7 84 106 24 65 167 121 52 162

Q. Started
1 156 22 149 130 50 16 36 44

R. Stifle
56 96 153 25 145 138 20 48 101

S. Came into money
45 32 119 78 146 66 87 174 163

T. Wholly
89 143 47 31 39 134 58 86

U. Loud, shrill cry
171 26 154 104 91 13

Solution on page 288

1 Q	2 N		3 O	4 M	5 H		6 J	7 P	8 N	9 F		10 H	11 F	12 I	13 U	14 K	15 E
	16 Q	17 A	18 N		19 G	20 R	21 J	22 Q	23 L		24 P	25 R		26 U	27 D	28 N	29 E	30 A	31 T
32 S	33 B		34 M	35 B		36 Q	37 C	38 B	39 T	40 M		41 I	42 D	43 F		44 Q	45 S	46 N	47 T		48 R
49 M	50 Q	51 H		52 P	53 O	54 I	55 B	56 R		57 J	58 T	59 K	60 M	61 A		62 I	63 F	64 B		65 P	66 S
67 E	68 F		69 K	70 E	71 M	72 A		73 D	74 L	75 J	76 I		77 J	78 S	79 D	80 B	81 A	82 E	83 H	84 P	85 G
86 T		87 S	88 O	89 T	90 L		91 U	92 D	93 C		94 O	95 I	96 R	97 B		98 K	99 M	100 O	101 R	102 N	103 A
104 U	105 H		106 P	107 I	108 C	109 F	110 J	111 A	112 G		113 D	114 G	115 E		116 G	117 D	118 H	119 S		120 A	121 P
122 H	123 E		124 B	125 J	126 C		127 O	128 K	129 F	130 Q	131 L	132 N	133 A	134 T		135 J	136 G	137 C	138 R	139 I
140 O	141 N		142 E	143 T	144 K	145 R	146 S	147 M	148 B	149 Q	150 C	151 L	152 G		153 R	154 U	155 I	156 Q	157 N	158 H
159 E	160 F	161 J	162 P	163 S		164 L	165 D	166 E	167 P	168 G	169 A	170 M	171 U		172 I	173 C	174 S		175 L	176 O	177 C

244

A. Methodical $\overline{22}\ \overline{153}\ \overline{40}\ \overline{86}\ \overline{101}\ \overline{110}\ \overline{132}\ \overline{37}\ \overline{57}\ \overline{126}$

B. Not so plump $\overline{35}\ \overline{47}\ \overline{7}\ \overline{129}\ \overline{44}\ \overline{31}\ \overline{105}$

C. Symbol $\overline{94}\ \overline{99}\ \overline{106}\ \overline{82}\ \overline{125}\ \overline{10}$

D. Go over, as old arguments $\overline{70}\ \overline{3}\ \overline{154}\ \overline{75}\ \overline{49}\ \overline{20}$

E. Carpet fluff $\overline{27}\ \overline{21}\ \overline{55}\ \overline{139}$

F. Den of ___ $\overline{18}\ \overline{87}\ \overline{92}\ \overline{73}\ \overline{50}\ \overline{100}\ \overline{65}\ \overline{142}$

G. African nation $\overline{2}\ \overline{128}\ \overline{5}\ \overline{17}\ \overline{51}\ \overline{118}\ \overline{114}$

H. Don't look a ___ in the mouth: 2 wds. $\overline{130}\ \overline{152}\ \overline{85}\ \overline{60}\ \overline{30}\ \overline{140}\ \overline{52}\ \overline{34}\ \overline{146}$

I. Approaches $\overline{148}\ \overline{71}\ \overline{43}\ \overline{137}\ \overline{25}$

J. Stop ___: 3 wds. $\overline{36}\ \overline{169}\ \overline{147}\ \overline{90}\ \overline{96}\ \overline{113}\ \overline{48}$

K. Rebound $\overline{167}\ \overline{64}\ \overline{156}\ \overline{123}\ \overline{150}\ \overline{9}\ \overline{112}\ \overline{46}$

L. Empty talk $\overline{29}\ \overline{103}\ \overline{11}\ \overline{88}\ \overline{56}\ \overline{81}\ \overline{61}$

M. Concealed $\overline{14}\ \overline{164}\ \overline{42}\ \overline{120}\ \overline{135}\ \overline{58}$

N. Treated $\overline{131}\ \overline{24}\ \overline{4}\ \overline{83}\ \overline{77}\ \overline{98}\ \overline{45}$

O. Not judgmental $\overline{74}\ \overline{32}\ \overline{159}\ \overline{67}\ \overline{155}\ \overline{124}\ \overline{138}\ \overline{23}\ \overline{38}\ \overline{165}$

P. Allude $\overline{119}\ \overline{72}\ \overline{145}\ \overline{168}\ \overline{62}$

Q. Thunder $\overline{141}\ \overline{54}\ \overline{91}\ \overline{117}\ \overline{115}\ \overline{89}$

R. Canary color $\overline{68}\ \overline{33}\ \overline{107}\ \overline{6}\ \overline{53}\ \overline{143}$

S. Great disorder $\overline{8}\ \overline{163}\ \overline{69}\ \overline{16}\ \overline{39}\ \overline{76}\ \overline{108}\ \overline{19}$

T. Wife of Theseus $\overline{121}\ \overline{157}\ \overline{1}\ \overline{102}\ \overline{166}\ \overline{63}\ \overline{104}$

U. Submit for approval $\overline{41}\ \overline{80}\ \overline{12}\ \overline{149}\ \overline{84}\ \overline{122}$

V. Socially active: 3 wds. $\overline{144}\ \overline{93}\ \overline{134}\ \overline{151}\ \overline{28}\ \overline{133}\ \overline{79}\ \overline{158}\ \overline{95}$

W. Wall recess $\overline{97}\ \overline{161}\ \overline{162}\ \overline{111}\ \overline{116}$

X. Supernatural tale: 2 wds. $\overline{59}\ \overline{160}\ \overline{66}\ \overline{13}\ \overline{26}\ \overline{109}\ \overline{127}\ \overline{15}\ \overline{136}\ \overline{78}$

Solution on page 288

1 T	2 G		3 D	4 N	5 G	6 R	7 B	8 S	9 K	10 C	11 L	12 U	13 X		14 M	15 X	16 S
17 G		18 F	19 S		20 D	21 E	22 A		23 O	24 N	25 I	26 X	27 E	28 V		29 L	30 H
31 B		32 O	33 R	34 H	35 B		36 J	37 A		38 O		39 S	40 A	41 U	42 M		43 I	44 B	45 N		46 K
47 B	48 J		49 D	50 F	51 G	52 H	53 R	54 Q	55 E	56 L	57 A	58 M	59 X		60 H	61 L	62 P	63 T	64 K	65 F	66 X
67 O	68 R		69 S	70 D	71 I		72 P	73 F	74 O	75 D	76 S	77 N	78 X		79 V	80 U	81 L	82 C		83 N	84 U
85 H	86 A	87 F	88 L	89 Q	90 J		91 Q	92 F	93 V	94 C		95 V	96 J	97 W	98 N		99 C	100 F	101 A	102 T
103 L	104 T	105 B	106 C	107 R	108 S	109 X		110 A	111 W	112 K		113 J	114 G	115 Q	116 W		117 Q	118 G	119 P	120 M
121 T	122 U	123 K	124 O	125 C	126 A	127 X	128 G	129 B	130 H		131 N	132 A	133 V		134 V	135 M	136 X	137 I	138 O	139 E	140 H
	141 Q	142 F		143 R	144 V	145 P	146 H		147 J	148 I	149 U		150 K	151 V	152 H		153 A	154 D
	155 O		156 K	157 T	158 V		159 O	160 X	161 W		162 W	163 S	164 M	165 O	166 T	167 K	168 P	169 J

Crostic 12

A. Jest — $\overline{54}\ \overline{112}\ \overline{58}\ \overline{93}\ \overline{70}\ \overline{170}\ \overline{13}\ \overline{4}\ \overline{135}$

B. Meaningful — $\overline{36}\ \overline{183}\ \overline{85}\ \overline{149}\ \overline{167}\ \overline{197}\ \overline{45}\ \overline{118}\ \overline{105}$

C. Top effort: 2 wds. — $\overline{129}\ \overline{181}\ \overline{37}\ \overline{83}\ \overline{109}\ \overline{136}\ \overline{20}\ \overline{50}\ \overline{176}$

D. Season beginning Ash Wednesday — $\overline{44}\ \overline{179}\ \overline{152}\ \overline{22}$

E. If it happens: 3 wds. — $\overline{1}\ \overline{71}\ \overline{106}\ \overline{6}\ \overline{142}\ \overline{117}\ \overline{24}\ \overline{166}\ \overline{15}\ \overline{123}$

F. Contract — $\overline{98}\ \overline{186}\ \overline{19}\ \overline{102}\ \overline{43}\ \overline{79}\ \overline{38}\ \overline{92}\ \overline{2}$

G. Shakespearean hero — $\overline{158}\ \overline{21}\ \overline{175}\ \overline{51}\ \overline{101}\ \overline{5}\ \overline{40}$

H. Unusually small thing — $\overline{163}\ \overline{126}\ \overline{25}\ \overline{154}\ \overline{52}\ \overline{27}$

I. Stretch out — $\overline{187}\ \overline{87}\ \overline{28}\ \overline{62}\ \overline{53}\ \overline{94}\ \overline{130}\ \overline{49}$

J. In a difficult position: 3 wds. — $\overline{169}\ \overline{173}\ \overline{96}\ \overline{161}\ \overline{195}\ \overline{180}\ \overline{31}\ \overline{74}\ \overline{12}$

K. Large, shorthaired dog — $\overline{26}\ \overline{127}\ \overline{65}\ \overline{46}\ \overline{90}\ \overline{155}\ \overline{113}$

L. Power — $\overline{7}\ \overline{145}\ \overline{35}\ \overline{116}\ \overline{72}\ \overline{188}$

M. Greek island — $\overline{75}\ \overline{59}\ \overline{77}\ \overline{111}\ \overline{198}\ \overline{148}$

N. Author Fleming — $\overline{3}\ \overline{120}\ \overline{194}$

O. Molar man — $\overline{199}\ \overline{153}\ \overline{121}\ \overline{160}\ \overline{184}\ \overline{80}\ \overline{131}$

P. Before this time — $\overline{107}\ \overline{78}\ \overline{56}\ \overline{10}\ \overline{30}\ \overline{165}$

Q. Pronunciation marks — $\overline{95}\ \overline{18}\ \overline{11}\ \overline{174}\ \overline{138}\ \overline{68}\ \overline{159}$

R. Japanese religion — $\overline{73}\ \overline{141}\ \overline{47}\ \overline{190}\ \overline{64}\ \overline{134}$

S. Brawl — $\overline{76}\ \overline{144}\ \overline{89}\ \overline{119}\ \overline{23}\ \overline{133}\ \overline{189}\ \overline{17}\ \overline{82}\ \overline{100}$

T. At sea — $\overline{132}\ \overline{114}\ \overline{8}\ \overline{88}\ \overline{63}\ \overline{66}\ \overline{42}\ \overline{32}$

U. Red gem — $\overline{67}\ \overline{104}\ \overline{128}\ \overline{99}$

V. Result — $\overline{171}\ \overline{61}\ \overline{168}\ \overline{191}\ \overline{14}\ \overline{97}\ \overline{41}$

W. Not conventional — $\overline{9}\ \overline{185}\ \overline{164}\ \overline{108}\ \overline{146}\ \overline{178}\ \overline{81}\ \overline{122}\ \overline{124}\ \overline{84}$

X. Contemporary — $\overline{86}\ \overline{139}\ \overline{196}\ \overline{151}\ \overline{57}\ \overline{39}$

Y. Brass instrument — $\overline{29}\ \overline{157}\ \overline{192}\ \overline{150}\ \overline{125}\ \overline{16}\ \overline{172}\ \overline{55}$

Z. Salary, for instance — $\overline{137}\ \overline{193}\ \overline{34}\ \overline{147}\ \overline{143}\ \overline{162}$

a. Spanish Arab — $\overline{103}\ \overline{91}\ \overline{60}\ \overline{33}$

b. Canine — $\overline{115}\ \overline{110}\ \overline{182}\ \overline{177}\ \overline{48}\ \overline{156}\ \overline{140}\ \overline{69}$

Solution on page 288

1 E	2 F		3 N	4 A		5 G	6 E	7 L		8 T	9 W	10 P	11 Q	12 J	13 A	14 V	15 E		16 Y
17 S		18 Q	19 F	20 C	21 G	22 D	23 S	24 E	25 H		26 K	27 H	28 I		29 Y	30 P		31 J	32 T	33 a	34 Z
35 L	36 B	37 C	38 F		39 X	40 G	41 V		42 T	43 F	44 D	45 B	46 K	47 R	48 b	49 I	50 C		51 G	52 H	53 I
54 A	55 Y	56 P	57 X		58 A	59 M	60 a	61 V	62 I	63 T	64 R	65 K		66 T	67 U		68 Q	69 b	70 A	71 E	72 L
73 R		74 J	75 M		76 S	77 M	78 P	79 F	80 O		81 W	82 S		83 C	84 W	85 B	86 X	87 I	88 T	89 S	90 K
91 a	92 F		93 A	94 I	95 Q	96 J		97 V	98 F	99 U		100 S	101 G	102 F	103 a		104 U	105 B	106 E	107 P	108W
109 C	110 b		111 M	112 A	113 K	114 T	115 b	116 L	117 E	118 B	119 S		120 N	121 O	122W	123 E	124W		125 Y	126 H
	127 K	128 U	129 C	130 I		131 O	132 T		133 S	134 R	135 A	136 C	137 Z	138 Q	139 X		140 b	141 R	142 E	143 Z
144 S	145 L	146W	147 Z		148 M	149 B	150 Y	151 X		152 D	153 O	154 H		155 K	156 b	157 Y	158 G	159 Q		160 O	161 J
162 Z		163 H	164W	165 P	166 E	167 B		168 V	169 J		170 A	171 V	172 Y	173 J	174 Q	175 G	176 C		177 b	178W	179 D
	180 J	181 C	182 b	183 B	184 O	185W	186 F	187 I	188 L		189 S	190 R	191 V	192 Y	193 Z	194 N	195 J	196 X	197 B	198 M	199 O

Crostic 13

A. Written oath
111 35 34 127 11 138 19 133 163

B. Chief support
3 88 107 213 21 58 69 187

C. Penetrating
20 60 57 211 28 156 184 44

D. Land turtle
195 123 45 54 189 22 12 177

E. Natural fabric
67 160 210 137 61 115

F. Musical accord
64 173 40 170 212 65 49

G. Medicinal potion
14 141 200 53 9 117

H. Leftovers
174 116 98 43 5 82 129 143

I. Small sailboat
100 74 63 7 105 55

J. Beaker's kin: 2 wds.
71 15 73 86 93 175 198 39

K. Barrier
85 201 165 192 101

L. Unduly demonstrative
95 157 161 150 41 83 172 171

M. Dr. Leary
158 162 97 149 24 203 90

N. Sandwich material: 2 wds.
75 119 108 8 126 176 197 31

O. Dumbfound
33 76 52 102 38 131 113 186 135

P. Bettor's reward
104 29 46 91 178 202

Q. Scott hero
190 78 147 13 94 26 125

R. Gruyere, e.g.
181 25 59 206 103 42

S. Well-off
48 155 179 36 27 66 191 145

T. Noisy insect
122 51 106 62 96 23

U. Perch
199 152 72 110 182

V. Patriotic song
56 194 68 1 132 144

W. Uncertain: 2 wds.
142 208 47 196 2 148 81

X. Close
30 79 80 10 120 167

Y. Indiana city: 2 wds.
92 37 134 168 124 209 121 6 136

Z. Accommodating
18 139 99 204 84 183 128 118

a. Paper measures
207 154 166 87 32

b. Salad plant
114 89 16 193 112 185

c. Waits: 2 wds.
164 77 17 109 130 169 188 159 151

d. Brass instrument
50 70 146 4 205 140 153 180

Solution on page 288

1 V	2 W	3 B	4 d	5 H	6 Y	7 I	8 N	9 G	10 X	11 A	12 D		13 Q	14 G	15 J
16 b		17 c	18 Z		19 A	20 C	21 B	22 D	23 T		24 M	25 R	26 Q	27 S	28 C	29 P	30 X
31 N	32 a		33 O	34 A		35 A	36 S	37 Y	38 O	39 J	40 F	41 L		42 R	43 H	44 C	45 D	46 P		47 W	48 S
49 F		50 d	51 T		52 O	53 G	54 D	55 I	56 V	57 C	58 B		59 R	60 C	61 E	62 T	63 I	64 F		65 F	66 S
67 E	68 V	69 B	70 d		71 J	72 U		73 J	74 I	75 N	76 O	77 c	78 Q	79 X		80 X	81 W		82 H	83 L	84 Z
85 K	86 J		87 a	88 B	89 b	90 M		91 P	92 Y		93 J	94 Q	95 L		96 T	97 M	98 H	99 Z	100 I	101 K	102 O
	103 R	104 P	105 I	106 T	107 B	108 N	109 c		110 U	111 A	112 b	113 O		114 b	115 E	116 H	117 G	118 Z	119 N		120 X
121 Y		122 T	123 D	124 Y	125 Q	126 N	127 A	128 Z	129 H		130 c	131 O	132 V	133 A	134 Y		135 O	136 Y	137 E	138 A	139 Z
140 d	141 G	142 W	143 H	144 V		145 S	146 d		147 Q	148 W	149 M	150 L	151 c		152 U	153 d	154 a	—	155 S	156 C	157 L
158 M	159 c		160 E	161 L		162 M	163 A	164 c		165 K	166 a	167 X	168 Y	169 c	170 F	171 L		172 L	173 F	174 H	175 J
176 N		177 D	178 P	179 S	180 d	181 R	182 U	183 Z	184 C	185 b	186 O	187 B		188 c	189 D	190 Q	191 S	192 K		193 b	194 V
195 D	196 W		197 N		198 J	199 U	200 G	201 K	202 P		203 M	204 Z	205 d	206 R	207 a	208 W	209 Y	210 E	211 C	212 F	213 B

247

Crostic 14

A. Possessive — 115 132 55 152 102 105 170

B. Unyielding — 88 78 84 116 103 21 10 64

C. "The Outsiders" author — 113 85 87 17 147 149

D. Situated in the adjacent house: hyph. — 8 157 39 163 131 91 12 109

E. Confection — 31 57 48 129 112 119 38 134 89

F. Times gone by: 2 wds. — 52 56 86 97 62 73 43 26 7

G. Friendly — 155 114 23 118 96 104 177 128 187 59

H. Governing principle in Greek philosophy — 42 123 153 160 167

I. Burial — 143 121 106 165 93 161 110 16 180

J. Perspectives — 66 148 137 5 3 37 126 13 95 60

K. Like some species — 174 135 107 65 176 145 50 166 15 35

L. Semiquaver — 20 76 138 81 54 120 146 71 164

M. Idle time of the year: hyph. — 181 124 25 127 140 6 185 172 44

N. Improbable: hyph. — 158 130 68 51 28 122 156 75 4 29

O. Prevented — 94 82 173 99 133 142 79 117

P. Mint plant — 27 9 53 30 125 2 151 144 175

Q. Carried out vigorously — 179 100 188 162 49 40 61 136

R. Pitiful — 1 58 18 168 186 22 32 90

S. Formed unusually: hyph. — 19 70 101 77 182 108 139 83 150

T. Bizarre — 169 98 11 69 178 46 159 183 141

U. Delicious — 36 67 72 14 47 24 74 184 34

V. Shook — 80 171 92 63 45 41 33 154 111

Solution on page 288

1 R	2 P	3 J	4 N		5 J	6 M	7 F		8 D	9 P	10 B		11 T	12 D	13 J	14 U	15 K
16 I	17 C		18 R	19 S		20 L	21 B	22 R	23 G	24 U	25 M	26 F		27 P	28 N		29 N	30 P	31 E
32 R	33 V	34 U	35 K		36 U	37 J		38 E	39 D	40 Q	41 V	42 H		43 F	44 M	45 V		46 T	47 U	48 E	49 Q
50 K	51 N	52 F	53 P	54 L		55 A	56 F	57 E	58 R	59 G	60 J		61 Q	62 F	63 V	64 B	65 K	66 J	67 U	68 N	69 T
70 S		71 L	72 U		73 F	74 U		75 N	76 L	77 S		78 B	79 O	80 V	81 L		82 O	83 S		84 B	85 C
86 F		87 C	88 B	89 E		90 R	91 D	92 V	93 I	94 O		95 J	96 G	97 F		98 T	99 O	100 Q	101 S	102 A	103 B
	104 G	105 A	106 I		107 K	108 S	109 D	110 I	111 V		112 E	113 C	114 G		115 A	116 B	117 O	118 G	119 E	120 L	121 I
122 N		123 H	124 M		125 P	126 J	127 M		128 G	129 E	130 N	131 D	132 A	133 O		134 E	135 K	136 Q		137 J	138 L
139 S	140 M	141 T	142 O	143 I	144 P	145 K		146 L	147 C		148 J	149 C	150 S	151 P	152 A	153 H	154 V	155 G	156 N	157 D
	158 N	159 T	160 H	161 I		162 Q	163 D	164 L	165 I	166 K	167 H		168 R	169 T		170 A	171 V	172 M	173 O	174 K
	175 P		176 K	177 G	178 T	179 Q		180 I	181 M		182 S	183 T	184 U	185 M	186 R	187 G	188 Q	

248

A. Clear adhesive: 2 wds.
$\overline{149}\ \overline{143}\ \overline{49}\ \overline{37}\ \overline{109}\ \overline{57}\ \overline{119}\ \overline{44}\ \overline{187}\ \overline{82}$

B. Eagle's claw
$\overline{96}\ \overline{52}\ \overline{162}\ \overline{120}\ \overline{171}$

C. Hard to pin down
$\overline{154}\ \overline{125}\ \overline{138}\ \overline{85}\ \overline{32}\ \overline{105}\ \overline{99}$

D. Said no
$\overline{3}\ \overline{151}\ \overline{10}\ \overline{40}\ \overline{122}\ \overline{163}\ \overline{87}$

E. Report from Rather
$\overline{101}\ \overline{108}\ \overline{56}\ \overline{95}\ \overline{54}\ \overline{117}\ \overline{31}\ \overline{90}$

F. Seventh heaven
$\overline{113}\ \overline{72}\ \overline{27}\ \overline{60}\ \overline{98}\ \overline{166}\ \overline{61}\ \overline{36}$

G. "I Got Rhythm" composer
$\overline{172}\ \overline{189}\ \overline{50}\ \overline{70}\ \overline{35}\ \overline{159}\ \overline{18}\ \overline{68}$

H. Loan percentage
$\overline{180}\ \overline{146}\ \overline{133}\ \overline{80}\ \overline{47}\ \overline{136}\ \overline{112}\ \overline{168}$

I. Arm joint
$\overline{106}\ \overline{161}\ \overline{88}\ \overline{24}\ \overline{75}$

J. Attorney's alma mater: 2 wds.
$\overline{124}\ \overline{29}\ \overline{129}\ \overline{100}\ \overline{155}\ \overline{174}\ \overline{71}\ \overline{65}\ \overline{77}$

K. Distributed: 2 wds.
$\overline{41}\ \overline{186}\ \overline{164}\ \overline{76}\ \overline{179}\ \overline{111}\ \overline{19}$

L. In progress: 2 wds.
$\overline{25}\ \overline{181}\ \overline{7}\ \overline{160}\ \overline{79}\ \overline{17}\ \overline{110}\ \overline{30}$

M. Yellow narcissus
$\overline{66}\ \overline{83}\ \overline{9}\ \overline{21}\ \overline{147}\ \overline{69}\ \overline{91}\ \overline{78}$

N. Of the teeth
$\overline{74}\ \overline{165}\ \overline{127}\ \overline{15}\ \overline{1}\ \overline{157}$

O. Teeny: hyph.
$\overline{58}\ \overline{134}\ \overline{177}\ \overline{158}\ \overline{107}\ \overline{140}\ \overline{6}\ \overline{26}\ \overline{16}$

P. Valerie Harper series
$\overline{121}\ \overline{135}\ \overline{64}\ \overline{139}\ \overline{123}$

Q. Vacant
$\overline{144}\ \overline{23}\ \overline{150}\ \overline{183}\ \overline{38}$

R. Used a credit card
$\overline{12}\ \overline{185}\ \overline{137}\ \overline{84}\ \overline{63}\ \overline{46}\ \overline{97}$

S. Last of a score
$\overline{34}\ \overline{148}\ \overline{86}\ \overline{73}\ \overline{130}\ \overline{11}\ \overline{4}\ \overline{176}\ \overline{115}$

T. Formfitting
$\overline{33}\ \overline{145}\ \overline{8}\ \overline{142}\ \overline{156}\ \overline{104}\ \overline{2}\ \overline{169}\ \overline{114}$

U. Country east of Austria
$\overline{81}\ \overline{89}\ \overline{190}\ \overline{178}\ \overline{175}\ \overline{152}\ \overline{167}$

V. Cider brandy
$\overline{67}\ \overline{188}\ \overline{45}\ \overline{103}\ \overline{42}\ \overline{93}\ \overline{22}\ \overline{59}\ \overline{126}$

W. Elephant driver
$\overline{51}\ \overline{5}\ \overline{131}\ \overline{184}\ \overline{94}\ \overline{173}$

X. Pine away
$\overline{28}\ \overline{132}\ \overline{53}\ \overline{182}\ \overline{13}\ \overline{170}\ \overline{62}\ \overline{20}$

Y. Cause and ———
$\overline{116}\ \overline{48}\ \overline{153}\ \overline{141}\ \overline{118}\ \overline{102}$

Z. Play a flute
$\overline{92}\ \overline{39}\ \overline{128}\ \overline{43}\ \overline{14}\ \overline{55}$

Solution on page 288

1 N		2 T	3 D	4 S	5 W	6 O		7 L	8 T	9 M	10 D	11 S	12 R	13 X	14 Z	15 N	16 O
17 L	18 G	19 K	20 X		21 M	22 V	23 Q	24 I	25 L	26 O		27 F	28 X	29 J	30 L	31 E		32 C
33 T		34 S	35 G	36 F	37 A		38 Q	39 Z	40 D		41 K	42 V	43 Z		44 A		45 V	46 R	47 H	48 Y	49 A
50 G	51 W	52 B	53 X	54 E	55 Z		56 E	57 A	58 O	59 V	60 F		61 F	62 X		63 R	64 P	65 J	66 M		67 V
68 G	69 M		70 G	71 J	72 F	73 S	74 N		75 I	76 K	77 J	78 M		79 L	80 H	81 U	82 A	83 M	84 R	85 C	86 S
87 D		88 I	89 U	90 E		91 M	92 Z		93 V	94 W	95 E	96 B		97 R	98 F	99 C	100 J	101 E	102 Y		103 V
104 T	105 C	106 I		107 O	108 E	109 A	110 L	111 K	112 H	113 F		114 T	115 S	116 Y		117 E	118 Y	119 A	120 B	121 P	122 D
	123 P	124 J	125 C		126 V	127 N	128 Z	129 J		130 S	131 W	132 X	133 H		134 O	135 P	136 H		137 R	138 C	139 P
140 O	141 Y	142 T	143 A	144 Q		145 T	146 H	147 M	148 S	149 A		150 Q	151 D	152 U	153 Y	154 C	155 J	156 T	157 N	158 O
	159 G	160 L	161 I	162 B		163 D	164 K	165 N	166 F	167 U	168 H	169 T	170 X	171 B	172 G		173 W	174 J	175 U	176 S
	177 O		178 U	179 K	180 H	181 L	182 X		183 Q	184 W		185 R	186 K	187 A	188 V	189 G	190 U	

Crostic 16

A. Center of attention
$\overline{51}\ \overline{190}\ \overline{64}\ \overline{185}\ \overline{44}\ \overline{151}\ \overline{105}\ \overline{153}\ \overline{20}$

B. Seeding place for mollusks: 2 wds.
$\overline{100}\ \overline{81}\ \overline{88}\ \overline{139}\ \overline{96}\ \overline{129}\ \overline{195}\ \overline{46}\ \overline{22}$

C. Type of cake: hyph.
$\overline{89}\ \overline{180}\ \overline{15}\ \overline{56}\ \overline{99}\ \overline{150}\ \overline{119}\ \overline{49}\ \overline{42}\ \overline{138}$

D. Capital of Pakistan
$\overline{69}\ \overline{102}\ \overline{178}\ \overline{28}\ \overline{141}\ \overline{53}\ \overline{186}\ \overline{19}\ \overline{93}$

E. Trace
$\overline{60}\ \overline{75}\ \overline{67}\ \overline{182}\ \overline{1}\ \overline{50}$

F. Reluctant
$\overline{33}\ \overline{120}\ \overline{61}\ \overline{5}\ \overline{193}$

G. Plant growth
$\overline{45}\ \overline{14}\ \overline{91}\ \overline{86}\ \overline{183}\ \overline{78}\ \overline{134}\ \overline{171}\ \overline{106}\ \overline{157}$

H. Ageless
$\overline{123}\ \overline{13}\ \overline{7}\ \overline{175}\ \overline{172}\ \overline{104}\ \overline{10}\ \overline{65}\ \overline{144}\ \overline{3}$

I. Hives
$\overline{169}\ \overline{92}\ \overline{164}\ \overline{148}\ \overline{47}$

J. Beguile
$\overline{135}\ \overline{191}\ \overline{121}\ \overline{152}\ \overline{160}\ \overline{26}\ \overline{158}$

K. Marina: 2 wds.
$\overline{4}\ \overline{72}\ \overline{132}\ \overline{48}\ \overline{197}\ \overline{52}\ \overline{156}\ \overline{84}\ \overline{17}\ \overline{166}$

L. Chances
$\overline{24}\ \overline{147}\ \overline{11}\ \overline{122}$

M. Exotic
$\overline{161}\ \overline{124}\ \overline{108}\ \overline{165}\ \overline{114}\ \overline{63}\ \overline{80}\ \overline{168}\ \overline{187}\ \overline{98}$

N. Paid
$\overline{29}\ \overline{77}\ \overline{155}\ \overline{32}\ \overline{125}\ \overline{66}\ \overline{137}\ \overline{23}$

O. Represent with symbols
$\overline{57}\ \overline{43}\ \overline{94}\ \overline{113}\ \overline{68}\ \overline{110}$

P. Academician
$\overline{181}\ \overline{37}\ \overline{25}\ \overline{149}\ \overline{127}\ \overline{39}\ \overline{34}$

Q. Attempts
$\overline{154}\ \overline{2}\ \overline{163}\ \overline{177}\ \overline{90}\ \overline{145}\ \overline{107}\ \overline{189}\ \overline{118}\ \overline{38}$

R. Watch closely: 3 wds.
$\overline{87}\ \overline{196}\ \overline{167}\ \overline{8}\ \overline{117}\ \overline{146}\ \overline{111}\ \overline{35}\ \overline{179}\ \overline{62}$

S. As a result of: 2 wds.
$\overline{9}\ \overline{31}\ \overline{142}\ \overline{71}\ \overline{58}\ \overline{109}\ \overline{12}$

T. Covenant
$\overline{170}\ \overline{21}\ \overline{73}\ \overline{74}\ \overline{6}\ \overline{82}\ \overline{115}\ \overline{162}\ \overline{116}$

U. Effigies
$\overline{140}\ \overline{136}\ \overline{83}\ \overline{192}\ \overline{76}\ \overline{159}$

V. Prattler
$\overline{18}\ \overline{126}\ \overline{194}\ \overline{103}\ \overline{143}\ \overline{173}\ \overline{54}\ \overline{27}\ \overline{70}\ \overline{131}$

W. Small antelope: hyph.
$\overline{41}\ \overline{97}\ \overline{30}\ \overline{174}\ \overline{59}\ \overline{55}$

X. Suddenly
$\overline{36}\ \overline{176}\ \overline{130}\ \overline{188}\ \overline{40}\ \overline{128}\ \overline{101}\ \overline{184}\ \overline{85}$

Y. Circumference
$\overline{112}\ \overline{133}\ \overline{79}\ \overline{16}\ \overline{95}$

Solution on page 288

1 E	2 Q	3 H	4 K		5 F	6 T	7 H	8 R		9 S	10 H		11 L	12 S	13 H	14 G	15 C
16 Y	17 K	18 V	19 D	20 A	21 T	22 B		23 N	24 L	25 P	26 J		27 V	28 D	29 N	30 W		31 S	32 N	33 F	34 P
	35 R	36 X	37 P	38 Q		39 P	40 X	41 W		42 C	43 O	44 A	45 G	46 B	47 I		48 K	49 C	50 E	51 A
52 K	53 D	54 V	55 W	56 C	57 O	58 S		59 W	60 E		61 F	62 R		63 M	64 A	65 H	66 N	67 E	68 O	69 D	70 V
71 S		72 K	73 T		74 T	75 E	76 U		77 N	78 G	79 Y	80 M	81 B		82 T	83 U	84 K	85 X	86 G	87 R	88 B
	89 C	90 Q	91 G	92 I	93 D		94 O	95 Y	96 B	97 W	98 M		99 C	100 B	101 X	102 D		103 V	104 H		105 A
106 G		107 Q	108 M	109 S	110 O	111 R		112 Y	113 O	114 M	115 T		116 T	117 R	118 Q		119 C	120 F	121 J	122 L
123 H	124 M		125 N	126 V	127 P	128 X	129 B		130 X	131 V	132 K	133 Y	134 G	135 J	136 U	137 N	138 C	139 B		140 U	141 D
142 S	143 V	144 H	145 Q	146 R	147 L		148 I	149 P	150 C	151 A	152 J		153 A	154 Q	155 N	156 K	157 G	158 J		159 U	160 J
161 M	162 T	163 Q	164 I		165 M	166 K	167 R		168 M	169 I		170 T	171 G	172 H	173 V		174 W	175 H	176 X	177 Q	178 D
179 R	180 C	181 P	182 E		183 G	184 X	185 A		186 D	187 M	188 X	189 Q		190 A	191 J	192 U		193 F	194 V	195 B	196 R	197 K

Crostic 17

A. Navigational aid
$\overline{198}\ \overline{112}\ \overline{157}\ \overline{41}\ \overline{47}\ \overline{16}\ \overline{133}\ \overline{78}\ \overline{141}\ \overline{94}$

B. Darwinian theory
$\overline{73}\ \overline{191}\ \overline{38}\ \overline{79}\ \overline{23}\ \overline{52}\ \overline{65}\ \overline{29}\ \overline{5}$

C. Pollyanna attitude
$\overline{62}\ \overline{43}\ \overline{124}\ \overline{32}\ \overline{164}\ \overline{190}\ \overline{115}\ \overline{101}$

D. Determined
$\overline{131}\ \overline{67}\ \overline{105}\ \overline{118}\ \overline{123}\ \overline{56}\ \overline{113}\ \overline{178}$

E. Antitheses
$\overline{147}\ \overline{25}\ \overline{44}\ \overline{159}\ \overline{149}\ \overline{1}\ \overline{129}\ \overline{163}\ \overline{90}$

F. Day of rest
$\overline{75}\ \overline{17}\ \overline{92}\ \overline{8}\ \overline{194}\ \overline{110}\ \overline{53}$

G. Climatic zone
$\overline{37}\ \overline{176}\ \overline{151}\ \overline{87}\ \overline{98}\ \overline{148}\ \overline{165}\ \overline{182}\ \overline{83}$

H. Competent
$\overline{14}\ \overline{33}\ \overline{30}\ \overline{76}\ \overline{134}\ \overline{195}\ \overline{114}\ \overline{162}\ \overline{61}$

I. Unusual items
$\overline{137}\ \overline{187}\ \overline{13}\ \overline{54}\ \overline{31}\ \overline{185}\ \overline{106}\ \overline{28}\ \overline{86}$

J. Likely
$\overline{55}\ \overline{84}\ \overline{107}\ \overline{72}\ \overline{161}\ \overline{117}\ \overline{197}\ \overline{181}$

K. Impromptu: hyph.
$\overline{81}\ \overline{66}\ \overline{63}\ \overline{139}\ \overline{154}\ \overline{167}\ \overline{99}\ \overline{136}\ \overline{175}\ \overline{77}$

L. Ceremony of admission
$\overline{155}\ \overline{144}\ \overline{91}\ \overline{128}\ \overline{11}\ \overline{42}\ \overline{70}\ \overline{173}\ \overline{169}\ \overline{4}$

M. Written with symbols
$\overline{50}\ \overline{96}\ \overline{153}\ \overline{127}\ \overline{7}\ \overline{68}\ \overline{125}\ \overline{89}\ \overline{109}\ \overline{10}$

N. Completely
$\overline{158}\ \overline{120}\ \overline{111}\ \overline{95}\ \overline{59}\ \overline{80}\ \overline{184}\ \overline{189}\ \overline{93}\ \overline{45}$

O. Password
$\overline{36}\ \overline{160}\ \overline{46}\ \overline{39}\ \overline{97}\ \overline{100}\ \overline{64}\ \overline{171}\ \overline{138}\ \overline{48}$

P. Small, circular drum
$\overline{18}\ \overline{143}\ \overline{170}\ \overline{82}\ \overline{26}\ \overline{74}\ \overline{57}\ \overline{35}\ \overline{179}\ \overline{34}$

Q. Air base near Omaha, Nebraska
$\overline{88}\ \overline{146}\ \overline{174}\ \overline{188}\ \overline{15}\ \overline{132}$

R. Nonsense
$\overline{22}\ \overline{135}\ \overline{102}\ \overline{58}\ \overline{186}\ \overline{2}\ \overline{150}\ \overline{180}\ \overline{51}$

S. Sculled
$\overline{140}\ \overline{103}\ \overline{24}\ \overline{152}\ \overline{145}$

T. Bullwinkle's enemy Nogoodnik
$\overline{108}\ \overline{116}\ \overline{19}\ \overline{121}\ \overline{168}\ \overline{183}\ \overline{3}$

U. Capital of Iowa: 2 wds.
$\overline{166}\ \overline{9}\ \overline{104}\ \overline{126}\ \overline{6}\ \overline{49}\ \overline{156}\ \overline{40}\ \overline{69}$

V. Hoisted
$\overline{21}\ \overline{122}\ \overline{192}\ \overline{119}\ \overline{196}\ \overline{142}\ \overline{12}\ \overline{172}$

W. Moira Shearer film with "The": 2 wds.
$\overline{177}\ \overline{85}\ \overline{193}\ \overline{27}\ \overline{20}\ \overline{71}\ \overline{130}\ \overline{60}$

Solution on page 288

1 E		2 R	3 T	4 L	5 B	6 U	7 M		8 F	9 U	10 M	11 L	12 V	13 I	14 H		15 Q
16 A	17 F	18 P		19 T	20 W	21 V		22 R	23 B	24 S	25 E	26 P	27 W	28 I		29 B	30 H
	31 I	32 C	33 H	34 P		35 P	36 O		37 G	38 B		39 O	40 U		41 A	42 L	43 C	44 E	45 N		46 O
	47 A	48 O	49 U	50 M	51 R		52 B	53 F	54 I		55 J	56 D	57 P	58 R	59 N	60 W	61 H		62 C	63 K
64 O	65 B	66 K	67 D		68 M	69 U		70 L	71 W		72 J	73 B		74 P	75 F	76 H	77 K	78 A	79 B		80 N
81 K		82 P	83 G		84 J	85 W	86 I	87 G	88 Q	89 M	90 E	91 L	92 F	93 N	94 A		95 N	96 M		97 O	98 G
	99 K	100 O	101 C	102 R	103 S	104 U	105 D	106 I	107 J	108 T	109 M	110 F	111 N		112 A	113 D		114 H	115 C		116 T
117 J	118 D	119 V	120 N		121 T	122 V	123 D		124 C	125 M		126 U	127 M	128 L	129 E	130 W	131 D		132 Q	133 A
134 H	135 R	136 K	137 I	138 O		139 K	140 S		141 A	142 V	143 P	144 L	145 S		146 Q	147 E	148 G		149 E	150 R	151 G
152 S	153 M	154 K	155 L	156 U	157 A		158 N	159 E		160 O	161 J	162 H	163 E		164 C	165 G	166 U	167 K		168 T	169 L
	170 P	171 O		172 V	173 L	174 Q	175 K	176 G	177 W	178 D	179 P	180 R	181 J		182 G	183 T	184 N	185 I
	186 R	187 I	188 Q		189 N	190 C	191 B	192 V	193 W		194 F	195 H		196 V	197 J	198 A

251

Crostic 18

A. Computer components — 74 67 56 98 8 127 144 39 201 54

B. Medication — 146 119 63 82 160 126 106 179 69 149

C. Sailing vessel's lookout: hyph. — 113 83 136 97 29 166 3 124 178

D. Kitchen appliance — 197 115 5 135 121 42 59 155 52 164

E. Desert waterhole — 36 194 142 133 171

F. Sleeping garment — 109 11 25 140 138 176 35 18 148 104

G. "M*A*S*H" star: 2 wds. — 61 19 103 85 204 30 66 34

H. German air fleet — 102 123 73 86 132 112 14 89 177

I. Supper engagement: 2 wds. — 65 158 47 50 203 40 196 1 114 101

J. Speaker's platform — 193 55 128 118

K. Logical thinking — 15 187 81 199 93 62

L. Book of the Bible — 120 125 174 145 6 165 200 2 12

M. Shorten — 161 41 157 205 96 100 31 16 37 110

N. Ace-flyer Jimmy ___ — 53 90 129 152 105 134 21 44 169

O. Tiny hatchery fish — 94 48 24 159 181 9 168 141 107 173

P. Female theater guides — 137 206 22 33 91 77 80 185 71 153

Q. Actress Nettleton — 180 45 26 108

R. Legal action — 43 84 27 28 162 13 49 198 184 192

S. Son of Seth — 88 130 79 182

T. One-god believer — 92 150 95 190 154 78 20 147 122 60

U. Too heavy — 72 70 99 76 163 51 23 17 186 143

V. Prohibitive word: hyph. — 195 46 58 116

W. Recreation spots: 2 wds. — 131 7 64 139 156 202 38 189 32 175

X. Showing deference — 167 57 4 68 151 111 172 117 188

Y. Lads — 10 75 191 183 87 170

Solution on page 288

1 I		2 L	3 C	4 X	5 D		6 L	7 W	8 A	9 O	10 Y		11 F	12 L
13 R		14 H	15 K	16 M	17 U	18 F	19 G	20 T		21 N	22 P	23 U	24 O	25 F		26 Q	27 R
28 R	29 C		30 G	31 M	32 W	33 P		34 G		35 F	36 E	37 M	▬	38 W	39 A	40 I		41 M	42 D	43 R
44 N	45 Q	46 V	47 I		48 O	49 R		50 I	51 U	52 D	53 N	54 A		55 J		56 A	57 X	58 V	59 D	60 T	61 G
62 K	63 B		64 W	65 I	66 G	67 A	68 X	69 B	70 U	71 P		72 U	73 H		74 A	75 Y	76 U	77 P		78 T	79 S
80 P		81 K	82 B	83 C		84 R	85 G		86 H	87 Y	88 S		89 H	90 N	91 P	92 T		93 K	94 O		95 T
96 M	97 C		98 A	99 U	100 M	101 I	102 H	103 G	104 F	105 N	106 B	107 O	108 Q		109 F	110 M	111 X		112 H	113 C	114 I
115 D	116 V	117 X	118 J		119 B	120 L	121 D		122 T	123 H	124 C	125 L	126 B	127 A	128 J	129 N	130 S	131 W			132 H	133 E
134 N	135 D	136 C	137 P	138 F		139 W	140 F	141 O	142 E		143 U	144 A	145 L		146 B	147 T	148 F		149 B	150 T	151 X
152 N	153 P		154 T	155 D	156 W		157 M	158 I	159 O		160 B	161 M	162 R		163 U	164 D	165 L	166 C	167 X	168 O	169 N
170 Y		171 E	172 X	173 O	174 L	175 W		176 F	177 H	178 C	179 B	180 Q	181 O	182 S		183 Y	184 R		185 P	186 U	187 K
	188 X	189 W	190 T	191 Y	192 R	193 J		194 E	195 V	196 I		197 D	198 R	199 K	200 L	201 A	202 W	203 I	204 G	205 M	206 P

252

Window Boxes

There is a common 4-letter word hidden in each strip of letters in Column I. Find the words by thinking of the strips in Column II as open and closed windows and then matching each letter strip with its correct window strip so that the 4-letter word will show. There is only one correct solution for all ten strips.

Solution on page 287

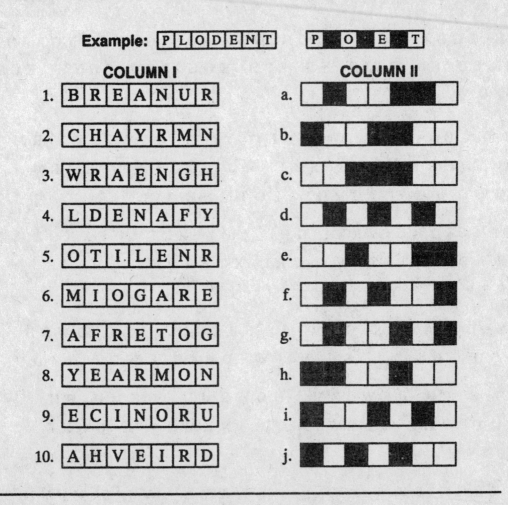

Example: P L O D E N T   P O E T

COLUMN I

1. B R E A N U R
2. C H A Y R M N
3. W R A E N G H
4. L D E N A F Y
5. O T I L E N R
6. M I O G A R E
7. A F R E T O G
8. Y E A R M O N
9. E C I N O R U
10. A H V E I R D

COLUMN II

a.
b.
c.
d.
e.
f.
g.
h.
i.
j.

Exploraword

How many 4-letter words can you form from the letters of the given word? A letter may be used only as many times as it appears in the given word. Proper names, contractions, and foreign words are not allowed.

Our list of 68 words on page 289

P E D E S T A L

CRYPTOGRAMS

Each of these cryptograms is a sentence in a substitution code. One letter of the alphabet is substituted for the correct letter. THE SMART CAT might become MRX DGYUM LYM. M is substituted for T, R for H, X for E, etc. One way to break the code is to look for repeated letters. E, T, A, O, N, R, and I are the most often used letters. A single letter is usually A or I; OF, IS, and IT are common two-letter words; try THE or AND for a three-letter group. The code is different for each cryptogram.

Solutions on page 289

1. KCB YGDJO YFZ LFOB DGXWO ZG YB YGXJO
   WBMBD SB FSJB KG ZBB KGG RFD OGYW KCB
   DGFO.

2. KM KGC AJ QGOI WJRC YMMYK YKGY PKMO
   KM AQHRMC, HY RJJXMC GA HB G EHEM
   JDWGO PGA UMHOW LOTMHRMC.

3. KNB KZDRUG FXI QFL YBX KZI ZIFXK:
   XTRRDRU TSZDVV FRL XTRRDRU LBNR
   SIBSVI.

4. L ALOS ADHX GJAOB, SBESILJAAU GWSH
   ZWSU JNS ZJOSH VU ESDEAS GWD JHHDU RS.

5. NKMH PH BKWLZM, UQHGML. NKMH PH
   ALQXDYM, GMYMZWAM. NKMH PH GQXDA,
   IXIDYM.

6. XYXHGX FV FOCXH: "BI ZVA LVT'F HFVN
   JQXMMBTM, B'YY HNYBF AN FPV IVQ VTO,
   XTL FUOT ZVA'YY JO FUO FUBQL YXQMOHF
   HFXFO!"

7. YBKP-EBYTBHX ZY XIB PENZX MP
   LZYHZTKZDB; XIB YBDYB MP LZCDZXJ
   CEMFY FZXI XIB QUZKZXJ XM YQJ DM XM
   MDBYBKP.

254

8. W XRB XJPRGJE WA WVLYO OSMJJ BJWME
XJNRMJ SQE KWMJAOE OSQAD SJ VRJE, WAV
WXRLO OIR BJWME WNOJM SJ OSQADE SJ
VRJE.

9. GB GD Q TEEI XSQM BE QGK Q SGBBSW
NGTNWH BNQM UEZH BQHTWB DE QD BE
KQLW UEZH DNEB DZHW, RZB MEB DE
NGTN BNQB UEZ EAWHDNEEB BNW KQHL.

10. S YTEEDYYPTC ASBBJSVD BDLTJBDY
PSCCJZV JZ CUID ASZH MJADY, SCFSHY
FJMW MWD YSAD GDBYUZ.

11. ADPI KAQ FPQFEP EQTP PBMD QKDPY, KDPS
LQI'K EQQR BK PBMD QKDPY, KDPS EQQR HI
KDP VBWP LHYPMKHQI.

12. UPWS ZOQOQDOZ, CGSYVPTY SYO WPL YCW C
WHLMHLT WIOGG ONOZB LHTYS, HS ZHWOW
CTCHL SYO LOES QVZLHLT.

13. E NDT DJP MRRTPAEMUP M BDDV NDTH
YPUUPT, LMGEJB IDTQPV DJ AMREUDY LEYY
MJV YPMTJPV FPGPTMY VDKPJ ADTVEMY
IMWF UD FMW JDULEJB.

14. MFGFBL GNCCFRF RMHSWHLF: ''Q VHX NB LEF
SFHB'X CQXL, TWL BNTNSU QB LEF
FOACNUOFBL NZZQGFX XFFOX LN PBNV LEF
SFHB.''

MASTERWORDS

Using only the 10 letters given below, fill in the diagram forming words across and down to achieve the highest possible score. Each letter has a given value, so try to use the high-value letters as much as possible. You may repeat letters as often as you wish, even within words. Do not repeat words in the diagram. Foreign words, abbreviations, and words starting with a capital letter are not allowed.

When the diagram is completely filled, add up your score. Count across only, each letter, line by line. Put the total for each line in the boxes at the right.

Our solution with a score of 350 points on page 289

A₄ B₁ E₃ I₅ L₂ N₅ O₁ R₃ S₂ T₄

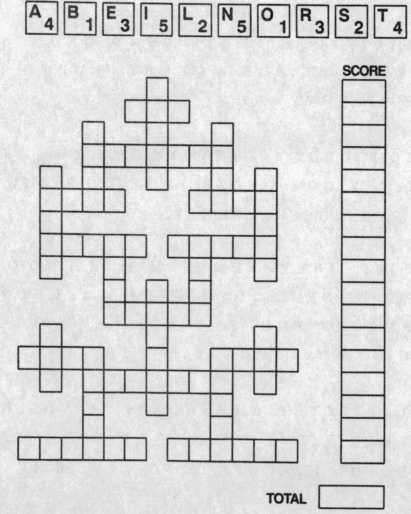

SCORE

TOTAL

256

ANAGRAM MAGIC SQUARE

Find an anagram for the 5-letter word in each box. The anagram will answer one of the clues. Put the number of that clue into the small square and write the anagram on the dash. The numbers in each row and column will add up to 65. Write the first letter of each anagram on the correspondingly numbered dash at the bottom of the page; and, presto!, the Anagram Magic saying will appear. To start you off, we have put in one anagram and its clue number and set its first letter on the proper dash at the bottom of the page.   Solution on page 289

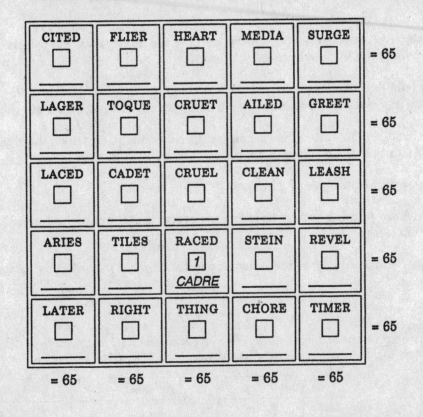

CITED ☐ ___	FLIER ☐ ___	HEART ☐ ___	MEDIA ☐ ___	SURGE ☐ ___	= 65
LAGER ☐ ___	TOQUE ☐ ___	CRUET ☐ ___	AILED ☐ ___	GREET ☐ ___	= 65
LACED ☐ ___	CADET ☐ ___	CRUEL ☐ ___	CLEAN ☐ ___	LEASH ☐ ___	= 65
ARIES ☐ ___	TILES ☐ ___	RACED ☐1☐ CADRE	STEIN ☐ ___	REVEL ☐ ___	= 65
LATER ☐ ___	RIGHT ☐ ___	THING ☐ ___	CHORE ☐ ___	TIMER ☐ ___	= 65

= 65   = 65   = 65   = 65   = 65

1. Framework
2. Dark yellow
3. Desires
4. Princely
5. Emulated Meryl Streep
6. Circumference
7. Ground
8. Model
9. Fissile rock
10. Bring up
11. Command
12. Cite
13. Stomach problem
14. Map within a map
15. Slacken
16. White heron
17. Transfer design
18. Key
19. It has a thousand eyes
20. Targeted
21. Puncture
22. Simple machine
23. Warning
24. Ransack
25. Armistice

C
— —
1 2 3 4 5 6 7 8 9 10 11 12 13 14 15 16 17 18 19 20 21 22 23 24 25

LOGIC PROBLEM

COMMUNITY ART

Last week, the volunteers at the Baybridge Community Center were delighted when each of five local artists (one of whom is Ricki) donated a painting to the center. Each painting was in a different-colored frame and hung in a different room (one was the foyer). Each painting was in a different genre (one was abstract). From the information provided, determine the frame color of each artist's painting, the room in which each painting was placed, and the genre of each painting. (Note: All names are gender neutral.)

1. The painting framed in red (which was hung in the library) was not the one painted by Robin (who painted the surrealist painting).

2. Lesley (who isn't the one who used photorealism in his or her painting) framed her painting in green. Lesley's painting was hung in neither the kitchen nor the game room.

3. The painting in the white frame is neither the cubist painting, which was painted by a man and was hung in the meeting room, nor the one hung in the kitchen.

4. Courtney framed his painting in blue.

5. Chris (whose painting was not hung in the library) isn't the one who donated the painting framed in tan.

6. The man who painted the impressionist painting did not frame his painting in red.

This chart is to help you record information from the clues as well as the facts you deduce by combining information from different clues. We suggest you use an "X" for a "no" and a "•" for a "yes."

		COLOR					ROOM					GENRE				
		BLUE	GREEN	RED	TAN	WHITE	FOYER	GAME ROOM	KITCHEN	LIBRARY	MEETING ROOM	ABSTRACT	CUBIST	IMPRESSIONIST	PHOTOREALISTIC	SURREALIST
ARTIST	CHRIS															
ARTIST	COURTNEY															
ARTIST	LESLEY															
ARTIST	RICKI															
ARTIST	ROBIN															
GENRE	ABSTRACT															
GENRE	CUBIST															
GENRE	IMPRESSIONIST															
GENRE	PHOTOREALISTIC															
GENRE	SURREALIST															
ROOM	FOYER															
ROOM	GAME ROOM															
ROOM	KITCHEN															
ROOM	LIBRARY															
ROOM	MEETING ROOM															

Solution on page 289

MAZE

Find your way through this maze from the arrow at the top to the one at the bottom.
Solution on page 290

CIRCLES IN THE SQUARE

The twenty 5-letter words all fit in the diagram. All words begin and end in a dark circle. Horizontal words read from left to right; all other words from top to bottom. We have set one letter to get you started.

Solution on page 290

BEAST	LINED	NOVEL	ROWAN
BLIMP	LOFTY	PAUSE	TALON
BROWN	NANNY	PECAN	TAPER
DAISY	NOMAD	PROUD	TOWEL
EMEND	NOOSE	REGAL	TROOP

260

SIMON SAYS

Start with POST OFFICE and follow the directions carefully to discover a phrase that is apropos.

Solution on page 290

1. Print the words POST OFFICE.

1. _____

2. Change the first vowel from the left to an A.

2. _____

3. Insert a D to the left of the C.

3. _____

4. Reverse the order of the first four letters from the left.

4. _____

5. Change the F's to G's.

5. _____

6. Insert an N to the left of each G.

6. _____

7. Switch the O and the I.

7. _____

8. Insert an R to the left of the O.

8. _____

9. Move the second N from the left to the right of the O.

9. _____

10. Insert an M to the right of the A.

10. _____

11. Change the first consonant from the right to an S.

11. _____

12. Delete the E.

12. _____

13. Insert a U to the right of the O.

13. _____

14. Switch the first and second letters from the left.

14. _____

NUMBER JUMBLE

Using the numbers 1, 3, 5, and 9, which four-number combination is missing?

Solution on page 290

1593 5319 9351 5193

3195 3951 9531 1395

5139 1359 3519 9315

1953 3915 9153

5931 9513 5391 1935

3159

3591 1539 ? 9135

SCRAMBLE ACROSS

Unscramble each group of letters in the diagram on the top to form a word and put it into the corresponding group of squares in the diagram on the bottom. Do this for ACROSS WORDS ONLY. The completed diagram on the bottom will be a crossword puzzle with words reading across and down. For groups of letters that can make more than one word across, solve across and down together.

Solution on page 290

FILL-IN

The entries for this puzzle are given to you, listed alphabetically according to length. Across and Down words are all mixed together, and you are to find their proper places in the diagram.

Solution on page 290

3 Letters
Ace
Aga
Aim
Bed
Bee
Bud
Ela
Ere
Err
Hot
Hut
Lad ✓

Lag
Let
Nor
O'er
Oil
Pin
Pod
Pop
Pro
Res
Set
Sly
Sur

Tau
Ten
Tin

4 Letters
Aden
Amid
Anns
Edge
Eire
Fume
Isle
Nuns

Ogee
Paid
Pass
Pole
Read
Sari
Silo
Spit
Tear
Tsar

5 Letters
Amass

Astir
Cedes
Pones
Pulse
Roams
Spate
Spurn
Tonal
Tress

6 Letters
Elicit
Script
Smiles
Stains

7 Letters
Edifies
Imitate

8 Letters
Laudable
Ordinary

9 Letters
Annuities
Dismissal

ALPHABET PLUS

Form common 5-letter words by rearranging each word and adding the letter of the alphabet shown with it. The word ARENA (the letters of NEAR plus the letter A) has been filled in for you.

Our solution on page 290

A + NEAR = __ARENA__

B + LATE = _____

C + ROVE = _____

D + ABLE = _____

E + CHAR = _____

F + TEAR = _____

G + PEAR = _____

H + CRIB = _____

I + ONES = _____

J + ROAM = _____

K + LEAN = _____

L + MACE = _____

M + ROAR = _____

N + CASK = _____

O + DARN = _____

P + PLEA = _____

Q + SUET = _____

R + COAT = _____

S + RIFT = _____

T + TRUE = _____

U + CONE = _____

V + TAIL = _____

W + TAKE = _____

X + REAL = _____

Y + LIED = _____

Z + RACY = _____

Numberboxes

Using the hints below, correctly place the numbers 1 through 9 into the diagram.

Solution on page 290

1. 5 is top center.

2. 3 is directly below 1.

3. 4 is directly left of 5.

4. 7 is two squares to the right of 9.

5. 8 is two squares to the left of 6.

6. 1 is directly right of 9.

7. 2 is two squares directly above 6.

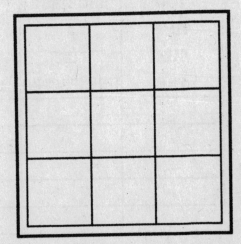

TELEPHONE CALL

Can you tell which one of these phones is ringing? Its number has 1 even and 2 odd digits and is divisible by 3.

Solution on page 290

Suspended Sentence

The words in each vertical column go into the spaces directly below them, but not necessarily in the order they appear. When you have placed all the words in their correct spaces, you will be able to read a quotation across the diagram from left to right.

Solution on page 290

FOR	PUT	RECORDED	THE	RAIN
YOU	SHORTEST	RAINY	OF	AWAY
TIME	A	ARRIVAL	PERIOD	OF
THE	LIES	SOME	MONEY	AND
THE	UNEXPECTED	BETWEEN	DAY	MINUTE

SYLLASTEPS

CAL	LIG	RA	PHY
A	CU	I	TY
AD	U	LA	TOR
LAC	ER	A	TION
COM	PRO	MIS	ER
IM	PU	RI	TIES
IN	SCRU	TA	BLE
RE	LO	CA	TION

CROSS NUMBERS

4	80	50	14	8	12
32	4	5	2	10	52
21	3	16	6	2	58
5	8	17	11	28	3
4	5	10	6	7	5
5	26	19	32	30	14

BRICK BY BRICK

C	R	I	B		D	A	M	S		O	M	E	N	S
L	A	N	A		E	M	I	T		R	O	D	E	O
A	N	T	S		C	A	F	E	T	E	R	I	A	S
M	E	E	K	E	R		F	A	R		O	T	T	O
P	E	R		D	E	E		M	I	A	S			
			L	E	G	E	N	D		A	M	E	N	D	S
S	T	O	R	Y		S	I	L	L	Y		O	R	A
H	O	P	E		H	U	L	A	S		S	T	A	N
A	G	E		F	E	E	L	S		A	R	E	T	E
M	A	R	B	L	E		Y	E	L	L	O	W		
			R	U	D	E		R	A	M		O	S	E
S	A	R	A		E	R	S		B	A	R	R	E	L
P	R	O	V	I	D	E	N	C	E		E	T	T	A
E	L	L	E	N		C	O	O	L		S	H	O	T
D	O	E	R	S		T	W	O	S			T	Y	N	E

FOUR CORNERS

B	U	M	P
A	S	E	A
L	E	S	S
D	R	A	T

C	R	A	B
H	A	L	O
O	R	A	L
P	E	S	T

C	L	A	P
H	I	R	E
E	V	E	R
F	E	A	T

F	I	S	H
I	D	L	E
S	E	A	R
T	A	P	E

AROUND THE BLOCK

BLOCKBUILDERS
SIDNEY POITIER

TRIANGLE QUOTE
Self-help is the best help.

ABACUS

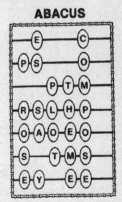

CHIPS
Nothing is harder to resist than a bit of flattery.

PUZZLE DERBY
1. FALLacious, 2. JUMPer, 3. gRUNion, 4. ColLIEs, 5. PoSITion, 6. HercuLEAN, 7. SWAYze, 8. JERKwater, 9. UnderSTAND, 10. WALKout. All answers contain the names of body movements. Win: Horse O; Place: Horse U; Show: Horse E.

MARBLES
CREPT (clockwise from upper left: R C P T; center: E)

GUESS WHO
1. Bob Denver, 2. Dan Rather, 3. Dolly Parton, 4. Jay Leno, 5. Lee Marvin, 6. Mae West, 7. Mel Gibson, 8. Woody Allen.

BOWL GAME
STRIKES: 1. Motherland, 2. Specialist, 3. Penetrated, 4. Vegetables, 5. Storehouse, 6. Receptions, 7. Fingernail, 8. Pawnbroker, 9. Spectacles, 10. Reschedule. SPARES: 1. Alder, Month; 2. Spice, Tails; 3. Drape, Tenet; 4. Bevel, Stage; 5. Hoses, Route; 6. Niece, Sport; 7. Elfin, Grain; 8. Brawn, Poker; 9. Place, Sects; 10. Cruel, Heeds.

ROULETTE
1. Lather, 2. Forest, 3. Intone, 4. Antler, 5. Allays, 6. Noodle, 7. Retina, 8. Arrest, 9. Beware, 10. Strive, 11. Needle, 12. Solder, 13. Total, 14. Outer, 15. Worse, 16. Liter, 17. Ego, 18. And, 19. Era, 20. Did, 21. Evens, 22. Needy, 23. Longs, 24. Ravel.
QUOTE: Life is an abnormal business.

ROUNDERS
Solitaire, Bridge, Canasta.

LETTER SCORE
1. Outwit, 2. Newts, 3. Awry, 4. Gadfly, 5. Zebra, 6. Godfather, 7. Oppose, 8. Flexible, 9. Gauze, 10. Bulletproof.

MATCH-UP
3 and 8 match. (Differences: 1. Foot, 2. Motion lines, 4. Buttons, 5. Head, 6. Eye, 7. Ball, 9. Flippers.)

BULL'S-EYE SPIRAL
OUT: 1. Delivers, 9. Pacers, 15. Retrace, 22. Sorest, 28. Until, 33. Nude, 37. Live, 41. Decal, 46. Presser, 53. Denim, 58. Redraw, 64. Dessert, 71. Cadet, 76. Roper.
IN: 80. Reported, 72. Actress, 65. Edward, 59. Ermine, 53. Dresser, 46. Place, 41. Deviled, 34. Unlit, 29. Nuts, 25. Erose, 20. Carters, 13. Recaps, 7. Reviled.

WORDFINDER
ACROSS: Crochet, Prone, Fortify, Vanish, Sweeten, Talcum, Helpful, Tomato, Priest, Bridge, Tooth.
DOWN: Python, Stared, Javelin, Variety, Weariest, Pattern, Cartoons, Talent, Postage, Bargain, School.

DART GAME
Gavel, Glory, Gourd, Guest, Graph.

PULLING STRINGS
1. Yule, 2. Honeysuckle, 3. Soy, 4. Leeks, 5. Chosen.

FINISH THE FOURS
Literary character: Count of Monte Cristo

WHEELS
A. 1. Preach, 2. Defray, 3. Firmly, 4. Subtle, 5. Donate, 6. Sailor, 7. Hinder, 8. Convey.
A happy family is but an earlier heaven.
B. 1. School, 2. Repeat, 3. Rustic, 4. Signal, 5. Sphinx, 6. Walrus, 7. Prince, 8. Ignore.
To some, reducing is wishful shrinking.

QUOTAGRAMS
A. Do noble things, do not dream them all day long.
B. Several excuses are always less convincing than one.
C. Expedients are for the hour, but principles are for the ages.
A. 1. Dean, 2. Moment, 3. Loyal, 4. Bland, 5. Delight, 6. Hood, 7. Strong.
B. 1. Scene, 2. Relevant, 3. Sways, 4. Choice, 5. Annals, 6. Vixen, 7. Sour, 8. Gales.
C. 1. Tutored, 2. Sheep, 3. Heir, 4. Appraise, 5. Greet, 6. Buffoon, 7. Christen, 8. Relax.

CATEGORIES
SIGNS: Capricorn, Libra, Aquarius, Sagittarius, Pisces.
ROOMS: Closet, Library, Attic, Studio, Parlor.
CAPITALS: Copenhagen, London, Athens, Stockholm, Paris.
BEVERAGES: Coffee, Lemonade, Ale, Soda, Punch.
BIBLE: Cain, Lazarus, Adam, Samson, Peter.

PLACES, PLEASE

E	L	L	T	K	S	S	S	A	P	Y	B	E
T	D	L	C	S	T	Y	A	N	G	L	E	S
A	A	I	A	O	L	A	E	R	E	S	A	U
L	L	P	T	H	A	W	E	S	E	P	R	M
S	A	E	E	N	X	N	S	R	I	A	D	E
R	E	S	A	R	E	U	R	E	K	A	S	B
N	O	O	C	C	A	R	A	P	T	U	R	E
I	O	S	H	T	R	E	U	A	A	U	E	N
W	R	O	T	E	M	S	D	P	L	A	C	E
I	E	R	U	P	U	T	U	E	T	M	O	A
D	G	A	A	R	F	F	S	N	E	I	L	T
E	I	N	R	A	F	U	T	N	A	R	O	H
R	T	I	N	Y	S	L	S	Y	A	P	R	N

TILE PATTERNS

6	2	4	1
1	4	3	6
3	5	2	1
2	6	1	3
6	2	5	2

RIDDLE ME THIS

1. Nine, 2. Happiness, 3. Noise, 4. Canvas.

PATCHWORK QUOTE

There is no money in poetry, but then there is no poetry in money either. (Robert Graves)

PHOTO FINISH

5 matches. (1. Fewer lines on sail, 2. No background, 3. Black on bottom of sail, 4. No water lines.)

THREE TO ONE

1. Headrest, 2. Notation, 3. Orchestrate, 4. Dentistry, 5. Reindeer, 6. Finalist, 7. Alphabet, 8. Informant, 9. Vanilla, 10. Taxicab.

HUBCAPS

1. Expand, Repair, Depart; 2. Salami, Splash, Inlaid; 3. Ascend, Recent, Accept.
BONUS WORD: Palace

SPLIT PERSONALITIES

1. Billie Jean King, 2. Steffi Graf, 3. Arthur Ashe, 4. Stefan Edberg, 5. Gabriela Sabatini, 6. Chris Evert, 7. Martina Navratilova, 8. Jimmy Connors.

LUCKY CLOVER

MIND BOGGLER

$$
\begin{array}{r}
5\,9\,4\,9 \\
-\,3\,5\,9\,4 \\
\hline
2\,3\,5\,5
\end{array}
$$

CRACKERJACKS

GROUND BEEF

BLIPS

Had, Hag, Hay, Hen, Hex, Hey, Hub, Hue, Hug.

GUEST STAR

1. Hazel, 2. Naive, 3. Tiara, 4. Again, 5. Excel.

GUEST STAR: Ethan Allen

WORD DIALS

1. Chapel, Forbid, Hectic, Jalopy. FISH: CARP

2. Phobia, Expose, Dinghy, Gazebo. FISH: SHAD

SHUFFLE

A. 1. Gerald Ford, 2. Bill Clinton, 3. Jimmy Carter, 4. Ronald Reagan.
B. 1. Patricia Nixon, 2. Bess Truman, 3. Barbara Bush, 4. Eleanor Roosevelt.

CRYPTO-TRIVIA

Piggy banks were not originally made in the shape of a pig. In the Middle Ages, kitchen utensils were made from an orange clay called "pygg." This clay was used to make cups, dishes, pots, and jars. People often saved money in their "pygg jars." Even when pygg was no longer used, the name remained. The pygg jars became pig banks when potters made the banks in the shape of the animal, the pig.

FOUR SQUARE

T	E	A	M	W	O	R	K
A	L	T	O	E	R	I	E
L	E	O	S	R	A	C	Y
L	E	N	S	E	L	K	S
T	A	R	T	S	H	U	T
A	R	I	A	T	A	R	O
L	I	N	K	E	R	I	N
E	D	G	E	W	I	S	E

FIRST AND LAST

I	A	N	A	V	A	K	E	M	B
S	H	P	L	Q	H	T	R	V	R
T	A	R	N	T	T	B	O	G	O
U	B	U	B	A	R	A	V	L	L
O	E	T	L	C	A	S	A	L	D
L	L	A	B	T	E	K	R	A	E
S	C	A	L	O	R	G	E	T	R
E	T	T	A	T	A	N	R	S	Y
Q	U	E	A	S	E	K	T	S	A
T	E	K	P	E	C	H	D	R

1. Basketball, 2. Louisiana, 3. Alphabet, 4. Turntable, 5. Earthquake, 6. Embroidery, 7. Yardstick, 8. Keepsake, 9. Etiquette, 10. Escalator, 11. Rangers, 12. Star, 13. Rally, 14. Yogurt.

WHAT'S LEFT?

Good questions outrank easy answers.

SCRAMBLED VEGETABLES

Radish, Pepper, Carrot, Potato, Celery, Squash, Turnip.

SLIDE-O-RAMA

Cape, Coat, Cowl, Gown, Hood, Muff, Robe, Ruff, Slip, Suit, Wrap.

HOW MANY SQUARES?

10 (ABGF, BCHG, BDOM, CEQN, CING, DEKI, GHNM, IKQO, JLRP, NOTS)

HEADINGS

1. Memory, Cordless, Dial, Speaker, Touch-tone.

2. Brush, Scraper, Roller, Thinner, Tint.

3. Fuchsia, Hyacinth, Wisteria, Wild rose, Daisy, Tulip.

FRAMEWORK 1

FRAMEWORK 5

FRAMEWORK 9

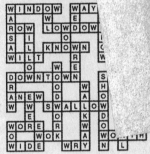

FRAMEWORK 2

FRAMEWORK 6

FRAMEWORK 10

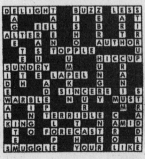

FRAMEWORK 3

FRAMEWORK 7

FRAMEWORK 11

FRAMEWORK 4

FRAMEWORK 8

FRAMEWORK 12

FILL-IN

CIRCLES IN THE SQUARE

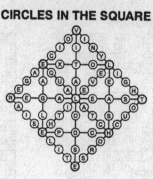

MASTERWORDS

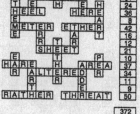

LETTERBOXES

NINE OF DIAMONDS

1. Patterns, 2. Reminder, 3. Migrated, 4. Contains, 5. Condense, 6. Happened, 7. Inventor, 8. Sawhorse, 9. Sapphire.

WORD MERGERS

1. Aim, Fly; Family.
2. Air, Fun; Unfair.
3. Fist, Say; Satisfy.
4. Has, Made; Ashamed.
5. Chop, Main; Champion.
6. Core, Dirt; Director.
7. Coin, Tune; Continue.

DAISY

Reach, Panic, Tonic, Elect, Acute.
BONUS WORD: Carpet

SQUARES

1. Maintain, 2. Hesitate, 3. Escalate, 4. Skillful, 5. Diplomat, 6. Aromatic, 7. Official.

THREE'S COMPANY

1. May, November, September; 2. Dagger, Knife, Stiletto; 3. Cow, Filly, Vixen; 4. Aunt, Sister, Uncle; 5. Ford, Lincoln, Mercury; 6. Birch, Cottonwood, Magnolia; 7. Cleaver, June, Ward; 8. Cutters, Schooners, Sloops; 9. Jefferson, Roosevelt, Washington; 10. Jupiter, Thor, Zeus; 11. Ewe, Kayak, Pop; 12. Cadillac, Detroit, Lansing; 13. Child, Toddler, Tot; 14. Creed, Dogma, Tenet; 15. Celtics, Clippers, Pistons.

HOP, SKIP, AND JUMP
NUTRITION

ROUNDERS

Backgammon, Chess, Checkers.

INSERT-A-WORD

1. Minnow, 2. Resigned, 3. Boredom, 4. Dictate, 5. Warrant, 6. Draperies, 7. Tribune, 8. Brisket, 9. Patient, 10. Blowout.

ESCALATORS

1.

F	FROSTY	STORY	TROY	S
L	SAILED	IDEAS	SIDE	A
Y	YOUTHS	SOUTH	HOST	U
I	RECIPE	CREEP	PEER	C
N	PLANES	LAPSE	SLAP	E
G	GRATES	STARE	EAST	R

2.

T	LASTED	LEADS	SLED	A
R	RATING	GIANT	TINA	G
A	REPAID	PRIDE	DRIP	E
V	RAVENS	SNARE	EARS	N
E	CLOSED	CLODS	SOLD	C
L	REALLY	RELAY	LEAR	Y

3.

M	STREAM	TEARS	STAR	E
A	SAWING	WINGS	SWIG	N
G	GLANCE	CLEAN	CANE	L
N	REASON	AROSE	SORE	A
I	INSERT	RENTS	NEST	R
F	GOLFED	LODGE	DOLE	G
Y	OYSTER	STORE	ROTS	E

4.

T	DEPOTS	POSED	SPED	O
R	CARROT	ACTOR	COAT	R
I	RAISIN	RAINS	AIRS	N
M	FLAMES	FALSE	SELF	A
M	SIMMER	MISER	SIRE	M
I	PRAISE	PEARS	RAPS	E
N	TENNIS	STEIN	SITE	N
G	GATHER	EARTH	HEAR	T

LETTER TILES

```
      S H E
L A T E R
O P E R A
P E W
```

TILES
PASSIONATE

MIDDLE OF THE ROAD
Every dogma has its day.

THREE TO ONE

1. Doorstep, 2. Consonant, 3. Lonesome, 4. Diplomat, 5. Illusion.

PAIRS IN RHYME

1. Peas and carrots, 2. Cat and mouse, 3. Hand and foot, 4. Here and now, 5. Shoes and socks.

HALFTIME

Andrew, Arthur, Calvin, Dennis, Dwight, Gordon, Joseph, Martin, Norman, Robert, Victor, Warren.

HUBCAPS

1. Petite, Satire, Mutiny; 2. Rocker, Nickel, Cuckoo; 3. Teeter, Poetry, Pretty.
BONUS WORD: Ticket

QUOTEFALLS

1. If you cannot win, make the fellow ahead of you break the record.
2. When a man is wrapped up in himself, he makes a pretty small package.
3. Idealism increases in direct proportion to one's distance from the problem.

AROUND THE BLOCK

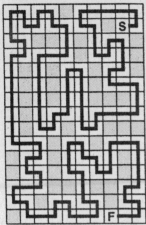

PICTURE THIS

TAKEOUTS
4 football players are left.

JIGSAW PUZZLE

CODEBREAKER
1. Paste, 2. Drink, 3. Knead, 4. Raise, 5. Irate, 6. Earns, 7. Naked, 8. Tapir, 9. Satin, 10. Adept.

ALPHABET SOUP

AMAZING QUOTE

Hard work consists of an accumulation of easy things that you didn't do when you should have.

YOU KNOW THE ODDS
1. Checking account, 2. Deposit, 3. Money order, 4. Balance, 5. Promissory note, 6. Liability.

SHUFFLE
1. Roast beef, 2. Chicken gumbo, 3. Filet mignon, 4. Peking duck, 5. Swiss steak, 6. Irish stew, 7. Veal scallopine, 8. Welsh rabbit, 9. Lobster Newburg, 10. Quiche Lorraine.

HEADINGS
1. Madrid, Beijing, Seoul, Calcutta, Moscow, Paris.
2. Let It Be, Something, She Loves You, Get Back, Yesterday, Hey Jude.
3. Caterpillar, Alice, Walrus, Cheshire Cat, Dormouse.

ANAGRAM MAGIC SQUARE
1. Aside, 2. Sitar, 3. March, 4. Infer, 5. Leash, 6. Early, 7. Alter, 8. Dries, 9. Drain, 10. Shelf, 11. Table, 12. Ogles, 13. Yemen, 14. Onset, 15. Usage, 16. Ridge, 17. Flier, 18. Aunts, 19. Cadet, 20. Evens, 21. Votes, 22. Asset, 23. Leeks, 24. Umber, 25. Easel.
SAYING: A smile adds to your face value.

MAZE

NINE OF DIAMONDS

1. Strainer, 2. Scramble, 3. Lectured, 4. Indicate, 5. Discover, 6. Improved, 7. Cardigan, 8. Recorder, 9. Reproach.

THE SHADOW
7 matches. (Differences: 1. Rabbit missing, 2. Wand missing, 3. Two wands, 4. Rabbit's ear, 5. Confetti reversed and rabbits moved, 6. Rabbit moved, 8. Rabbit wearing hat.)

JIGSAW SQUARES
A lady had William Gladstone and Benjamin Disraeli as dinner partners on succeeding nights. Asked to compare them, she said: "I was convinced Gladstone was the most fascinating person on earth, until Disraeli's manner persuaded me that I was the most fascinating."

PYRAMID POWER

1. Aspect, 2. Aspens, 3. Assess, 4. Covens, 5. Denial, 6. Hornet, 7. Impala, 8. Linens, 9. Livens, 10. Nectar, 11. Palate, 12. Scones, 13. Shrimp, 14. Target, 15. Thrive, 16. Throne.

MIDDLE OF THE ROAD
Many are called but few get up.

WORD CALCULATOR
1. Wither, 2. Studio, 3. Bisque, 4. Museum, 5. Pewter, 6. Design, 7. Gravel, 8. Faucet.

START AND FINISH
1. Hush, 2. Plump, 3. Window, 4. Bulb, 5. Nation, 6. Depend, 7. Laurel, 8. Chic, 9. Rigor, 10. Medium.

CHANGAWORD
1. Make, Take, Tame, Time.
2. Turn, Burn, Barn, Bark, Back.
3. Home, Hose, Host, Hoot, Soot, Soon.
4. Take, Lake, Lace, Lack, Lock, Look, Loop.

FLOWER POWER
C: 1. Crack, 2. Chino, 3. Wring, 4. Bland, 5. Cline, 6. Plaza, 7. Stamp, 8. Slams, 9. Grist, 10. Dread, 11. Cloak, 12. Breed, 13. Greet, 14. Trine, 15. Graze, 16. Flare, 17. Prove, 18. Chalk.
CC: 1. Chore, 2. Crave, 3. Whale, 4. Brick, 5. Clink, 6. Plano, 7. Sling, 8. Stand, 9. Glaze, 10. Drama, 11. Crimp, 12. Bless, 13. Groat, 14. Tread, 15. Greek, 16. Fried, 17. Plant, 18. Craze.

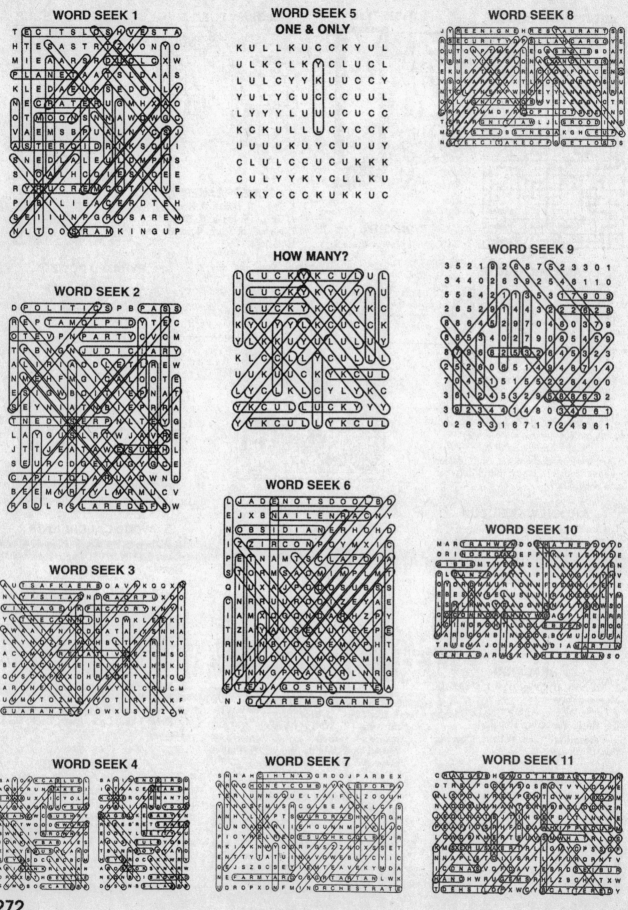

WORD SEEK 1

WORD SEEK 5
ONE & ONLY

WORD SEEK 8

HOW MANY?

WORD SEEK 9

WORD SEEK 2

WORD SEEK 6

WORD SEEK 3

WORD SEEK 10

WORD SEEK 4

WORD SEEK 7

WORD SEEK 11

WORD SEEK 1
WIZARD'S WORDS

The astronomer was asked, "How's business?" He replied, "Things are looking up."

WORD SEEK 3 WORD LIST

Alligator, Breakfast, Caramel, Daughter, Expensive, Factory, Guarantee, Humorous, Innocent, Jasmine, Knowledge, Language, Moccasin, Nephew, Organize, Partner, Quotation, Relative, Satisfy, Tradition, Uproar, Vintage, Waterfall, Xenon, Yesterday, Zinnia.

WORD SEEK 7 WORD LIST

Auctioneer, Blockhouse, Confident, Diagonal, Eardrum, Farmyard, Gender, Honeycomb, Intern, Jester, Knock, Loophole, Myself, Nasty, Orchestrate, Propel, Quadrate, Raisin, Shortcake, Tartan, Underplay, Value, Weather, Xanthic, Yiddish, Zombi.

WORD SEEK 10 WORD LIST

(Bea) Arthur, (Tom) Bosley, (Raymond) Burr, (William) Conrad, (Bill) Cosby, (William) Daniels, (Tony) Danza, (Bob) Denver, (Buddy) Ebsen, (John) Forsythe, (William) Frawley, (James) Garner, (Marla) Gibbs, (Sharon) Gless, (Andy) Griffith, (Fred) Gwynne, (Larry) Hagman, (Sherman) Hemsley, (Howard) Hesseman, (Ron) Howard, (Kate) Jackson, (Julie) Kavner, (Ted) Knight, (Michael) Landon, (Gavin) MacLeod, (Lee) Majors, (Pamela Sue) Martin, (Rue) McClanahan, (Mary Tyler) Moore, (Harry) Morgan, (Bob) Newhart, (Carroll) O'Connor, (William) Shatner, (Susan) St. James, (Robert) Urich, (Betty) White, (Robert) Young.

CRYPTO-FAMILIES

1. FRUIT: Pear, Tangerine, Apricot, Cantaloupe, Honeydew, Orange, Kiwi, Cherry, Grape, Peach.

2. COMMUNICATION: Poster, Magazine, Radio, Newspaper, Memo, Speech, Cablegram, Satellite, Telephone, Letter.

3. DOG: Boxer, Husky, Pointer, Poodle, Greyhound, Collie, Akita, Beagle, Dachshund, Airedale.

4. ICE CREAM: Maple walnut, Bubble gum, Vanilla, Coffee, Fudge ripple, Butter pecan, Chocolate, Peppermint, Strawberry, Pistachio.

5. NONSENSE: Mumbo jumbo, Gobbledygook, Tommyrot, Balderdash, Fiddlefaddle, Bunkum, Poppycock, Flimflam, Hogwash, Claptrap.

6. CARDS!: Canasta, Euchre, Bridge, Poker, Whist, Blackjack, Hearts, Pinochle, Casino, Gin rummy.

SECRET WORD

1. Grand, 2. Havoc, 3. Panes, 4. Chord, 5. Block, 6. Mirth.

1. Thugs, Hound, Orate, Upset, Shrug, Aesop, Nurse, Dupes; 2. Drive, Incas, Shore, Ovens, Reach, Dries, Evans, Raise; 3. World, Ideal, Notes, Drips, Owlet, Wiper, Swear; 4. Handy, Actor, Remit, Meant, Other, Nadir, Yacht; 5. Omits, Brick, Strum, Toils, Roles, Umber, Crumb, Trick; 6. Herod, Islam, Later, Aimed, Royal, Ideas, Thyme, Yodel.

CRYPTOGRAMS

1. An optimist thinks the glass is half full; a pessimist thinks the glass is half empty. A realist knows that if he sticks around, he's eventually going to have to wash the glass.

2. A friend was telling me about a choir he had heard that had sung without any instrumental backing. He explained, "And they performed without musical accomplishment."

3. English usage is sometimes more than mere taste, judgment, and education — sometimes it's sheer luck, like getting across a street.

4. Whether at work or at play, it's a lot more fun if, while you are doing the one, you don't constantly feel you ought to be doing the other.

5. The pleasure we derive from doing favors is partly in the feeling it gives us that we are not altogether worthless.

6. The Ten Commandments are short and to the point simply because they were given to us directly, without the help of lawyers.

7. It is more important to know where you are going than to get there quickly. Do not mistake activity for achievement.

8. Earnest people are often people who habitually look on the serious side of things that have no serious side.

9. Silence may save you from being wrong and looking foolish, but it will also deprive you of the possibility of being right.

10. The exchange of Christmas presents ought to be reciprocal rather than retaliatory.

11. Never explain — your friends do not need it, and your enemies will not believe it anyway.

12. If you don't get everything you want, think of the things you don't get that you don't want.

13. A boy is grown up when he walks around the puddle.

14. It's a fact: A really big man never blows his knows.

MISSING DOMINOES

CIRCLES IN THE SQUARE

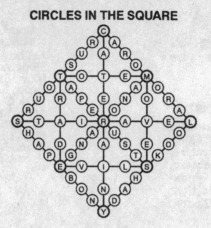

RINGMASTER

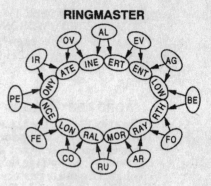

CODEWORD

1-S, 2-I, 3-O, 4-J, 5-D, 6-U, 7-A, 8-K, 9-W, 10-F, 11-L, 12-B, 13-Z, 14-E, 15-P, 16-G, 17-X, 18-C, 19-V, 20-Q, 21-N, 22-Y, 23-M, 24-R, 25-T, 26-H.

ONE AND ONLY

POINT THE WAY

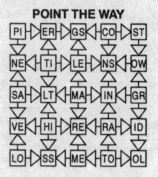

WINDOW BOXES

1-f Room, 2-c Just, 3-e Echo, 4-g Olio, 5-h Vice, 6-i Zero, 7-j Blue, 8-b Loft, 9-a Lazy, 10-d Know.

ROUNDERS

1. Clemson, 2. Rutgers, 3. Stanford, 4. Columbia, 5. Marquette, 6. Georgetown, 7. Bucknell, 8. Duquesne, 9. Villanova.

PUZZLE DERBY

1. Boxer, 2. Chestnut, 3. Scant, 4. Ajar, 5. Garbage, 6. Stink, 7. Cabin, 8. Bowler, 9. Trivial, 10. Ransack.
Win: I; Place: A; Show: E.
All answers contain names of containers.

THREE FROM NINE

1. Leather, Proxy, Ess; 2. Tadpole, Lunch, Arc; 3. Offense, Roust, Apt; 4. Apricot, Erupt, Nil; 5. Village, Spine, Rut; 6. Jittery, Manse, Own; 7. Granite, Diner, Nog; 8. Paisley, Cloud, Arm; 9. Toccata, Prism, Rug.

CATEGORIES

MUSICAL INSTRUMENTS: Banjo, Irish harp, Recorder, Clarinet, Harmonica.
WORLD CAPITALS: Brussels, Islamabad, Rangoon, Cairo, Helsinki.
SPORTS: Bowling, Ice hockey, Racquetball, Cricket, Handball.
COMEDIANS: (Jack) Benny, (Eric) Idle, (Carl) Reiner, (Bill) Cosby, (Bob) Hope.
DESSERTS: Baklava, Ice cream, Rice pudding, Cheesecake, Hermit.

SHARE-A-LETTER

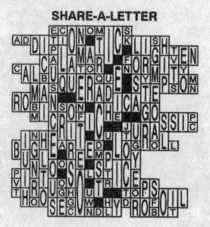

TURN A PHRASE

We confess to little faults only to persuade others that we have no great ones.

MATCHMAKER

Tennessee-Michigan, Hank-Aaron, Elate-Depress, Six-Eight, Ending-Finale, Banal-Ordinary, Orange-Rind, Orville-Wilbur, Travel-Agent, Solid-Liquid, Acute-Keen, Raven-Ibis, Egg-Nog.
SONG TITLE: These Boots Are Made for Walkin'

COMMON COMBOS

1. Train, 2. Hall, 3. Flag, 4. Cross, 5. Mail, 6. Look, 7. Light, 8. Jack.

A FEW CHOICE WORDS

1. Comedy, 2. Permit, 3. Nimble, 4. Walrus, 5. Bright, 6. Quaint.

WORD MATH

1. English pub, 2. Earthbound, 3. Money talks.

PATCHWORK QUOTE

There are two ways of meeting difficulties. You alter the difficulties or you can alter yourself to meet them.

GUESS WHO

1. John Paul Jones, 2. Bill Blass, 3. Lena Horne, 4. Emile Zola, 5. Bob Dole, 6. Jean Simmons, 7. Lorne Greene, 8. Zane Grey, 9. Grant Wood, 10. Bobby Unser, 11. Tom Clancy, 12. Clint Black.

LUCKY SCORE

1. Variety (68), 2. Review (68), 3. Leave (55), 4. Livelier (97), 5. Eleven (62), 6. Valley (64), 7. Reveille (83), 8. Valve (62), 9. Evolve (66), 10. Level (56).
TOTAL: 681

ALPHABET PLUS

Chain, Abide, Acorn, Solid, Forge, Front, Night, Latch, Giant, Major, Brick, Decal, Frame, Along, Olive, Depot, Qualm, Frost, Gloss, Fetch, Suave, Overt, Brown, Boxer, Ready, Graze.

PUZZLE IN THE ROUND

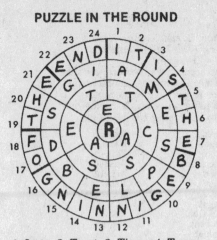

1. Irate, 2. Treat, 3. Timer, 4. Terms, 5. Trace, 6. Reach, 7. Scare, 8. Crabs, 9. Spear, 10. Grasp, 11. Rails, 12. Snarl, 13. Nears, 14. Arise, 15. Barns, 16. Brags, 17. Adore, 18. Fared, 19. Tears, 20. Share, 21. Greet, 22. Egret, 23. Inter, 24. Tried.
SAYING: It is the beginning of the end.

SYLLACROSTIC

Mae West: Too much of a good thing can be wonderful.
1. Mallard, 2. Acquit, 3. Embellish, 4. Wadi, 5. Education, 6. Standing, 7. Titanic, 8. Tortilla, 9. Ostentation, 10. Overabsorb, 11. Macabre, 12. Undertow, 13. Centavo, 14. Halloween, 15. Ousted, 16. Feline, 17. Arthur, 18. Ganef, 19. Ormolu, 20. Occasional.

WORD SEEK 4 WORD LIST

Babies'-breath, Baby bath, Baby blue, Backbend, Backbite, Backbone, Bail bond, Baked beans, Bankbook, Bareback, Baseball, Baseborn, Bat boy, Beachballs, Beanbags, Bedbug, Beetle-browed, Bellboys, Bell buoy, Big Ben, Blackbeard, Blackberry, Blackboard, Bluebell, Bluebird, Bock beer, Bonbon, Boo-boo, Bosom buddy, Browbeat, Brown bears, Brown betty, Bunk beds, Busboy, Bush baby, Busybody, Bye-bye.

QUOTAGRAMS

A. Friendships multiply joys and divide griefs.
B. Ego creeps in on little cat feet and fogs up the mind.
C. A truth that's told with bad intent beats all the lies you can invent.
A: 1. Jury, 2. Dives, 3. Springy, 4. Fiddled, 5. Impose, 6. Nail, 7. Shift.
B: 1. Flamenco, 2. Dipped, 3. Threaten, 4. Geese, 5. Fiction, 6. Gluttons.
C: 1. Lethal, 2. Taunt, 3. Nebula, 4. Whined, 5. Ditto, 6. Oaths, 7. Battery, 8. Vital, 9. Hints, 10. Scent.

DIAGRAMLESS FILL-IN

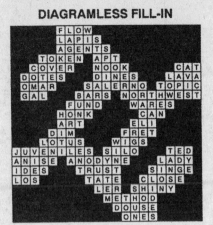

CHAIN WORDS

Laugh, Graph, Chart, Chars, Crash, Flash, Blaze, Phase, Shape, Shale, Leash, Least.

FRAMEWORK 4 RELATED WORDS

Alley, Avenue, Boulevard, Cul-de-sac, Highway, Interstate, Lane, Route, Street, Turnpike.

FLOWER POWER

C: 1. Shady, 2. Study, 3. Songs, 4. Gangs, 5. Banes, 6. Ravel, 7. Fives, 8. Liven, 9. Genie, 10. Reeve, 11. Glass, 12. Klutz, 13. Saute, 14. Chill, 15. Spill, 16. Shied, 17. Cheer, 18. Stria.

CC: 1. Steel, 2. Shred, 3. Stair, 4. Gouda, 5. Bandy, 6. Rangy, 7. Fangs, 8. Lives, 9. Gives, 10. Revel, 11. Genes, 12. Klein, 13. Slave, 14. Cause, 15. Shuts, 16. Spitz, 17. Chile, 18. Shill.

QUOTEFALLS

1. Successful men follow the same advice they prescribe for others.
2. When a child pays attention to his parents, they're probably whispering.
3. Travelers can tell when it's vacation time: the regular roads are closed and the detours are open.
4. A businessman who came up the hard way observes that about all you can do on a shoestring these days is trip.

SECRET WORD

1. Agent, 2. Steam, 3. Month, 4. Chief, 5. Medal, 6. Usher.
1. Dogma, Ebony, Limbo, Equip, Gouda, Amble, Talon, Eland.
2. Round, Adult, Douse, Imago, Astir, Trump, Opens, Rogue.
3. Heart, Outre, Roman, Odium, Spear, Crash, Orate, Pound, Ergot.
4. Prate, Ready, Eclat, Shaft, Ideal, Dices, Elgar, Neath, Tramp.
5. Drift, Edgar, Cruel, Onset, Riots, Artel, Trend, Idaho, Omens, Noise.
6. Birds, Radio, Itchy, Datum, Estop, Surly, Marco, Adept, Ideas, Daily.

MASTERWORDS

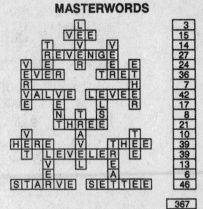

CRYPTOGRAMS

1. Children are very adept at comprehending modern statistics. When they say, "Everyone else is allowed to," it usually is based on a survey of one.

2. All mankind is divided into three classes: those who are immovable; those who are movable; and those who move. (Benjamin Franklin)

3. People are finding that a simpler lifestyle provides greater satisfaction than a relentless pursuit of materialism. (Laurence S. Rockefeller)

4. Do a disagreeable job today instead of tomorrow. You will save twenty-four hours of dreading to do it, while having twenty-four hours to savor the feeling that the job is done.

5. It's time to diet and exercise when you accept the fact that you can fool some of the people all of the time and all of the people some of the time — but not while you're wearing a bathing suit.

6. Senator to colleagues: "Life in the Senate is getting too complicated. It's impossible to sidestep one issue without stepping on another one."

7. You can drive through some big game compounds. This makes it easier for animals to observe humans in their natural habitat, the automobile.

8. Show me a man with his head held high and I'll show you a man who cannot get used to his bifocals.

9. I think the most satisfying thing I've ever done is fill out my tax return in Roman numerals.

10. Government never furthered any enterprise but by the alacrity with which it got out of its way.

11. Why is a paper tissue so small when you use it for your nose, and so large when it finds its way into the washing machine?

12. How a man plays the game shows something of his character; how he loses shows all of it.

13. How come the mighty Bengal tiger is an endangered species while the puny mosquito flourishes?

CODEWORD

1-R, 2-Y, 3-W, 4-E, 5-H, 6-Z, 7-T, 8-L, 9-Q, 10-B, 11-S, 12-I, 13-K, 14-G, 15-X, 16-U, 17-P, 18-N, 19-F, 20-C, 21-V, 22-A, 23-D, 24-M, 25-O, 26-J.

CRYPTOGRAMS

1. The most irritating person at a class reunion is the guy who has both hair and money.

2. He who expects nothing will never be disappointed.

3. Nowadays, it seems to take half as long to get into debt and twice as long to get out.

4. Open meetings often reveal a lot of closed minds.

5. One thing we all know about the speed of light is that it gets here too early in the morning.

6. Note to summer vacationers: When you're advised to travel light, they mean your suitcase, not your wallet.

7. The trouble with telling a good story is that it reminds the other guy of a dull one.

8. The greatest underdeveloped territory on earth is the area lying between human ears.

9. The concert of nations has each country singing in a different key.

10. A business is too big when it takes a week for gossip to go from one end of the office to the other.

11. If you make a right turn from the left lane, you're probably just careless, and not really what the guy behind you called you.

12. It's almost impossible to see the silver lining when you're living in a fog.

13. No matter how much you try to improve on Mother Nature, you're not kidding Father Time.

14. The United States would be better off if we had less conversation and more conservation.

15. The amount of sleep required by the average person is usually ten minutes more.

16. When some people talk about their family tree, they usually trim off a branch here and there.

17. Resisting temptation is a lot easier when we think we'll probably get another chance later on down the line.

CROSTIC 1

Author: (Mark) Twain
Source: (The Late) Benjamin Franklin

What an adroit old adventurer the subject of this memoir was! In order to get a chance to fly his kite on Sunday he used to hang a key on the string and let on to be fishing for lightning.

A. Tragedy
B. Wrestle
C. Artist
D. Infectious
E. Noonday
F. Bushtit
G. Egotism
H. Nugget
I. John Doe
J. Adherent
K. Monkish
L. Inveigh
M. Natch
N. Fatherly
O. Rushed
P. Affront
Q. Natasha
R. Knothole
S. Longbow
T. Idiotic
U. Neared

CROSTIC 2

Author: L.P. Holmes
Source: Catch and Saddle

Two people, total strangers . . . are thrown together in a situation from which neither emerge quite the same . . . They have lost something or they have gained something. One thing is certain . . . like it or not, a certain bond has been established between them.

A. Lengthwise
B. Phone booth
C. Horseshoe
D. Open letter
E. Limitation
F. Marionette
G. Even-steven
H. Son
I. Chattering
J. Abstemious
K. Theme song
L. Cow
M. Highwayman
N. At the worst
O. Nightshirt
P. Deliberate
Q. Sheathe
R. Arithmetic
S. Degenerate
T. Definition
U. Loganberry
V. Earthquake

CROSTIC 3

Author: (James Frances Johnson with) Floyd Miller
Source: (The Man Who Sold) the Eiffel Tower

All of America's gold rushes and . . . oil booms and . . . homesteading migration were nothing compared to the Florida land boom of the mid-twenties. Millions of Americans poured into the peninsula . . . There were twenty-five thousand real estate agents in Miami alone.

A. French
B. Little Toot
C. Off and on
D. Young
E. Dwight Eisenhower
F. Merchant marine
G. Immediate
H. Laminates
I. Luminous
J. Etruscans
K. Ramada
L. Torpedo
M. Hashed
N. Empowers
O. Edibles
P. India
Q. Favorite Martian
R. Fools
S. Emotional
T. Loopholes
U. Tents
V. Obligation
W. White Angel
X. Endings
Y. Remade

CROSTIC 4

Author: Mike Sheridan
Source: Hawaii ... Naturally (Sky
Magazine, March 1986)
Few places on earth offer such a win-
ning combination of diverse climate,
dramatic scenery, exquisite beaches,
flowers, and trees as Hawaii. That
makes the Aloha State a true paradise,
and a prime destination for individuals
who want more than just a tan.

A. Monotone
B. Innuendo
C. Kiwi
D. Erstwhile
E. Suffixes
F. Hatteras
G. Empires
H. Rotator cuff
I. Incisor
J. Decisive
K. Adamant
L. Noticed
M. Hawser
N. Atlanta Braves

O. White Heat
P. Acquiesced
Q. Imminent
R. Indicator
S. Nathan Hale
T. Awash
U. Tarawa
V. Urban
W. Rajahs
X. Agitated
Y. Lopped off
Z. Lessee
a. Yams

CROSTIC 5

Author: Debby Wood
Source: The Gift Is in the Mail
(Shopper 11/89)
Now that the Christmas shopping
season is in full swing, catalogs are
arriving by the bundle each day. Many
of them obviously should have been
delivered to Donald Trump's house instead of mine, judging from the prices
of the merchandise.

A. Deceive
B. English
C. Baffled
D. Better
   half
E. Yachtsman
F. Whiplash
G. Objection
H. Opportune
I. David Niven
J. Touch up
K. Hemmed in
L. Everybody
M. Guess

N. Inchon
O. Falsify
P. Through
Q. Idols
R. Sour mash
S. Ignorant
T. Nothing
U. Touts
V. Harassed
W. Egrets
X. Midas
Y. Aware
Z. Idles
a. Lemmon

CROSTIC 6

Author: P(eg) Bracken
Source: Resolutions, Anyone?
I know one thing—it's easier to make
resolutions for other people on an
I'll-make-them-you-keep-them basis,
than it is to make them for oneself. I
do this often, for I've always been
courageous about facing up to faults,
if they are someone else's.

A. Profitable
B. Behemoth
C. Roommate
D. Amoles
E. Cogwheel
F. Kentucky
G. Emotional
H. Nemesis
I. Repeal
J. Eiffel
K. Soft-shoe
L. Offstage
M. Louisiana

N. Up for it
O. Toughest
P. Interview
Q. Ohio
R. Nebraska
S. Settee
T. Arkansas
U. Notorious
V. Youthful
W. Onionskin
X. Neediest
Y. Empathy

CROSTIC 7

Author: (Mary Andrews) Ayres
Source: Emphasis on Good News
America needs more "Happy Talk." More
emphasis on good news, more mass
entertainment built around the good
things. More articles to inspire us. More
music that makes us want to sing.

A. Austere
B. Yarmuk
C. Ragtime
D. Enrich
E. Stemmed
F. Episode
G. Mast
H. Presto
I. Hunts
J. Angora
K. Senate
L. Impart

M. Shimmer
N. Oblate
O. Nominal
P. Gnomes
Q. Occult
R. Ominous
S. Distort
T. Nainsook
U. Epergne
V. Whist
W. Shadow

CROSTIC 8

Author: Thomas Paine
Source: Rights of Man
Ignorance is of a peculiar nature; once
dispelled, it is impossible to
reestablish it. It is not originally a
thing of itself, but is only the absence
of knowledge; and though man may be
kept ignorant, he cannot be made
ignorant.

A. Tongue-tied
B. Honeycomb
C. On the take
D. Misspent
E. Acrobat
F. Sarongs
G. Pantywaist
H. Allocation
I. Incinerate
J. National
K. Engulfed

L. Raphael
M. Indelible
N. Giblets
O. Hobby-horse
P. Take off
Q. Slip in
R. Olden times
S. Fighting
T. Missouri
U. Argued
V. Nicotine

CROSTIC 9

Author: (James) Thurber
Source: Here Lies Miss Groby
Miss Groby taught me English com-
position thirty years ago ... The shape
of a sentence crucified on a blackboard
(parsed, she called it) brought a light
to her eye ... You remember her. You
must have had her, too.

A. The creeps
B. Have at
C. Unhitch
D. Rub out
E. Babyish
F. Echoic
G. Roughish
H. Homely
I. Ephraim
J. Ragbag
K. Eat dirt
L. Leads on

M. In charge
N. Eyesome
O. Stodgy
P. Madmen
Q. In that
R. Sumac
S. Sees to
T. Go to seed
U. Reproof
V. Of a truth
W. Biller
X. Yokelry

SUM TOTALS

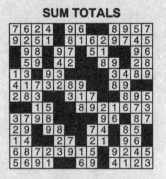

WINDOW BOXES

1-f Fear, 2-j Carp, 3-b Step, 4-e Grin, 5-d Cloy, 6-g Must, 7-i Idea, 8-h Sour, 9-c Alit, 10-a Town.

ALPHABET PLUS

Canal, Labor, Vocal, Flood, Niece, Stiff, Anger, Usher, Radio, Jaunt, Token, Slope, Lamps, Uncle, Choir, Taped, Quits, Carry, Study, Other, Unite, Waver, Vowel, Relax, Diary, Razor.

JIGSAW SQUARES

General Dwight Eisenhower used to demonstrate leadership with a simple piece of string. He would put it on a table and say, "Pull it and it'll follow wherever you wish. Push it and it will go nowhere at all. And it's just that way when it comes to leading people."

CATEGORIES

CAPITALS: Halifax, Ottawa, Victoria, Edmonton, Regina.
MONOPOLY: Hotels, Oriental Ave., Ventnor Ave., Electric Company, Reading RR.
SHAKESPEARE: Hamlet, Othello, Viola, Emilia, Romeo.
GODS: Hermes, Odin, Vulcan, Eros, Ra.
ARTISTS: Hopper, O'Keeffe, Velasquez, Eakins, Rembrandt.

SCOREBOARD

The following is our order of play. The words before and after a slash (/) were formed in the same play. Our running tally is in parentheses.

Re (2), Are (5), Pare (9), Ode (12), Rot (18), Rare/Ad (24), Cab/Cad/Be (37), Foot (45), Spare (56), No (58), Best/Odes (76), Lees (86), Cabin (96), Cabins (108), Skim (116), Rote (124), Jet (128), On (130), Exes/Bests (150), Quit/Li (157), Hexes/Oh (164), Id (166), Toque (176), Wan/Won (182), Skims (197), Us (201), La (210), Aura/Am (220), Zag (227), Envy (231), Xi/In (235), Tram (242).

ABACUS

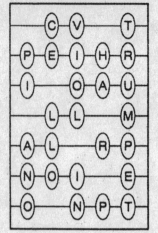

COMMON DENOMINATOR

Rhinoceros (All words are animals.)

WORD MATH

	0	1	2	3	4	5	6	7	8	9
1.	F	O	R	C	E/P	L	A	Y	S	
2.	E	A	R	T	H	L	I	N	G	S
3.	S	W	I	T	C	H	E	D/O	O	N
4.	C	O	N	F	U	S	E	D	L	Y
5.	S	E	C	O	N	D/H	A	L	F	
6.	B	I	G/C	A	R	T	O	N	S	

BULL'S-EYE SPIRAL

OUTWARD: 1. Diaper, 7. Placid, 13. Arab, 17. Mammals, 24. Ignite, 30. Embargo, 37. Malaria, 44. Persevere, 53. Ferret, 59. Sorrel, 65. Letter, 71. Rages, 76. Ulcer.
INWARD: 80. Recluse, 73. Garret, 67. Teller, 61. Roster, 55. Refer, 50. Eves, 46. Repair, 40. Alamo, 35. Grab, 31. Meeting, 24. Islam, 19. Mamba, 14. Radical, 7. Prepaid.

SIMON SAYS

1. LADYSSLIPPER
2. LLADYYSSLIPPER
3. LLADYYSSLLITHER
4. DALLYYSSLLITHER
5. DALLYSSLLITHEYR
6. DALLYOFLLITHEYR
7. DLLIALLYOFTHEYR
8. DLIALYOFTHELLYR
9. DLIALYOFTHEVALLYR
10. LILYOFTHEVALLEY
11. UIUOFTHEAUUE
12. EUUAEHTFOUIU
13. EUUAEHTTFOUIU
14. BEUUAEHTTOUIU
15. BUAEHTTUIU
16. BUIUTTHEAU
17. BUIUTTHECUP
18. BUTTHECUP
19. BUTTERCUP

NUMBERBOXES

9	4	3
2	8	5
6	1	7

CRYPTO-GEOGRAPHY

San Francisco, California
Rudyard Kipling lamented, "San Francisco has only one drawback — 'tis hard to leave." This important center for industry, commerce, tourism, and finance is also known for its constant climate and hillside views.

BOWL GAME

STRIKES: 1. Ultrasonic, 2. Serpentine, 3. Irrelevant, 4. Contribute, 5. Torrential, 6. Fiberglass, 7. Discretion, 8. Automobile, 9. Expatriate, 10. Literature.
SPARES: 1. Count, Rails; 2. Serene, Pint; 3. Lever, Train; 4. Butter, Coin; 5. Toner, Trial; 6. Glares, Fibs; 7. Coins, Tired; 8. Bootie, Maul; 9. Repeat, Taxi; 10. Retail, True.

ANAGRAM MAGIC SQUARE

1. Laden, 2. Omits, 3. Shelf, 4. Taper, 5. Tames, 6. Ideas, 7. Manor, 8. Epics, 9. Items, 10. State, 11. Nears, 12. Earth, 13. Viand, 14. Edges, 15. Rocks, 16. Frost, 17. Ocean, 18. Usage, 19. Naked, 20. Defer, 21. Abets, 22. Glean, 23. Arise, 24. Infer, 25. Nepal.
QUOTE: Lost time is never found again.

ESCALATORS

1

DAMPEN	P	NAMED	A	MEND
PEANUT	U	PATEN	N	TAPE
STABLE	B	STEAL	T	LEAS
CHAPEL	L	PEACH	H	CAPE
SENIOR	I	SNORE	O	ERNS
SOLVED	S	LOVED	L	DOVE
HAIRDO	H	RADIO	O	RAID
DANGER	E	GRAND	G	DARN
PRAYED	D	REPAY	Y	PARE

2

BASKET	B	STEAK	T	SAKE
APACHE	A	CHEAP	H	PACE
DIREST	T	SIRED	E	RIDS
CATHER	T	REACH	H	CARE
EASTER	E	STARE	A	REST
ARDENT	N	TRADE	T	DEAR
DETACH	D	CHEAT	C	HATE
ASHORE	O	SHARE	H	SEAR
DAWDLE	W	ADDLE	E	LADD
ANSWER	N	SWEAR	S	WARE

278

JIGSAW PUZZLE

COMPLETE-A-WORD

1. Sing/Listing, 2. None/Nominee, 3. Hard/Charade, 4. Make/Mistake, 5. Akin/Parking, 6. Fate/Feather, 7. Rely/Orderly, 8. City/Society.

SHUFFLE

1. Abandon-Desert, 2. Baffle-Confound, 3. Calamity-Disaster, 4. Delicate-Dainty, 5. Profits-Earnings, 6. Fabric-Material, 7. Habitual-Regular, 8. Jealous-Envious, 9. Kindle-Ignite, 10. Latent-Concealed.

WORD MATH

	0	1	2	3	4	5	6	7	8	9
1.	D	R	A	N	K/	J	U	I	C	E
2.	S	H	O	R	T/	C	A	B	L	E
3.	H	O	U	S	E/	P	A	I	N	T
4.	F	R	O	Z	E	N/	M	I	L	K
5.	B	Y	-	P	R	O	D	U	C	T
6.	B	R	I	D	L	E/	P	A	T	H

HEADINGS

1. Drum, Shirt, Darts, Train, Headset, Candy, Trumpet, Tricycle, Skateboard.
2. Collie, Mastiff, Boxer, Chow, Terrier, Pointer, Greyhound, Dachshund, Dalmatian.
3. Eland, Hyena, Zebra, Jackal, Lion, Giraffe, Chameleon, Ostrich, Warthog.

SIMON SAYS

1. CANDYSTRIPER
2. CANDHSTRIPER
3. CAANDHSTRIIPEER
4. CAANDHFSTRIIPEER
5. CAANHDFSTRIIPEER
6. CAANHDFSTRSSPEER
7. OAANHDFSTRSSPEER
8. OAANHDFSTLSSPEER
9. OAANHDFTLSSPEERS
10. OAAONHDFTLSSPEERS
11. OAAONDFTLSSHPEERS
12. OAAONDFTLSSHEPERS
13. OAAONEFTLSSHEPERS
14. AAONEOFTLSSHEPERS
15. AAONEOFTSSHELPERS
16. ANAONEOFTSSHELPERS
17. ONEOFTANASSHELPERS
18. ONEOFSANATSHELPERS
19. ONEOFSANTASHELPERS

THREESOMES

QUICK QUOTE

It's difficult to keep your mind and your mouth open at the same time.

1. A Touch of Mink, 2. Domino theory, 3. My Fair Lady, 4. Student Prince, 5. Oedipus, 6. The Tenth Man, 7. Chorus Line.

ROUNDABOUT

1. Sandal, 3. Waving, 5. Inseam, 7. Marina, 9. Indian, 11. Nature, 13. Grudge, 15. Agenda, 17. Adagio, 19. Pikers, 21. Ordeal, 23. Bantam.
ANSWER TO RIDDLE: Swimming pool.

SYLLACROSTIC

(Joe) Murray: Marriage should be a duet—when one sings, the other claps.

1. Monoglot, 2. Undertow, 3. Rebekah, 4. Radiate, 5. Abdomen, 6. Yoko, 7. Maturation, 8. Avarice, 9. Regardless, 10. Rabbi, 11. Institution, 12. Amusing, 13. Generous, 14. Encouragement, 15. Seismograph, 16. Hesitate, 17. Oregano, 18. Unimportant, 19. Lagomorph, 20. Desirable, 21. Benefactor, 22. Eccentric, 23. Appraisal, 24. Daphnia, 25. Upkeep, 26. Ethos.

LOGIC PROBLEM

(Clue numbers in parentheses)
Prize amts. were $10,000, $15,000, $20,000, $25,000, and $30,000 (intro.). Baldwin [2 times more money than Paul (5)] didn't win $10,000 [no $5,000], $15,000 [no $7,500], $25,000 [Gina (2)], or $30,000 (5); Baldwin won $20,000, and Paul won $10,000 (5). Ms. Weber won ½ as much as Westdale Mall winner (1), so didn't win $10,000 [Paul], $20,000 [no $40,000], $25,000 [no $50,000], or $30,000 [no $60,000]; she won $15,000, and the Westdale Mall winner won $30,000 (1). The Eastville Mall winner won more than Baldwin [$20,000] (5), so won $25,000 [only possible]. Weber [hat (1)], who won $15,000, isn't the Eastville Mall [$25,000], Westdale Mall [$30,000], Northport Mall [wedding gift (3)], or Center City Mall winner [sofa (6)]; she's the Southtown winner. McNeily didn't win $10,000 or $30,000 (4); she won $25,000, and Robert won $30,000 (4). Henry didn't win $15,000 [Ms. Weber]; he won $20,000. Karen won $15,000. Henry isn't the Center City Mall winner (6); Paul is. Henry is the Northport Mall winner. Crawford isn't the Westdale Mall winner (1); Dunne is. Crawford is the Center City Mall winner.
In summary:
Gina McNeily, Eastville, $25,000
Henry Baldwin, Northport, $20,000
Karen Weber, Southtown, $15,000
Paul Crawford, Center City, $10,000
Robert Dunne, Westdale, $30,000

CODEWORD

1-F, 2-D, 3-G, 4-H, 5-Q, 6-J, 7-S, 8-A, 9-U, 10-T, 11-V, 12-P, 13-K, 14-R, 15-Y, 16-M, 17-O, 18-I, 19-N, 20-E, 21-X, 22-W, 23-B, 24-Z, 25-C, 26-L.

PICTURE THIS

CHANGAWORD

1. Drop, Crop, Coop, Hoop, Hood, Hold.
2. Head, Heat, Beat, Boat, Boot, Foot.
3. Gain, Lain, Laid, Lard, Lord, Lore, Lose.
4. Show, Shot, Soot, Sort, Sore, Sire, Hire, Hide.

BOOKWORMS

A little boy of zest and energy was given a crocus bud by his mother. His delight was boundless. He took it carefully in his small fist and fell asleep with it unharmed. When she looked in on him later in the evening, it had come into bloom.

BULL'S-EYE SPIRAL

OUT: 1. Retract, 8. Piece, 13. Remotely, 21. Tsar, 25. Abode, 30. Resume, 36. Nome, 40. Name, 44. Opera, 49. Flat, 53. Ivan, 57. Nehru, 62. Open, 66. Utter, 71. Frog, 75. Ire, 78. Tag.
IN: 80. Gate, 76. Rigor, 71. Fret, 67. Tune, 63. Pour, 59. Henna, 54. Vital, 49. Fare, 45. Poem, 41. Anemone, 34. Muse, 30. Redo, 26. Bara, 22. Style, 17. Tome, 13. Receipt, 6. Carter.

FLOWER POWER

C: 1. Abide, 2. Alive, 3. Erode, 4. Grunt, 5. Prose, 6. Crack, 7. Poach, 8. Tract, 9. Trail, 10. Teary, 11. Trade, 12. Tenet, 13. Paned, 14. Horae, 15. Delta, 16. Baste, 17. Serve, 18. Goods.

CC: 1. Aorta, 2. Above, 3. Elide, 4. Grids, 5. Prove, 6. Crude, 7. Prone, 8. Toast, 9. Trace, 10. Track, 11. Teach, 12. Trait, 13. Pearl, 14. Handy, 15. Donee, 16. Beret, 17. Salad, 18. Geste.

FRAMEWORK 13

FRAMEWORK 14

FRAMEWORK 15

FRAMEWORK 16

FRAMEWORK 17

FRAMEWORK 18

FRAMEWORK 19

FRAMEWORK 20

FRAMEWORK 21

FRAMEWORK 22

FRAMEWORK 23

FRAMEWORK 24

FRAMEWORK 25

FRAMEWORK 26

PICTURE PAIRS

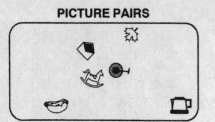

ACROSS AND DOWN

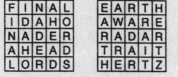

	A
F	I	N	A	L
I	D	A	H	O
N	A	D	E	R
A	H	E	A	D
L	O	R	D	S

	B
E	A	R	T	H
A	W	A	R	E
R	A	D	A	R
T	R	A	I	T
H	E	R	T	Z

DOUBLE TROUBLE

FLOWER POWER

C: 1. Habit, 2. Hover, 3. Revel, 4. Divan, 5. Cater, 6. Sedan, 7. Males, 8. Loser, 9. Sinew, 10. Rayon, 11. Poled, 12. Fever, 13. Bowed, 14. Cowed, 15. Totem, 16. Paten, 17. Siren, 18. Cavil.

CC: 1. Harem, 2. Haven, 3. Robin, 4. Devil, 5. Civet, 6. Saver, 7. Metal, 8. Laden, 9. Solar, 10. Risen, 11. Panes, 12. Foyer, 13. Below, 14. Coven, 15. Towed, 16. Power, 17. Sated, 18. Cited.

LUCKY STAR

1-2. Table, 3-4. Clean, 5-6. Fault, 7-8. Plain, 9-10. Night, 11-12. Cheap.

PATCHWORK QUOTE

Those who know human nature will acknowledge what strength lighthearted nonsense gives hard-working people.

FRAMEWORK 14
MYSTERY GUEST

Kierkegaard

FRAMEWORK 23 MESSAGE

All that glitters is not gold.

WHEELS

A. 1. Cougar, 2. Ardent, 3. Famous, 4. Hombre, 5. Bandit, 6. Dacron, 7. Logjam, 8. Pigeon.

MESSAGE: Laughter is a form of internal jogging.

B. 1. Proper, 2. Accept, 3. Option, 4. Egoism, 5. Barely, 6. Abrupt, 7. Oxford, 8. Eaglet.

MESSAGE: People apt to promise are apt to forget.

CIRCLES IN THE SQUARE

SQUARES

1. Overtook, 2. Repulsed, 3. Ointment, 4. Extended, 5. Amenable, 6. Function, 7. Bubbling, 8. Corporal, 9. Recovery.

ANAGRAMS PLUS

1. Tennis, 2. Cricket, 3. Polo, 4. Racing, 5. Soccer, 6. Rugby, 7. Golf, 8. Skating, 9. Track, 10. Bowling.

WHAT'S NEXT?

1. 20, 8, 5.
2. 18, 15, 1, 4.
3. 20, 15.
4. 19, 21, 3, 3, 5, 19, 19.
5. 9, 19.
6. 1, 12, 23, 1, 25, 19.
7. 21, 14, 4, 5, 18.
8. 3, 15, 14, 19, 20, 18, 21, 3, 20, 9, 15, 14.
QUOTATION: The road to success is always under construction.

SIMON SAYS

1. GRATITUDE
2. GSITITUDE
3. GSITITUPE
4. SITITUPE
5. SITIVUPE
6. SITIVEUP
7. SITIVE
8. THINSITIVE
9. THANSITIVE
10. THANSITIVKING
11. STHANITIVKING
12. STHANITIVKINGPOSE
13. STHANIVKINGPOSITE
14. THANIVKINGPOSIT
15. THANIVEKINGPOSIT
16. THANKINGIVEPOSIT
17. THANKINGPOSITIVE
18. POSITIVE THANKING

SPINWHEEL

OUT: 1. Drawer, 3. Apparel, 6. Big, 7. Elder, 9. Castle, 11. Boots, 13. Pat.

IN: 14. Taps, 12. Too, 11. Belt, 10. Sacred, 8. Legible, 5. Rap, 4. Pare, 2. Ward.

MIND TICKLER

The pieman offered to sell Simon two 5 ounce tarts and five 3 ounce tarts weighing a total of 25 ounces and costing $1.48. Instead, Simon bought five 5 ounce tarts and one 3 ounce tart weighing a total of 28 ounces, but only costing $1.40.

YOU KNOW THE ODDS

1. Gift shop, 2. Supermarket, 3. Movie theater, 4. Bookstore, 5. Boutique.

WINDOW BOXES

1-g Goal, 2-j Echo, 3-d Jowl, 4-c Whim, 5-h Arch, 6-i Dump, 7-a Roam, 8-f Pork, 9-b Obey, 10-e Huge.

THE SHADOW

4 matches. (Differences: 1. Stars, 2. Baseball, 3. Switch plate, 5. Apron string, 6. Plant, 7. Bangs, 8. Counter.)

CATEGORIES

EUROPEAN COUNTRIES: Czech Republic, Ukraine, Portugal, Ireland, Denmark.

THEATER PEOPLE: Costumer, Understudy, Playwright, Ingenue, Director.

ORGANIZATIONS: Club, Union, Party, Institution, Denomination.

CAR PARTS: Carburetor, Universal, Piston, Ignition, Dashboard.

IMPRACTICAL PEOPLE: Castlebuilder, Utopian, Pollyanna, Idealist, Daydreamer.

281

MISSING DOMINOES

SUNRAYS

Sole, Rain, Dole, Sari, Lode, Airs, Noel, Said, Lone, Raid, Lose, Arid.

CHANGAWORD

1. Card, Care, Came, Game.
2. Take, Tale, Tile, File, Five.
3. Fold, Bold, Bond, Band, Hand.
4. Play, Clay, Clap, Chap, Chip.

ANACROSS

1. Acrobat, 2. Fancied, 3. Gratify, 4. Abraded, 5. Elegant, 6. Ottoman, 7. Signora.

OUTLINED WORD: Octagon

PHRASAGRAMS

1. Pop the question, 2. Cold as ice, 3. Take it easy, 4. Spill the beans, 5. Let off steam, 6. Bury the hatchet, 7. Rock the boat, 8. Steal the show.

MATCH-UP

2 and 7 match. (Differences: 1. Filled-in bar, 3. Passengers, 4. Extra vertical line, 5. Striped pennant, 6. Designs on balloon, 8. Eyes in banner, 9. Filled-in top.)

MATCHMAKER

Outcast-Exile, Notion-Idea, Expert-Skilled, Silly-Goose, Tiger-Ocelot, Early-Overdue, Parallel-Divergent, Again-Anew, Top-Dog, African-Violet, Tool-Implement, Instant-Coffee, Mockingbird-Eagle.
SAYING: One step at a time is good advice.

BIG QUESTION

1. Gorilla, 2. Launch, 3. Chamber, 4. Berth, 5. Thesis, 6. Sister, 7. Terrific, 8. Fickle, 9. Lewis, 10. Wisdom, 11. Domain, 12. Inside, 13. Devout, 14. Outlet, 15. Tardy, 16. Year, 17. Artist, 18. Traffic, 19. Candle, 20. Lens, 21. Salem, 22. Emerge, 23. Gear, 24. Resign.
ANSWER TO RIDDLE: Deflated

FANCY FIVES

1. Scale, 2. Crash, 3. Alarm, 4. Storm, 5. Flute, 6. Grope, 7. Guess, 8. Ruble, 9. Globe, 10. Cruel, 11. Rouge, 12. Shrub, 13. Shout, 14. Grass, 15. Cream, 16. Voile, 17. Tribe, 18. Tempt, 19. Rapid, 20. Smart, 21. Clove, 22. Wrote, 23. Water, 24. Diner, 25. Raise.

SLIDE-O-RAMA

Acre, Foot, Gram, Inch, Mile, Mole, Pace, Palm, Peck, Pica, Pint, Pole, Yard.

CROSSBLOCKS

1. Ca/v/e/rn, S/n/ac/k, La/un/d/er, Si/m/p/le.
BONUS: Ca/n/d/le
2. Sp/r/in/g, D/ec/la/re, C/h/i/me, M/e/d/al.
BONUS: Sp/ec/i/al

TAKE A LETTER

1. Alcott, Miller, Updike; 2. Austen, Ferber, Irving; 3. Capote, Holmes, Wilder; 4. Bronte, Huxley, London.

RINGERS

1. Idiot, Zebra, Older, Vocal; 2. Garbs, Aimed, Those, Orbit; 3. Coach, Water, Droop, Agile; 4. Raven, Tonic, Feast, Usual; 5. Zesty, Price, Cloak, Oozed.

CRYPTO-FAMILIES

1. RACETRACK: Jockey, Thoroughbred, Sulky driver, Harness racing, Post position, Starting gate, Photo finish, Homestretch, Grandstand, Silks.
2. CITIES: Key West, Terre Haute, Cedar Rapids, New York, Baton Rouge, Des Moines, Little Rock, Sioux Falls, Las Vegas, Palm Beach.
3. RELATIVE: Aunt, Mother, Husband, Sister, Wife, Father, Uncle, Brother, Cousin, Daughter.
4. THEATER: Balcony, Aisle, Curtain, Backstage, Wings, Box seat, Orchestra pit, Apron, Props, Footlights.
5. GEESE: Bird, Flock, Honk, Gander, Web-footed, Gosling, Feather, Waterfowl, Eggs, Long-necked.
6. SIGNS: This Side Up, Dead End, Out To Lunch, Don't Walk, One Way, School Zone, Garage Sale, Wet Paint, No U-turn, Fragile.

CODEWORD

1-F, 2-D, 3-J, 4-C, 5-N, 6-W, 7-Z, 8-G, 9-Y, 10-M, 11-E, 12-Q, 13-B, 14-I, 15-P, 16-R, 17-S, 18-V, 19-T, 20-O, 21-A, 22-X, 23-H, 24-L, 25-U, 26-K.

SUM WORDS

1. Name + Trowel = Watermelon
2. Root + Simple = Metropolis

SPECULATION

1. Trips, 2. Whist, 3. Spur, 4. Transit, 5. Nitro, 6. Weirs.
SAYING: When it rains, it pours.

RHYME TIME

1. Damp champ, 2. Rude dude, 3. Bold hold, 4. Top cop, 5. Lone throne, 6. Cool mule, 7. Great state.

WHICH WAY WORDS

1. Wharf, 2. Doorstep, 3. Churlish, 4. Mask, 5. Operetta, 6. Concord, 7. Plucky, 8. Crops, 9. Lupine, 10. Readily, 11. Change, 12. Orlon, 13. Nature.
RELATED WORDS: Woodchuck, Armadillo, Crocodile, Porcupine, Orangutan.

UNSCRAMBLERS

1-K Shanghai, China; 2-H Naples, Italy; 3-G Ankara, Turkey; 4-L Yokohama, Japan; 5-I Alexandria, Egypt; 6-B Sydney, Australia; 7-J Budapest, Hungary; 8-E Athens, Greece; 9-F Bogota, Colombia; 10-C Montreal, Canada; 11-D Madrid, Spain; 12-A Calcutta, India.

ANAGRAM MAGIC SQUARE

1. Faces, 2. Olive, 3. Raged, 4. Teach, 5. Urban, 6. Nears, 7. Edger, 8. Idler, 9. Spree, 10. Adder, 11. Nadir, 12. Acerb, 13. Ladle, 14. Lapse, 15. Yanks, 16. Taper, 17. Ogres, 18. Torte, 19. Heirs, 20. Edict, 21. Bagel, 22. Rabid, 23. Abode, 24. Verdi, 25. Educe.
SAYING: Fortune is an ally to the brave.

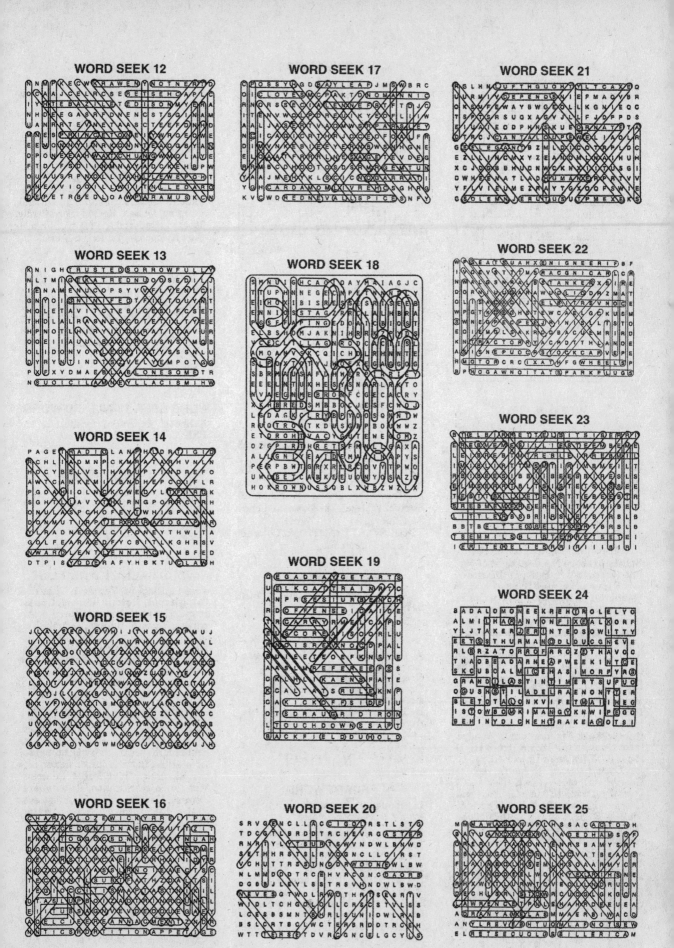

283

ALPHABET SOUP

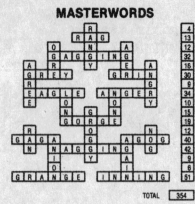

WORD MATH

	0	1	2	3	4	5	6	7	8	9
1.	C	O	L	D/	T	U	R	K	E	Y
2.	R	E	S	U	M	P	T	I	O	N
3.	S	P	E	C	U	L	A	T	O	R
4.	W	I	S	H/	M	E/	L	U	C	K
5.	R	O	U	N	D/	S	T	E	A	K
6.	D	I	S	P	U	T	A	B	L	E

LOGIC PROBLEM

(Clue numbers in parentheses)

Balloons [above Noelle's, right of parrots (2)] aren't A, B (1), D [Martin K (6)], E [peacocks (6)], F [E peacocks], or G [above N] (1); they're C, parrots B, and Noelle's J. Eddie's [children, right of geese, above Jill's [right of Olive's (3) (3)] isn't A, B [parrots], C [balloons], D [right of balloons], E [peacocks], or F [right of peacocks]; it's G, geese F, Jill's N, and Olive's M. Dogs [top (7)] aren't D (1); they're A. Roses [above tiger (7)] are D and tiger K. Betty's [right of Vicki's [trees (4)] (4)] is I and Vicki's H. Rita's is B (4). Peter's [rainbow (5)] isn't C [balloons], D [roses], E [peacocks], or F [geese]; it's L. Wendy's [above mouse (8)] isn't A [trees H], D [tiger K], E [rainbow L], or F [illus., 1); it's C and mouse J. Alan's [left of George's (5)] isn't A (1), E [Eddie's G, geese F] (1), or F [Eddie's G]; it's D and George's E. Foster's isn't F (1); it's A. Ida's is F. Bells aren't Betty's (1) or Olive's (3); they're Jill's. Irises aren't I (1); they're M. Ship is I.

In summary:

A, Foster, dogs; B, Rita, parrots; C, Wendy, balloons; D, Alan, roses; E, George, peacocks; F, Ida, geese; G, Eddie, children; H, Vicki, trees; I, Betty, ship; J, Noelle, mouse; K, Martin, tiger; L, Peter, rainbow; M, Olive, irises; N, Jill, bells.

MASTERWORDS

TOTAL [354]

PUZZLE IN THE ROUND

1. Close, 2. Loose, 3. Bells, 4. Boles, 5. Relic, 6. Alice, 7. Lined, 8. Olein, 9. Diner, 10. Aired, 11. Trice, 12. Icier, 13. Rouse, 14. Nurse, 15. Arise, 16. Slier, 17. Tamer, 18. Oater, 19. Tenor, 20. Route, 21. Metal, 22. Elate, 23. Leans, 24. Stale.

TOURIST ATTRACTION: Colorado National Monument

COMMON COMBOS

1. Golf, 2. Paper, 3. Summer, 4. Bird, 5. Wood.

MIXMASTER

A. Can't see the wood for the trees.
Across: 1-d. Sharp, 2-c. Moist, 3-a. Occur, 4-e. Under, 5-b. Write.
Down: 1-e. Topic, 2-b. Italy, 3-d. Clean, 4-c. Cease, 5-a. Yacht.
B. Take the wind out of one's sails.
Across: 1-c. Grown, 2-b. Wrist, 3-d. Zebra, 4-a. Knock, 5-e. Thumb.
Down: 1-b. Banjo, 2-a. Stare, 3-d. Image, 4-c. Train, 5-e. Drive.

SECRET WORD

1. Spout, 2. Trace, 3. Jumpy, 4. Amity, 5. Plain, 6. Notes.

1. Farce, After, Urges, Copes, Erupt, Togas; 2. Facts, Often, Lower, Laces, Owner, Wolfs; 3. Joins, Inure, Tenor, Trump, Enjoy, Ramps, Yearn; 4. Horne, Amino, Ruins, Money, Oaths, North, Youth; 5. Grape, Rouge, Arose, Smile, Spine, Large, Amend, Nudge, Dumps; 6. Radio, Edits, Maine, Imbue, Nurse, Debit, Emirs, Rabid, Sober.

WORD SEEK 12 MYSTERY STATE

New Jersey, The Garden State, Eastern Goldfinch, Violet, Red Oak

WORD SEEK 13 WORD LIST

Absolutely, Beautifully, Cyclist, Defining, Essay, Friendly, Gallant, Hurtle, Imitation, Jitterbug, Knighthood, Lonesome, Malicious, Navigation, Official, Painting, Queen, Rested, Sorrowfully, Trusted, Undertake, Visiting, Whimsically, Xylophone, Yardstick, Zebra.

WORD SEEK 14 WORD LIST

Rational, Launch, Heroic, Channel, Legislator, Rhapsody, Youth, Habit, Talent, Thread, Drawn, Normal, Linear, Radio, Optic, Clamp, Prudent, Trifle, Eddy, Yeast, Terror, Relic, Claw, Westward, Drift, Trap, Pagoda, Airfield, Digit, Tried.

WORD SEEK 19 WIZARD WORDS

A brutal aspect of football is the PRICE OF SEATS.

WORD SEEK 20 WORD LIST

Serve, Verge, Genie, Niece, Cello, Logic, Crust, Rusty, Style, Least, Aster, Terse, Seven, Endow, Dowel, Elbow, Bowed, Edict, Thumb, Broad, Adult, Torch, Horse.

WORD SEEK 21 WORD LIST

Jungle, Elegant, Tangent, Thoughtful, Limpid, Detour, Rustic, Cantaloupe, Eclipse, Exempt, Tortilla, Archives, Situate, Endive, Exactly, Yellow, Winch, Humane, Exodus, Somewhat, Trauma, Angels, Solemn, Needle, Erased, Depends, Solo, Ornate, Earnings, Suture.

WORD SEEK 23 WORD LIST

Belies, Berries, Better, Billet, Bitter, Blister, Briberies, Bristle, Brittle, Emblem, Esteem, Imbibe, Immerse, Irresistible, Letter, Limber, Litter, Littler, Member, Miller, Millet, Miseries, Missile, Mister, Relies, Remembers, Remiss, Resemble, Resist, Restless, Retire, Riblet, Series, Settee, Setter, Settle, Silliest, Simile, Simmer, Sister, Sitters, Slimmest, Sterile, Street, Teller, Terrible, Tester, Timber, Titter, Treble, Tremble, Trestle.

WORD SEEK 25 MYSTERY STATE

Massachusetts; (The) Bay State; Mayflower; Chickadee; American elm.

SPANNERS

CIRCLES IN THE SQUARE

PICTURE THIS

ALPHABET SOUP

WORD MERGERS

1. Punt, Red; Prudent.
2. Race, Tin; Certain.
3. Anti, Gave; Navigate.
4. Lend, Rave; Lavender.
5. Came, Ruin; Manicure.
6. Tor, Elate; Tolerate.
7. Need, Mist; Sediment.
8. Sport, Nice; Inspector.

IN OTHER WORDS

I see politics enter land.
PRESIDENTIAL
ELECTIONS

SUNRAYS

Pane, Told, Pain, Lode, Pint, Deal, Into, Pled, Anti, Plod, Neat, Idol.

SPELL & SCORE

1. Glance, 2. Broad, 3. Swing, 4. Jet, 5. Crawl, 6. Wreath, 7. Burro, 8. Knot, 9. Twirl, 10. Why.

STRETCH LETTERS

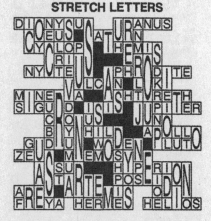

TAKE A LETTER

1. Carols, Spirit, Wreath; 2. Icicle, Lights, Spruce; 3. Manger, Ribbon, String; 4. Herald, Sleigh, Tinsel.

ANAGRAM MAGIC SQUARE

1. Deuce, 2. Oland, 3. Nadir, 4. Tears, 5. Shrub, 6. Evans, 7. Nacre, 8. Dared, 9. Bales, 10. O'Hare, 11. Yeats, 12. Share, 13. Orang, 14. Nosed, 15. Maple, 16. Edits, 17. Nines, 18. Swing, 19. Extra, 20. Relax, 21. Races, 22. Abler, 23. Nancy, 24. Doles, 25. Stint.

SAYING: Don't send boys on men's errands.

FILL-IN

SYLLACROSTIC

E.G. Leterman: If your conscience won't stop you, pray for cold feet.
1. Endow, 2. Giotto, 3. Lemon, 4. Epithet, 5. Tarsus, 6. Experiment, 7. Romeo, 8. Make-up, 9. Artery, 10. Nuncio, 11. Inconnu, 12. Fillip, 13. Yonder, 14. Ottawa, 15. Uruguay, 16. Relief, 17. Castro, 18. Orator, 19. Nordic, 20. Sorrento, 21. Casual, 22. Identified, 23. Engulf, 24. Negative, 25. Cottage, 26. Enlist.

QUOTEFALLS

1. You don't just stumble into the future. You create your own future.

2. With a laugh and a smile you can make even a lousy day worth living.

3. Probably nothing in the world arouses more false hopes than the first four hours of a diet.

4. Tart words make no friends. A spoonful of honey will catch more flies than a gallon of vinegar.

LOGIC PROBLEM

(Clue numbers in parentheses)
Mos. are Aug., Sept., Oct., Nov., and Dec. (intro.). One with OH and hiking (1) doesn't have Italy, Greece (1), France [camping or riding (3)], or Spain (5); it has Britain. It won't be Aug. (1); it'll be Sept., and the Aug. issue will have the skiing article (2). ME will be earlier than OH [Sept.] (1); it will be Aug. Dec. [France (3)] has camping or riding (3), so won't have FL or IA [Spain and sailing, in some order (5)]; it'll have TX. FL [Spain or sailing (5)] won't go with Italy [not with sailing (4)] or Greece (6); it'll go with Spain, and IA will go with sailing (5). FL won't go with riding (6); TX will. FL will go with camping. Italy won't go with sailing (4); Greece will. Italy will go with skiing. Oct. won't have sailing (4); it'll have camping. Nov. will have sailing.

In summary:
Aug., Maine, Italy, skiing
Sept., Ohio, Britain, hiking
Oct., Florida, Spain, camping
Nov., Iowa, Greece, sailing
Dec., Texas, France, riding

LETTERDROP

1. A watched pot never boils.
2. Leave well enough alone.

CRYPTO-FAMILIES

1. CLASSROOM: Computer, Teacher, Students, Seats, Blackboard, Eraser, Books, Desk, Maps, Chalk.

2. WORK: Slave, Labor, Toil, Drudge, Strive, Struggle, Operate, Sweat, Produce, Endeavor.

3. JOBS TODAY: Plumber, Mechanic, Clerk, Editor, Barber, Architect, Carpenter, Mason, Welder, Trucker.

4. SUBJECTS: English, History, Arithmetic, Chemistry, Latin, Geography, Civics, Algebra, Physics, Sociology.

5. ARTS AND CRAFTS: Basketry, Macrame, Quilting, Decoupage, Ceramics, Embroidery, Origami, Needlepoint, Calligraphy, Batik.

6. JOBS OF OLD: Chandler, Regrater, Furrier, Chapman, Cambist, Fletcher, Slubber, Wainwright, Armorer, Saddler.

CRYPTOGRAMS

1. The rocking chair was invented for the man who doesn't need to work, can't sit still, and likes to make noise.

2. I'm careful of the words I say, to keep them soft and sweet. I never know from day to day which ones I'll have to eat.

3. When you walk in the park in the spring, you realize love is a great game. In fact, it's the only game where the players want to stay on the bench. (Bob Hope)

4. Be patient with the girl who walks to the front seat late for church in order to show off a new hat. In a few years she will drop into the back seat to get out quickly if the baby cries.

5. A child enters your home and makes so much noise for twenty years you can hardly stand it — then departs, leaving the house so silent you think you will go mad.

6. To really enjoy the better things in life, one must first have experienced the things they are better than. (Oscar Homolka)

7. Remember not only to say the right thing in the right place, but far more difficult still, to leave unsaid the wrong thing at the tempting moment. (Benjamin Franklin)

8. We have to learn to be our own best friends because we fall too easily into the trap of being our own worst enemies.

9. Never argue at the dinner table, for the one who is not hungry always gets the best of the argument.

10. Making the decision to have a child — it's momentous. It is to decide forever to have your heart go walking around outside your body.

11. A wise old owl lived in an oak; the more he saw the less he spoke; the less he spoke the more he heard: why can't we all be like that bird?

12. Never miss an opportunity to make others happy — even if you have to leave them alone to do it.

13. Don't be conceited. Just because you're sitting in the front seat doesn't mean you're driving the car.

MIXED BAG

Bow, Fore, Stern, Bridge, Steamer, Porthole, Gangplank, Staterooms, Starboard, Lifeboat, Hawsers, Sailor, Yacht, Buoy, Aft.
QUOTE: There were two lofty ships, from old England they set sail.

JIGSAW PUZZLE

```
E A S T          T A B
G L E E          W I L E
G L A N D      F A C E T
      R O T O R
      O N I O N
      P E N D
            F
          T O O L
      G U I D E
      I S L E S
S P A R K    S A T I N
E A R L      N O N E
E Y E        D E N T
```

JIGSAW SQUARES

In the hectic holidays ahead, the best gift you can give costs nothing. It takes only a moment to deliver it, but the memory of it can last a lifetime. It's the one thing people can wear that never goes out of style, and one size fits everyone. It's called a smile. (Reader's Digest, Dec. 1987)

TRIPLEX

A: 1. Scram, 2. Prove, 3. Amati, 4. Riata, 5. Titan, 6. Attar, 7. Nepal, 8: Bizet.
B: 1. Amuse, 2. Verse, 3. Tiger, 4. Taste, 5. Anode, 6. Aruba, 7. Altar, 8. Ethel.
C: 1. Serac, 2. Sepia, 3. Error, 4. Tempo, 5. Devil, 6. Baha'i, 7. Argon, 8. Eliza.
CITY AND STATE: Spartanburg, South Carolina.

LOGIC PROBLEM

(Clue numbers in parentheses)
The week begins on Sun., and the game times were 12 p.m., 2:30 p.m., 5:30 p.m., 6 p.m., and 8:30 p.m. (intro.). Steve watched the Seahawks (4). George's game was Sun. (5). Ed's game was at 6 p.m. (7). The Sat. game was at 2:30 (6). The Sat. game (2:30, last] wasn't Ed's [6:00], John's (1), or Steve's [Seahawks] (6); it was Troy's. The 49ers game started at noon [earliest] (3). It wasn't John's (1), Ed's [6 p.m.], or Troy's [2:30]; it was George's. The Broncos aren't John's (1) or Troy's [Sat.] team (6); they're Ed's [6 p.m.] John's game was later than the Broncos' [6 p.m.] (1); it was at 8:30 [latest]. His team isn't the Cowboys (2); it's the Raiders. Troy's team is the Cowboys [2:30]. The Fri. game was 3 hours later than Cowboys game (2); it was at 5:30. It wasn't Ed's [6 p.m.] or John's [8:30]; it was Steve's. John's game was played Mon. and Ed's Bronco game Thurs (1).
In summary:
Ed, Broncos, Thurs., 6:00 p.m.
George, 49ers, Sun., 12:00 p.m.
John, Raiders, Mon., 8:30 p.m.
Steve, Seahawks, Fri., 5:30 p.m.
Troy, Cowboys, Sat., 2:30 p.m.

CHAIN WORDS

Ketch, Fetch, Bring, Brine, Bribe, Tribe, Tripe, Gripe, Grape, Shape, Shale, Leash.

THREE'S COMPANY

1. Baritone, Soprano, Tenor; 2. Supreme, Topmost, Unsurpassed; 3. Anne, Elizabeth, Mary; 4. Banana, Orange, Plum; 5. Hook, Rod, Sinker; 6. Superior, Tahoe, Victoria; 7. Date, Engagement, Meeting; 8. Alberta, Ontario, Quebec; 9. Antonio, Diego, Francisco; 10. Emerald, Lime, Olive; 11. Bolero, Jitterbug, Reel; 12. Collie, Mastiff, Rottweiler.

ANAGRAM MAGIC SQUARE

1. Trail, 2. Hares, 3. Elbow, 4. Cheap, 5. Owner, 6. Mates, 7. Manor, 8. Angel, 9. Nepal, 10. Decor, 11. Outer, 12. Flair, 13. Clasp, 14. Urges, 15. Sleek, 16. Three, 17. Overt, 18. Medal, 19. Idols, 20. Stage, 21. Grade, 22. Ridge, 23. Exalt, 24. Askew, 25. Tenor.
SAYING: The command of custom is great.

QUICK QUOTES

1. A critic is a man who knows the way but can't drive the car.
2. The only way to have a friend is to be one.
3. Character is something you either have or are.

1. A. Winter, B. Watch, C. Stack, D. Harmony, E. Smoke, F. Data, G. Comet, H. Bewitch, I. Vine, J. Straw, K. Obvious.
2. A. Violet, B. Fable, C. Donate, D. Winner, E. Honeybee, F. Yeast, G. Worthy.
3. A. Higher, B. Vacancy, C. Tourist, D. Rehearse, E. Rehire, F. Tomatoes.

CRYPTO-FAMILIES

1. OILS: Peanut, Baby, Safflower, Olive, Canola, Cottonseed, Sesame, Linseed, Soybean, Corn.
2. CITY STREETS: Policeman, Vendors, Pretzels, Hot dogs, Pedestrians, Subways, Taxicab, Skyscraper, Newsstand, Boutiques.
3. TREE CITY NAMES: Pinehurst, Larchmont, Oakland, Cedar Rapids, Maplewood, Palm Springs, Birch Run, Walnut Creek, Beech Grove, Fircrest.
4. INSECTS: Boll weevil, Cricket, Grasshopper, Honeybee, Katydid, Ladybug, Mosquito, Wasp, Gypsy moth, Termite.
5. COLORFUL: Red herring, Greenhorn, Blue ribbon, Ivory tower, Orange stick, White water, Rose window, Silver spoon, Coral reef, Pink elephant.
6. U.S. 5-LETTER CITIES: Miami, Tulsa, Flint, Boise, Fargo, Sitka, Butte, Dover, Selma, Omaha.

SIMON SAYS
1. WATERCOOLER
2. WATERCIILER
3. TATERCIILET
4. TATERCIIDLET
5. TATERCIDILET
6. TELIDICRETAT
7. TSLIDICRSTAT
8. TSLIICRSTADT
9. TLIIRSTADT
10. THLIIRSTADT
11. THLIRSTAIDT
12. THLIRSTAIDIT
13. THKIRSTAIDIT
14. THIRSTAIDKIT

TRIANGLE QUOTE
Easier said than done.

FORE 'N' AFT
1. Soot, 2. Opted, 3. Liar, 4. Torso, 5. Ohio, 6. In-law, 7. Wins, 8. Elfin.
MESSAGE: Slow down.

COMMON COMBOS
1. Glass, 2. Minute, 3. Magic, 4. Plate, 5. Watch, 6. Top, 7. Table, 8. Hair, 9. Down, 10. Double.

CROSSOUT QUOTE
It's so simple to be wise—just think of something stupid to say. Then say the opposite.

UPS AND DOWNS
1. Peanut butter, 2. Tuna fish, 3. Genoa salami, 4. American cheese, 5. Roast beef.

SPLIT PERSONALITIES
1. Jimmy Connors, 2. Jack Kramer, 3. Chris Evert, 4. Michael Chang, 5. Rod Laver, 6. Althea Gibson, 7. Steffi Graf, 8. Jennifer Capriati.

HOW MANY SQUARES?
18 (ABMK, CDPN, EFLK, EGSQ, FGML, FHTR, GHNM, GIUS, HION, HJVT, IJPO, KLRQ, KMXW, LMSR, MNTS, NOUT, NPZY, OPVU)

ANAGRAM QUOTES
1. The trouble with being on time is that nobody is there to appreciate it.

2. A person afraid of work must be brave enough to face poverty.

3. It takes a heap of payments to make a house your home.

FILL-IN

SPELLBOUND
Mosque (6), Pray (4), Sting (5), Cajole (6), Whiz (4), Flaxen (6), Brick (5), Avowed (6), Ruin (4), Godly (5), Azure (5) + 10 (bonus) = 66.

TRADE-OFF
1. Curtly, Curtsy; 2. Legion, Lesion; 3. Barter, Carter; 4. Assort, Assert; 5. Billet, Bullet.

CODEWORD

1-G, 2-I, 3-A, 4-H, 5-J, 6-K, 7-N, 8-U, 9-P, 10-X, 11-O, 12-E, 13-D, 14-Z, 15-C, 16-W, 17-R, 18-M, 19-V, 20-B, 21-Y, 22-L, 23-Q, 24-S, 25-F, 26-T.

DART GAME
Bravo, Brown, Batik, Bluff, Bugle.

DAISY
Offer, Nifty, Aloof, Chief, Lofty.
BONUS WORD: Falcon

SATELLITES
Soda, Sofa, Soliloquy, Soloist, Solution, Sonar, Sonata, Sorority.

LINKWORDS
1. Bed, 2. Mill, 3. Milk, 4. Free, 5. Cup, 6. Play, 7. Key, 8. Work, 9. Lamp, 10. Pea.

TAKE A LETTER
1. Gopher, Impala, Weasel; 2. Gerbil, Jackal, Ocelot; 3. Alpaca, Cougar, Donkey; 4. Coyote, Monkey, Rabbit.

SCRAMBLE ACROSS

CROSSED NAMES
1. Phil Donahue, 2. Ann Landers, 3. George Burns.

OBSERVATION POST
1. None
2. A, B, C, D, H, J, K, M, N
3. G, O, P, Q
4. E, F, H, I, J, K, L, N
5. B, C, D

STAR WORDS
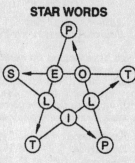

TILES
OCCASIONAL

WORD MERGERS
1. Rob, Sew; Browse.
2. Dog, Ran; Dragon.
3. Get, Man; Magnet.
4. Car, Tree; Terrace.
5. Bit, Rely; Liberty.
6. Grim, Lip; Pilgrim.
7. Song, Tick; Stocking.

BUILDING BLOCKS
Noise, Sponge, Reason, Ominous, Handsome.

THREE FROM NINE
1. Prevent, Lunch, Owe; 2. Swallow, Loose, Hoe; 3. Cracker, Stoop, Boo.

SQUARES
1. Blossoms, 2. Fidelity, 3. Affinity, 4. Athletic, 5. Journeys, 6. Bulletin, 7. Mountain.

WINDOW BOXES
1-g Beau, 2-j Hymn, 3-e Wren, 4-f Leaf, 5-i Tier, 6-h Ogre, 7-b Frog, 8-a Yarn, 9-c Ecru, 10-d Avid.

CRYPTO-LIMERICK
There once was a musician named Sloan,
Who wanted to play the trombone.
But one day when he tried,
It just wouldn't slide,
And he knew that his chance was blown.

CRYPTO-FAMILIES
1. SKIING: Poles, Lift, Slope, Scarf, Jacket, Trail, Jump, Goggles, Mogul.
2. HOCKEY: Puck, Slap shot, Skates, Net, Stick, Rink, Helmet, Hat trick, Mask.
3. SNOW: Ball, Bank, Flake, Plow, Blower, Drift, Tire, Mobile, Man.
4. WHITE: Wall, Elephant, Cap, Flag, Sale, Space, Knight, Lie, Wash.

CROSTIC 10

Author: (Jean) Kerr
Source: (Please) Don't Eat the Daisies

If you have formed the habit of checking on every new diet that comes along, you will find that, mercifully, they all blur together, leaving you with only one definite piece of information: french-fried potatoes are out.

A. Knighthood
B. Encourage
C. Relative
D. Rhyolite
E. Difficulty
F. Overflow
G. Night owl
H. Truthful
I. Elementary
J. Amphibian
K. Toffee
L. Typhoon
M. Honeymoon
N. Effective
O. Doughboy
P. Allowance
Q. Initiated
R. Suffocate
S. Inherited
T. Entirely
U. Scream

CROSTIC 11

Author: Sterling North
Source: Hurry, Spring!

An Englishman's home is his castle. The nest of a bird and the surrounding territory are equally well defended . . . "Mine, mine, mine," warbles the male bird protecting his territory. "Wife and chi, chi, chi, chi, children."

A. Scientific
B. Thinner
C. Emblem
D. Rehash
E. Lint
F. Iniquity
G. Nigeria
H. Gift horse
I. Nears
J. On a dime
K. Ricochet
L. Twaddle
M. Hidden
N. Handled
O. Uncritical
P. Refer
Q. Rumble
R. Yellow
S. Shambles
T. Phaedra
U. Render
V. In the swim
W. Niche
X. Ghost story

CROSTIC 12

Author: William Plomer
Source: (Peter's Quotations:) Ideas for Our Time

It is the function of creative men to perceive the relations between thoughts, or things, or forms of expression that may seem utterly different, and to be able to combine them into some new forms — the power to connect the seemingly unconnected.

A. Witticism
B. Important
C. Level best
D. Lent
E. In the event
F. Agreement
G. Macbeth
H. Peewee
I. Lengthen
J. On the spot
K. Mastiff
L. Energy
M. Rhodes
N. Ian
O. Dentist
P. Erenow
Q. Accents
R. Shinto
S. Fisticuffs
T. Offshore
U. Ruby
V. Outcome
W. Unorthodox
X. Recent
Y. Trombone
Z. Income
a. Moor
b. Eyetooth

CROSTIC 13

Author: A(ndrew) Mitchell
Source: (Vanishing Paradise) The Tropical Rainforest

Hummingbirds need to visit thousands of flowers every day to extract enough nectar to survive . . . At night many of the smaller species save energy by lowering their metabolism to about one-fifth of its daytime value, effectively going into a brief hibernation.

A. Affidavit
B. Mainstay
C. Incisive
D. Tortoise
E. Cotton
F. Harmony
G. Elixir
H. Leavings
I. Lugger
J. Test tube
K. Hedge
L. Effusive
M. Timothy
N. Rye bread
O. Overwhelm
P. Payoff
Q. Ivanhoe
R. Cheese
S. Affluent
T. Locust
U. Roost
V. Anthem
W. In doubt
X. Nearby
Y. Fort Wayne
Z. Obliging
a. Reams
b. Endive
c. Sits tight
d. Trombone

CROSTIC 14

Author: (Samuel) Johnson
Source: Lives of the Poets

Pope was not content to satisfy, he desired to excel and therefore always endeavored to do his best; he did not court the candor, but dared the judgment of his reader, and expecting no indulgence from others, he showed none to himself.

A. Jealous
B. Obdurate
C. Hinton
D. Next-door
E. Sweetmeat
F. Olden days
G. Neighborly
H. Logos
I. Interment
J. Viewpoints
K. Endangered
L. Sixteenth
M. Off-season
N. Far-fetched
O. Thwarted
P. Horehound
Q. Enforced
R. Pathetic
S. Odd-shaped
T. Eccentric
U. Toothsome
V. Shuddered

CROSTIC 15

Author: (Richard L.) Sterne
Source: (John) Gielgud Directs (Richard Burton in) Hamlet

A great difficulty . . . with . . . famous plays is that you get a performance which is good and sound, well rehearsed, but it just doesn't live because the actors all know that the audience knows perfectly well everything that's going to happen.

A. Scotch tape
B. Talon
C. Elusive
D. Refused
E. Newscast
F. Euphoria
G. Gershwin
H. Interest
I. Elbow
J. Law school
K. Gave out
L. Under way
M. Daffodil
N. Dental
O. Itsy-bitsy
P. Rhoda
Q. Empty
R. Charged
S. Twentieth
T. Skintight
U. Hungary
V. Applejack
W. Mahout
X. Languish
Y. Effect
Z. Tootle

CROSTIC 16

Author: Louis L. Vine
Source: Your Neurotic Dog

Only tame or domesticated dogs bark. Wild dogs and wolves howl. Barking is an imitation. As the early masters urged their dogs to go after game, the dogs, in their excitement, imitated their humans' sounds and in time developed the barking habit.

A. Limelight
B. Oyster bed
C. Upside-down
D. Islamabad
E. Shadow
F. Loath
G. Vegetation
H. Immemorial
I. Nests
J. Engross
K. Yacht basin
L. Odds
M. Unfamiliar
N. Remitted
O. Notate
P. Egghead
Q. Undertakes
R. Ride herd on
S. Owing to
T. Testament
U. Images
V. Chatterbox
W. Dik-dik
X. Overnight
Y. Girth

CROSTIC 17

Author: Leo Rosten
Source: Points to Ponder

I cannot believe that the purpose of life is to be "happy." I think the purpose of life is to be useful, to be responsible, to be compassionate. It is, above all, to matter, to count, to stand for something, to have made some difference that you lived at all.

A. Lighthouse
B. Evolution
C. Optimism
D. Resolute
E. Opposites
F. Sabbath
G. Temperate
H. Effective
I. Novelties
J. Probable
K. Off-the-cuff
L. Initiation
M. Notational
N. Teetotally
O. Shibboleth
P. Tambourine
Q. Offutt
R. Poppycock
S. Oared
T. Natasha
U. Des Moines
V. Elevated
W. Red shoes

CROSTIC 18

Author: (John D.) MacDonald
Source: (The) Dreadful Lemon Sky

A news story is a fragile thing. It is like a hot-air balloon. It needs a constant additive of more hot air in the form of new revelations, new actions, new suspicions. Without this, the air cools, the big bag wrinkles, sighs, settles to the ground and disappears.

A. Microchips
B. Antibiotic
C. Crow's-nest
D. Dishwasher
E. Oasis
F. Nightshirt
G. Alan Alda
H. Luftwaffe
I. Dinner date
J. Dais
K. Reason
L. Ephesians
M. Abbreviate
N. Doolittle
O. Fingerling
P. Usherettes
Q. Lois
R. Litigation
S. Enos
T. Monotheist
U. Overweight
V. No-no
W. State parks
X. Kowtowing
Y. Youths

WINDOW BOXES
1-c Oath, 2-e Undo, 3-a Deal, 4-h Jump, 5-b Peak, 6-j Vary, 7-g Earn, 8-d Knot, 9-f Quiz, 10-i Wave.

ANAGRAM MAGIC SQUARE
1. Cadre, 2. Ocher, 3. Urges, 4. Regal, 5. Acted, 6. Girth, 7. Earth, 8. Ideal, 9. Shale, 10. Raise, 11. Edict, 12. Quote, 13. Ulcer, 14. Inset, 15. Remit, 16. Egret, 17. Decal, 18. Islet, 19. Night, 20. Aimed, 21. Lance, 22. Lever, 23. Alert, 24. Rifle, 25. Truce.
SAYING: Courage is required in all art.

EXPLORAWORD
Alee, Ales, Alps, Aped, Apes, Apse, Dale, Daps, Date, Deal, Deep, Dees, Dele, Ease, East, Eats, Eels, Else, Lade, Lads, Laps, Last, Late, Lead, Leap, Leas, Lees, Lest, Lets, Pads, Pale, Pals, Past, Pate, Pats, Peal, Peas, Peat, Peel, Pelt, Pest, Pets, Plat, Plea, Pled, Sale, Salt, Sate, Seal, Seat, Seed, Seep, Sept, Seta, Slap, Slat, Sled, Spat, Sped, Step, Tads, Tale, Tape, Taps, Teal, Teas, Teed, Tees.

LOGIC PROBLEM
(Clue numbers in parentheses)
The red-framed painting [library (1)] wasn't painted by Robin (1), Lesley [green (2)], Courtney [blue (4)], or Chris (5); it was painted by Ricki. Chris didn't paint the tan-framed painting (5); Robin did. Chris painted the white-framed painting. Lesley [female (2)] didn't paint the surrealist [Robin (1)], photorealistic (2), cubist [male (3)], or impressionist painting [male (6)]; she painted the abstract painting. Lesley's painting [abstract] wasn't hung in the kitchen, game room (2), or meeting room [cubist (3)]; it was hung in the foyer. Ricki [red, library] didn't paint the cubist [meeting room] or the impressionist painting (6); Ricki painted the photorealistic painting. Chris's painting [white] wasn't hung in the meeting room or kitchen (3); it was hung in the game room. Robin's surrealist painting wasn't hung in the meeting room [cubist]; it was hung in the kitchen. Courtney's painting was hung in the meeting room. Chris painted the impressionist painting.

In summary:
Chris, white, game room, impressionist
Courtney, blue, meeting room, cubist
Lesley, green, foyer, abstract
Ricki, red, library, photorealistic
Robin, tan, kitchen, surrealist

MASTERWORDS

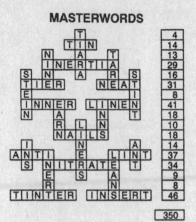

	4
	14
	13
	29
	16
	31
	8
	41
	18
	10
	18
	14
	37
	34
	9
	8
	46

350

CRYPTOGRAMS
1. The world was made round so we would never be able to see too far down the road.

2. He had so many gold teeth that when he smiled it looked as if a pipe organ was being unveiled.

3. Two things are bad for the heart: running uphill and running down people.

4. I like long walks, especially when they are taken by people who annoy me.

5. When in charge, ponder. When in trouble, delegate. When in doubt, mumble.

6. Alaska to Texas: "If you don't stop bragging, I'll split up two for one, and then you'll be the third largest state!"

7. Self-respect is the fruit of discipline; the sense of dignity grows with the ability to say no to oneself.

8. A boy becomes an adult three years before his parents think he does, and about two years after he thinks he does.

9. It is a good plan to aim a little higher than your target so as to make your shot sure, but not so high that you overshoot the mark.

10. A successful marriage requires falling in love many times, always with the same person.

11. When two people love each other, they don't look at each other, they look in the same direction.

12. Just remember, although the sun has a sinking spell every night, it rises again the next morning.

13. I for one appreciate a good form letter, having worked on Capitol Hill and learned several dozen cordial ways to say nothing.

14. Recent college graduate: "I was on the dean's list, but nobody in the employment offices seems to know the dean."

NUMBERBOXES

4	5	2
9	1	7
8	3	6

MAZE

SCRAMBLE ACROSS

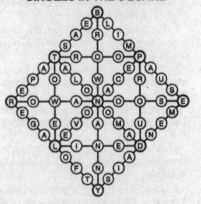

CIRCLES IN THE SQUARE

NUMBER JUMBLE
5913

TELEPHONE CALL
192

SUSPENDED SENTENCE
The shortest recorded period of time lies between the minute you put some money away for a rainy day and the unexpected arrival of rain.

SIMON SAYS
1. POSTOFFICE
2. PASTOFFICE
3. PASTOFFIDCE
4. TSAPOFFIDCE
5. TSAPOGGIDCE
6. TSAPONGNGIDCE
7. TSAPINGNGODCE
8. TSAPINGNGRODCE
9. TSAPINGGRONDCE
10. TSAMPINGGRONDCE
11. TSAMPINGGRONDSE
12. TSAMPINGGRONDS
13. TSAMPINGGROUNDS
14. STAMPINGGROUNDS

FILL-IN

P	O	L	E		R	E	S		A	D	E	N
R	E	A	D		O	I	L		S	I	L	O
O	R	D	I	N	A	R	Y		T	S	A	R
			F	U	M	E		A	I	M		
S	T	A	I	N	S		S	C	R	I	P	T
P	O	N	E	S		B	E	E		S	U	R
A	N	N	S		H	U	T		I	S	L	E
T	A	U		P	O	D		A	M	A	S	S
E	L	I	C	I	T		S	M	I	L	E	S
		T	E	N		S	P	I	T			
P	A	I	D		L	A	U	D	A	B	L	E
O	G	E	E		E	R	R		T	E	A	R
P	A	S	S		T	I	N		E	D	G	E

ALPHABET PLUS
Arena, Table, Cover, Blade, Reach, After, Grape, Birch, Noise, Major, Ankle, Camel, Armor, Snack, Adorn, Apple, Quest, Actor, First, Utter, Ounce, Vital, Tweak, Relax, Yield, Crazy.

FRAMEWORK FIRST WORDS
Framework 2: Surrey
Framework 3: WV4090
Framework 4: Street
Framework 5: Stream
Framework 6: Midway
Framework 7: 64815
Framework 8: Sparse
Framework 10: Window
Framework 11: 20713
Framework 12: Delight
Framework 14: Circus
Framework 15: Puff
Framework 17: Fantasia
Framework 18: Salt
Framework 19: September
Framework 20: Post
Framework 21: Muffin
Framework 22: Purist
Framework 23: Drive
Framework 24: Kayak
Framework 25: Serve
Framework 26: 91856